CRITICAL PEDAGOGY,
THE STATE,
AND
CULTURAL STRUGGLE

Teacher Empowerment and School Reform

Henry A. Giroux & Peter L. McLaren, editors
Department of Educational Leadership
Miami University–Oxford, Ohio

In an age when liberalism and radicalism have come under severe attack, American education faces an unprecedented challenge. The challenge has now moved beyond the search for more humanistic approaches to schooling and the quest for educational equality. Today's challenge is the struggle to rebuild a democratic tradition presently in retreat.

Laboring in a climate of anti-intellectualism and cultural ethnocentrism, educators are witnessing the systematic reduction of pedagogical skills and the disempowerment of the teaching profession; the continuation of privilege for select numbers of students on the basis of race, class, and gender; and the proliferation of corporate management pedagogies and state-mandated curricula that prescribe a narrow and sterile range of literacies and conceptions of what it means to be a citizen.

Under the editorship of Henry A. Giroux and Peter L. McLaren, this series will feature works within the critical educational tradition that define, analyze, and offer solutions to the growing dilemmas facing the nation's teachers and school systems. The series will also feature British and Canadian analyses of current educational conditions.

CRITICAL PEDAGOGY, THE STATE, and CULTURAL STRUGGLE

edited by

HENRY A. GIROUX and PETER L. McLAREN

State University
of New York
Press

Published by
State University of New York Press, Albany

© 1989 State University of New York

For information, address State University of New York
Press, State University Plaza, Albany, NY 12246

Library of Congress Cataloging-in-Publication Data

Critical pedagogy, the state, and cultural struggle / Henry A. Giroux
and Peter McLaren, editors.
    p. cm. – (SUNY series in teacher empowerment and school
reform)
    Includes index.
    ISBN 0–7914–0036–0. – ISBN 0–7914–0037–9 (pbk.)
    1. Educational sociology–United States. 2. Educational
anthropology–United States. 3. Educational–United States–
Philosophy. I. Giroux, Henry A. II. McLaren, Peter, 1948–
III. Series.
LC191.4.C75   1989   89–4176
370.19–dc19   CIP

10 9 8 7 6 5 4 3 2 1

Dedicated to the memory of Laurie McDade

CONTENTS

ACKNOWLEDGMENTS

We wish to acknowledge our indebtedness to Jeanne Brady Giroux and Jenny McLaren for their unwavering encouragement and for their helpful suggestions in putting together this project.

Walter Feinberg, "Fixing the Schools: The Ideological Turn." Originally appeared in *Issues in Education* 3 (1985), pp. 113–138.

Michelle Fine, "Silencing and Nurturing Voice in an Improbable Context: Urban Adolescents in Public School," has been reprinted with permission from *Language Arts,* 64:2 (Feb. 1987), pp. 157–174.

Henry. A. Giroux and Roger Simon, "Popular Culture and Critical Pedagogy: Everyday Life as a Basis for Curriculum Knowledge" has been reprinted with permission from the *Boston University Journal of Education* 170, no. 1, (1988).

Sections of Peter McLaren, "On Ideology and Education: Critical Pedagogy and the Cultural Politics of Resistance," have appeared in *Educational Theory* 37, no. 3 (1987): 301–326 and in *Social Text* 19/20 (Fall, 1988): 153–185 and have been reprinted with permission.

Introduction

Schooling, Cultural Politics, and the Struggle for Democracy

Henry A. Giroux
Peter McLaren

As the Age of Reagan comes to a close, a new stage in the national debate about the future of public schooling in the United States is beginning to develop. The growing interest in such a debate can be seen not only in the ongoing announcements by both of the major political parties but also in the increasing concern by members of the general public to improve the quality of American schools. There is little doubt that the ferment that has characterized the educational debate of the 1980s will continue; hopefully, the second stage of this debate will raise a new set of questions, provide a new language of analysis, and embrace a different set of interests for defining the purpose and meaning of public education.

All of the essays written for this collection are concerned with this debate and the significance it has for addressing some of the more important issues and problems the present generation of Americans will have to confront and think about in the near future. These chapters are bound together by a common concern. It is a concern for linking the issue of educational reform to the broader considerations of democracy, the ethical and political character of fundamental social relations, and the demands of critical citizenship. As different as these contributions appear in both their theoretical focus and their ideological representation, they all point to a number of important elements for creating a new public philosophy of education. This is a philosophy for the postmodern era. It is not one that seeks ideal fathers through the grand narratives that characterized the work of Marx, Freud, Durkheim, or Parsons; nor is it one that looks for salvation in the textual wizardry of the new poststructuralists. It is a philosophy that is decidedly concrete. It is one that embraces a politics of difference, that links questions of history and structural formations, that views ideology and human agency as a source of educational change, and that integrates macro- and microanalyses with a focus on the specificity of voices, desires, events, and cultural forms that give meaning and substance to everyday life. Characterizing the contributions in this volume is a theoretical openness and a spirit of hope, a belief that schools are places where students can find their voices, reclaim and affirm their histories, and develop a sense of self and collective identity amidst the language of larger public loyalties and social relations. But there is also a spirit of historicity that informs the various positions that make up this book, a sense of the need to push the history of recent decades against the grain in order both to question its purchase on knowledge as received truth and to shift the debate on educational reform from one dependent on a claim to a privileged reading of the past to one committed to a provisional and relational understanding of truth and commitment to investigating culture, teaching, and learning as a set of historically and socially constructed practices. In short, the spirit of hope and historicity which informs the contributions to this volume does not see the mechanisms of injustice as indelibly inscribed in the social order but rather as open to change and reconstruction through a critical rethinking of and commitment to the meaning and purpose of schooling in our society.

With this in mind we want to argue that the current debate about education represents more than a commentary on the state of public education in this country; it is fundamentally a debate about the relevance of democracy, social criticism, and the status of utopian thought in constructing both our dreams and the symbols and stories we devise in order to give meaning to our lives. The debate has taken a serious turn in the last decade. Under the guise of attempting to revitalize the language of conservative ethics, the Reagan agenda has, in reality, launched a dangerous attack on some of the most fundamental aspects of democratic public life. What has been valorized in this language is not the issue of reclaiming public schools as agencies of social justice or critical democracy, but a view of schooling that disdains the democratic implications of pluralism, rejects a notion of learning which regards excellence and equity as mutually constitutive, and argues for a return to the old transmission model of learning.

It is worth noting that since the early 1980s the conservatives have dominated the debate over public education and have consistently put liberals and other groups of progressive stripe in the uncomfortable position of defending failed, abandoned, or unpopular policies and programs initiated in the 1960s, even though it is recognized that many of these programs and policies were either never properly implemented or were not given an adequate chance at achieving their expected results. The power of the conservative initiative resides, in part, in its ability to link schooling to the ideology of the marketplace and to successfully champion the so-called virtues of Western civilization. In addition, it has doggedly defended a programmatic policy of school reform based on jargon-filled and undifferentiated conceptions of authority, citizenship, and discipline. Unlike many radical and progressive critics of the 1960s, conservatives have not merely argued that schools have failed in their primary vision of creating a literate and industrious citizenry; they have also attempted to develop both an analysis of the failure of public schooling and a program for curing the affliction. Through the sponsorship of a number of national reports, from *A Nation at Risk* to *American Education: Making It Work*, the Reagan administration had been able to set the agenda for both defining and addressing what it labeled the "crisis in education." To be sure, the conservative analysis is by no means original, but in the absence of an alternative position which is capable of publicly contesting the assumptions that have informed the Reagan-inspired education agenda, right-wing conservatives will continue to dominate the upcoming debate on education.

In our view, the debate over public education has been predictably one-sided in that the conservatives have set the agenda for such a debate and initiated a plethora of policy studies designed to implement their own educational initiatives. The success of the conservative educational agenda also points to a fundamental failure among progressive and radical educators to generate a public discourse on schooling. This is not to suggest that there has been an absence of writing on educational issues among leftist critics. In fact, the body of literature that has emerged in the last decade is duly impressive. One major problem facing the recent outpouring of critical discourse on schooling is that over the years it has become largely academicized. It has lost sight of its fundamental mission of mobilizing public sentiment toward a renewed vision of community; it has failed to recognize the general relevance of education as a public service and the importance of deliberately translating educational theory into a community-related discourse capable of reaching into and animating public culture and life. In effect, critical and radical writings on schooling have become ghettoized within the ivory tower, reflecting a failure to take seriously the fact that education as a terrain of struggle is central to the reconstruction of public life and, as such, must be understood in vernacular as well as scholarly terms. This, of course, is not to downgrade the importance of scholarly discourse on schooling, nor publications which serve to disseminate tracts and treatises on important epistemological and theoretical concerns. It is simply to highlight the fact that the assault on grand narratives should take place not only in the paper chase of the academy but also in classrooms of resistance and in communities struggling for a better life through a variety of public spheres.

In the upcoming debate on education in the United States, critical educators need to regain the ideological and political initiative. Such a project should at the very least embody four challenges: first, the major assumptions that characterize the conservative critique of education must be effectively challenged and refuted; second, the programmatic reforms put forth by the Reagan administration and taken up by the Bush presidency must be unmasked for what they really are: part of a major assault on the egalitarian ideology of public education as well as the principles of equity and democracy; third, a new critical language of schooling must emerge in order to formulate its own ciriticisms of schools as part of a wider project of possibility, one which provides an educational vision capable of mobilizing not only the middle class, but also those minorities of race, class, and gender who have been largely excluded from the language and practice of school reform for the past eight years; and finally, it is imperative that progressive educators put forth a federal policy for funding public education as part of an alternative program for economic growth. Before indicating how the articles in this book contribute to a public discourse of educational reform, we want to address briefly some of the issues we have raised as part of a wider debate on educational critique and transformation.

Challenging the conservative discourse of schooling

The Reagan conservatives have developed their analysis of public schooling in the United States in opposition to a number of advances associated with the progressive educational reforms of the 1960s and 1970s. Ironically, the ascendency of the conservative critique of schooling began with the radical criticisms of schooling in the 1960s. Radicals and progressives argued for greater access to higher education for black and other minority students through a policy of open admissions; they criticized the schools for being merely adjuncts to the labor market; they challenged the racist, sexist, and culturally biased nature of the curriculum at all levels of schooling; they opposed school hierarchies which discriminated against women teachers and staff, which silenced a developing social conscience among students, and which excluded minorities; they challenged the tracking procedures in elementary and secondary schools which slotted minorities and other disadvantaged groups into vocational schooling; and they were instrumental in providing the impetus for a number of important federal entitlement programs in such areas as bilingual, compensatory, and special education. In

short, these educational critics attempted to democratize access to and outcomes of both public schooling and higher education, to make school curricula relevant to the lives of children, and to shape federal policy that
would actively provide the financial support and national leadership to ensure that schooling in this country functions as a vehicle of social and economic mobility. Although the progressive educational movements of the
1960s and 1970s helped to inaugurate a number of important legislative
programs, they unfortunately often exaggerated the concept of personal
freedom, which at times collapsed into a form of vapid anti-intellectualism;
they often legitimated infantile as opposed to theoretically mature forms
of scholarship; moreover, they argued for a child-centered pedagogy which
amounted to a romantic celebration of student culture and experience
that made progressive reform patterns appear unrealistic – if not damagingly
counterproductive – to the aspirations of parents of minority and working-
class students and inhibited a more thorough theoretical investigation into
other crucial aspects of racial and class domination.

The Reagan conservatives attacked this legacy of reform on a number
of ideological and political fronts. Not surprisingly in an age of corporatist
politics, the initial line of attack centered on redefining the purpose of public schools as agents of social discipline and economic regulation. Under
the guise of proclaiming a national crisis in the schools, the conservatives
have willfully misread and consistently argued against the reforms of the
1960s and 1970s, claiming that they both compromised the academic rigor
of the public school curriculum and contributed to declining teacher and
student performance. Most strikingly preposterous was the attempt to fasten
the blame for the lagging domestic performance of the United States economy and its shrinking preeminence in the international marketplace on the
failure of the schools to prepare adequately its young citizenry to be capable
of reinvigorating corporate and industrial America. From such a human
capital perspective, schools are important only to the degree that they provide the forms of knowledge, skills, social practices, and entrepreneurial
values necessary to produce a labor force capable of aggressively competing
in world markets. Today, as in previous decades, a concern with social transformation and critical citizenship has been replaced by a preoccupation
with forging a school-business alliance. In the spirit of neoclassical economics, state boards of education continue to encourage schools to enter part-
nerships with industry, with its stress on producing efficient workers. The
present-day culture of schooling appears more and more bent on producing
what Andre Gorz calls "adapted individuals," by which he refers to "exactly
the kind of people that capitalist industry needs . . . those who will put
up with the regimentation, repression, discipline and deliberately unat-

tractive programs . . . [those who] are ideologically reliable, and who will not be tempted to use their technical knowledge to their own political advantage."[1]

As part of the excellence movement ushered in by the Reagan administration, we see a continual emphasis on the vocationalization of learning and the deskilling of teachers in our public schools, all of which reaches its apogee in the "teacher-proofed" curriculum, which creates a nondialectical separation of conception from execution and effectively reduces teachers to the status of technicians or state-sponsored functionaries. To assert that schools serve as meritocratic institutions for the purpose of fostering equality of opportunity and outcome simply registers, in this context, as a quaint oversimplification which masks schooling's socially and culturally reproductive dimensions.

The more this logic plays itself out in the contemporary educational scene, the more schools serve to multiply injustice under the banner of excellence, and the less likely it is that excellence will be equated with the development of pedagogical practices designed to foster critical intelligence and public conscience. In effect, the term *excellence* is reduced to a code word for legitimating the interests and values of the rich and the privileged. Within this perspective, remedial programs which try to extricate the lowly from their benighted condition label such students as "deprived" or "deviant" youth. This labeling not only serves to entrap students within the contours of a professional discourse, doubly confirming the legitimating power of school practices, but also serves to reproduce intergenerational continuity by defining who are to become members of the elite class and who are to occupy the subaltern caste.

Common perspectives animating this conservative position—and the privileged groups whose claim to power depend on its propagation and legitimation—consider social inequities to inhere in human nature and the inherent imperfection of groups marginalized by poverty, race, and gender. The logic of this position collapses into a defense of racial, class, and gender inequalities under the pretext of essentializing human nature by holding responsible for their own history and present conditions disadvantaged groups whose real powerlessness assures them of failure within the cultural and economic frames of reference set by dominant groups. The perspective that disadvantaged students should be the focus of special programs to remediate their deficiencies is in many respects as impoverishing and debilitating as the social and economic circumstances of which they are perennial victims since it impresses upon the disenfranchised that it is their personal shortcomings as minority or economically disadvantaged groups which prevent them from joining the elite tracks that lead to university life and a better future. Nowhere does this perspective address or attempt to illuminate the lived subordination of students as it pertains to relations of power that constrain possibilities for empowerment within the dominant culture; and nowhere are relations of power and social structures acknowledged as working together as codeterminants of school failure. Within this view of excellence, learning is linked to acquiring "the basics" and uncritically adopting values consistent with industrial discipline and social conformity.

By separating equity from excellence, conservatives have managed to criticize radical and progressive reformers for linking academic achievement to the principles of social justice and equality while simultaneously redefining public schooling in relation to the imperatives of the economy and the marketplace. Consequently, when the Reagan administration trumpeted the term *excellence* as its clarion call for school reform, it usually meant that public schools should offer more rigorous science and math curricula – a notion in keeping with the conservative idea that scientific know-how and technical proficiency are equivalent to industrial progress. The language of "achievement," "excellence," "discipline," and "goal orientation" effectively meant deemphasizing liberal and creative arts and stressing "job skills" curriculum more in keeping with vocational education and returning to the authoritarian classroom armed with the four Rs curriculum (which for President George Bush means "reading, 'riting, 'rithmetic, and respect").

A critical theory of schooling needs to both criticize this position and, in a clear and discernible public language, drastically redefine the relationship between schooling and education. In the words of John Dewey, this means invoking a choice between education as a function of society and society as a function of education. The major economic problems faced by the United States have not been caused by public education, although the economic crisis has certainly had a significant impact on the problems schools are experiencing. Unemployment, declining productivity, inflation, and the persistence of vast inequalities in wealth and power among the general population have little to do with the declining academic achievement of American students. For example, high levels of unemployment and declining productivity have more to do with bad investment policies and the crisis within the world economy than with a decline in school-produced skills. Moreover, recent empirical studies make abundantly clear that the employment growth in the next few decades will be dominated by low-level jobs primarily in the service industries and will require little education and fewer higher-order intellectual and technical skills.

This is not to suggest that critical educators should disavow the importance of schools in educating youth with the basic skills that can be used to find employment. But it must be stressed that being educated for occupational mobility must also include learning knowledge and skills of a different order of intellectual complexity from what has been advocated by the Reagan administration. In this case, we are referring to learning which is tied to forms of self- and social empowerment. Education for the future means that students will need to acquire advanced levels of economic literacy that will allow them not only to work in the marketplace but also to transform it as part of a broader struggle to create a more egalitarian and just society. Similarly, critical educators will need to address and promote policies for forging new linkages between schools and communities in relation to the issues of job creation and public service. For instance, a national youth service corps could provide students with the opportunity to integrate social reform, academic credit, and civic education. Finally, as part of an attempt to promote an ethic of civic and social responsibility, critical educators need to argue for forms of schooling that do not reduce the capacity for learning to economic or technical considerations: that is, critical educators need to develop an educational discourse that connects the purpose and practice of schooling to a public philosophy in which learning is seen as part of a wider discourse of freedom and democratic struggle.

The Reagan approach to public school reform has shifted in recent years, as reflected in a spate of recent publications either produced by the United States Department of Education or endorsed publicly by its administration. We refer here to former Education Secretary William J. Bennett's report, *American Education: Making Work*; Allan Bloom's *The Closing of the American Mind*; and E. D. Hirsch's *Cultural Literacy*. Rather than abandoning the old technicist discourse which reduces schooling to job training, Bennett has added to it the notion of cultural uniformity. Public schools are now defended as both cultural *and* industrial sites. For example, Bennett's call for more curricular content and increased standardized testing is a thinly disguised attempt to impose cultural uniformity on the schools, to make school content irrelevant to the culturally specific traditions, experiences, and histories the students bring to schools, and to deskill teachers by forcing them to concentrate on delivering a curriculum that is both prepackaged and intellectually vapid. Rather than raising questions regarding how schools actively silence students, how the hidden curriculum of tracking works to marginalize and ensure failure for working-class and minority students, or how the dominant culture excludes the voices, dreams, and collective memories of subordinate groups, Bennett argues that equal opportunity can be achieved through more rigorous academic discipline and by instilling in parents greater educational expectations for their children. Such prescriptions remain ominously silent with respect to the forms of moral and social regulation that schools embody which benefit the students of the rich and the privileged, and the particularly odious forms of discrimination based on race. Similarly, Bennett's proposals render invisible the suffering and the social and political hardships that students from subordinate groups frequently face both in and out of schools.

Bennett's perspective trivializes the meaning of education through both a neglect of the larger social and political issues facing our society at the present moment and an unwillingness to expand the task of reform in terms of a more critical theory of ethics and curriculum. His prescriptions for pedagogical reform embody an equally truncated vision. For example, the attributes he associates with good teaching sound as if they were taken from the scripts of the Mr. Roger's children show: a good teacher is usually white and middle class, has a necessary grasp of his or her subject matter, communicates effectively by finding a style least offensive to the majority, vigorously avoids any serious challenge to prevailing accepted mores or the social relations which reinforce them, and exhibits an unflinching moral character. In the language of educational Reaganism, this translates into teaching the so-called canon of Western virtues, transmitting standardized and politically inoffensive content to students in ways that can be measured empirically and rendered morally neutral, adopting a work ethic that is scornful of unions, and equating school achievement with raising students' SAT scores and implementing tougher forms of classroom management. Bennett's general formula for classroom teaching, if accepted, turns teachers into hapless clerks or servants of the empire. But Reagan isn't content with an educational theory based solely on the values implicit in the Mr. Roger's view of the world. Teaching in the ghetto calls for an altogether different model. Reagan's view that educators also need to "get tough" was clearly reflected in public praise for the authoritarian tactics of Joe Clark, a New Jersey high school principal. Clark has gained his reputation by imposing his form of "educational leadership" on a school of inner-city students. It is a leadership style and pedagogical philosophy that has distinguished Clark through his intimidation of teachers who disagree with him, his expulsion of over nine hundred students whom he has labeled as perverts and troublemakers, and his imposing a schoolwide military model of top-down discipline. For example, students who commit infractions are made to sing the school anthem over the public intercom system. Clark, who wields a bullhorn and baseball bat as the trademarks of his educational philosophy, claims he has restored law and order to the school while simultaneously raising students' test scores. That these "gains" (which themselves are suspect) have taken place amidst the humiliation of both students and teachers, the expulsion of students who are most in need of schooling, and the creation of a police state atmosphere appears to heighten rather than diminish the stature of Joe Clark in the eyes of the Reagan administration. Such mean-spirited tactics have no place in a democratic classroom; they simply serve as a prescription for powerlessness and social conformity.

Central to Bennett's view, which is a popularized version of much of what can be found in the works of Bloom and Hirsch, and which is indicative of the recent ideological turn the Reagan administration has made in its language of educational reform, is the notion that it is not just the American economy which is at risk in the present failure of our schools, but the very notion of Western civilization itself. Rather than becoming an object of engagement and analysis, culture is to be understood through either the wisdom of the Great Books or a view of cultural restoration that is ironically paraded as cultural literacy. Within Bennett's social vision, cultural and social difference quickly becomes labeled as deficit, as the Other, as deviancy in need of psychological tending and control. At stake in this perspective is a view of history, culture, and politics committed to cleansing democracy of its critical and emancipatory possibilities. Similarly, in this perspective, the languages, cultures, and historical legacies of minorities, women, blacks, and other subordinate groups are actively silenced under the rubric of teaching as a fundamental act of national patriotism.

Following Bennett's lead, Bush conservatives seek to promulgate a view of education designed to rewrite the past from the perspective of the privileged and the powerful; this is a perspective that disdains both the democratic possibilities of pluralism and forms of pedagogy that critically engage issues central to developing an informed democratic public. Critical educators must offer a more progressive view of cultural literacy based on a respect for the languages and traditions that, as June Jordan has remarked, "conform to the truth of our many selves and would . . . lead us into the equality of power that a democratic state must represent."[2]

There is little doubt that the legacy of Reagan conservatism will continue to display an instinctive hostility to the democratic implications of public education. This is clear from the rhetoric structuring educational reforms at the level of state policy and in the rhetoric of liberal and conservative reformers, in which an image of schooling is evoked that enlarges corporate and hegemonic cultural concerns while diminishing a view of schooling dedicated to educating students for the ethical and political demands of democratic culture and public responsibility. The challenge that this view poses for critical educators should not be underestimated; there is a real urgency for educators to construct new frames of reference for the debate over educational reform by reclaiming schools in the interest of creating citizens capable of exhibiting civic courage, extending democratic possibilities, combating domestic tyranny, preventing assaults on human freedom and dignity, and struggling for cultural justice. It is important, especially at this time in our history, that a public discourse in education be developed that speaks not merely to adapting citizens to the existing configurations of power, but to creating a language of possibility and political imagination that will resuscitate the goals of self-determination and social transformation.

Schooling for democracy and civic courage: Elements of an educational platform

Within the last decade, a group of critical educational theorists has emerged that has combined the best work of social theorists such as John Dewey, John Childs, Paulo Freire, and Antonio Gramsci in a attempt to extend and advance an emancipatory vision of public schooling. In this work, schooling is viewed as a form of cultural politics, one which focuses on the centrality of power and struggle in defining both the nature and purpose of what it means to be educated. Within this perspective, schooling always represents an introduction to, preparation for, and legitimation of particular forms of social life. Rejecting the traditional view of instruction and learning as a neutral process antiseptically removed from the contexts of history, power, and ideology, critical educational theory begins with the assumption that schools are essential sites for organizing knowledge, power, and desire in the service of extending individual capacities and social possibilities. At the core of this discourse has been a twofold task. First, as a language of protest, critical educational theory has attempted to develop a counterlogic to those relations of power and ideologies in American society that mask a totalitarian ethics and strip critical ethical discourse from public life. This logic has pointed to the importance of developing an educational language that moves beyond moral outrage in order to provide a critical account of how individuals are constituted within schools as human agents within different moral and ethical discourses and experiences. Second, this perspective has attempted to develop a critical theory of education as part of a radical theory of ethics aimed at constructing a new vision of the future. In this view, American schooling becomes a vital sphere for extending civil rights, fighting for cultural justice, and developing new forms of democratic public life within a life-affirming public culture.

Critical educators need to revitalize this critical tradition by appropriating the best of its insights from the ghettoized language and sphere of academic life. In addition to a purely academic language of schooling, we need a public language, one that is theoretically rigorous, publicly accessible, and ethically grounded; called for is a language which refuses to reconcile schooling with inequality, which actively abandons those forms of pedagogical silencing which prevent us from becoming aware of and offended by the structures of oppression at work in both institutional and everyday life. We need a language that reconstructs schooling as a form of cultural politics, that links the construction of school knowledge to the concerns of everyday culture, that redefines the language of reform in unequivocal terms, and that situates the debate over education as part of a wider struggle for democracy itself. This wider struggle for democracy and social reform calls for an ethical conversion to the priority of labor over capital and to the elimination of economic and social injustices.

A critique of the conservative agenda for education should begin by defending schools as democratic public spheres responsible for providing an indispensable public service to the nation: that of awakening the moral, political, and civic responsibilities of its youth. More specifically, critical educators need to put forth a clearer vision of what education is supposed to do outside the imperatives of industry and why it is important as a public rather than merely private endeavor underwritten by the principles of liberal capitalism. By linking public education to the imperatives of a critical democracy rather than to the narrow imperatives of the marketplace, the debate on the meaning and nature of public education can be situated within the broader context of issues concerned with critical citizenship, politics, and the dignity of human life. In this view it becomes possible to provide a rationale and purpose for public education which aims at developing critical citizens and reconstructing community life by extending the principles of social justice to all spheres of economic, political, and cultural life. By viewing public schools as primary to the formation of a critical and engaged citizenry, schools can be envisioned as a social site from which to organize the energies of a moral vision. This means challenging the sterile instrumentalism, selfishness, and contempt for democratic community that has become the hallmark of the Reagan era. It means recognizing and struggling against the structured injustices in society which prevent us from extending our solidarity to those "others" who strain under the weight of various forms of oppression and exploitation. It also means enhancing and ennobling the meaning and purpose of education by giving it a truly central place in the social life of the nation, where it can become a public forum for addressing the needs of the poor, the dispossessed, and the disenfranchised.

A critical educational theory also needs to redefine the public role of what it means to be a teacher. Developing a public philosophy that offers the promise of reforming schools as part of a wider revitalization of public life has important implications for redefining the nature and purpose of teaching itself. The Reagan era has seriously undermined the possibilities for teachers to extend the role that schools might play as democratic public spheres. In fact, the Republican agenda for schooling, with its emphasis on standardized testing, massive accountability schemes for teacher evaluation, standardized curricula, and top-down, get-tough approaches to school discipline, has further contributed to the deskilling and disempowerment of teachers. There is a growing need to generate policies that improve the working conditions of teachers as well as dignify their role as public servants. Instead of defining teachers as clerks or technicians, we should reconceive the role of teachers as engaged and transformative intellectuals. This means viewing teachers as professionals who are able and willing to reflect upon the ideological principles that inform their practice, who connect pedagogical theory and practice to wider social issues, and who work together to share ideas, exercise power over the conditions of their labor, and embody in their teaching a vision of a better and more humane life. Central to this position is the need for critical educators to fight for reforms that enable teachers to work under conditions in which they have time to reflect critically, conduct collaborative research, engage in dialogue with their students, and learn about the communities in which their schools and others are located. At the very least this means significantly raising teacher salaries; extending opportunities for sabbaticals; redistributing power in schools among teachers and administrators; providing school systems with increased funding for in-service programs; creating national public information networks that provide resources and funds for teachers to engage in individual or collective research projects related to their teaching; and forming teacher-parent resource centers that offer opportunities for teachers, parents, and community people to work together more closely in shaping school policy. Finally, schools must be given the resources to help meet the social, cultural, economic, and political problems they encounter. Drugs, teenage pregnancy, illiteracy, nutrition, and health care are not problems the schools can ignore; new policy initiatives need to be formulated and put to work regarding how schools can function as a community resource, initiatives which view students as active agents working within wider cultural and political contexts.

Another issue of central importance that needs to be addressed more forcefully by critical educators is learning for empowerment. Reagan conservatives have consistently defined learning in ways that ignore the diversity of experiences, traditions, voices, histories, and community traditions that students bring to school. Cultural difference has often been treated as a deficit. A curriculum policy must be put forth that argues for the importance of drawing upon the cultural resources that students bring to schools as a basis for developing new skills and engaging existing knowledge claims. This concept suggests advocating curriculum policies and modes of pedagogy that both confirm and critically engage the knowledge and experience through which students give meaning to their lives. In effect, it suggests taking seriously, as a crucial aspect of learning, the experiences of students mediated by their own histories, languages, and traditions. This is not meant to imply that a student's experience should be romantically celebrated or unqualifiably endorsed; on the contrary, it means developing a critically affirmative language that works both *with and on* the experiences that students bring to the classroom. Although this approach is often designed to valorize the language forms, modes of reasoning, dispositions, and histories that students use in defining the world, it is also meant to make student experience an object of critical analysis and debate. Similarly, it means teaching students how to identify, unravel, and critically appropriate the codes, vocabularies, and deep grammar of different cultural traditions. Such a pedagogy provides the foundation for developing curricula and pedagogical models that replace the authoritative language of recitation and imposition with an approach that allows students to speak from their own histories and traditions while simultaneously challenging the very grounds of knowledge and power that work to silence them. Such a pedagogy makes possible a variety of human capacities which expand the range of social identities students may become. A curriculum which respects the diversity of student voices also provides a fundamental referent for legitimizing the principle of democratic tolerance as an essential condition for forms of solidarity rooted in the principles of trust, sharing, and a commitment to improving the quality of human life. Schools need to incorporate the diverse and contradictory stories that structure the interplay of experience, identity, and possibility that students bring to the classroom. As we have argued elsewhere, for many students schools are places of "dead time," holding centers that have little or nothing to do with either their lives or their dreams. Reversing that experience for students must be a central issue in reconstructing a new educational policy.[3]

Finally, critical educators need to address the role the federal government should assume in financing its school reform movement. While fighting to restructure the economy in ways that would bring it into greater harmony with forms of democratic socialism, critical educators must not forget that enduring qualitative educational improvements cannot take place without adequate funding. Four issues need to be dealt with in innovative ways. First, new revenue sources have to be developed as an alternative to the inequitable property tax system that privileges the students of the wealthy and the rich. Such sources might include taxing large corporations through a corporate profit tax; developing a graduated income tax; instituting a corporate property tax; or placing a hefty tax on real estate speculation. During the last decade, federal funding for military expenditures has doubled while educational funding has been cut by 15 percent. Needless to say, these priorities have to change so that the American government can demonstrate a commitment to life and education over death and militarism. Second, the problem of financing school reform must be tied to the wider issue of developing an alternative economic program committed to full employment or at the very least to extensive youth employment through the creation of programs in the public sector. Similarly, the federal government must make available the resources to ensure that qualified students can afford to enter and finish college. This means massively increasing the amount of money available for college loans, scholarships, and grants. Third, a major financial commitment must be made to the underprivileged and those youth who are labeled at risk. This might take the form of investing in a national family literacy campaign, providing health and nutrition programs for the poor while struggling at the federal level for forms of socialized medicine and a national day care plan, and doubling the financial commitment to Head Start programs. Fourth, although the issue of federal financing for educational reform does not exhaust the debate about improving the quality of education in this country, it needs to be argued that money does make a difference in providing suitable conditions for teachers to work, children to learn, and productive school programs to continue and succeed. Schools with broken toilets, inadequate school supplies, low teacher salaries, lead-filled paint, and limited resources for substitute teachers fail to educate, in part, because they lack financial resources. This situation points to the importance of the critical educators not only fighting for policies aimed at increasing federal spending on education, but also targeting financial aid for those populations labeled at risk.

At the current time, critical educators have a historic opportunity to reclaim the importance of public schooling as a basis for critical citizenship, civic responsibility, and democratic public life. Setting a new theoretical and ethical context for the debate on educational reform that will take place in the 1990s is a challenge that must not go unanswered. Central to this challenge is the need for education to develop a new public language of vision and hope that speaks to new forms of political and cultural analysis, and a deepening and extension of the range of democratic social relations and practices in our schools and classrooms.

Re-presenting the text

The purpose of this book is to provide a series of articles that we believe demonstrate the basic elements of what we call a "language of critique and possibility." Central to this language is a new vision of educational reform consistent with the civic hopes and democratic possibilities that public education has long held for most Americans. The aim of such a language is fourfold: to define the purpose of schooling as part of a democratic public philosophy; to reconstruct the theory-and-practice relationship as a normative, political endeavor whose importance is defined by a project of democratic empowerment rather than the technical mastery of skills; to develop a cultural politics of schooling in relation to a politics of difference and cultural justice that enables both teachers and students to speak from their own voices, histories, and experiences; and to provide the theoretical basis for a critical pedagogy that incorporates those knowledge forms and social practices that constitute the spheres of popular and everyday life.

Although united by a critical relationship to the prevailing orthodoxies in educational theory and practice, the essays included in this volume span a wide range of topics, are animated by different concerns, and are structured by a variety of theoretical discourses. As disparate in scope and specificity in relation to the issues as these essays are, the central themes engaged by each of the contributors and the continuity of assumptions linking them nevertheless converge to introduce modes of critical inquiry that contribute to a deeper understanding of schooling as a form of cultural politics. Taken together, these essays are devoted in their diverse ways to developing and demonstrating the importance of the aforementioned aims that we believe are central to developing a critical theory of schooling. The four sections that make up this book parallel the lines of inquiry we have attempted to define in this introduction. In what follows, we will briefly summarize each of these sections along with their respective articles.

The contributions that make up Part 1 of this volume, which deals with schooling and the struggle for public life, direct themselves in varying degrees to the task of rethinking the nature and purpose of schooling. Such a "rethinking" is not meant to occur at the conceptual or analytical level alone, but rather as part of a new democratic philosophy that grounds itself not only in a professional pedagogical discourse, but also in a language of public life. Underwriting these essays is both a criticism of the neoconservative and liberal discourses that currently structure the logic of the new reform platforms endorsing the move towards national educational "excellence" and a materialist challenge to the "academicized" direction presently undertaken by some theorists in the critical educational tradition itself.

Signaling the emergence of the categories of culture and politics into our understanding of how schools work, and seeking to redefine the role of knowledge within the contexts of cultural and curriculum studies, these contributions strongly suggest that the categories which we use to understand and explain the purpose and process of schooling must be made as multifarious, as nuanced, and as variable in detail as the technologies of power that structure the social relations of classroom life; furthermore, they must become part of a critical vernacular that attempts to break free from the preserve of the academy where debates on the purpose and effects of schooling too often are radically disjoined from the manifold relations of everyday life, including struggles that take place within neighborhoods; churches; youth, minority, and women's communities; and workplace-based communities of resistance: in short, within those very sites which set the preconditions for group formations and social action capable of vitiating the discourse of privatization and individualism common to our postmodern condition. In addition to calling for a new critical vernacular for analyzing the social, economic, and political contexts of school-society relations, these essays stress the importance of redefining the very nature and function of schooling itself; that is, rather than conceiving schools to be monolithically present as learning institutions, these essays urge us to rethink the contribution of schools to society in terms of public spheres designed to intervene in the serial, the mechanical, and the mass-produced aspects of everyday life in which inequality is able to reproduce itself. In this way schools become agencies for reconstructing and transforming the dominant status quo culture. What these essays collectively achieve is to rescue the term *culture* from its New Right and liberal status as a Platonic time capsule of elite knowledge or a community register of statistics and facts, and situate it in the nexus of power and knowledge and the contextual relations of class, gender, and race. The end result is the creation of a tactical and strategic connection among critical theory, pedagogical practice, and public philosophy which is designed to provide educators with a more productive and illuminating model for understanding and transforming existing relations of power and privilege in the classroom and the wider social sphere. What emerges from these attempts are the beginnings of a new public discourse formulated for use among those groups of educators, parents, administrators, and public servants who wish to develop a critical theory of practice learning for the modern age.

Martin Carnoy begins with the position that schools have become a product of both "reproductive" forces–attempts by the dominant class to impose its concept of the world on the mass of students–and "democratizing" forces–attempts by subordinate groups to shape schools and school expansion to contribute to the development of their cultures in the context of an American capitalist development that serves them and not solely the business class. Carnoy argues that prevailing interpretations of school reform have, for the most part, failed to take into account an analysis of culture in relation to the state. Examining the role of schooling in the conflict between dominant and subordinate ideologies and the role of cultural resistance in American schools, Carnoy urges schools to participate in the expansion of mass culture and in the weakening of the grasp of dominant business ideologies as relate to education. Schools, claims Carnoy, should serve as sites dedicated to counterhegemonic struggle and resistance. Whether or not schools can become agents of counterhegemony–of a change in the dominant culture–involves a struggle more over the *control* of schools than the *content* of schooling, especially in relation to the dominant culture's control over access to knowledge. Carnoy maintains that it is with social movements outside the school that the future of counterhegemony resides, since these groups can help schooling make an impact on American mass culture and on history and who gets to make it.

Samuel Bowles and Herbert Gintis maintain that liberal educational theory, grounded as it is in neoclassical economics, with its propensity to partition learning (human development) from choosing (human freedom), is prone to obfuscate the issue of domination in the educative process in which the freedom of the student is completely subordinated to an institutional will in which preferences are externally imposed. The authors stress a "becoming-by-action" model of individual choice as a means of correcting the arrested development of liberal educational theory. This means exercising one's freedom to choose independently of collective sentiment, and entering into mutual, reciprocal, and participatory action with others to achieve commonly defined goals. By reconstituting liberal political philosophy in this way, the authors claim that it becomes more compatible with a democratic theory of education by constructing a space for individuals to develop their preferences, their capacities for social participation, and their ability to make critical and informed choices.

Michael Apple directs his attention toward the advent of the neoconservative consensus in the United States which has, regrettably, received the approbation of many of our social institutions such as the schools. To a large extent, the discourse of the New Right has laundered the term *culture* of its dialectical and political dimensions, deflecting attention away from the significance of popular culture as a category for understanding the manner in which student subjectivities are constructed in opposition to the goals and intentions of many school programs. Apple is primarily concerned with the process by which dominant beliefs become dominant—how they "win ascendency" through a specific and contingent process of ideological struggle. Maintaining that in order to fully comprehend the terms of the current debate in educational reform one must have a clear grasp of "society's already unequal cultural, economic, and political dynamics that provide the center of gravity around which education functions," Apple links these dynamics to the debate over property and person rights at a time of grave economic crisis in the United States.

Apple skillfully charts out how conservative ideologies appeal to people, not by creating a false consensus but by working on reorganizing the feelings, the contradictory lived experiences, and the popular sentiments of large groups of individuals by manipulating their perceived needs, fears, and hopes. Tracing historically the political, economic, and ideological reasons why the social democratic consensus that led to the extension of person rights in education, politics, and the economy has slowly faded, Apple documents how the new "hegemonic bloc" of neoconservative thinking and practices is being constructed, and how it relates to critical concerns surrounding the curriculum.

Miriam David offers an astute examination of how home-school relations are built into the formation of the capitalist educational system. She pays particular attention to the structuring of parental responsibility for children and the role of the school in promoting traditional family models. One of her central concerns is that the gendered division of labor in parenting largely operates unproblematically, reinforcing gender differences in both family, educational, and work activities in adulthood. Furthermore, she describes how the current call for educational reform and a return to more rigorous academic standards by the Thatcher government, in power since 1979, has sustained old educational inequalities while recreating new ones, often reducing parents to the role of ungendered consumers shopping for a middle-class product. In particular, David discusses how traditional family models fostered by the school condemn minority children by judging their patterns of family socialization against Eurocentric, Christian standards. Recent British initiatives in the area of multicultural education are uncovered to reveal a denigration of minority children and their cultures and their differential subjugation according to race, class, and gender. David describes how, within such a logic, schooling serves to replicate appropriate parental behaviors and roles by requiring certain forms of parental involvement in the schools while at the same time serving to structure the role of teachers as types of surrogate parents and parents as types of adjunct teachers.

The contributions in Part 2, which examine rethinking schooling as the language of reform, seek to capture a greater historical and contextual understanding of the relation of schooling to the wider social order and the role that teachers can play as critical agents of social change, capable of effecting a new relationship between theory and practice and action and reflection. It becomes clear from these essays that what is needed, if schools are to truly make a difference, is a language of reform that is born of a socially and morally insurgent imagination, one that involves both critique and hope, that challenges and engages the educators who choose to appropriate it, and, at the same time, that provokes those interested in educational reform to rethink and reshape the specificities of their experiences as teachers, administrators, parents, and students with respect to the aims and purposes of present-day schooling. Highly critical of the mechanical, efficiency-oriented approach to schooling that has dominated the language of school reform over the last two decades, these contributors seek in their analyses to liberate reason and evaluation from the obviousness of the literal and the measurable and to distinguish practical and emancipatory knowledge from the merely technical and skill-oriented knowledge that has seeped into mainstream curriculum thinking from the ever-present discourse of scientism. The new language of school reform that must gain ascendency over the next decade has to be built on a new ethical and intellectual foundation that can effectively countermand the ideological shift taking place in education toward the New Right. Such a foundation must rest on a preferred commitment to assist the disadvantaged and disenfranchised, to search for new forms of solidarity in the ongoing struggle against oppression, and to construct new forms of citizenship which move beyond a focus on individual virtue and the dangers of personalized moral transgression. Rather, the new model of citizenship that needs to be mobilized in our classrooms must begin to consider the meaning of cooperative learning, collective struggle for the common good, and a greater understanding of the sociology of oppression and the structural dimensions of evil that often occupy the very foundation of our social relations and our cultural, economic, and institutional life.

Like Michael Apple, Walter Feinberg rejects the view that has prevailed in the Age of Reagan: that schools should serve as a bulwark for national defense interests and as a recruitment center for participants in our industrialized economy. He reports on the ideological shift that is occurring in disparate fields today which suggests the need to drastically reform the voice of institutionalized authority which has served as a major mechanism of large-scale social inequality. Discussing in detail the various reform documents and reports on the crisis in American schooling as part of a wider ideological shift in American society, Feinberg seeks to build an intellectual and moral tradition that will enable students to begin to reflect on the ideological and material shortcomings of the present era.

Philip Wexler argues that the history of the curriculum can essentially be seen in the victory of scientism over humanism, a victory in which the scientific has replaced humanity, spirit, and reason. Current attempts by the school reform movement to redefine knowledge as skill and information echo, for Wexler, Horkheimer and Adorno's notion that a culture of scientism would reinforce a rationalized and alienating daily social life. Wexler sees the advent of postmodernism as the antithesis of scientism, yet at the same time he claims that the ironic revolts of postmodernism really reflect yet another form of scientism in that both scientism and postmodernism dissolve into the deeper logic of commodity culture. Wexler maintains that postmodernism ended when it could no longer provide any values as an alternative to the marketplace.

Drawing upon his own ethnographic research, Wexler reveals that the most powerful aspect of the sociality of the school is its institutional authority to define legitimate knowledge and personnel, and that the informal social lives of students largely support the institutional production of stratified identities. Although there are students who actively resist the social rules and rites of the school, each form of student opposition is paired with a pattern of student affirmation. Together, the paired identities follow the overarching institutional class form of the school. Although the split identities of the students are unified under the class character of the institution as "symbolic economies of identity," Wexler claims that the fusion of identity and institution is so pervasive in schools that the basic binary conception of resistance and domination that has gained ascendency in critical studies of schooling is no longer serviceable for our understanding of the hegemonic operations within the cultural field of school life. Against the backdrop of a failed oppositional culture, Wexler argues for a "new science" which would offer a revolutionary openness presently derived by contemporary culture and social relations. This opening, he contends, can be found in the specificity of history and scientific practice.

Richard Smith and Anna Zantiotis's contribution illustrates how teacher education has come to constitute a social form of practicality that is fundamentally preoccupied with the specifics of occupational needs. In fact, this social form has, over the years, solidified into a regime of truth in which the source of knowledge, skills, and attitudes for the production of knowledge about teaching and for teacher preparation has become located in the objective relations of teaching itself: that is, from within its own performative text. In other words, the "doing" of teaching has become privileged over the ability and necessity of teachers to reflect critically on what constitutes the ideological dimensions of pedagogy. Through an explication of dominant, realist, and avant-garde discourses on teacher education and their historical situatedness, Smith and Zantiotis argue for an approach to teacher education that takes seriously the political, economic, and social implications of schooling and the part played by teacher education as a site for the production of knowledge.

All of the authors in Part 3, which focuses on the relationships among schooling, ideology, and student voice, address in different terms how schooling functions as a cultural and political site that embodies a project of transformation and regulation. Schooling in this section is viewed as a form of cultural politics, that is, as a place in which a sense of identity, worth, meaning, and value is constructed through social relations which legitimate particular knowledge forms, ideologies, and ways of life. As the introduction to particular ways of life, schooling is analyzed as a site where students are both enabled and silenced, where meaning is produced within specific arrangements of power, and where contradictions and tensions emerge between the human capacities students bring to schools and the social forms that mediate them. In many ways, schooling is a process of marking off culturally desired forms of meaning and practice; it is an ideological practice that implicates the wider society, the institutional life of the school, the familial patterns in the surrounding community, and the lives of the students and teachers in the production of stories and narratives that challenge as well as produce particular forms of oppression and violence. But is is also a site that expands human capacities through practices that celebrate a pedagogy of and for difference, that presupposes the importance of democratic community, that inextricably connects student achievement with the ability to take risks, and that affirms the voices of teachers and students while simultaneously encouraging them to be self-reflective and more socially critical.

Henry A. Giroux explores some of these issues by addressing three important themes. First, he argues for a new public philosophy to provide schools with a sense of purpose and meaning that supports the education of students as critical risk-taking citizens; second, he calls for a theory of ethics that provides the referent for teachers to act as engaged and connected intellectuals; third, he maintains that existing forms of radical educational theory have failed to appropriate some of the more important theoretical gains being made in the wider fields of social theory. In keeping with this position, he then draws from some of the theoretical work being done in literary and cultural studies to develop what he calls a "pedagogy of and for difference."

Michelle Fine, in her article, "Silencing and Nurturing Voice in an Improbable Context: Urban Adolescents in Public School," analyzes the various mechanisms through which the practice of silencing works in schools to undermine the project of individual and social empowerment. Focusing on the ways in which minority students from low-income families are positioned within pedagogical and administrative practices in a New York public school, Fine demonstrates how power, knowledge, and ideology structure curriculum, pedagogy, and school regulations so as to shut down and disconnect the voices, experiences, and histories of subordinate groups. But Fine is not content just to analytically map how the practice of silencing works through various aspects of the everyday workings of schools; she is most concerned with developing a theoretical, political, and ethical case for naming oppression. For Fine, this means developing an educational theory and practice that recognizes and addresses the importance of affirming and legitimating the various voices that give meaning to the diverse groups of disempowered students that increasingly inhabit American schools.

Peter McLaren's essay on ideology and education addresses the importance of breaking away from the heritage of Marxian categories in order to readmit hope and possibility into the language of educational theory and practice. Specifically, McLaren focuses his critique on Marxian orthodoxy and its one-sided view of ideology, particularly its failure to recognize the limits of meaning and rationality as the exclusive terrain of both subjectivity and subjection. For McLaren, ideology better serves as a critical and empowering referent when it expands its focus to include not only the production of meaning but also the production of desire and the mobilization of affect. McLaren attempts to expand our understanding of how power both enables and constrains in various ways through practices that focus on the body as a central terrain of struggle: that is, he investigates as a pedagogical and ideological issue how the body becomes the site at which desire is mobilized, pleasure is experienced, joy is invested, and humiliation administered. In sum, McLaren charts out the fundamental elements of a theory of the body and desire as part of a wider theory of how students come to be positioned with the matrix of knowledge, desire, and power.

In Part 4, the authors take up various theoretical positions regarding the relationship between popular culture and critical pedagogy. What unites the articles in this section is the refusal to view popular culture as either merely vulgar knowledge or as an unproblematic and romanticized sphere of resistance and opposition. Instead, it is viewed as a site of struggle and

contestation, an important cultural and social terrain that authorizes, en-
dows, and sometimes imperils youth and their identities and which simultaneously serves to empower or disempower them. The authors recognize
that educators who refuse to acknowledge popular culture as a significant
basis of knowledge often devalue students by refusing to work with the
knowledge that students actually have and in doing so eliminate the possibility of developing a pedagogy that links school knowledge to the differing
subject relations that help to constitute their everyday lives. It becomes
clear in this section that a more critical theory of schooling demands that
teachers be more attentive to the ways in which students make both affective and semantic investments as part of their attempt to regulate and give
meaning to their lives. This suggests that educators make popular culture
a legitimate object of school knowledge so as to deepen the relationship
between schooling and everyday life and to better grasp as a basis for critical
analysis the totality of elements that organize student identities, experiences, and cultures.

In his study of children's literature, Joel Taxel argues that such literature
has to be analyzed as more than simply a hegemonic discourse. In effect,
Taxel examines such texts as part of a wider struggle over a selective tradition
and its relationship to complex and sometimes contradictory ideologies and
messages. For Taxel, reading texts is a form of cultural politics and demands
a theory of learning that views knowledge as a contested terrain, as a reposi-
tory where meaning is produced within, outside, and between dominant
and subordinate traditions, that is, among the discourses of dominant,
mass, and popular cultures.

David Shumway makes a strong case for using popular culture in the
classroom by examining the importance of teaching rock 'n' roll. For Shumway, rock 'n' roll cannot be treated merely as music, but as a cultural form
that embodies codes, conventions, rules, and values that transcend their
being relegated either to the status of folk culture or an uncritical populist
tradition. Shumway argues that using rock 'n' roll in the classroom provides
a counterpoint to the way the body is shaped and policed in schools. Popular culture presents another body to students, one that is in-formed by
pleasure and joy, as well as a body that refuses regimentation and deadening habit. Rock 'n' roll in this view is itself a contradictory form, containing elements of both domination and emancipation, and as such needs
to be developed and analyzed as part of a critical pedagogy. For Shumway,
rock 'n' roll, like any other popular form, should be treated as text and
needs to be read critically, especially when it plays such a powerful role in
shaping students' perceptions and social practices. In effect, a critical pedagogy of the popular is important in Shumway's view because it helps stu-

dents learn skills regarding how their own interests are being either reproduced or severed through particular cultural forms.

In the final article of this section, Giroux and Simon argue that both
pedagogy and popular culture have been ignored by critical and radical
educational theorists. They proceed to outline the basic elements of a critical pedagogy and then raise some serious issues about how to rethink the
notion of the popular and what this rethinking might suggest for incorporating the latter into a critical pedagogy. They finish by raising a number
of questions that have been asked by students and educators who have trav-
eled the difficult journey from critical educational theory to classroom practice. The questions suggested and the problems raised serve as a reminder
that a critical pedagogy is never finished, that it is always in a state of tension because it is supportive of a cultural politics that defines itself through
a project of hope and possibility.

PART ONE

Schooling and Public Life

Education, State, and Culture in American Society

Martin Carnoy

More than in any other modern nation, the American state (defined as the set of political institutions at the federal, state, and local level) has founded its political legitimacy and economic development policy on incorporating heterogeneous waves of immigration into a mass national "culture." Public schools were designed to play an important role in this process. From their beginnings in Massachusetts as a broader public (rather than individual village or town) institution, the state (in its more general meaning, as used in this essay) attempted to define knowledge (curriculum, texts), who would be permitted to transmit knowledge (teacher credentialing), and what the transmission process was to be (how classrooms and schools would be organized).

There have been many interpretations of this early school reform (see, for example, Katz, 1970; Bowles and Gintis, 1975; Tyack, 1982). Some have argued that it was primarily aimed at socializing an Irish immigrant and other lower-class "rabble" into a disciplined labor force for fledgling New England industries. Others suggest that it was a political response to demands for state-regulated schooling and school expansion by a broad-based social movement which saw higher-quality schooling as fundamental to social mobility in a rapidly changing Massachusetts economy.

The difference between these interpretations is crucial for any understanding of culture and the relation between public education and culture. The first interpretation argues that schools impose a dominant ideology on a resisting mass whose own culture is destroyed in the process. Young people from subordinate groups, in that model, are implicitly relegated to whatever role the dominant class has in store for them – they are separated from a culture (and knowledge) that they understand and control and are reintegrated into a set of necessarily alienating norms and values that are unknowable and uncontrollable. Accepting this dominant-class view of their roles – in this interpretation – is tantamount to becoming "separated," with all that that implies for self-image and psychological well-being. Resistance to incorporation is tantamount to self-preservation, to developing alternative possibilities that are rooted in mass culture, including mass knowledge and mass morality.

The second interpretation claims that schools incorporate students into a set of norms and values that already reflect mass culture. In this interpretation, a business or capitalist culture has always existed in America, but this has only been one of many influences on mass education, and not necessarily the dominant one. In that interpretation, acceptance of school norms and the cognitive curriculum is the condition for integration and assimilation. Far from separation, it is the minimum condition of avoiding alienation, for school socialization and knowledge transmission provide the keys to becoming a full participant-member of dominant mass culture. Resistance, in this interpretation, is self-marginalization.

The problem with both these interpretations is that neither develops a clear and consistent analysis of the state and culture. It is the state which perpetrates the reform. Henry Levin and I (Carnoy and Levin, 1985) have argued that the democratic capitalist state necessarily has to pursue contradictory aims in its education policy. On the one hand, it must socialize and train labor for capitalist production. Part of the socialization is to make the inequalities, injustices, and hierarchies of capitalist production appear as natural consequences of economic and social life and to promote capitalism as the most efficient and just of all economic systems. This "reproductive" role of the state and the schools creates and imposes an ideological representation of dominant male business culture. It also necessarily subordinates all other cultures, including those of European and Asian immigrant groups, blacks, Hispanics, women, "assimilated" working people, and even property-owning populist farmers – as they struggle to survive within corporate capitalism. Subordination means subjugating their cultural development to the business class's conception of knowledge, human relations, economic roles and rewards, justice, language, and morality.

On the other hand, schools in America have also been charged with inculcating children with democratic ideals and – as an important institution in a democratic state – with responding to demands on the state for equalizing access to material goods and services, particularly education itself. Schools have therefore been an important focus of social movements clamoring for greater economic and social equality. If it is assumed that schools are also charged with "democratizing" American society and have been shaped historically by the masses contesting business ideology, the socialization and knowledge transmission taking place in American schools cannot be seen as simply the imposition of a business ideology on subordinate groups. To take such a view would require assuming either that all educational expansion and reform over the past 150 years have been a creation of the business class or that the masses demand more schooling because they are fully accepting of the business conception of educational form and content.

Levin and I argue that American education is a product of both "reproductive" forces—attempts by the dominant class to impose its concept of the world on the mass of youth in school—and "democratizing" forces—attempts by subordinate groups to shape schools and school expansion to contribute to the development of their cultures in the context of an American capitalist development that serves them and not just the business class.

Critical analyses of American education have stressed only its negative and exclusionary aspects—the schools' "hidden" message of subordination and failure designed to cull out those youngsters unable to handle the common curriculum. Even today, in an era when approximately 35 percent of eighteen- to twenty-year-olds enter postsecondary education, 25 percent of high school students do not finish twelfth grade with their class. More than 50 percent never enter any kind of college. A high fraction of these is black or Hispanic.

In our view, the educational system's failure to socialize young people adequately—even socially marginalized minorities—should not be necessarily seen as schools' *purposeful* objective, even in their reproductive role. We argue that the negative message and the failure to impart cognitive skills to a significant fraction of youth are probably dysfunctional even to reproducing a class division of labor and capitalist relations of production. They are particularly dysfunctional to developing the state's legitimacy among those groups whose children fail in school.

In this essay, I develop a model for understanding the role of ideology and cultural resistance in American schools. I depart from the important contributions made by Giroux (1981), Apple (1982), Willis (1977), and others. I find that the nature and meaning of resistance in schools is a highly complex issue in a democratic capitalist society. Business ideology has been and continues to be shaped by social movements and wherever schools have changed as a result of such movements. Today's American public schools are not elitist institutions. They welcome academic success by all social classes. Yet they also tend to define learning and knowledge in ways that make academic success particularly difficult for children from lower-income families and from certain groups. We know that fundamental skills taught in schools (language skills, math, and science) can be learned more effectively by all children than they are now and can certainly be taught in ways that certain groups, now effectively excluded, would find much more accessible. This is not a "resolvable" paradox, but rather–in the view presented below–a paradox that implies exploitable political space for those that are willing to engage in the struggle for change.

Schools and the state

Schools in America are largely public institutions. As such, they are subject to direct political pressures that are conditioned by the overall conflict between capital and labor, by the changing structure of the labor market, and by various social movements seeking greater equality. Educational institutions are therefore not just reproducers of dominant-class conceptions of what and how much schooling should be provided; public schools also reflect social demands. Attempts by the capitalist state to reproduce the relations of production and the class division of labor confront social movements that demand more public resources for their needs and more say in how those resources are to be used. The capitalist state and its educational system are therefore more than just a means for co-opting social demands, or for simply manipulating them to satisfy dominant-class needs. Social demands shape the state and education.

These demands usually emerge from the defensive position in which subordinate groups find themselves in a society dominated by business-class values and norms. The reforms demanded may therefore appear as co-opted or manipulated. But to assume that they are completely manipulated is to underestimate subordinate groups' consciousness of their dominated position in capitalist society. Such an assumption relegates all popular action to the realm of an unconscious and inevitable reproduction of capitalist relations of production and/or assigns ultimate control of the political process to the business class (what Gramsci called "passive revolution"). But a social conflict theory of the state (see Poulantzas, 1978) argues that popular action speaks authentically to mass needs. That the reforms achieved by such action may be partially altered by capitalist class power acting through the state apparatuses does not negate the authenticity of the social movements themselves.

In the social conflict theory, the struggle of dominated groups to change the conditions that oppress them and the attempts of dominant groups to reproduce the conditions of their dominance are the key to understanding changes in the economy, in social relations, and in the culture. These changes, in turn, are reflected in state policies and in public schooling, both prime targets of the conflict.

The nature of the conflict in each historical period is qualitatively different because the structures of production, the state, the schools, and other institutions keep changing as a result of previous conflict. For example, the conflict between labor and capital in the nineteenth century contributed to a transformation of the dominant form of capitalist enterprise from a small, competitive firm to a giant corporate oligopoly. With the crisis of corporate capitalism in the 1930s and the conflict that was part of that crisis, the state became involved in the production process (albeit indirectly), especially in the distribution of output. After the Second World War, transnational capital became the dominant form of capitalist production. Labor struggles have changed and so have social movements. They condition social change and are also profoundly conditioned by it.

Various fractions of the business class attempt to fashion education and other state apparatuses for the reproduction of capitalist production (primarily to make it more profitable and less conflictive), and social movements attempt to fashion these same institutions in ways that better serve workers, women, minorities, or certain groups—religious and otherwise— that feel threatened by state secularism, the advance of minorities, or the more equal role of women in society. As capitalism changes, some of the demands made by business groups on the schools also change, although the underlying theme of reproducing the relations remains the same. Similarly, the demands of social movements have changed with social change, even though the underlying theme of extending or maintaining their rights as citizens and workers has not. Furthermore, the demands of some social movements are not inconsistent with the demands of business, particularly when their focus is on strengthening discipline in the classroom, concentrating curriculum on the three Rs, increasing graduation requirements, or excluding certain books from the classroom because they offend Fundamentalist religious interpretations. Education can thus be understood in the context of a complex social conflict that changes as a result of previous struggle.

The changing organization of production is central to this understanding because—in capitalist society—social conflict is so deeply rooted in that organization. Capitalist production (and from what we have seen historically, production in bureaucratic socialist societies as well—see Carnoy and Samoff, forthcoming) is marked by a social division of labor that separates intellectual work from manual work, by a separation of technology from the process of work, by the use of science and technology to rationalize power, and by an organic relation between knowledge and power.

As part of this reproductive dynamic, the state incorporates these divisions into all its apparatuses. Moreover, the state helps reproduce capitalist relations of production under changing conditions of production by taking knowledge and attempting to transform it into language and rituals that separate that knowledge from consumers and workers. The state regularly legitimizes business ideology by transforming self-serving economic and social views into technocratic "facts" and decisions allegedly based on "scientific" studies and "expertise." In the state, the knowledge-power relation is not only an ideological legitimization; the separation of intellectual from manual work concerns science itself. The state incorporates science into the mechanisms of power; intellectual experts as a body of specialists are controlled through their financial dependence on modern state apparatuses. Most professionals have become state functionaries, in one form or another. In the United States, 33 percent of all university graduates are directly employed by the federal, state, or local government, many in public education itself. Twenty-five percent of scientists and engineers depend on military spending alone (DeGrasse, 1983, p. 101).

At the same time, social movements make demands on the state for increased protection *against* experts and technology, as well as for increased access to information. For example, blacks have fought for years against the "expert" opinion that they were not ready for equal treatment in schools and the workplace. The ideological battles on U. S. Vietnam policy were carried out on the field of information and expertise reaching the American public. Unions have had a long conflict with business and much of the "official" medical organizations over the expert definition of and responsibility for health hazards on the job. Environmental organizations spend much of their energy fighting government and business experts with expertise of their own on pollution and the protection of natural resources. The antinuclear movement has challenged expert opinion on nuclear power plants, arms, and, most recently, the massive Strategic Defense Initiative. All these conflicts are carried out in the state apparatuses, through legislative challenges, in the courts, and through the agencies whose charge is to protect the public against excesses of the private market.

As part of its democratic dynamic, therefore, the capitalist state can produce knowledge that protects the public and extends democratic control over private production. The democratic dynamic also conflicts with the state's use of knowledge for reproduction. Some state agencies may produce knowledge and expertise that contradict that of other agencies. Thus reproductive and democratic dynamics conflict within the state itself.

Education is, of course, part of the state apparatus. Besides contributing, first, to the reproduction of the class structure through the distribution of youth into the various functions of the labor force on the basis of their educational qualifications and, second, to the reproduction of the relations through an ideological inculcation of bourgeois values (see Althusser, 1971), the educational system provides the technical skills and know-how necessary for the continued accumulation of capital. The schools not only distribute knowledge; they produce it. Workers pay for the education of their children, and part of the return to these expenditures goes to maintain the rate of profit.

The production of knowledge is carried out not only through teaching students, but also through state spending on research in public and private universities and research institutions. The state plays an increasingly important role in guiding the direction of innovation by investing heavily in research and development. The space program, defense expenditures, grants to universities—all contribute to a particular direction of innovation, one that assists in raising profits to private capital, but also one that expands development, raises wages, and increases access to higher education for working-class and minority youth.

Furthermore, the educational apparatus itself is an important source of employment and upward mobility for lower-income and economically marginalized groups in society. In advanced industrial societies, the teachers and administrators of the school system form part of the "new petty bourgeoisie" (Poulantzas, 1975), which is drawn from sections of the working class and provides upward mobility for women and minority males. More than half of all the women and minority men professionals in the United States are employed by the government, mostly in local government, and primarily in the educational system (see Carnoy, Shearer, and Rumberger, 1983), although this percentage has fallen in the 1970s and 1980s. Salaries in government employment for these groups average higher (in the same education and age category) than in the private sector. The schools are therefore also employers and contribute—through that employment—to expanding opportunities for subordinate groups.

The educational system is not simply an instrument of business or of other dominant groups to shape youth—according to social-class origin, race, ethnicity, or gender—into some conception held by these groups of what social roles these youth should fill. Schooling is the product of conflict between the dominant and the dominated. Conflicts in the production sector, for example, affect schools, just as they condition all state apparatuses. The more general political and social conflict between different visions of the future of American society which takes place in the democratic political arena also encompasses the schools. Education is at once the result of contradictions and the source of new contradictions. It is an arena of conflict over the production of knowledge, ideology, and employment, a place where social movements try to meet their needs and fight for the expansion of their access to resources and citizenship rights, and where business attempts to reproduce its hegemony.

Because public education is not completely obedient to the reproductive imperative, it may not contribute optimally to creating an "ideal" division of labor or to the socialization of youth into the process of smooth capital accumulation. In that case, business groups and their political allies (religious hierarchies, for example, some union leadership, and ethnic groups who are ideologically committed to a strongly anti-Soviet foreign policy) will attempt to reproduce those relations either by tightening discipline of labor in production, by pressuring the state bureaucracy to act in a way that disciplines labor and other subordinate groups, or by bringing the educational system back into line by means of business-inspired educational reform. Thus, the development of contradictions in education is not the end of the dialectical process created by the tension between the democratic and reproductive dynamics. The process continues from one round to the next.

Culture and ideology

The American Heritage Dictionary (Second College Edition, 1985) defines *culture* as the "totality of socially transmitted behavior patterns, arts, beliefs, institutions, and all other products of human work and thought characteristic of a community or population." In a politically democratic, capitalist, industrialized society, especially one that is composed of a number of relatively separate immigrant communities from every continent with rather different immigrant histories, this "totality of socially transmitted behavior patterns" is difficult to define.

The difficulty derives both from the openly contested concept of culture between the dominant and dominated groups in capitalist society and the overlay of the multiplicity of immigrant cultures particular to the United States (also characteristic of other countries such as Canada, Australia, Argentina, and Brazil). Throughout U. S. history, dominant groups have attempted to impose a set of values and norms on subordinate groups. Some subordinate groups were so marginalized that they were excluded even from this imposition. Native Americans, blacks, and later, Mexican and Asian immigrants were outside the boundaries of national definition required to be socialized into some version of the dominant culture.

The "culture" which the dominant group imposes is not the culture of the business class itself, but some ahistorical version of it which we can call "ideology." I say "ahistorical" because ideology, unlike culture, does not include the specific history-making capability of culture, which is reserved for the dominant group to whom the culture belongs and which they alone have the capacity to create. Were the dominant group to impose its culture on subordinate groups, that would imply that the subordinate groups would, by accepting that imposition, also be receiving the capacity to shape and develop the dominant business class culture in their own image. This is not what the dominant group has in mind at all.

Ideology, to the contrary, has no historical component. That is not to say it does not have a history. But its history is one that is shaped by the dominant group. Ideology is the dominant group's conception of what the subordinate group should aspire to – that is, what the subordinate group should take as its values and norms. Business-class culture for workers is to work hard and productively for honest wages, save, stay sober, raise a solid family, aspire to be an entrepreneur, be loyal to the firm, and so forth. Male business culture for women is to work in supportive female occupations when young, marry, raise a family, support the husband in his work, and inculcate the children with the values of hard work, savings, loyalty, and honesty. Business culture for immigrants is to assimilate themselves into the American work ethic, save for the future, and climb up the ladder of American opportunity. For white male workers and immigrants, this version of business culture holds out the possibility of enormous financial success – striking it rich – and ascendency into the business class itself. Indeed, capitalist or business ideology was the first cultural representation in history that made membership in the dominant class theoretically accessible to all – at least (until recently), all white males.

One of the most important manifestations of the successful imposition in America of dominant-group ideology has been increased material consumption. The very expansion of consumption by subordinate groups has enabled them to possess the symbolic accoutrements of the dominant business culture, a culture that stresses its accomplishments above all in material terms. Thus, a suit and a tie, a beautiful dress, an automobile, a house in the suburbs, and eventually travel to Florida and foreign lands and dinners in restaurants with expensive wine were and are apparent manifestations of "incorporation" into the dominant culture.

Is such increased consumption purely ideological? In part it is. Subordinate groups will always consume a "lesser" and interpretive version of what the dominant group consumes. What is desirable consumption is also defined by the dominant groups. In that definition, whatever subordinate groups consume is not as "beautiful," not as interesting, not as satisfying as what the dominant group consumes. Therefore, subordinate groups will always aspire to consume more. But since they will not be determining what "beautiful," "interesting," and "satisfying" consumption is (an activity left to the dominant group), they will never be able to get enough.

Yet, more consumption is also a victory for subordinate groups. Achieving higher levels of consumption allows for more leisure if one chooses to take it, makes life more pleasant, increases options. Moreover, not all subordinate groups have necessarily accepted dominant-group versions of "beautiful" and "satisfying." Therefore, as consumption expands, those groups have been able to influence standards of satisfaction and taste. In that sense, subordinate-group culture is developed through increased consumption — seized, as it were, from ideology and transformed in new forms of popular culture.

Imposing the ideological representation of dominant culture in capitalist America has meant, first and foremost, to inculcate the primacy of private property and individual freedom. Nevertheless, the American constitution, for all its compromises, and for all its exclusivity (only white males over twenty-one years old were included in the political definition of citizenship), created the basis not only for defining American culture in the image of the dominant class at the time, but — as important — for contesting that definition within the context of the Bill of Rights. The democratization of culture has occurred as part and parcel of the struggle for participation in setting the political agenda — through suffrage, through unions, through civil rights struggles by minority groups.

It may seem unusual to discuss culture in terms of political conflict. In the United States and other politically democratic capitalist societies, it was and is precisely through such struggles that culture becomes constantly redefined. In large part this is the case because of the nature of the capitalist state, which — in order to reproduce capitalist relations of production — must reincorporate the class-race-ethnic-gender self-identifying individuals into capitalist society as citizen-individuals, separated from their class, race, ethnic, and even gender identification and, instead, viewing themselves as members of the nation-state. As individual members of the nation-state, judged — as individuals — by its laws, workers no longer see themselves as politically different from employers, blacks are politically no different from whites, Chinese-Americans no different from Italian-Americans, and women no different from men.

Yet the U. S. state itself is a capitalist state, whose bureaucracy, for various reasons (see Carnoy, 1984), is committed to enhancing and developing the accumulation of capital in the hands of private business. The American nation-state has been and continues to be dominated by a business-class hegemony. America's dominant culture, in that sense, has to be defined as a business culture, and reincorporated individuals must be reincorporated believing in and living business-dominated culture. However, in order for the culture of private property or business to dominate, it was necessary, from the very beginning of the American state, to provide the means by which citizen-individuals could act politically as equal political participants—in other words, to act politically autonomously from their economic position. It is from this individual political action that workers, blacks, ethnic groups, and women could reconstitute elements of their own culture and reinject those elements into the definition of the broader notion of the people-nation's values and norms.

On the one hand, then, the dominant groups in American society attempt to impose on subordinate groups a version of the dominant culture (ideology) through the workplace, the schools, and the media. The principal characteristics of ideology are (a) its ahistoricity for those who accept it, and (b) its potential rewards. Thus, by conforming to the dominant-group definition of individual reintegration into the nation-state, individuals separate themselves from their previous class or group culture and accept—in principle—an ahistorical (from a cultural perspective) participation in the dominant-class project. On the other hand, in order to persuade subordinate groups to conform to this separation and reintegration, the dominant group has to provide some type of history-making and influencing capability to those who accept, whether it be an increased probability of material success (sharing, as Przeworski and Wallerstein [1982] have argued, in the profits of capitalist production) or of being socially approved (Durkheim, 1949). Becoming an individual reintegrated in the dominant-group version of the nation-state also gives the individual in a democracy the right to participate—as a citizen-individual, theoretically acting separately from class origins or race or gender—in political choices that have cultural implications—and therefore to influence cultural change through political change.

And, finally, in a democracy, members of subordinate groups, at considerable material and social cost to themselves, can resist acceptance of dominant-group ideology. They can choose to develop their subordinate-group cultures within the context of the hegemony of dominant-group ideology. From the position of this development they can challenge dominant-group hegemony through social movements couched in subordinate-group culture. Even in this case, the culture that is developed by counterhegemonic social movements is necessarily influenced by hegemonic ideology. In order to appeal to the mass of a subordinate group, counterhegemonic movements must usually couch their message in some version of hegemonic ideology, and must use the means of hegemonic ideology—the media, the courts, the ballot box, that is, the political space of capitalist democracy.

The process of cultural domination and cultural change in an advanced capitalist society is therefore complex. The dominant business group attempts to impose an ideology on subordinate groups that purports to reward them materially and socially and that gives them the right to sanction politically the policies of the dominant groups themselves through elections. Some resist the ideology, attempting to remain in the "comfort" of their own history. They may or may not try to change dominant culture. The individuals who accept this domination pay the potential cost of cultural alienation, yet even they can exercise some influence on economic and social policy through political participation. The influence of those individuals on dominant culture is diluted by their acceptance of business hegemony. They have bought the underlying norms and values that separate them from their own history; hence it is difficult for them to alter the historical process as led by the business class.

But, as the rise of religious fundamentalism in America and of fascism in Europe suggests, the alienation among the working class and the peasants from this acceptance of the dominant business (capitalist) ideology is great enough among the individuals from these subordinate groups that they search for new forms of social indentification and reintegration through religious salvation, hypernationalism, and other forms of moral crusades. These expressions of working-class and peasant culture, perverted by their passage through a prism of ideological acceptance (and resulting cultural loss), have been able to shape the political course of capitalist states, posing significant contradictions for capitalist development in its national context. The cultural change that results from these subordinate-group influences (expressed through political conflict in the capitalist state) is not completely controlled by the dominant business class, or even totally in its interest. This implies that in such situations, "accepting" subordinate groups (in Gramsci's terms, "organic intellectuals") can shape dominant culture, producing a form of "popularized" capitalist culture.

Resistant groups also assault business culture from time to time, either to overthrow it completely (to seize the history-making process, hence culture, from the dominant class) or to be included in the dominant history-making process on their terms. As I have suggested elsewhere (Carnoy and Samoff, forthcoming), democratic capitalist states are impressively resistant to overthrow precisely because they are able to accommodate subordinate groups in that process, significantly changing the distribution of material rewards, increasing participation in political decision making, and even allowing business culture to change (the Swedish case is a good example, or the United States in the 1930s, or, in terms of the civil rights movement, in the 1960s).

These cases also suggest that the dominant business culture can be changed by resistance movements in ways that popularize it. Such popularization can be viewed either as "passive revolution" (in Gramsci's terms), or, alternatively, as a genuine alteration of dominant culture (in the history-making sense) in favor of subordinate groups. Even resistant groups bring a hegemonic-influenced version of their culture into the conflict, but the difference between that version and the elements of subordinate culture that emerge from groups *accepting* reintegration into dominant-group ideology lies in the relatively "unalienated" nature of the resisters' subordinate culture. There is an interesting paradox here: resisting subordinate groups are defined as "alienated," and hence in conflict with dominant-group culture. But this term is—in our sense— incorrect, since it is their relative *lack* of alienation from culture—their own culture— that enables them to shape dominant culture in their own image. It is the members of subordinate groups that accept the ideological form of culture who end up forcing an alienated form of their influence on the business class.

Dominant culture can therefore change. It can become more inclusive and more "popular." It can include more of the values and norms associated with subordinate-group—working class, women, blacks, and other minorities—cultures. This "popularization" of dominated cultures includes changes in some of its most profound elements, such as language and the conception of human relations. But the dominant group is more willing and able to accept influence and change from those subordinate groups that have "accepted" dominant-group ideology. These groups are, first of all, politically crucial to reproducing business-class hegemony. Their acceptance reaffirms the universality and inclusiveness of dominant culture, and hence legitimizes the leadership of that class in capitalist societies.

Second, the demands of those subordinate groups emerge from a necessary alienation from dominant culture. Their acceptance has yielded them some substance (a greater share of profits in the form of higher wages—see Przeworski and Wallerstein, 1982—but also many symbols without substance), individual membership in the people-nation without political power, higher wages without financial security, and education without social mobility. But rather than reject those symbols, they attempt to expand them in their own image. In this expansion, nationalism (a primary element of the business-class ideology accepted by these subordinate groups) becomes hopelessly enmeshed with Fundamentalist religion, the nuclear family, some forms of racism and xenophobia, and small town communalism—all part of a "populist," free-farmer, rural, traditional culture.

Since these subordinate-group values are framed within dominant-class ideology, they can usually be easily incorporated into it. But ideological change gradually seeps back into culture itself, altering the norms and values of the dominant group. Dominance in a democracy requires hegemonic leadership but also a cameleonlike hegemony that takes on the colors of its subordinate-group allies.

Yet in democracies the influence of alienated, subordinate culture is limited by the extent to which this alienation is felt—and in the same way— by the mass of subordinated employed labor, women, and minorities. Historically there has been direct conflict between the values promoted by alienated, "accepting" groups and other groups. The chauvinistic interpretation of "popular" values is even more exclusive in some ways than business culture, since it emanates from the alienated insecurity of jilted and unrequited acceptance. In a real political sense it makes itself self-limiting in any people-nation where the majority cannot be brought into the version of nationalism defined by these groups.

For dominant-group culture to change, however, both "accepting" and "resisting" subordinate groups have to engage themselves politically in the arena of the contested state. For those groups who resist dominant ideology, the issue is primarily whether rewards of engagement are worth the risks of cultural alienation. The principal reward is to change the rules of the game (dominant culture) sufficiently to make individual and group development possible with the minimun psychological cost—in other words, to allow for an authentic cultural development for these groups within the framework of the capitalist economy.

Some argue that this goal is an impossibility—a contradiction in terms. In that political position, the only alternatives are overthrow of the capitalist, patriarchic state (changing control of the history-making mechanism) or cultural separatism. The Black Panthers is an example of the first, and the black separatist movement of the 1960s of the second. I have suggested that the democratic capitalist state is relatively flexible in making concessions to social movements, albeit after long struggles. Neither are those concessions what struggling groups contesting dominant history-making power might have hoped for. So there is risk in subordinate groups engaging dominant culture within the democratic framework, and this risk leads logically to the position that such engagement is futile and even destructive of whatever cultural authenticity subordinate groups may have. The only possible course for imposing true pluralism, coming from such a position, then, is revolution. Gramsci (1971) developed the concept of 'counterhegemony' to describe the process of building a revolutionary culture rooted in existing subordinate culture shaped and extended through a revolutionary political party. The aim of that party, as Gramsci saw it, was to develop an alternative to dominant-class capitalist values and norms, and, on the basis of that revolutionary culture, to overthrow the capitalist state.

The very flexibility of the advanced capitalist state makes it unlikely that overthrow will succeed. Neither are the rules of the political game which subordinate groups must play in the democratic capitalist structure shaped solely by the dominant business class. From its very origins, capitalist democracy was a concession to a limited subset of subordinate groups. Subsequently, this concession was expanded to include others through political conflict. Business-class culture, based on the hierarchy of capitalist production, was irrevocably altered to allow yeoman farmers, then male workers, then black males, then women, and finally youth, to formally enter into the shaping of the culture through political participation. The resulting political rules are set in the context of business culture but are also the product of previous political engagements by subordinate groups (see Bowles and Gintis, 1986).

Voluntary separatism is the second form of subordinate-culture development. Whereas counterhegemony entails using political space in the advanced capitalist democratic state to develop revolutionary possibilities, separatism avoids political engagement. Separatism has been rather successful in America. Many immigrant groups were able to develop their community economies by maintaining a high degree of separation and nonengagement. At one extreme, the Pennsylvania Amish have rejected all modernization for the past 150 years, developing a highly efficient, unmechanized agriculture. They have maintained their cultural identity by rejecting all but economic interaction with the outside community. Although they are formally U. S. citizens, they do not exercise the political rights of citizenship, except to take advantage of the freedom to live separately. To a different degree, Jewish, Japanese, and Italian (among others) immigrants also developed an economic and cultural autarky that attempted to maintain traditional values and norms within the context of a powerful business-class culture. For these groups, this was possible because their commercial acumen enabled them to justify maintaining nonmodern, assimilated values. There was no inherent contradiction between their cultural identity and the dominant-class ideology (except that many Jews and Italians, for example, also brought socialist values with them from Europe—but these were "modern" reactions to capitalism rather than their traditional cultural norms). Relative separation only enhanced their capability to succeed materially in conditions of assimilation marked by severe discrimination and exploitation.

Other subordinate groups have not found it easy to progress materially and—simultaneously—to maintain their cultural identity. Blacks, pre–Second World War Chinese immigrants, and Hispanics came to the United States from traditional or feudal peasant land tenure systems without the tools to compete successfully with capitalist culture on its own grounds. Other groups, such as Poles and Russians, faced similar problems. But because of severe discrimination, blacks, Chinese, and Hispanics maintained their traditional culture through a forced separation from the dominant hegemony. There was, indeed, no attempt to reintegrate them as individual members of the people-nation; their labor was exploited as a group, or subclass. None of these groups had any connection to the contested development of American business culture until well into the twentieth century. Neither were they able to turn their separation to their advantage because they lacked the dominant-class business skills to accumulate sufficient capital within each of their communities.[1]

For the materially successful separated groups, acceptance of dominant-class ideology was a natural outcome of their economic development. Material success was itself a legitimation of that ideology, even though it was achieved largely through maintaining cultural identity and sociopolitical separation. For the superexploited groups, to the contrary, acceptance of the dominant ideology necessarily meant (and means) the constant affirmation of their marginalization to dominant culture – their placement *outside* the history-making capacity of that culture.

The principal alternatives to the self-alienation implied by that marginalization are two: (1) continued cultural separation under new conditions controlled by the groups themselves, this time with adequate economic skills to accumulate community capital (much in the tradition of earlier immigrant groups; and (2) political engagement, such as the civil rights movement, to alter the terms under which reincorporation takes place – thus implicitly altering the nature of the subordinate group's future cultural development as it becomes reincorporated into the dominant ideology.

The post–Second World War Chinese community and Cuban immigrants have followed the first alternative. The black community has tended to follow the second, and so have – to a much lesser extent – Hispanics. However, many individuals in the latter two groups have chosen (or have felt forced) to separate themselves into new forms of marginalized, individualist, apolitical, nonengaging, cultural identities that incorporate some elements of dominant-class ideology (consumerism, for example) and reject others (success in school, saving, employee loyalty, long-term employment), particularly those that symbolize subordination of Anglo culture and power.

These new forms of marginalized identities, or *exit*, are apolitical because they do not have a political motive. They do not engage the dominant culture. Nevertheless, they can have political meaning if the dominant group perceives that this exit is either a threat to the legitimacy of the dominant culture or a threat to the reproduction of an adequately large, productive labor force. The threat to the legitimacy of the dominant culture may come from the development of an extensive underground economy and society based on crime and illegal drugs, where—as in New York or Miami—the dominant urban society is seriously affected. The threat to the reproduction of an adequate labor force occurs when large-scale defections from high school leave significant portions of the population underskilled relative to the future configuration of jobs—as in the case of Hispanics in California. In such situations of implicit threat to the reproductive needs of the dominant hegemony, the passive resistance of subordinate groups[2] may produce changed conditions for the resisting groups even without their organizing into a social movement. Yet it is more likely that, without a visible movement, the dominant-group reaction will be increased coercion rather than attempts to compromise with subordinate-group culture. Indeed, the larger marginalized community may also perceive exit as enough of a threat to its own aspirations and cultural development (in its struggle with the dominant ideology) that combating exit becomes a focus of subordinate-group social organizing.

Before turning to the role of schooling in this conflict between subordinate culture and dominant ideology, I want to suggest that not only do subordinate groups react to the dominant ideology in America, but that dominant groups also react to such reactions. Hegemony *is* important to the business class for the reproduction of its political power and its control of economic resources. When challenged, dominant groups will attempt to avoid giving in, or at least will try to absorb the challenge in a way that sharply reduces the potential effect of compromise on the dominant group's capacity to make history.

Subordinate groups do succeed in winning concessions and gaining a foothold in dominant-class culture, usually in periods when the dominant class is divided on how to deal with subordinate-group demands or, as in the 1930s, is too weakened to prepare an adequate response (see Skocpol, 1981). But the business class does not give up once such concessions are made. New leadership subgroups within the larger business community use whatever political space that may develop (a slowdown in social movement activity, as in the 1980s, for example) to reorganize themselves and attempt to restore a form of dominant culture more favorable to the reproduction of capitalist relations of production and capital accumulation under business's control.

These new attempts at business hegemony must, however, appear in forms different from the past. There is no going back in culture. It is the history-making aspect of culture and the control of translating that culture into ideology that can and does change. This is what the new leadership of the dominant group tries to reestablish. In different periods of history, then, dominant American culture changes as a result of assaults by subordinate-group social movements, and then changes again as the business class attempts to reestablish a "purer" and—at the same time—more "up-to-date" form a business values and norms, still grounded in the basics of control of capital accumulation and the relations of production.

This is the process we have witnessed at the end of the 1970s and during the Reagan presidency. American business culture had been assaulted almost continuously from the 1930s into the early 1970s. With Reagan, new elements of the business class—mostly from the South and West—succeeded in reestablishing the dominance of business ideology in American white workers, in a significant percentage of women, and in some minority groups.

Education and culture

The public educational system is an important state institution. As such, it sits at the center of the conflict between the dominant business ideology—crucial for the reproduction of business dominance itself—and the subordinate culture, struggling for a say in the way American society develops.

In my interpretation of this conflict, young people from subordinate groups are confronted in American schools by a complex set of possibilities and choices. First, the fact that the mass of working-class children, including marginalized minorities, have access to high school and even college today is the result of a long struggle by subordinate groups for greater access to education. To accommodate this large influx of lower-social-class children, the educational system has had to change constantly. Second, the norms and values represented by the schooling process are not just those of business ideology. They also contain democratic, mass ideals of equality (even in terms of outcomes), participation, altruism, public service, and a just state that corrects the worst excesses of the free market.

Even so, many students—especially from lower-income families—have a difficult time in school. The school assumes that the family will also educate the child in a way consistent with the school's version of mass culture—a culture that accepts the basic tenets of business ideology. If the child's culture is not consistent with the school's, there has to be a clash. In younger children, this conflict appears as difficulties in grasping the curriculum. As they fall far behind, lagging behind usually turns into a direct conflict with the institution of schooling. As early as fifth and sixth grade, this frustration turns into "trouble making." A number of analysts have called such conflict "resistance," where resistance is identified with Gramsci's concept of counter-hegemony. We have argued, however, that *exit*—acting out against or dropping out from the school–without political engagement is not resistance. Rather, it is essentially a personal attempt to escape from a costly, painful situation. And the only way that such exit becomes political is when the larger community–either the dominant business class or subordinate groups themselves–make school frustration and dropout a political issue.

But many students who easily learn the required curriculum also conflict with the school as they get older. They understand–at a rather sophisticated level–that the school's vision of society is not theirs. Their conflict *is* resistance. They see the school as a barrier to the cultural development of their subordinate group because it prevents them, as a member of a particular group, from realizing their learning possibilities in terms that they can control.

I have argued that to understand whether schools can change to accommodate this resistance requires an analysis of the state. The schools are an apparatus of that state. This essay has claimed that the American education system has changed and it also has not changed. Furthermore, it changes in favor of accommodating resistance in some periods of history–associated with powerful social movements demanding such accommodation–and in favor of ignoring and even crushing resistance in other periods, when the dominant business class is able to reorganize its thoughts and regain political power.

Can the schools become the agent of counterhegemony–of a change in dominant *culture*? I have argued that the principal struggle over the power to influence a people-nation's history is in the state apparatuses, including in the educational apparatus. But it happens that this struggle occurs more over *control* of schools than over the *content* of schooling. This is not just a coincidence. Subordinate groups are much less concerned with the content of dominant-group ideology than they are with its exclusivity, that is, its control over access to knowledge. To subordinate groups, exclusivity appears as the main barrier to political power, and hence to a voice in the way dominant culture develops.

From inside the schools, the view is somewhat different. Students from subordinate groups, especially marginalized groups, face a curriculum which demands a certain kind of learning. The method of teaching this curriculum assumes a desire to succeed on the school's (and society's) terms, no matter how irrelevant or uninteresting the content. As subordinate-group students grow older, many, encountering difficulties, react unpolitically to the pain of school by tuning out and dropping out.

Teachers and principals can play an important role in holding such students in school. They can do so by altering the teaching method and the curriculum. The important constraint on well-intentioned school officials–a constraint placed there as much by activist subordinate groups as by state curriculum requirements—is that the learning objectives realized by the larger, "mainstream" culture (not necessarily associated with the dominant elite, but rather with a more popularized, middle-class norm) are met by subordinate, marginalized youth. In simple terms, this means high school completion followed by college entrance.

The point I have tried to make here is that this is not the usual conception of counterhegemony. On the one hand, it requires rejecting business ideology as practiced by the school, since that ideology has always tended to relegate "marginalized," lower-social-class youth to a stratum of work and social participation that demands only a minimum of school-based knowledge. Access to that knowledge means access to participation in the economic and political process, and access means struggling against the ideology of exclusiveness. On the other hand, this concept of counterhegemony requires accepting the mass culture (which includes business ideology) as practiced by the school, since it is that culture which permits influencing history (culture) by subordinate groups. Indeed, it is that culture that argues for general access to dominant knowledge for all.

Teachers and students struggling for change in this context are therefore inevitably committed to struggling for student learning and "success" in generally accepted terms but necessarily also struggling for using different tools. It is the search for and use of those tools that require imagination and political conflict with business ideology. But the struggle can also rely on underlying democratic norms (as much part of the schools' agenda as the reproduction of the dominant ideology) to advance change which succeeds in making marginalized students more successful.

Those in the schools committed to change would also do well to keep Gramsci's conception of counterhegemony in mind. Gramsci viewed the primary counterhegemonic educational institution as the revolutionary party. In the American context—and in industrial capitalist democracies in general—there are no revolutionary political parties. But there are social movements that work partly within political parties. These—such as the civil rights movement, and antiwar movement, La Raza, the women's movement, and the children's rights movement—have all affected what goes on in schools, and have created openings for change. Those in the schools who would have an impact on the development of American mass culture—on history and who gets to make it—have their best chance to make that impact by working with such movements.

Yet working with subordinate-group movements makes clear to teachers and organizers who are not members of those groups that there has been an important change in demands on schools in the last decade. The goal in the 1960s was equal access. Now the goal is equal outcome (see *Our Children at Risk*, 1985). Success in school for marginalized students means, in today's cultural struggle, inclusion and incorporation. But it also means changing state apparatuses to serve these students by making such apparatuses impart modern technology and knowledge to everyone. It is resistance to expand mass culture and to weaken once again the hold that business ideology exerts over the public sector's principal institutions.

Can There Be a Liberal Philosophy of Education in a Democratic Society?

Samuel Bowles
Herbert Gintis

Liberalism promises the universal extension of democracy, equality, liberty, and the material prerequisites of personal fulfillment. Unlike the "pie in the sky" salvation offered by many social faiths, this promise can only be delivered in the tangible here and now. Moreover, liberalism's vision has been a tool of liberation, bred and nourished through two centureis of struggle, at once idealistic and earthly, by oppressed groups in unequal and hierarchical societies. Nevertheless, liberalism cannot make good its promise, for it supports a vision of economic justice allowing a small minority to wield economic power independent of the will of the majority.

A progressive vision for social change in liberal societies must attempt to fulfill liberalism's promise rather than negate it.[1] What is the role of liberal educational theory in such a progressive vision? In this paper we shall argue that the liberal concept of human nature forces us to separate what are in fact integrally interrelated aspects of human welfare: learning (human development) and choosing (human freedom). By so doing, liberal educational theory justifies schooling as a form of domination in which the freedom of the student is completely subordinated to an institutional will. An adequate conception of human nature must recognize that learning occurs through choosing, implying that human development occurs through the exercise of freedom. Such a concept allows the fulfillment of the liberal vision and corresponds to the notion of progressive social change as the full democratization of social life.

Two fundamental partitions are central to the liberal philosophical tradition spanning the three centuries from the contributions of Thomas Hobbes and John Locke in the seventeenth century to the great liberal thinkers of the twentieth century. First, social space is divided into a private and a public realm. The public realm of social space is considered to be the state, whereas the private realm is constituted by the family and the capitalist economy. Second, individuals are partitioned into two groups: rational agents whose intentions and choices are the subject of the explicit political and economic theory of liberalism, and those who for reasons of age, incapacity, or citizenship are excluded from this privileged category. The logic of liberal political philosophy may be underlined if we term the first *choosers* and the second *learners*.

As a result of this partition of individuals into learners and choosers, liberal political philosophy has a defect which renders its model of choice incompatible with a democratic theory of education. This is the assumption that the individual enters into a choice situation with externally constituted goals – the "preferences" of neoclassical economics, and the "interests" of political science. Thus where the problem of intentional action – agency – arises, and hence where considerations of liberty and democratic accountability apply, individuals can be taken as given. This handy fiction makes the argument for individual liberty extremely simple and elegant: consider, for instance, the following well-known passage from John Stuart Mill's *On Liberty*:[2] "The only purpose for which power can be rightfully exercised over any member of a civilized community against his will is to prevent harm to others. His own good . . . is not a sufficient warrant."

Yet taking preferences as given, while allowing us to recognize democracy's contribution to the proper aggregation of wants, obscures the contribution of democratic institutions to human development – their unique capacity to foster in people the ability intelligently and creatively to control their lives. Liberalism tells us that people make decisions. But the liberal conception of action must be reconstructed to recognize that decisions also make people.[3]

Of course the liberal model of the individual recognizes that preferences and capacities are formed somewhere. Its error is to assume that where individuals are in the process of becoming, problems of agency and choice are absent. For instance, Mill's famous proclamation of the inviolability of individual preferences cited above is followed immediately by the less frequently cited proviso:

It is, perhaps, hardly necessary to say that . . . we are not speaking of children or of young persons below the age which the law may fix as that of manhood or womanhood . . . [who] . . . must be protected against their own actions . . . For the same reason we may leave out of consideration those backward states of society in which the race itself may be considered as in its nonage. . . . Despotism is a legitimate mode of government in dealing with barbarians, provided the end be their improvement.

Mill here erects an opposition between *choosers* on the one hand and *learners* on the other, and justifies a system of relations of domination and subordination between the former and the latter. This opposition is characteristic of liberal discourse in general. Choosers are the knights in shining armor of liberalism, whereas learners represent a residual category: individuals whose statuses do not include, and whose behavior does not support (be it temporarily or *in perpetuum*), the right of free choice—in short, those who are not deemed to be rational agents.[4]

The status of chooser has always applied in liberal discourse to educated, propertied, white male heads of households, and variously through history to others as well. The status of learner has always applied in liberal discourse to children, prisoners, the insane, and the uncivilized. It has also applied variously to women, servants, workers, and specific races and cultures which, by virtue of their biological constitution or social station, are deemed to be more or less permanently denied the status of rational agent.

The learning-choosing opposition, in addition to permeating liberal consciousness, is reflected in the very taxonomy of the traditional social sciences. Economics and political science deal with choosers, and exhibit scant concern for the formation of wills, whereas sociology, anthropology, and psychology deal with learners in the process of formation of wills, hence lying outside the logic of choice. Perhaps it is for this reason that the maximizing models of economics found a ready welcome in political science but are yet to make serious inroads into the other social sciences.

If we combine the learning-choosing partition with the private-public distinction, we arrive at four basic types of action accessible to liberal theory: learning in the private sphere, choosing in the private sphere, learning in the public sphere, and choosing in the public sphere. Contemporary liberals prescribe a set of favored social institutions to regulate each type of action, some of which are illustrated in Figure 1.

The crux of the liberal learning-choosing partition can be summarized by reference to Figure 1. First, institutions deemed educational or correctional are exempted from scrutiny according to the principles of rational agency, freedom, and choice. Within the liberal discourse one does not ask, for instance, whether schools are democratic. Since such favored institutions of learning as families and schools are not required to be accountable to their participants, central forms of domination governing personal development are obscured.

Second, liberalism relegates choice to an arena of personal autonomy ostensibly devoid of developmental potential. Although liberal institu-

Figure 1:

The Liberal Partitions and Favored Social Institutions

Action	Social Sphere	
	Private	*Public*
Learning	Patriarchal families	Hierarchical schools
Choosing	Competitive markets	Democratic elections

tions—market and ballot box—are praised as sensitively attuned to expressing the wills of consumers and citizens, this sensitivity fails to extend to a most central area of personal control: the choice as to how individuals are to develop their preferences, their capacities for social participation, and their abilities to make critical and informed choices. Liberalism claims that the marketplace and the ballot box allow people to get what they want. But liberalism is silent on how people might get to be what they want to be, and how they might get to want what they want to want.

This defect in the liberal model of action helps us understand how the golden age of free trade and the "democratic revolution" also saw the birth of systems of institutional dependence (e.g., compulsory education) and social control (e.g., conscription) to an extent unparalleled in human history. Our point here is hardly to mourn some fictitious idyllic past when popular forces impressed upon society a free and democratic structure of personal development. Forms of domination (class, ethnic, patriarchal, religious, and other) clearly underlay personal formation in precapitalist society. Indeed, the expansionary tendency of personal rights has doubtless undermined many such ancient forms of oppression. We suggest, rather, that it is in the nature of the learning-choosing partition systematically to obfuscate the issue of domination in human development; that the liberal state cannot account for its own manner of imposing preferences is simply a case in point.

In our view, learning and choosing represent polar categories of a more general form of social action. In place of the archetypal 'child' and 'adult' of liberal theory, we say that the individual constitutes preferences and develops personal powers by acting in the world. This model thus supplements Mill's vision of the rational chooser with Marx's conception of the formative power of action. For it was the Marx of *Capital* who stressed that labor is a process going on between man and nature, a process in which man, through his own activity, initiates, regulates, and controls the material reactions between himself and nature. He confronts nature as one of her own forces . . . By thus acting on the external world and changing it, he at the same time changes his own nature.[5]

Using this becoming-by-acting model, schools, families, workplaces, the electoral process, playgrounds, town meetings, sports arenas, markets, and hospitals can all be assessed according to the same criteria: those of liberty, popular accountability, and contribution to personal development. Our unification of learning and choosing, in rejecting the traditional status of the child, also thereby rejects the status of adult. Those traditional liberal defenses of liberty based on the sanctity of individual preferences are thus severely compromised.

When individuals are at once choosers and learners, the boundaries between liberty, popular sovereignty, and legitimate authority become blurred. A simple example should illustrate our point here. Ought the producer or consumer to determine the nature of a service delivered? If the consumer is considered a chooser, the service is called a "commodity," and consumer sovereignty is deemed to hold. If, by contrast, the consumer is considered a learner (a child), the preferences of others count. Schools, for instance, teach what children *should* know, not what they *wish* to know. If we reject the learning-choosing dichotomy, however, we must search for new principles to resolve the issue.

How do we deal, for example, with the case of the craft which considers not only what consumers want, but what will also contribute to the development of consumers' capacities to appreciate? Or, again, how do we deal with students who fully accept the notion of learning and perhaps even revere the superior wisdom of their teachers, but wish to participate in making educational policy? These, we submit, are not anomalous cases. They are the rule, not the exception to the rule.

The use of a becoming-by-acting model of individual choice provides educational philosophy, not with a set of ready-made political slogans, but rather with a challenging intellectual enterprise: how can the centrality of individual choice and the commitment to liberty and popular sovereignty be preserved, while at the same time the myths of the autonomous individual and the fully formed chooser are rejected?

We address this problem by recognizing that personal development is in general best served through an interaction of two strategies: exercising one's freedom to choose independently of collective sentiment, and entering into mutual, reciprocal, and participatory action with others to achieve commonly defined goals. These two strategies are precisely Albert Hirschman's twin notions of 'exit' and 'voice'.[6]

The critique of the liberal model of action in terms of exit and voice is then simply stated. By taking preferences and interests as pregiven, liberalism equates agency with exit. Individuals exercise their rights either through market and ballot box. Both involve presenting a menu of alternatives, of which the preferred can be chosen by the individual in social isolation. The power of the chooser, then, is limited to his or her ability to abandon a product or a political party—that is, to exit. The market economy and the liberal democratic state, then, stress exit to the virtual exclusion of voice, and representation as opposed to the virtual exclusion of participation. The balance of exit and voice upon which personal development depends is thus not permitted to develop.

The instrumental theory of action, of course, simply bypasses these concerns, for it cannot accommodate the insight that we become who we are in part through what we do. According to the principle of learning through choosing, by contrast, individuals and groups in general participate not merely to meet preexisting ends, but also to constitute themselves, or to reaffirm themselves, as persons and groups with particular and desired attributes.[7]

It follows that preferences are as much formed as revealed in the exercise of choice. Individuals choose in order to become, and the nature of the opportunities given for the expression of choice will affect the formation of wills. One thus does not merely register one's preferences in giving to charity or voting; rather, one constitutes and reaffirms oneself as a charitable person or a good citizen. Similarly, in volunteering for combat the soldier is not merely registering his preference for victory, nor even expressing his status as a brave man; rather, he is constituting and reaffirming his character as brave. Finally, a worker who joins a strike is not simply opting for one social outcome as opposed to another. Such a worker is in addition affirming his or her status in social life, and his or her dignity by virtue of, or even despite, that status.

The great liberal thinkers themselves did not pretend that choice based on instrumental action could form the universal model of social practice. Obligation, loyalty, love, shame, civic virtue, and a host of other sentiments and commitments were variously held to be essential influences upon social action. Even Bernard Mandeville, who shocked his eighteenth-century readers with *The Fable of the Bees*, did not envision that private greed would yield public virtue in all realms of society, but rather focused on the economy. Early liberal economic thinkers—notably Smith and Bentham—showed a lively interest in both the learning and choosing aspects of economic life, pondering the kinds of human beings that the emerging capitalist system would produce and advocating institutions to guide and correct this process.

The celebrated ability of markets to reconcile individual interests and collective rationality—or at least to substantially attenuate the contradiction between the two—was always viewed as conditional on a kind of morality and moral action. We could hardly agree more with Denis Patrick Obrien on this point:[8]

> While the classical writers were the earliest fully to appreciate the allocative mechanism of the market, and the power, subtlety and efficiency of this mechanism, they were perfectly clear that it could operate only within a framework of restrictions. Such restrictions were partly legal and partly religious, moral and conventional; and they were designed to ensure the coincidence of self and community interest.

The early liberals recognized that the perpetuation of these moral, religious, and conventional commitments could not be taken for granted. But later views, particularly those inspired by the instrumental conception of action exemplified by neoclassical economics, came to embrace a much simpler view of the nature of the individual as exogenous to social life. Custom, community, and commitment might still be the bedrock of social interaction, but liberal thinkers—rejecting the activism on behalf of tradition of Edmund Burke and other conservatives—increasingly saw these as the result of a more or less historical legacy rather than the outcomes of ongoing projects of cultural reproduction. Thus the problem of the reproduction of a culture consistent with the workings of the market, the ballot box, and the other institutions advocated by liberalism dropped from theoretical debate.

To some extent the eclipse of cultural practices as a theoretical concern has flowed from the logic of liberal discourse itself. By couching its fundamental principles in terms of an individual and asocial conception of rights, liberal discourse makes difficult the expression of solidarity and cooperation as goals of political practices. With the ascendency of liberalism, observed Otto Gierke, the "sovereignty of the state and the sovereignty of the individual were steadily on their way towards becoming the two central axioms from which all theories of social structure would proceed, and whose relationship to each other would be the focus of all theoretical controversy."[9]

Indeed, virtually the only forms of social solidarity explicitly sanctioned in liberal discourse are nationality, based on common citizenship, and kinship, based on the family. It is perhaps for this reason that among the most effective forms of "the politics of becoming" in some advanced capitalist countries today are nationalism and the antifeminist defense of the patriarchal family.

Paradoxically, the disappearance from theoretical discussion of this problem of cultural reproduction in the nineteenth century coincided with a growing awareness that heightened labor mobility, urbanization, economic dynamism, and other upshots of the growth of the capitalist economy itself had undermined many traditional bases of morality and social control. Thus just as the issue of cultural reproduction fell from theoretical view, it began to assume immense practical importance in the minds and work of the growing army of reformers and administrators who since the nineteenth century have attempted to construct (mostly state) surrogates for the rapidly eroding family, neighborhood community, craft guild, church, community, and the like. The result was the construction of compulsory schools, asylums, and prisons during an era which prided itself on tearing down other walls in the interest of economic freedom.

A fundamental problem of liberal social theory, then, is that it takes as axiomatic the reproduction of those cultural, moral, and economic conditions which are necessary to make good the normative claims made on behalf of its favored institutions. The task of cultural reproduction falls in important measure to schooling, but schools are arenas of learning, not of choosing, and thus, as we have seen, lie almost totally outside the boundaries of the explicit liberal theory itself. Schools, of course, are only a part of the process of social reproduction: we become who we are as much through what we learn in our economic and political activities as through our schooling. But liberalism – either as a philosophy or as an approach to social science – is not only temperamentally ill-disposed but conceptually ill-equipped to address the problem of the forms of learning promoted by the spread of markets and elections as the dominant framework for choosing.

Thus we may broaden considerably the assessment of liberal educational theory offered in our previous work, *Schooling in Capitalist Society*.[10] In our consideration of the educational theory of John Dewey, for example, we limited our critique to a single point: the triple objectives of human development, social equality, and smooth acculturation to adult life are simply inconsistent in a capitalist society. We certainly made note in *Schooling* of the improbable liberal assumption that individual development is exogenous to social processes. But beyond this we did not question the philosophical foundations of liberal educational theory.

Yet our critique of the instrumental conception of action bears the unavoidable implication that a viable theory of education in a democratic society requires the rejection of the fundamental liberal partition of individuals into learners and choosers and its replacement by a theory which takes account of the manner in which class relationships, the state, the family, and other structures regulate our own individual and collective projects to shape who we are.

Such a theory of education must develop a conception of personal development in which schooling is treated as a means of rendering students capable of controlling their lives as citizens, family members, workers, and community members, and in which the educational process induces students to control increasingly substantial spheres of their education as they move from early to later levels of schooling. No doubt there are formidable obstacles in the development of such a philosophy of educational structure. But it remains central to the growth of an effective movement for an emancipatory educational system.

The Politics of Common Sense: Schooling, Populism, and the New Right

Michael W. Apple

The conventional approach to understanding how ideology operates assumes by and large that ideology is "inscribed in" people simply because they are in a particular class position. Either the power of dominant ideas is a given in which dominance is guaranteed or the differences in "inscribed" class cultures and ideologies will generate significant class conflict. In either case, ideology is seen as something that somehow makes its effects felt on people in the economy, in politics, in culture and education, and in the home without too much effort. It is simply *there*. The common sense of people becomes common sense "naturally" as they go about their daily lives, lives that are prestructured by their class position. If you know someone's location in the class structure, you know their sets of political, economic, and cultural beliefs and you don't really have to inquire into *how* dominant beliefs actually do become dominant. It is usually not assumed that these ideas "should positively have to *win* ascendency (rather than being ascribed it) through a specific and contingent (in the sense of open-ended, not totally determined) process of ideological struggle.[1]

Yet the current political situation in many Western capitalist nations presents us with evidence that such a conventional story is more than a little inadequate in understanding the shifts that are occurring in people's common sense. We are seeing a pattern of conflicts within dominant groups that has led to significant changes in their own positions, and, even more importantly, we are witnessing how elements of ideologies of groups in dominance become truly *popular*. There is a rupture in the accepted beliefs of many segments of the public which have historically been less powerful,[2] a rupture that has been worked upon and expanded by economically and politically strong forces in the society. And these ideological shifts in common sense are having a profound impact on how a large portion of the public thinks about the role of education in that society.

In this chapter, I shall describe and analyze a number of these most important changes in popular conceptions. A particular concern will be how ideologies actually become a part of the popular consciousness of classes and class fractions which are not among the elite. In order to understand this, I shall employ theoretical work on the nature of how ideology functions that has developed over the past decade. I don't want to do this because of some disembodied commitment to the importance of "grand theory." Indeed, as I have argued at greater length in *Teachers and Texts*, we have been much too abstract in our attempts to analyze the role of education in the maintenance and subversion of social and cultural power.[3] Rather, I intend to provide an instance in the use of theories to uncover the limits and possibilities of cultural and political action by actually applying them to a concrete situation that is of major importance today, the New Right's reconstruction of our ideas about equality.

Stuart Hall stresses exactly this point in his criticisms of the abstractness of much critical literature on culture and power in the last two decades. After a period of "intense theorization," a movement has grown that has criticized "the hyperabstraction and overtheoreticism that has characterized theoretical speculation, since . . . the early 1970s." As he puts it, in what seemed to be the pursuit of theory for its own sake, "we have abandoned the problems of concrete historical analysis."[4] How do we counteract this tendency? Theoretical analysis should be there to allow us to "grasp, understand, and explain – to produce a more adequate knowledge of – the historical world and its processes; and thereby to inform our practice so that we may transform it."[5] This is what I shall do here.

Reconstructing education

Concepts do not remain still very long. They have wings, so to speak, and can be induced to fly from place to place. It is this context that defines their meaning. As Wittgenstein so nicely reminded us, one should look for the meaning of language in its specific contextual use. This is especially important in understanding political and educational concepts, since they are part of a larger social context, a context that is constantly shifting and that is subject to severe ideological conflicts. Education itself is an arena in which these ideological conflicts work themselves out. It is one of the major sites in which different groups with distinct political, economic, and cultural visions attempt to define what the socially legitimate means and what the ends of a society are to be.

In this chapter, I want to situate the concern with *equality* in education within these larger conflicts. I shall place its shifting meanings both within the breakdown of the largely liberal consensus that guided much educational and social policy since the Second World War and within the growth of the New Right and conservative movements over the past two decades that have had a good deal of success in redefining what education is *for* and in shifting the ideological texture of the society profoundly to the right.[6] In the process, I want to document how new social movements gain the ability to redefine – often, though not always, in retrogressive ways – the terms of debate in education, social welfare, and other areas of the common good. At root, my claim will be that it is impossible to fully comprehend the shifting fortunes of the assemblage of concepts surrounding *equality* (equality of opportunity, equity, etc.) unless we have a much clearer picture of the society's already unequal cultural, economic, and political dynamics that provide the center of gravity around which education functions.

As I have argued at considerably greater length elsewhere, what we are witnessing today is nothing less than the recurrent conflict between *property rights* and *person rights* that has been a central tension in our economy.[7] Gintis defines the differences between property rights and person rights in the following way.

A *property right* vests in individuals the power to enter into social relationships on the basis and extent of their property. This may include economic rights of unrestricted use, free contract, and voluntary exchange; political rights of participation and influence; and cultural rights of access to the social means for the transmission of knowledge and the reproduction and transformation of consciousness. A *person right* vests in individuals the power to enter into these social relationships on the basis of simple membership in the social collectivity. Thus, person rights involve equal treatment of citizens, freedom of expression and movement, equal access to participation in decision-making in social institutions, and reciprocity in relations of power and authority.[8]

It is not surprising that in our society dominant groups "have fairly consistently defended the prerogatives of property," and subordinate groups on the whole have sought to advance "the prerogatives of persons."[9] In times of severe upheaval, these conflicts become even more intense, and, given the current balance of power in society, advocates of property rights have once again been able to advance their claims for the restoration and expansion of their prerogatives not only in education but in all of our social institutions.

The United States economy is in the midst of one of the most powerful structural crises it has experienced since the depression. In order to solve it on terms acceptable to dominant interests, as many aspects of the society as possible need to be pressured into conforming with the requirements of international competition, reindustrialization, and (in the words of the National Commission on Excellence in Education) "rearmament." The gains made by women and men in employment, health and safety, welfare programs, affirmative action, legal rights, and education must be rescinded since "they are too expensive" both economically and ideologically.

Both of these latter words are important. Not only are fiscal resources scarce (in part because current policies transfer them to the military), but people must be convinced that their belief that person rights come first is simply wrong or outmoded given current "realities." Thus, intense pressure must be brought to bear through legislation, persuasion, administrative rules, and ideological maneuvering to create the conditions that right-wing groups believe are necessary to meet these requirements.[10]

In the process, not just in the United States, but in Britain and Australia as well, the emphasis of public policy has materially changed from issues of employing the state to overcome disadvantage. Equality, no matter how limited or broadly conceived, has become redefined. No longer is it seen as linked to past *group* oppression and disadvantagement. It is simply now a case of guaranteeing *individual choice* under the conditions of a "free market."[11] Thus, the current emphasis on *excellence* (a word with multiple meanings and social uses) has shifted educational discourse so that underachievement is once again increasingly seen as largely the fault of the student. Student failure, which was at least partly interpreted as the fault of severely deficient educational policies and practices, is now being seen as the result of what might be called the biological and economic marketplace. This is evidenced in the growth of forms of social Darwinist thinking in education and in public policy in general.[12] In a similar way, behind a good deal of the rhetorical artifice of concern about the achievement levels in, say, inner-city schools, notions of choice have begun to evolve in which deep-seated school problems will be solved by establishing free competition over students. These notions assume that by expanding the capitalist marketplace to schools we will somehow compensate for the decades of economic and educational neglect experienced by the communities in which these schools are found.[13] Finally, there are concerted attacks on teachers (and curricula) based on a profound mistrust of their quality and commitments.

All of this has led to an array of educational conflicts that have been instrumental in shifting the debates over education profoundly to the right.

The effects of this shift can be seen in a number of educational policies and proposals now gaining momentum throughout the country: (1) proposals for voucher plans and tax credits to make schools more like the idealized free market economy; (2) the movement in state legislatures and state departments of education to "raise standards" and to mandate both teacher and student "competencies" and basic curricular goals and knowledge, thereby centralizing even more at a state level the control of teaching and curricula; (3) the increasingly effective assaults on the school curriculum for its supposedly antifamily and anti-free-enterprise bias, its "secular humanism," and its lack of patriotism; and (4) the growing pressure to make the needs of business and industry into the primary goals of the educational system.[14] These are major alterations, ones that have taken years to show their effects. Though I shall paint in rather broad strokes here, an outline of the social and ideological dynamics of how this has occurred should be visible.

The restoration politics of authoritarian populism

The first thing to ask about an ideology is not what is false about it, but what is true. What are its connections to lived experience? Ideologies, properly conceived, do not dupe people. To be effective they must connect to real problems, real experiences.[15] As I shall document, the movement away from social democratic principles and an acceptance of more right-wing positions in social and educational policy occur precisely because conservative groups have been able to work on popular sentiments, to reorganize feelings, and in the process to win adherents.

Important ideological shifts take place not only by powerful groups "substituting one, whole, new conception of the world for another." Often, these shifts occur through the presentation of novel combinations of old and new elements.[16] Let us take the positions of the Reagan administration as a case in point, for, as Clark and Astuto have demonstrated in education and Piven and Cloward and Raskin have shown in the larger areas of social policy, significant and enduring alterations have occurred in the ways that policies are carried out and in the content of those policies.[17]

The success of the policies of the Reagan administration, like that of Thatcherism in Britain, should not simply be evaluated in electoral terms. The policies need to be judged by their success as well in disorganizing other more progressive groups, in shifting the terms of political, economic, and cultural debate onto the terrain favored by capital and the Right.[18] In these terms, there can be no doubt that the current right-wing resurgence has accomplished no small amount in its attempt to construct the conditions that will put it in a hegemonic position.

The Right in the United States and Britain has thoroughly renovated and reformed itself. It has developed strategies based upon what might best be called an *authoritarian populism*.[19] As Hall has defined this, such a policy is based on an increasingly close relationsip between government and the capitalist economy, a radical decline in the institutions and power of political democracy, and attempts at curtailing "liberties" that have been gained in the past. This is coupled with attempts to build a consensus, one that is widespread, in support of these actions.[20] The New Right's "authoritarian populism"[12] has exceptionally long roots in the history of the United States. The political culture here has always been influenced by the values of the dissenting Protestantism of the seventeenth century. Such roots become even more evident in periods of intense social change and crisis.[22] As Burnham has put it:

> Whenever and wherever the pressures of "modernization"—secularity, urbanization, the growing importance of science—have become unusually intense, episodes of revivalism and culture-issue politics have swept over the social landscape. In all such cases since at least the end of the Civil War, such movements have been more or less explicitly reactionary, and have frequently been linked with other kinds of reaction in explicitly political ways.[23]

The New Right works on these roots in creative ways, modernizing them and creating a new synthesis of their varied elements by linking them to current fears. In so doing, the Right has been able to rearticulate traditional political and cultural themes and because of this has effectively mobilized a large amount of mass support.

As I noted, part of the strategy has been the attempted dismantling of the welfare state and of the benefits that working people, people of color, and women (these categories are obviously not mutually exclusive) have won over decades of hard work. This has been done under the guise of anti-statism, of keeping government "off the backs of the people," and of "free enterprise." Yet, at the same time, in many valuative, political, and economic areas the current government is extremely state-centrist, both in its outlook, and very importantly in its day-to-day operations.[24]

One of the major aims of a rightist restoration politics is to struggle in not one but many different arenas at the same time, not only in the economic sphere but in education and elsewhere as well. This aim is grounded in the realization that economic dominance must be coupled to "political, moral, and intellectual leadership" if a group is to be truly dominant and if it wants to genuinely restructure a social formation. Thus, as both Reaganism and Thatcherism recognize so clearly, to win in the state you must also win in civil society.[25] As the noted Italian political theorist Antonio Gramsci would put it, what we are seeing is a war of position. "It takes place where the whole relation of the state to civil society, to 'the people' and to popular struggles, to the individual and to the economic life of society has been thoroughly reorganized, where 'all the elements change.'"[26]

The Right then has set itself an immense task, to create a truly "organic ideology," one that seeks to spread throughout society and to create a new form of "national popular will." It seeks to intervene "on the terrain of ordinary, contradictory common-sense," to "interrupt, renovate, and transform in a more systematic direction" people's practical consciousness. It is this restructuring of common sense, which is itself the already complex and contradictory result of previous struggles and accords, which becomes the object of the cultural battles now being waged.[27]

In this restructuring, Reaganism and Thatcherism did not create some sort of false consciousness, creating ways of seeing that had little connection with reality. Rather, they "operated directly on the real and manifestly contradictory experiences" of a large portion of the population. They did connect with the perceived needs, fears, and hopes of groups of people who felt threatened by the range of problems associated with the crises in authority relations, in the economy, and in politics.[28]

What has been accomplished has been a successful translation of an economic doctrine into the language of experience, moral imperative, and common sense. The free market ethic has been combined with a populist politics. This has meant the blending together of a "rich mix" of themes that have had a long history—nation, family, duty, authority, standards, and traditionalism—with other thematic elements that have also struck a resonant chord during a time of crisis. These latter themes include self-interest, competitive individualism (what I have elsewhere called the "possessive individual"),[29] and antistatism. In this way, a reactionary common sense is partly created.[30]

The sphere of education has been one of the most successful areas in which the Right has been ascendent. The social democratic goal of expanding equality of opportunity (itself a rather limited reform) has lost much of its political potency and its ability to mobilize people. The "panic" over falling standards and illiteracy, the fears of violence in schools, the concern with the destruction of family values and religiosity, all have had an effect. These fears are exacerbated, and used, by dominant groups within politics and the economy who have been able to move the debate on education (and all things social) onto their own terrain, the terrain of standardization, productivity, and industrial needs.[31] Since so many parents *are* justifiably concerned about the economic futures of their children—in an economy that is increasingly conditioned by lowered wages, unemployment, capital flight, and insecurity[32] – rightist discourse connects with the experiences of many working-class and lower-middle-class people.

However, although this conservative conceptual and ideological apparatus does appear to be rapidly gaining ground, one of the most critical issues remains to be answered. How *is* such an ideological vision legitimated and accepted? How was this done?[33]

Understanding the crisis

The right-wing resurgence is not simply a reflection of the current crisis. Rather, it is itself a response to that crisis.[34] Beginning in the immediate post–Second World War years, the political culture of the United States was increasingly characterized by American imperial might, economic affluence, and cultural optimism. This period lasted for more than two decades. Socially and politically, it was a time of what has been called the *social democratic accord*, in which government increasingly became an arena for a focus on the conditions required for equality of opportunity. Commodity-driven prosperity, the extension of rights and liberties to new groups, and the expansion of welfare provisions provided the conditions for this compromise both between capital and labor and with historically more dispossessed groups such as blacks and women. This accord has become mired in crisis since the late 1960s and early 1970s.[35] Allen Hunter gives an excellent description of this accord.

From the end of World War II until the early 1970s world capitalism experienced the longest period of sustained economic growth in its history. In the United States a new "social structure of accumulation"–"the specific institutional environment within which the capitalist accumulation process is organized"–was articulated around several prominent features: the broadly shared goal of sustained economic growth, Keynesianism, elite pluralist democracy, an imperial America prosecuting a cold war, anti-communism at home and abroad, stability or incremental change in race relations and a stable home life in a buoyant, commodity-driven consumer culture. Together these crystallized a basic consensus and a set of social and political institutions which was hegemonic for two decades.[36]

At the very center of this hegemonic accord was a compromise reached between capital and labor in which labor accepted what might be called "the logic of profitability and markets as the guiding principles of resource allocation." In return it received "an assurance that minimal living standards, trade union rights and liberal democratic rights would be protected."[37] These democratic rights were further extended to the poor, women, and people of color as these groups expanded their own struggles to overcome racially and sexually discriminatory practices.[38] Yet this extension of (limited) rights could not last, given the economic and ideological crises that soon beset American society, a set of crises that challenged the very core of the social democratic accord.

The dislocations of the 1960s and 1970s–the struggle for racial and sexual equality, military adventures such as Vietnam, Watergate, the resilience of the economic crisis–produced both shock and fear. "Mainstream culture" was shaken to its very roots in many ways. Widely shared notions of family, community, and nation were dramatically altered. Just as importantly, no new principle of cohesion emerged that was sufficiently compelling to recreate a cultural center. As economic, political, and valuative stability (and military supremacy) seemed to disappear, the polity was itself "balkanized." Social movements based on difference–regional, racial, sexual, religious–became more visible.[39] The sense of what Marcus Raskin has called "the common good" was fractured.[40]

Traditional social democratic "statist" solutions which in education, welfare, health, and other similar areas took the form of large-scale attempts at federal intervention to increase opportunities or to provide a minimal level of support were seen as being part of the problem, not as part of the solution. Traditional conservative positions were more easily dismissed as well. After all, the society on which they were based was clearly being altered. The cultural center could be *built* (and it had to be built by well-funded and well-organized political and cultural action) around the principles of the New Right. The New Right confronts the "moral, existential, [and economic] choas of the preceding decades" with a network of exceedingly well-organized and financially secure organizations incorporating "an aggressive political style, on outspoken religious and cultural traditionalism and a clear populist commitment."[41]

In different words, the project was aimed at constructing a "new majority" that would "dismantle the welfare state, legislate a return to traditional morality, and stem the tide of political and cultural dislocation which the 1960's and 1970's represented." Using a populist political strategy (now in combination with an aggressive executive branch of the government), it marshaled an assault on "liberalism and secular humanism" and linked that assault (to what some observers have argued was "an obsession with individual guilt and responsibility where social questions are concerned [crime, sex, education, poverty])" with strong beliefs against government intervention.[42]

The class, racial, and sexual specificities here are significant. The movement to create a conservative cultural consensus in part builds on the hostilities of the working and lower middle classes toward those above and below them and is fueled as well by a very real sense of antagonism against the new middle class. State bureaucrats and administrators, educators, journalists, planners, and so on all share part of the blame for the social dislocations these groups have experienced.[43] Race, gender, and class themes abound here, a point to which I shall return in the next section of my analysis.

This movement is of course enhanced within academic and government circles by a group of policy-oriented neoconservatives who have become the organic intellectuals for much of the rightist resurgence. A society based on individualism, market-based opportunities, and the drastic reduction of both state intervention and state support—these currents run deep in their work.[44] They provide a counterpart to the New Right and are themselves part of the inherently unstable alliance that has been formed.

Building the new accord

Almost all of the reform-minded social movements—including the feminist, gay and lesbian, student and other movements of the 1960s—drew upon the struggle by blacks "as a central organizational fact or as a defining political metaphor and inspiration."[45] These social movements infused new social meanings into politics, economics, and culture. These are not separate spheres. All three of these levels exist simultaneously. New social meanings about the importance of person rights infused individual identity, family, and community, and penetrated state institutions and market relationships. These emerging social movements expanded the concerns of politics to all aspects of the "terrain of everyday life." Person rights took on ever more importance in nearly all of our institutions, as evidenced in aggressive affirmative action programs, widespread welfare and educational activist programs, and so on.[46] In education this was very clear in the growth of bilingual programs and in the development of women's, black, Hispanic, and native American studies in high schools and colleges.

There are a number of reasons that the state was the chief target of these earlier social movements for gaining person rights. First, the state was the "factor of cohesion in society" and had historically maintained and organized practices and policies that embodied the tension between property rights and person rights.[47] As such a factor of cohesion, it was natural to focus on it. Second, "the state was traversed by the same antagonisms which penetrated the larger society, antagonisms that were themselves the results of past cycles of [social] struggle." Openings in the state could be gained because of this. Footholds in state institutions dealing with education and social services could be deepened.[48]

Yet even with these gains, the earlier coalitions began to disintegrate.

In the minority communities, class polarization deepened. The majority of barrio and ghetto residents "remained locked in poverty," while a relatively small portion of the black and brown population were able to take advantage of educational opportunities and new jobs (the latter being largely within the state itself).[49] With the emerging crisis in the economy, something of a zero-sum game developed in which progressive social movements had to fight over a limited share of resources and power. Antagonistic rather than complementary relationships developed among groups. Minority groups, for example, and the largely white and middle-class women's movement had difficulty integrating their programs, goals, and strategies.

This stiuation was exacerbated by the fact that, unfortunately, given the construction of a zero-sum game by dominant groups, the gains made by women sometimes came at the expense of blacks and browns. Furthermore, leaders of many of these movements had been absorbed into state-sponsored programs, which–although the adoption of such programs *was* in part a victory–had the latent affect of cutting off leaders from their grass roots constituency and lessened the militancy at this level. This situation often resulted in what has been called the "ghettoization" of movements within state institutions as movement demands were partly adopted in their most moderate forms into programs sponsored by the state. Militancy is transformed into constituency.[50]

The splits in these movements occurred as well because of strategic divisions, divisions that were paradoxically the results of the movements' own successes. Thus, for example, those women who aimed their work within existing political and economic channels *could* point to gains in employment within the state and in the economic sphere. Other, more radical, members saw such "progress" as "too little, too late."

Nowhere is this problem more apparent than in the black movement in the United States. It is worth quoting one of the best analyses of the history of these divisions at length.

The movement's limits also arose from the strategic divisions that befell it as a result of its own successes. Here the black movement's fate is illustrative. Only in the South, while fighting against a backward political structure and overt cultural oppression, had the black movement been able to maintain a *de*-centered unity, even when internal debates were fierce. Once it moved north, the black movement began to split, because competing political projects, linked to different segments of the community, sought either integration in the (reformed) mainstream, or more radical transformation of the dominant racial order.

After initial victories against segregation were won, one sector of the movement was thus reconstituted as an interest-group, seeking an end to racism understood as discrimination and prejudice, and turning its back on the oppositional "politics of identity." Once the organized black movement became a mere constituency, though, it found itself locked in a bear hug with the state institutions whose programs it had itself demanded, while simultaneously isolated from the core institutions of the modern state.[51]

In the process, those sectors of the movement that were the most radical were marginalized or, and—this must not be forgotten—were simply repressed by the state.[52]

Even though there were major gains, the movements' integration into the state latently created conditions that were disastrous in the fight for equality. A mass-based militant grass roots movement was defused into a constituency, dependent on the state itself. *And very importantly, when the neoconservative and right-wing movements evolved with their decidedly antistatist themes, the gains that were made in the state came increasingly under attack and the ability to recreate a large-scale grass roots movement to defend these gains was weakened considerably.*[53] Thus, when there are right-wing attacks on the more progressive national and local educational policies and practices that have benefited people of color, it becomes increasingly difficult to develop broad-based coalitions to counter these offensives.

In their failure to consolidate a new "radical" democratic politics, one with majoritarian aspirations, the new social movements of the 1960s and 1970s "provided the political space in which right wing reaction could incubate and develop its political agenda."[54] Thus, state reforms won by, say, minority movements in the 1960s in the United States, and the new definitions of person rights embodied in these reforms, "provided a formidable range of targets for the 'counter-reformers' of the 1970s." Neoconservatives and the New Right carried on their own political "project." They were able to rearticulate particular ideological themes and to restructure them around a political movement once again.[55] And these themes *were* linked to the dreams, hopes, and fears of many individuals.

Let us examine this in somewhat more detail. Behind the conservative restoration is a clear sense of loss: of control, of economic and personal security, of the knowledge and values that should be passed on to children, of visions of what counts as sacred texts and authority. The binary opposition of we/they becomes very important here. "We" are law-abiding, "hard working, decent, virtuous, and homogeneous." The "theys" are very different. They are "lazy, immoral, permissive, heterogenous."[56] These binary oppositions distance most people of color, women, gays, and others from the community of worthy individuals. The subjects of discrimination are now no longer those groups who have been historically oppressed, but are instead the "real Americans" who embody the idealized virtues of a romanticized past. The "theys" are undeserving. They are getting something for nothing. Policies supporting them are "sapping our way of life," most of our economic resources, and creating government control of our lives.[57]

These processes of ideological distancing make it possible for antiblack and antifeminist sentiments to seem no longer racist and sexist because they link so closely with other issues. Once again, Allen Hunter is helpful. "Racial rhetoric links with anti-welfare state sentiments, fits with the push for economic individualism: thus many voters who say they are not prejudiced (and may not be by some accounts) oppose welfare spending as unjust. Anti-feminist rhetoric . . . is articulated around defense of the family, traditional morality, and religious fundamentalism."[58] All of these elements can be integrated through the formation of ideological coalitions that enable many Americans who themselves feel under threat to turn against groups of people who are even less powerful than themselves. At the very same time, it enables them to "attack domination by liberal, statist elites."[59]

This ability to identify a range of "others" as enemies, as the source of the problems, is very significant. One of the major elements in this ideological formation has indeed been a belief that liberal elites within the state "were intruding themselves into home life, trying to impose their values." This was having serious negative effects on moral values and on traditional families. Much of the conservative criticism of textbooks and curricula rests on these feelings, for example. Although this position certainly exaggerated the impact of the "liberal elite," and although it certainly misrecognized the power of capital and of other dominant classes,[60] there was enough of an element of truth in it for the Right to use it in its attempts to dismantle the previous accord and build its own.

A new hegemonic accord is reached, then. It combines dominant economic and political elites intent on "modernizing" the economy, white working-class and middle-class groups concerned with security, the family, traditional knowledge and values, and economic conservatives.[61] It also includes a fraction of the new middle class, whose own advancement depends on the expanded use of accountability, efficiency, and management procedures which are their own cultural capital.[62] This coalition has partly succeeded in altering the very meaning of what it means to have a social goal of equality. The citizen as "free" consumer has replaced the previously emerging citizen as situated in structurally generated relations of domination. Thus, the common good is now to be regulated exclusively by the laws of the market, free competition, private ownership, and profitability. In essence, the definitions of freedom and equality are no longer democratic, but *commercial*.[63] This is particularly evident in the proposals for voucher plans as "solutions" to massive and historically rooted relations of economic and cultural inequality.

In sum, then, the Right in both the United States and Britain has succeeded in reversing a number of the historic post–Second World War trends.

It has begun to dismantle and erode the terms of the unwritten social contract
on which the social forces settled after the war. It has changed the currency of political thought and argument. Where previously social need had begun to establish its
own imperatives against the laws of market forces, now questions of "value for
money," the private right to dispose of one's own wealth, the equation between
freedom and the free market, have become the terms of trade, not just of political
debate . . . but in the thought and language of everyday calculation. There has
been a striking reversal of values: the aura that used to attach to the value of the
public welfare [that is, the value of the common good], now adheres to anything
that is private–or can be privatized. A major ideological reversal is in progress in
society at large; and the fact that is has not swept everything before it, and that
there are many significant points . . . of resistance, does not contradict the fact
that, conceived not in terms of outright victory but more in terms of the mastery
of an unstable equlibrium, [the Right] has . . . begun to reconstruct the social
order.[64]

This reconstruction is not imposed on unthinking subjects. It is not
done through the use of some right-wing attempt at what Freire has called
"banking," whereby knowledge and ideologies become common sense
simply by being poured into the heads of people. The ruling or dominant
conceptions of the world and of everyday life "do not directly prescribe the
mental content of the illusions that supposedly fill the heads of the dominated classes."[65] However, the meanings, interests, and languages we construct are bound up in the unequal relations of power that do exist. To speak
theoretically, the sphere of symbolic production is a contested terrain just
as other spheres of social life are. "The circle of dominant ideas does accumulate the symbolic power to map or classify the world for others," to
set limits on what appears rational and reasonable, indeed on what appears
sayable and thinkable.[66] This occurs *not* through imposition, but through
creatively working on existing themes, desires, and fears and reworking
them. Since the beliefs of people *are* contradictory and have tensions because they are what some have called polyvocal,[67] it is then possible to move
people in directions where one would least expect given their position in
society.

Thus, popular consciousness can be articulated to the Right precisely
because the feelings of hope and despair and the logic and language used
to express these are "polysemic" and can be attached to a variety of discourses. Hence, a male worker who has lost his job can be antagonistic to
the corporations who engaged in capital flight or can blame unions, people
of color, or women "who are taking men's jobs." The response is *constructed*,

not preordained, by the play of ideological forces in the larger society.[68] And, though this construction occurs on a contradictory and contested terrain, it is the Right that seems to have been more than a little successful in providing the discourse that organizes that terrain.

Will the Right succeed?

So far I have broadly traced out many of the political, economic, and ideological reasons that the social democratic consensus that led to the limited extension of person rights in education, politics, and the economy slowly disintegrated. At the same time, I have documented how a new "hegemonic bloc" is being formed, coalescing around New Right tactics and principles. The question remains: Will this accord be long lasting? Will it be able to inscribe its principles into the very heart of the American polity?

There are very real obstacles to the total consolidation within the state of the New Right political agenda. First, there has been something of a "great transformation" in, say, racial identities. Omi and Winant describe it thus: "The forging of new collective racial identities during the 1950s and 1960s has been the enduring legacy of the racial minority movements. Today, as gains won in the past are rolled back and most organizations prove unable to rally a mass constituency in racial minority communities, the persistence of the new racial identities developed during this period stands out as the single truly formidable obstacle to the consolidation of a newly repressive racial order."[69] Thus, even when social movements and political coalitions are fractured, when their leaders are co-opted, repressed, and sometimes killed, the racial subjectivity and self-awareness that were developed by these movements has taken permanent hold. "No amount of repression or cooptation [can] change that." In Omi and Winant's words, the genie is out of the bottle.[70] This is the case because, in essence, a new kind of person has been created within minority communities.[71] A new, and much more self-conscious, *collective* identity has been forged. Thus, for instance, in the struggles over the past three decades by people of color to have more control of education and to have it respond more directly to their own culture and collective histories, these people themselves were transformed in major ways.[72] "Social movements create collective identity by offering their adherents a different view of themselves and their world; different, that is, from the world view and self-concepts offered by the established social order. They do this by the process of *rearticulation*, which produces new subjectivity by making use of information and knowledge already present in the subject's mind. They take elements and themes of her/his culture and traditions and infuse them with new meaning."[73] These meanings will make it exceedingly difficult for the Right to incorporate the perspectives of people of color under its ideological umbrella and will continually create oppositional tendencies within the black and brown communities. The slow, but steady, growth in the power of people of color at a local level in these communities will serve as a countervailing force to the solidification of the new conservative accord.

Added to this is the fact that even within the new hegemonic bloc, even within the conservative restoration coalition, there are ideological strains that may have serious repercussions on its ability to be dominant for an extended period. These tensions are partly generated because of the class dynamics within the coalition. Fragile compromises may come apart because of the sometimes directly contradictory beliefs held by many of the partners in the new accord.

This can be seen in the example of two of the groups now involved in supporting the accord. There are both what can be called "residual" and "emergent" ideological systems or codes at work here. The residual culture and ideologies of the old middle class and of an upwardly mobile portion of the working class and lower middle class—stressing control, individual achievement, "morality," etc.—have been merged with the emergent code of a portion of the new middle class—getting ahead, technique, efficiency, bureaucratic advancement, and so on.[74]

These codes are in an inherently unstable relationship. The stress on New Right morality does not necessarily sit well with an amoral emphasis on careerism and economic norms. The merging of these codes can only last as long as paths to mobility are not blocked. The economy must pay off in jobs and mobility for the new middle class or the coalition is threatened. There is no guarantee, given the unstable nature of the economy and the kinds of jobs being created, that this payoff will occur.[75]

This tension can be seen in another way which shows again that, in the long run, the prospects for such a lasting ideological coalition are not necessarily good. Under the new, more conservative accord, the conditions for capital accumulation and profit must be enhanced by state activity as much as possible. Thus, the "free market" must be set loose. As many areas of public and private life as possible need to be brought into line with such privatized market principles, including the schools, health care, welfare, housing, and so on. Yet, in order to create profit, capitalism by and large also requires that traditional values are subverted. Commodity purchasing and market relations become the norm and older values of community, "sacred knowledge," and morality will need to be cast aside. This dynamic sets in motion the seeds of possible conflicts in the future between the economic modernizers and the New Right cultural traditionalists who make up a significant part of the coalition that has been built.[76] Furthermore, the competitive individualism now being so heavily promoted in educational reform movements in the United States may not respond well to the somewhat more collective senses of traditional working-class and poor groups.

Finally, there are counterhegemonic movements now being built within education itself. The older social democratic accord included many educators, union leaders, minority group members, and others. There are signs that the fracturing of this coalition may only be temporary. Take teachers, for instance. Even though salaries have been on the rise throughout the country, this rise has been countered by a rapid increase in the external control of teachers' work, the rationalization and deskilling of their jobs, and the growing blame of teachers and education in general for most of the major social ills that beset the economy.[77] Many teachers have organized around these issues, in a manner reminiscent of the earlier work of the Boston Women's Teachers' Group.[78] Furthermore, there are signs throughout the country of multiracial coalitions being built among elementary and secondary school teachers, university-based educators, and community members to collectively act on the conditions under which teachers work and to support the democratization of curriculum and teaching and a rededication to the equalization of access and outcomes in schooling. The Public Education Information Network based in St. Louis and the Rethinking Schools group based in Milwaukee provide but a few of these examples.[79]

Even given these emerging tensions within the conservative restoration and the increase once again of alliances to counter its attempted reconstruction of the politics and ethics of the common good, this does not mean we should be at all sanguine. It is possible that, because of these tensions and countermovements, the Right's economic program will fail. Yet its ultimate success may be in shifting the balance of class forces considerably to the right and in changing the very ways we consider the common good.[80] Privatization, profit, and greed may still substitute for any serious collective commitment.

We are, in fact, in danger both of forgetting the decades of hard work it took to put even a limited vision of equality on the social and educational agenda and of forgetting the reality of the oppressive conditions that exist for so many of our fellow Americans. The task of keeping alive in the minds of the people the collective memory of the struggle for equality, for person rights in *all* of the institutions of our society, is one of the most significant tasks educators can perform. In a time of conservative restoration, we cannot afford to ignore this task. This requires renewed attention to important curricular questions. Whose knowledge is taught? Why is it taught in this particular way to this particular group? How do we enable the histories and cultures of the majority of working people, of women, of people of color (these groups again are obviously not mutually exclusive) to be taught in responsible and responsive ways in schools? Given the fact that the collective memory that *now* is preserved in our educational institutions is more heavily influenced by dominant groups in society,[81] the continuing efforts to promote more democratic curricula and teaching are more important now than ever. For it should be clear that the movement toward an authoritarian populism will become even more legitimate if only the values embodied in the conservative restoration are made available in our public institutions. The widespread recognition that there were, are, and can be more equal modes of economic, political, and cultural life can only be accomplished by organized efforts to teach and expand this sense of difference. Clearly, there is educational work to be done.

4

Schooling and the Family

Miriam E. David

Home-school relations or the family-education couplet are still as familiar today as they were twenty, thirty, or even a hundred years ago, despite major transformations in both educational policy and the socioeconomic structure. The union remains as strong as in the old rhyme "love and marriage go together," but, as in that relationship, it is suffused with a variety of meanings to the different partners. Both draw their meanings from the wider, gendered society of which they are both a part. In popular discourse, as in the more analytical sociology of education, however, attention is rarely paid to these meanings and the inevitability of the union is taken for granted, despite the sexual and social differences clearly implied.

In this paper I want to tease out, from a feminist perspective, the various notions of family, and the related concepts of home and parent, that have become the staple of the political discourse of education. I want to assess the implications of these notions and their application to educational policy for women's lives by contrast to men's lives. What is the actual effect within school, between schools and families, within families, and in the workplace? What are the differential implications for schoolchildren as schoolgirls and schoolboys, as schoolgirl mothers or school-age parents, as mothers or fathers in the family, at home and at work?

Throughout the enduring popularity of the relationship between the family and school, the notions of the family, of the home and the parent, have rarely been seen as problematic. Perhaps more importantly, the gendered nature of the notions has rarely been called into question. Rather the family, in its various guises, has been treated as a valued political asset, with parties of all political persuasions claiming some notion of the family for its own. Yet a mere glance at the catalogue of terms developed both as policy proposals and instruments, as well as to rouse popular sentiments for educational progress and change, indicates both their problematic and gen-

50

dered nature–parental power, parental choice, good home-school relations, family-life education, parent and sex education, or education in sex
and personal relationships, poverty and home background, parental involvement and participation. All are resonant with a variety of conflicting
social and sexual meanings–differences in social class, in two- or one-
parent households, in the age of efficacy of parenting, and the quality and
sufficiency of the home.

The privacy of the family has tended to render it immune from public
scrutiny or appraisal. Hence, the terms used for policy proposals and instruments as well as in more popular discourse appear as ungendered and
even unisex: in particular, *parent* is used for both mothers and fathers where
their roles may not be interchangeable. It is also used as if it were a social
category. The model for the family in all of these discussions and debates
remains that of the traditional nuclear family, resident in its own private
home, with two parents in differential roles–a breadwinner father and an
economically dependent housewife/mother. Discussions of adequate home
background tend to reflect this two parent differentiated household. The
model, too, assumes a household with sufficient parental means to render
it self-sufficient; in other words, a relatively middle-class home. So family-
households which are not dependent upon male earnings or a wage are seen
to be a deviation from the norm, whether in terms of social class or gender.
Indeed, in previous analyses there has tended to be confusion over whether
working-class households are different by virtue of sources and types of income or the "working" status of the "parent", expecially calling into question "working mothers". Another household that is different from the
model is that of the lone-parent: most usually a lone-mother household
(in Britain, according to the most recent figures, lone-mother outnumber
lone-father households in the ratio 9 to 1). Even lone-mother households
vary in their social class home background as well as their origins. Those
created by divorce or separation may be of a very different socio-economic
status from those created by choice and different, yet again, from those
originating from teenage or schoolage parents. Yet these distinctions are
rarely taken account of in proposals to improve home-school relations, parental participation, parental involvement or parent power. On the other
hand, attempts to "reform" such latter families by means of parent education or education for family life are becoming more popular solutions to
what has often recently been termed "the problem of the family". (David,
1986a, p. 35).

Almost all educational policy assumes the necessity of both sustaining
and improving good home-school relations, yet it does not initiate discussion about the different needs and interests of various family members with

divergent home backgrounds as a prelude to proposals for change. Rather an identity of interests and needs is assumed, first, between families of widely divergent social class and economic positions, in which the market positions of the mothers especially, may necessitate paid employment; second, between lone- and two-parent households where, in the former, mothers are thereby expected to perform as both mothers and fathers; and third, between families with school-age parents, especially mothers and others. One reason, of course, is that these family-school relations are themselves part of the process of education; the assumption is that "proper" home circumstances, on the traditional model, provide the right model for socialization into adult parental roles, which will be gendered in similar ways. These notions are, however, not the preserve of conservative or right-wing political ideas alone. On the contrary, they have not been called into question by liberal or social democratic thinkers either. This is not to suggest that no relationship should exist between home and school, but rather that the umproblematic, clearly gendered division in parenting and family-school relations obviously renders problematic a whole range of progressive social and educational change, in particular the achievement of equal treatment between men and women in adult life, whether in the privacy of the family or in the more "public" world of the economic marketplace (David, 1987, p. 190).

The "problem" is most clearly in evidence with the almost universal acceptance, particularly in political discourse, of the present form of compulsory education: in Britain from the age of five years old to sixteen years old and in the United States from six years old to eighteen years old. Conventional discussions of the family-education couplet do not admit discussion of pre-school education or care as part of the education system; nor are the terms on which schooling is presented a factor for discussion. In other words, the hours of the school day, the length of the school term or semester, and the timing and length of the school holidays or vacations are all relatively fixed and immutable. Yet they themselves, let alone the more detailed relations within school, may militate against any change in gendered, adult relationships. In particular, school authorities or government itself thereby admits of no responsibility for children outside of this age and time limit. Children remain the sole responsibility of their parent(s) before the start of compulsory schooling, and at the beginning and end of the school day, school term and school year. In Britain, in addition, children over the age of compulsory schooling, without the benefit of access to further or higher education or an independent economic position, are becoming more firmly the responsibility of their parents again. In recent changes in the social security (social welfare) legislation, the state has reduced its own commitment to responsibility for housing of all unemployed teenagers and young adults below the age of twenty-five (Land, 1986).

Parent responsibility for children is indeed extensive and the provision of compulsory schooling therefore only provides a limited interruption in that responsibility to ensure the well-being of the next generation. But that parental responsibility is, of necessity, gendered: fathers engaged in full-time economic activity cannot perforce care for children below the age of compulsory schooling, nor in the school holidays and at the ends of the school day. For various historical reasons, having little to do with theories of child development, the lengths of the school day and school year are much shorter than the conventional working day and working year. Indeed, Tyack and Strober (1980) have argued that the relatively short length of the school year was fought for by teachers in the United States who needed to supplement their incomes with a second job. Be that as it may, the need to care for pre-school children and young school-age children is a responsibility that inevitably has to be shouldered by mothers, in the absence of collective or state responsibility. There is, however, growing evidence to suggest that older school-age children of parents who must, of necessity, work outside the home are "latchkey children"; for these children, public provision both before and after school is either absent or too costly to afford. Care in the school vacation remains the financial and social responsibility of parents: with similar attendant problems for some parents (New and David, 1985).

This structuring of parental responsibility for children sets the context for the form and characteristics of home-school relations, as well as for the lessons in family education. These lessons are framed around a particular work ethic for men and another "ethic" or morality for women and mothers (David, 1984). In other words, the form of compulsory schooling does not mark a break with past practices in family life and family responsibility. Given the historic reluctance on the part of any government, of whatever political persuasion, expressly to intervene in private family relationships, compulsory schooling does not represent the takeover of parental responsibility. Rather it is the expression of the need to complement particular types of family in their "work" of raising the next generation, illustrating the recognition that families alone cannot shoulder the responsibility and, moreover, that mothers at home cannot finally and alone wean children (boys especially) from the home to the rigors of the economic marketplace. Home-school relations are, then, almost literally built into the creation of a capitalist education system, which itself prefigures, for male children at least, the separation of home and work for adults. Indeed, the form of compulsory schooling–in addition to the length of the school day, school term or semester, and school year–builds on home-school relations. Not only does it require particular activities of mothers in ensuring the smooth running of the schools, but the school, in its daily representation of being "in loco parentis", stands in place of both parents and also attempts to replicate appropriate parental behavior and roles, through the structuring of teachers' activities and so forth (David, 1980). It is probably no accident that the majority of headteachers (principals) of primary schools are men, whereas the vast majority of classroom teachers are women. Indeed, in the early years of a child's schooling the necessity for the classroom teacher to be motherly is paramount. Most recently, Sarah Freedman has drawn attention to this situation as a continuing issue for American elementary schoolteachers (1987, pp. 41–57).

Dorothy Smith (1984) has most eloquently expressed, by citing a series of pamphlets produced by the Toronto school board, the range of expectations schools make of mothers in working in concert with the school. What comes through her account, however, is the knowledge and skills that mothers need to have acquired before becoming mothers in order to prepare pre-school children adequately for school. No longer is the expectation of care in the pre-school years adequate. Mothers are now expected to be the first educators of their children, rather than the kindergarten or equivalent being the first school. Home as the first school is very different from home of the past, not merely because mother has been transformed from housewife and nurse to teacher but also because of the "tools" required for the trade. In concert with this change in ideological expectation has grown up a vast array of advice to mothers through manuals, toys and materials to achieve such ends. A whole range of stores targeted on the "educative-mother" market have mushroomed over the last two decades. And professors of education have been deployed not only in providing advice in the form of books, magazines and manuals, but also in developing the wherewithal to achieve such developments. Indeed, in some bookstores nowadays it is impossible to know where schoolbooks end and home books begin. Home-school relations are now an essential and inextricable part of the paraphernalia of both home and school activities. Listening and learning with mother is a seamless web of activity from home to school and back again. Indeed, the growth of "homework" as a complement to the schoolwork of primary schoolchildren is a testimony to this sea change.

Mothers (and fathers, too, when available) are not only expected, then, to back up the work of the school at home, but they are now expected to participate in school activities during the school day–listening to young children learn to read, helping with mathematics, with craft work, and with outings and trips. Their potential involvement in the educational work of the primary school is now virtually endless (David, 1985).

This kind of involvement and set of sea changes in the presumptions about home-school relations build upon the various measures developed in the 1960s to improve upon the implementation of an agreed-upon political principle of equality of educational opportunity. All the social science evidence pointed to the necessity of breaking down the dissonance between home and school in an effort to improve the socioeconomic fates of those from poor and disadvantaged home backgrounds (see especially the Coleman Report, 1966). Educational disadvantage was seen to rest in the poverty of the home and family. Involing parents in their children's education was avowedly the way to break "the cycle of disadvantage." Plentiful solutions were proposed and developed by American educators, from Headstart, to Follow-Through, to Parent-Child Centres (see Grubb and Lazerson, 1983, for a detailed resume of these varied programs). Such solutions, on a more modest scale, were also developed in England and Wales in the wake of the Plowden Committee's report (New and David, 1985).

The aim was to reach the parents of disadvantaged children, so-called because of the judgement made of their home circumstances. The model of the advantaged child was that from the conventional nuclear family. In the beginning, the aim was partly met, but increasingly it has been twisted by a combination of parental circumstance and pressure so that the aim is no longer to bring disadvantaged children to the level of middle-class children (David, 1985). Rather, now it is the children of middle-class mothers, particularly those not involved in paid work outside the home, who are the chief beneficiaries of these revised schemes of parental involvement in primary education.

Over fifteen years ago Jencks and his coauthors (1972) pointed to the serendipity involved in these programs of compensatory education. They pointed out, in their reassessment of family and schooling in America, that despite the enormous resources allocated to such programs, educational achievement had more to do with "luck" than with home background. What Jencks and his coauthors did not analyze was the impact of maternal involvement as separate from parental or paternal, home background. This research has yet to be conducted in that systematic statistical fashion. Bowles and Gintis (1976) pointed to the inaccuracy and inadequacy of some of the analyses, in a limited kind of autocritique. They pointed to the systematic influence of class on the fates of working-class American men, although they did not acknowledge the sexism of their analysis.

Subsequently more ethnographic studies have shown the effects of such programs and their transformation to middle-class families. Raphaela Best (1982) has commented on how the boys she studied did not like their mothers' involvement with the school, since it made them feel babyish. The scheme certainly had a short-term effect, even if its influence did not last into adult educational achievement. Since this comment was only an aside from the major study of sexual differentiation in an elementary school in North Carolina, its effect is unlikely to have been followed through into adulthood.

Dorothy Smith (1984) and her associates at the Ontario Institute for Studies in Education (OISE), especially Alison Griffith (1984, 1986), have also shown the effects of such programmatic developments, not on the children but on the mothers themselves. Alison Griffith's particularly sensitive analysis of lone parents and their relationships with school demonstrates the veracity of the exclusionary nature of gendered home-school relations. Mothers alone are not able, for a variety of reasons, to participate in their children's schooling on a par with mothers in two-parent families. There is also some evidence of similar effects within British schooling (David, 1985). Moreover, it appears that new forms of discrimination may be beginning with these modified forms of mother-school relations. The HMI (Her Majesty's Inspectors) have pointed, in a series of commissioned reports on the effects of public expenditure cuts on the public provision of schooling, to the creation of new forms of disadvantage both between schools and within schools themselves. They remark in particular on the divisiveness of "parental contributions of both cash and labour" (1985, p. 9). This divisiveness increases disparities both among schools in different neighborhoods and within schools among families that can and cannot afford to contribute either financially or in terms of the skills they offer (David, 1985). Of course, there is also a gendered nature to the contributions—with fathers chiefly able to contribute cash and mothers, where they can, contributing their own time and skills either in or out of school. But clearly mothers from working-class families or lone parents who need to take paid employment cannot contribute in the same measure as mothers from middle-class households who do not need to have paid employment. So these new schemes are revising the kinds of social inequality created through schooling. If the social science research of the 1960s is correct in arguing that the effects of home background are crucial to equalizing educational achievement, then changes in educational policy which equalize opportunities for social class parental involvement in children's education will lead to inequalities in achievement based on inequalities between types of family and parental background. In particular, the evidence that has been collected to date, anecdotal for the most part, would appear to indicate that disparities are occurring among families around the question of maternal employment and status.

Most of the evidence discussed so far has related to elementary or primary schools. Indeed, most of the discussion about good home-school relations and parental involvement, in both popular discourse and the sociology of education, centers on early childhood education. However, the principle remains for secondary education, too, although here the form is usually rather different. Parental involvement, for example, is not usually taken to mean participation in daily school activities, but in PTA work or in home-based support for children's schoolwork. It could be assumed that differential maternal employment status would have less effect in this case. This is probably true, but the expectations of maternal, rather than paternal, home-based support are still more pressing. For example, standards of dress are still policed by the school and assumed to be mothers' "work" (David, 1984). Fathers, on the other hand, are still expected to be ultimately responsible for children's public behavior, such as non-attendance at school.

It is interesting to note, however, that sexual activity, which is almost always only an overt concern of secondary schools, at least in England, is also seen as a matter for gendered control. A recent cause célèbre in England highlighted this fact dramatically. A Mrs. Victoria Gillick took the British Government to court over the question of doctors giving contraceptive advice to children under the age of sixteen without parental consent. Although the whole issue was couched in gender-neutral language, the main concern of Mrs. Gillick was maternal protection of daughters (David, 1986b, pp. 50–51). Initially this concern was upheld by the law courts, but the House of Lords did not sustain it. However, subsequently the Government department responsible, the Department of Health and Social Security (DHSS), altered its advice to doctors to ensure that only in exceptional circumstances were girls to receive contraceptive advice without parental consent. This stance has been confirmed by HMI advice to schools (DES, 1986, p. 19). Given the growing numbers of lone-parent families and the fact of general maternal responsibilities for daughters, this advice clearly reinforces notions of maternal protectiveness. On the other hand, it also takes away from young teenage girls their autonomy as adolescent women and maintains them in childlike dependency within the family.

This approach is not at odds with the growing public concern about the "problem of schoolgirl mothers". Indeed, in Britain, as in the United States, there has been a growth in public policy solutions to this problem. The origins, however, of the solutions are rather different. In Britain, it is part of the question of "protectiveness" and also disapprobation for children becoming mothers inappropriately and unconventionally. In the United States it appears that the growth of school-age mother or parent units created by educational authorities derives more from policies to do with equal educational opportunities–Title IX of the Educational Amendments (Zellman, 1981; David, 1984).

A sensitive study of teenage mothers in England by Sue Sharpe (1987) points out how difficult it is for those of school age to continue with conventional, compulsory education:

Lyn went into school at fifteen when she was almost due to give birth. She was wearing big maternity clothes and felt "dead weird" being with everyone else in school uniform. It was break time and everyone was in the yard talking about her: "They won't come up to you because they think you're dirty because you got pregnant and you're only fourteen or fifteen . . . But because you're still at school they think you're dirty and disgusting and they call you a slag, but it could happen to them any day." (Sharpe, 1987, p. 71)

Those who attend special units "are treated more like adults" (p. 82). Sharpe then comments: "They benefitted both practically and emotionally compared to girls without such support, who suffered more from their lack of status and recognition as mothers. If there were more such places it would help combat the cycle of deprivation that young mothers can get trapped in. A fifteen-year-old girl having her first baby is twice as likely to live at the poverty level than a nineteen-year-old first time mother" (pp. 82–83). School-age motherhood is not an appropriate form of behavior and certainly is not part of the concept of parental involvement, even in secondary education.

Indeed, precisely because schoolchildren and mothers are seen as separate and not overlapping categories, school-age mothers are prevented from participating in conventional education and are often "punished" for breaking school rules. Indeed, maternal involvement has a clear and precise or particular meaning. It is confined to mothers of school-age, primary schoolchildren. Not only are school-age mothers excluded from compulsory schooling, but conventional mothers tend to be excluded from further and higher education. As Sharpe points out, they have to rely on "private" family rather than "public" policy solutions:

Returning to education at any time is not easy with small children, little money and few available childcare facilities, but it can be done. Sometimes if girls are living at home, they can reach some arrangement with one of the family to babysit while they go to further education college . . . Elaine left her son with her sister who also had a young child . . . Helen left her daughter with her mother while she continued to take her A levels at sixth form college . . . Rosemary waited until her three children were at school before she started studying again. (Sharpe, 1987, pp. 83–84)

As noted above, education authorities do not usually recognize pre-school child care as their responsibility; it is the responsibility of the mother. Hence mothers of pre-school children are de facto excluded from all levels of education unless they can reach some "private" solution. This solution itself is usually women's work and the work of mothers of other children (New and David, 1985). It is still rare for institutions of further and higher education in Britain to provide child care facilities, although some now do as a result of the pressure group activities of their maternal students or staff. Rather, such educational institutions seek to adapt their courses to the presumed needs of "mature" women students by providing part-time courses which usually match the hours of the school day. This approach presumes that such mother-students have school-age children. There is some anecdotal evidence to suggest that this solution of adapting courses for mature students does not necessarily accord with these students' needs or wishes (Wenman, 1987; Coley, 1987). It maintains such women in an unequal position in relation to both education and subsequent employment and may therefore have the continued effect of being discriminatory.

Exploring the meaning of family and parent in relation to secondary and further or higher education in this fashion is to digress from the conventional literature. There are, however, two related issues which can be explored here: one is the debate around the curriculum of secondary schools to incorporate either education for parenthood or sex education; the other is the discussion about achieving an education for all through new forms of multicultural and antiracist education which have implications for family life. But the "conventional" debate around secondary education and the family has, on the whole, shifted from a concern with equal educational opportunities for all to one about parental rights over their children's education. This is, of course, in the context of a shift in predominant political ideologies. It marks the demise of a liberal and social democratic political consensus and the ascendency, in Britain, of those who now style themselves the "Conservative Educationalists" (private communication from Chris Knight, 1987).

The debate about parent education or education for family life was initially sparked off by a concern about changing social trends in family life and, in particular, the growth of lone-parent families, especially those headed by teenage mothers (David, 1986a). Public policy solutions at first focused only on those who had become mothers unconventionally, providing for them through either special educational solutions or social service and social welfare agencies. This was not seen as part of the mainstream educational debate. However, some educators argued for a more mainstream "preventative" approach, through the curriculum of schools, rather than for an ex post facto approach. This stance chimed in well with those educators who were arguing for social or sex education on more progressive grounds (David, 1987). The debate quickly became passionate and embroiled with arguments about religious and sexual morality. In the event, the passion was sufficient to require amendments to the educational legislation around the question of teaching sex education. The clause in the 1986 Education Act required teachers to ensure that such teaching pay attention to "moral considerations and the value of family life" (DES, 1986, par. 46, p. 48). The implication is clear that lessons in sex education can only focus on traditional sexual morality and sexual relationships and their relations to gender roles in the family and the workplace. Changes in gender roles are clearly limited if the conventional nuclear family continues to have pride of place in lessons about family life. Moreover, in this curriculum matter, as in no other, both the government, through the 1980 Education Act, and the HMI, in their advice to schools, require consultation with parents. The HMI state

Although responsibility for the curriculum does not rest with parents it is important for schools to seek and give weight to the views of parents . . . The importance of sexual relationships in all our lives is such that sex education is a crucial part of preparing children for their lives now and in the future as adults and parents. In sex education factual information . . . is not more important than a consideration of the qualities of relationships in family life and of values . . . It is therefore quite common to find sex education taught as part of a programme of personal and social education, sometimes in conjunction with religious education. (DES, 1986, pp. 16–18)

Although sex education is now a conventional component of the curriculum of secondary schools, it has a special status both in that parents still have to be consulted about its content and in that it can be taught across a range of school subjects. At least this latter is recognition of how gender or sex roles pervade society and therefore the curriculum. Nevertheless, although gender-neutral language is usually invoked, it is apparent that gender difference is a normal part of the curriculum and will thereby influence adult, and parental, life.

This differentiation is clear in the discussion in Britain about developing a multi-ethnic or multi-cultural form of education, despite protestations to the contrary. Two issues may be used to highlight the matter: one is the cause célèbre in the Bradford education authority over the views of one of its headmasters, Ray Honeyford. The other is the more extensive discussion in the government-commissioned report on multi-ethnic education. Dr. Honeyford, the headmaster of a Bradford inner-city middle school (covering the age range of eight to twelve years) which caters to an over 90 percent Asian population, chose to voice his views about education in a new organ of the British right, the *Salisbury Review*, as well as in the more popular educational press. He was highly critical of the Asian family standards of upbringing and found them both linguistically and culturally lacking, judged against Eurocentric, Christian standards of behavior (Honeyford, 1983). This criticism sparked off a major educational political controversy, which ended with his dismissal by the Labour-held educational authority, but with a huge financial settlement, given his political acceptability to the Prime Minister, Mrs. Thatcher. He was invited to become a member of her educational "think-tank." The view that parents in general and mothers in particular should bring their children up according to rigid Christian norms has gained wide public acknowledgement.

These views were voiced more generally in the recommendations of the Swann report, entitled *Education for All* (Swann Report, 1985). The authors argued against mother-tongue teaching in early childhood education in favor of such education remaining the prerogative of the family: "a language learnt at mother's knee". As with Honeyford, such education was seen to be lacking for four reasons, all of which ignore the liberal premise that parental involvement in children's schooling enhances their educational achievement. The authors argued that mother-tongue teaching in school would merely delay a child's problems in learning; that it would lead to social divisions, if there were separate provisions; that it would lead to semilingualism (a similar indictment to Honeyford's); and that it should be part of a child's cultural heritage and therefore taught in the community, not in the school. There are clearly double standards at work here, since "cultural heritage" is conventionally taught in schools if it is British, Christian or secular culture. There is also the implied criticism of the quality of the cultural heritage. Honeyford's argument against such minority languages was only more explicit in its criticisms of the deficits of Asian language structures by comparison with European languages (Honeyford, 1983).

The Swann committee did, however, recommend instead bilingual education or "mother-tongue maintenance" at primary school, and opted for the possibility of a mother-tongue course for children at secondary schools as one of several "minority languages". To achieve this end in primary schools, it suggested using "bi-lingual resources" rather than special teachers or mothers' involvement in the primary school.

Such a role may be undertaken by a bilingual teacher, non-teaching assistant or nursery nurse already on the staff of the school, or even by a parent, or possibly by *fifth or sixth formers from local secondary schools as part of their child care courses* or community service experience. It should not be assumed, however, that the bilingual "resources" will as a matter of course relate to pupils from the same linguistic, cultural or ethnic groups when their backgrounds may be entirely different; nor should they be seen as "catering" just for the ethnic minority pupils but rather as an enrichment of the education of all pupils (1985, p. 408) (my emphasis).

In the case of ethnic minority children, parental participation is to be provided to a different standard. Mothers are still to be the first educators but are denied the opportunities now afforded the majority of mothers of primary schoolchildren. Despite the gender-neutral language, it is clear that it is girls from secondary schools who will be afforded opportunities to act as bilingual resources because it is only girls who take child care courses (Pugh and De'Ath 1984, p. 199). The report denigrates both minority ethnic cultures and at one and the same time provides gender-differentiated roles for parents.

However, it appears not to do so in its recommendations against separate schools, arguing against them on the grounds of equal opportunities. It acknowledges that separate schools are usually Islamic schools for secondary school girls. The argument against separate schools is therefore seen as a general argument against single-sex secondary schools for girls (Swann Report, 1985, p. 505). The authors criticize the schools for teaching "a way of life" rather than just subjects. This is clear, they state, from the policy on "school meals, physical education and religious instruction" (p. 503). The formal criticisms of the schools are on the grounds of sexual and social inequalities, but they appear more as a criticism of the minority ethnic culture than of the inequalities generated. The schools are seen to be inadequate in the careers' education they provide since the central focus is said to be "education for motherhood" (p. 507). The schools are also said to exacerbate girls' feelings of rejection. Neither of these criticisms appears to be very strong. There is very little evidence, in Britain at least, to suggest that marriage and motherhood, as an unpaid, full-time pre-occupation, do not play a major part in both the formal and informal curriculum of conventional British secondary schools. Moreover, their careers' education does not appear to be more progressive in the context of the "new" sex education. In addition, as Deem (1985), Shaw (1980), and Spender (1980) have shown, single-sex secondary schools for girls, whatever the curriculum, have a range of positive social effects. The criticisms seem to be a criticism of Muslim culture rather than an argument for sexual equality in education, given the weak arguments presented.

Careers' education for girls is not a strong point of secondary schools in England, whether or not they are "separate" schools. A government-initiated scheme–the Youth Training Scheme (YTS)–now provides places for all children who choose to leave at the school-leaving age of sixteen and cannot find a job. Now unemployed youthful school leavers aged sixteen are forced to accept a place on a training scheme for at least a year. The Women's National Commission (WNC), reviewing the impact of equal opportunities (1984) in such schemes, found that

it is common for *girl school leavers to be expected to help at home* for a period before finally going into the employment market. We were told of three categories of girls–
–Asian girls whose families seek to keep them at home;
–West Indian girls with working mothers;
–Girls in rural areas where jobs for women were often scarce–who might at the more mature age of 18 to 20 decide they want a YTS placement, but will by then have lost their opportunity. (1984, p. 15).

The WNC's solution is not to try to equalize the situation by making YTS more similar for boys and girls. Rather, it suggests a deferral policy: "A deferral system under which *urgent family responsibilities* might be one acceptable ground should be considered. If it became generally possible for girls to begin YTS at 18 or 19 this would prove a more appropriate age to interest girls, by then beyond the uncertainties of adolescence, in non-traditional work" (1984, p. 16, my emphasis). They assume that a short dose of family life is sufficient to encourage girls out of the home and into paid employment of a nontraditional, that is, masculine, type of work. But they reckon without all the other obstacles to such nontraditional work–lack of maternity leave and child care, lack of facilities for married women returners, lack of a peer group of women. Anna Pollert (1983) drew attention to the importance of such a group at work. In any event, the prior training for such "nontraditional" careers or jobs is lacking in British secondary schools. Little effort has been made to reduce gender stereotyping in the curriculum, and the gender-differentiated expectations of parenthood do not provide positive support for such developments. Rather there is reinforcement for gender difference in both family and work activities in adulthood.

However, the mainstream debate about family and schooling in Britain over the last decade has not been about these issues, which relate chiefly to women as pupils or mothers. It has shifted from a concern with equal opportunities to one of parental power and parental rights. Indeed, even the chief radical education authority in Britain–the Inner London Education Authority (ILEA)–whilst trying to resist these shifts in political mood centrally, has modified its commitment to implementing equal opportunities strongly. In a series of commissioned reports to discuss improvements in all levels of compulsory education in London, its commitment was to equal opportunities in the traditional social class mold. Despite its discovery that over a third of families in inner London were lone-parent families and that the majority of families were from minority ethnic backgrounds, its recommendations were all directed to increases in traditional kinds of parental involvement: "If we want children to achieve more, especially working class children, then improved home-school liaison and increased parental involvement must be a top priority. Cooperative home-school relations will enhance everything the school does" (Hargreaves Report, 1985, p. 14). To achieve this goal, increases in the number of representative parent governors, tutor group parents' associations and a home-school council are recommended. None of these solutions will deal with the problems for working mothers of school involvement, nor for ethnic minority parents of different interests. The authors of the report are very pessimistic about the possibility of achieving even the modest aims of the original principles of equality of educational opportunity. They dismiss it with the disclaimer that "there is very little the school can do towards removing poverty or improving the adverse social conditions in which many such parents live." (p. 13)

Indeed, this is a realistic assessment of the current political climate. The Conservative administrations, in power since 1979, have altered the terms of the debate and are no longer interested in trying to equalize opportunities between children of different home backgrounds. Their commitments, as expressed variously through pamphlets, books, and journals before their return to office, is to excellence and the maintenance of academic standards. Several new measures have signaled this change of mood, although no one piece of educational legislation has reinstated any form of parental rights in its entirety. A series of developments, however, give priority to parental rights and power over schemes of parental equality. For example, the 1980 Education Act gave parents the right to more information about how schools work in the form of prospectuses and aspects of the curriculum, to appeal against decisions made over pupil allocation to particular schools, and to involvement in school governing bodies. A modified form of parental privilege was also developed in the recreation of schemes of public financial support for a child's attendance at a private school—the Assisted Places Scheme. In more recent legislation, the 1986 Education Act, the system of parental governors has become more extensive, with a firmer system of election and the publication of annual reports. In Scotland, there are moves to extend schemes of parental choice to allow parents greater control over budgets, curricula and teacher appointments.

All of these schemes are directed at parents as the consumers of education, on the assumption that, as consumers, they will demand a good service. Indeed, Stuart Hall has described how some of the new proposals create an "educational supermarket" (1983, p. 9). Certainly, parents are seen as an ungendered social category and as only interested in shopping around for a quality product. But the content of the quality is assumed—a middle-class, academic education. No consideration is given to the parents who have neither the time nor ability to embark upon such a shopping spree—usually lone parents and working mothers. It is not toward them that such new educational endeavors are directed, but to the parents with entrepreneurial zeal.

In this process, educational inequalities are recreated and created. Unconventional parents are penalized through these new schemes both as parents of schoolchildren and if they are school-age parents, whereas entrepreneurial parents are rewarded and used to run the new "private" or "businesslike" schools. Indeed, the terrain of debate about family and schooling has shifted from opportunity to control. Parents are no longer involved in creating new opportunities for their children's generation; rather they are used to control and run the schools and the teachers within them. It seems that parent-teacher associations may have a completely different resonance in the next several years. They will no longer be associations for supporting together the school in which they are equal partners. Rather they will be more businesslike ventures in which some parents will control the work of teachers in the interests of ensuring that the children ultimately compete effectively in the marketplace. It is no longer true in Britain that it is only children that are the property of their parents. It seems that schools, too, are fast becoming parental property and are not subject to the regulation of the wider community, whose interests they ought to serve. Parental responsibility is now extensive—not only with respect to out of school time, but also in controlling school through its whole range of activities. Parents and the family are now crucial in the organization of education, but equal only in their formal access to power over schools.

PART TWO

Rethinking Schooling as the Language of Reform

Fixing the Schools:
The Ideological Turn

Walter Feinberg

The recent reports on educational reform, with their renewed emphasis on the academic side of the high school experience, have been favorably received. The many reports, documents, and books that have been delivered to the public in recent years decry the loss of purpose and intellectual vitality that the high school is depicted as once possessing. Although there are important variations on the theme, most call for a return to a core curriculum that is composed of traditional subject matter in science, mathematics, English, and social studies. In addition, many ask that students become familiar with the use of the computer – that they become computer literate.

Although a new emphasis on the intellectual side of secondary schools would certainly be a welcome change, with a few exceptions, the reports presented to the public are inappropriate guides for such a renaissance. Many are creatures of an ideological climate in which inquiry and dissent have been quieted and vocationalism, sometimes packaged as academic courses, is rampant. There are, of course, exceptions. Some of the documents represent serious attempts to understand the many problems that the schools face and to suggest viable ways to address them. Yet together the reports feed a questionable image of an educational system which has fallen away from a once golden age which, as the closing years of the century approach, we are called upon to recapture. For many, the prophet of this educational paradise lost was James Conant, whose wise counsel, we are told, was cast aside by the anarchy that has become known as the nineteen-sixties and seventies.

My own recollection of the period in which Conant wrote is different.

69

I recall it as a time of intense racial discrimination when even the most elementary formal rights were denied to black people, when sexual discrimination was unconsciously accepted as a part of the natural order of things, and when the call for equal opportunity beckoned white men only. I recall it as a time when racist, sexist, and militaristic images filled the pages of school textbooks unchallenged while the equivalent of today's "moral majority" readied themselves to protest the reading of *Catcher in the Rye*. All of this was not Conant's doing, of course, but neither was it Conant's seeing. To remember Conant is certainly to recall one who has become recognized as a remarkable educational statesman, but it is also to recall the key architect of the military-industrial-educational establishment, the person who sold education to the government as our answer to Sputnik.

Given the present ideological climate, Conant is an appropriate symbol. His no-nonsense approach to education vocationalized the liberal arts—scientists for the military and linguists for the state department. Yet, those who are advocating a core curriculum, as most of the reformers are doing, might recall the dual system that Conant proposed—academic disciplines for the talented few in the suburbs and behavioral control and vocational training for most of the youngsters in the slums.

If the gold-plated age is somewhat tarnished and the veneer worn, there is yet little doubt about what is represents. It speaks to a time when, *The Blackboard Jungle* notwithstanding, students were obedient, test scores were high, authority was respected, standards were clear, and the work ethic was in place.

To understand these newest educational proposals, one must view them within the context of the ideological climate of the present time. Some of the reports, and here *A Nation at Risk* must stand out,[1] contribute directly to an ascending ideology of statism and control. If discipline and order are not found in the school, they will not be found in the workplace, and production, consumption, and national power will suffer. Other documents, and here John Goodlad's *A Place Called School* is the most impressive, provide an instructive yet imcomplete account of schooling which remains to be filled in by the outcome of a larger ideological struggle.

My own view will obviously color this analysis. It is that schools are indeed in a critical situation, but not quite for the same reasons that have been given by many of the reports. I believe that schools should help students develop the intellectual equipment and the cultural perspective needed to reflect upon the value of the various choices and commitments that they are to make in the self-forming process of shaping a life. The schools are in a crisis because they are failing to meet this goal. To some extent this purpose provides the school with a negative mandate, one which is shared by parents and others charged with bringing up the young. It is to help a youngster avoid making an irreversible mistake, one that would be so damaging as to preclude or sharply curtail future choices. However, it provides a positive mandate as well: to help youngsters develop the modes of thinking and critical perspectives which will enable them to make wise choices and to participate critically in the activities of a political community.

It is this latter mandate which brings the schools into contact with general education and the liberal arts, but not the liberal arts as a set of prescribed materials selected by Mortimer Adler for some reason known only to himself and Aristotle. It is the liberal arts as they provide ways of reflecting on the life we are living and shaping. Indeed, there is nothing contradictory between a liberal and vocational education insofar as the vocational work provides a way for a student to try on different modes of being. There is only something wrong when the vocational work is taken up to preclude reflection and to reinforce an alreacy limited field.

Thus, when I speak of liberal education I have in mind a series of reflective activities in which youngsters use some available intellectual tools to reflect upon the shape that their life is taking. If science is taught, as I would expect it to be, it would be to learn how our environment sustains and influences the kinds of beings that we are, and the humanities would be taught to show how, through the development of culture, human beings come to interpret the nature of that being. When the National Commission, or the National Science Board, or the members of the Twentieth Century Fund Task Force write about the need for more science, math, and English, they do no have in mind the same things that I do. Rather, like Conant, they see these as weapons in a struggle for national survival, a belief which I do not wish to share. Even Adler, with all his It's-good-for-its-own-sake-so-let's-rub-their-nose-in-it argument, lets us know in the second volume that it's good for national defense too!

The fact is that there has been a lot of nonsense packaged under the heading of this or that national commission and this or that foundation report. Educational reports, especially those written by national commissions and educational foundations, are often about the business of creating social myths, and perhaps, as long as we understand this, we should not be too critical when we find that they have done their job well. There is art to the mythmakers' work, and such art should be understood.

The ideological turn

Although there is much conflict among the reports over important issues, together they reflect an ideological shift that is occurring in many fields.

In medicine, for example, the shift is represented by the slow abandonment of the quest for national health insurance, the rising acceptance of a multi-tiered system, the increase in for-profit health schemes, and a cap on payment for medicaid patients.[2] In civil rights and criminal justice the shift is reflected in the softening of affirmative action requirement and the weakening of interpretations of due process. One common way to view this shift is as a move from concerns about equality to concerns about efficiency, but I do not think that this description is completely accurate. For example, the reduced commitment to affirmative action has taken place within the context of a high unemployment rate. Unless one accepts a narrow, economic definition of efficiency, it is difficult to view as very efficient a society in which more than 7 percent of its population is forced to be unproductive. Moreover, the demand for efficiency in social service areas has been initiated as a response to an ever-increasing national debt which has developed as military expenditures have gone unchecked. In other words, inefficiency in national defense has sparked a concern for greater efficiency in social services and education. The ideological shift represents not a move from equality to efficiency but an attempt to reaffirm the legitimate basis of institutional authority and to quiet the various challenges that have arisen during the past fifteen years. This requires that the weight of the moral consensus be redistributed and that the voice of the institutional critics be muted.

In its attempt to reshape the moral consensus, education is actually following the lead of popular culture. In many of the most popular films of the late sixties and early seventies, such as *The Graduate*, authenticity and personal integrity were expressed as the supreme values standing in opposition to the established incentive and value systems. At the same time, the Free School Movement was at its height, and many saw in this movement a way in which students, too, could experience the same authenticity and integrity. Since the public schools were viewed as the antipathy of authenticity, they formed the background against which these values could be expressed and became to some the symbols of conformity and inauthenticity. By the middle of the 1970s, the American dream again became fashionable and the establishment stood as a barrier not to personal authenticity but to individual fame and fortune. The free school movement had passed, the reaction to public education was taking place in church-affiliated schools, and if there was a problem with the establishment, it was that it was not conformist enough. By the early 1980s, even the military, which had been out of favor during the Vietnam War, had a popular renaissance. The training sergeant in the film *An Officer and a Gentleman* (portrayed by a black actor) could bark at his recruits that killing women and children was one of the highest forms of patriotism. With Ronald Reagan calling the action in Southeast Asia a noble war, the audience could not help but read Vietnam into the script. On the campus, the CIA again began recruiting and ROTC regained the respectability it had lost.

The weight of the moral consensus was affected by other events as well. High unemployment and the rising rate of inflation provided the incentive for people to scramble for available jobs, and university students, faculty, and administrators strained to keep track of a constantly shifting market. The consensus was affected by the Soviet action in Afghanistan as well. It was an action which demonstrated that any superpower can have its Vietnam, licensing people to again use the behavior of "The Evil Empire" to the east as the measuring rod for its own morality.

The effect, of course, was to render the institutional criticisms and the values that generated them irrelevant—at least in the minds of many people. After all, what is the problem with a little inequality in the face of all of these dangers? It may be true, as the more radical critics have claimed, that the schools reproduce the relations of production, and perhaps the relations of production are a bit unequal, if not unjust. If the alternative is to turn over our industrial production to the Japanese, then we must continue to endure these inequities.

This is the climate in which the present reports on education have been issued. It is an atmosphere of threat and siege, a climate where a military-industrial giant is obsessed with the possibility of its own impotence. It is precisely the kind of climate where national chauvinism is likely to pass for educational wisdom.

Of course, it is the report by the National Commission on Excellence in Education, with all its talk of unilateral educational disarmament and its hyperbole about the rising tide of mediocrity, that best fits and reinforces this climate. It is not, however, the only one. The report by the National Science Board, published shortly before *A Nation at Risk*, anticipates its argument for school reform by linking schooling to the maintenance of economic strength and military security,[3] and *Making the Grade*, the report issued by the Twentieth Century Fund shortly after the publication of the National Commission on Excellence in Education, begins by endorsing the commission's concerns.[4] There are, as we shall see, different voices, other reports which do not play upon or consciously reinforce the agressive national agenda which has emerged with such force in recent years. Although few of these voices challenge directly the ideological direction established by *A Nation at Risk*, some say reasonable things about the quality of classroom life. Yet the present climate has surely circumscribed the educational debate and sharply curtailed some important understandings.

The creation of an educational ideology

It is *The Paideia Proposal*, not *A Nation at Risk*, which carries the subtitle "An Educational Manifesto." Yet, if a manifesto is judged by its propaganda value and its effectiveness as a mobilizer, that subtitle should have been awarded to the report by the members of the National Commission. Although Adler is certainly able to present his ideas in clear and simple terms, he does not have the same talent for the alarmist rhetoric that characterized the commission's argument. And although some of his arguments are certainly simplified, there are, especially in the third volume, some words about educational procedure and some examples of classroom practice which should be taken seriously. That he idealizes American democracy, as he does, and slips into arguments that link education to national defense helps to locate him ideologically. However, his attempt is to provide an educational treatise, and his work should be evaluated according to its success in doing so.

The same cannot be said for the report of the National Commission on Excellence in Education. The schools are a tool of national power, and because they are floundering, the nation is at risk. As a manifesto, it has done its job – alerting us to the fact that a problem exists in our nation's schools. This, however, is all that can be said. Instead of carefully characterizing the nature of that problem, it has offered a series of rhetorical slogans which lead not just to oversimplification, but to misrepresentation.

According to the authors of this report, if the United States wishes to maintain its industrial and military superiority, it must bring a halt to what it sees as the erosion of educational standards. The commission expresses optimism that this will be done because, as it patronizingly puts it, our citizens know that "education is one of the chief engines of a society's material well-being . . . Citizens also know in their bones that the safety of the United States depends principally on the wit, skill and spirit of the self-confident people, today and tomorrow."[5]

Although *A Nation at Risk* is only one of a number of reports that link industrial and military power to education, it is clearly the one that has received the most attention.[6] The fact is that there are many good reasons for improving our schools. However, the relationship between good schools and a strong military or an efficient, productive economy is much more complex than any of the reports acknowledge. Nevertheless, it does not take a sophisticated economist to see some of the flaws in the argument. For example, a number of the reports decry the decline in student test scores and the poor performance of students in the United States when compared to those from some other nations. Yet, although students in the

United States do not perform as well as those in France and England on a number of measured areas of achievement, there is no evidence to indicate that these lower scores have resulted in a comparably weaker military. Indeed, there is sufficient evidence to indicate that during the period when test scores have declined, the military has grown stronger.

The success that Japanese firms have had in penetrating the American market, along with the growing imbalance of trade between the two nations, has been an important factor in preparing the atmosphere for the reception of the reports. Indeed, *A Nation at Risk* identifies Japan as a major and troublesome source of industrial competition, which it is. In many respects Japan is performing for American education in the 1980's the same function that the Soviet Union performed in the 1950's. It is providing the dark incentive for restructuring the educational system. The reason for this is related to the large number of Toyotas and Hondas that are to be seen on the nation's roads and the equally impressive numbers of Sony televisions that are watched in American homes. The fact that Japanese students score quite high on standardized achievement tests while American students do not has not been lost on those who wish to find a reason for the decline in American industry that was evident a few years ago. The reasoning is simple and elegant, even if flawed. If Japanese children do well on standardized tests and if Japanese workers make more desirable cars than American workers, then if American youngsters would do better on standardized tests, American workers would make better cars. Although the logic may be wanting, the formula actually seems to work. American students have begun to do better on standardized tests and the automobile industry is now making record profits. Only a skeptic might point to the "voluntary" restrictions that Japan placed on exported automobiles to account for the revitalization of the American car industry, or to the benefits that have resulted to American industrialists by the taming of the work force.

There are, of course, many reasons besides schooling and test scores that could be provided for the recent growth of selected Japanese industry. The fact that Japan invests less than 1 percent of its GNP on defense means that, in contrast to the United States, a much larger proportion of its budget can be invested in industrial research. It also means that many more of its scientists and engineers are involved in consumer research rather than military research. Indeed, the link between a strong military and a weakened consumer industry may be much stronger than the link between a weak educational system and either a weakened military or a weakened industry. If test scores make the difference, then, of course, the industrial threat from Israel should at least equal that of Japan. Given the enfeebled state of Israel's economy, however, any suggestion to that effect would be properly taken as an absurdity.

Although the scores of Japanese students are indeed high, a closer look at the Japanese educational system suggests that it cannot be used to support many of the proposals put forward by some of the recent reports. For example, the reports are almost unanimous in calling for the development of some kind of merit pay system for teachers with rather steep differences in rewards. However, the formula for increasing salaries in Japan is, with minor exceptions, essentially based on seniority. Moreover, whereas teachers in the United States must usually undergo a trial period before receiving tenure, Japanese teachers are given tenure when they begin teaching. Many teachers in Japan would object to the recent reform proposals on the ground that they are too individualistic and would disrupt the cooperative activities of the schools.

I suspect that what is attractive about Japan to the American reformers is that it appears to be such a well-ordered society with a highly developed meritocracy. If one is willing to put aside Japan's discriminatory treatment of the Korean and Barakumin minorities, as well as the severe restrictions customarily placed on women, this appraisal is largely correct. However, in emphasizing the high achievement of Japanese students, little is made of those features of the Japanese system that are evidence of a commitment to equality or to the communal features of Japanese education. For example, the Japanese have a strong system of compensatory allocation which helps significantly to equalize the expenses that poor and wealthy districts provide for education. Moreover, there is some indication that this has an effect on measured achievement, since Japan reports a comparably small mean variation on tests. However, the measures that Japan has taken to advance the goal of equality were overlooked by the American educational reformers.

When the reports were published and as more and more educators began to cite with alarm the differences in the scores of American and Japanese youngsters, I began to wonder about the way in which the Japanese view their own educational system. I was fortunate to be invited to give some lectures in Japan and was thus provided the opportunity to talk to and interview a number of Japanese teachers, researchers, and educational officials.[7] Although I found considerable pride in the recent attention given to their schools, there were conflicting interpretations among the Japanese about the meaning of the high test scores. A considerable debate is taking place about whether these scores truly represent a high-quality educational system. Although there are many teachers who feel that the tests do help to motivate students, there are others who believe that they actually hurt the educational process. For example, in an interview with several teachers from one of the few prefectures where a science test is not required for placement into a high school, this concern was voiced with special eloquence by the head science teacher. He feared that if the students had to worry about passing the test he would no longer be able to teach them how to be scientific. When I pressed him for an explanation, he responded with an example. He noted that now he can take his junior high school students down to the pond, collect a sample of water, and spend a considerable amount of time helping them analyze all of the living organisms that can be found in it. However, if an examination in science were to be required, he would no longer be able to do that. He would have to teach them how to pass the test.

This teacher's opinion was echoed to some degree in an interview with Mr. Hisao Saito, the deputy director general of the Secretariat for the Provisional Council on Educational Reform.[8] He cited the intensity of competition fostered by the examination system as the most serious problem of Japanese education. When I asked whether he would be concerned if the reforms proposed by the council resulted in a decline in test scores, his response was that "we don't care about the results of achievement." His point was not that the commission is unconcerned about the level of achievement of Japanese children but rather that the present examination system and the intense competition that results are probably constraining certain forms of achievement. Of special concern are those forms having to do with creativity.

These concerns are not unrealistic. There is little doubt that the examinations drive the educational system. Students are required to take a test to determine the high school that they will attend and they are later required to take a test to determine whether they will be accepted to the university. In both instances, the mechanisms for selection place severe penalties on failure. For example, students apply for admission not only to the university, but to the high school as well, and they are allowed to apply to only one public high school. Although all public high schools in a perfecture administer the same examination, each sets its own standards for a passing score. Since the test for all public high schools is given on the same day and since students can only apply to one high school, failure means either that they must go to a private, more costly, and probably less prestigious high school or else, as is the case with very few students, they must seek employment.[9] Moreover, there is a very strict, informal system of high school ranking (from the most to the least prestigious), which gives each student a very clear understanding of his or her academic level. The high cost of failure requires that, before selecting the school they will apply to, junior high school students must have a clear understanding of their chances for being admitted. The fact that most students do attend a public high school means that this requirement is usually met. Fujita explains one of the mechanisms that is used:

Many junior and senior high schools arrange for their senior students to take several facsimile examinations by testing companies (usually six to twelve times a year). After every facsimile examination, students are informed of their test scores in each subject as well as the total, and the relative standings among the students who took the same combination of subjects and among those who plan to apply for the same high school or university. In addition to these facsimile examinations, students are given . . . mid-term and final examinations every trimester. Thus, as OECD examiners reported on Japanese education in 1971, "Students . . . become more interested in examination techniques than in real learning and maturation."[10]

Thus, instead of taking the level of performance on tests as a sign of educational health, there are many in Japan who view it as part of a rather serious educational problem, a problem that is fed by the large number of industries that have developed as a result of the examination system. Publication enterprises regularly detail the success that students from different schools have had in being accepted to the various universities. The success of a particular high school helps to determine its position in the informal ranking system. In addition, a large number of students attend privately owned cram schools, called Jukus, which are conducted after school hours and function to prepare students for the examination. The more elite cram schools require that students pass an entrance examination to be admitted, and I have been told that there are some which require that the child's mother remain home and not work outside of the house. In addition to the work at the regular school and the time spent in a Juku, many students are also tutored at home.[11]

Many Japanese are critical of this system, but it is unlikely that Japan will follow in Korea's footsteps and ban tutoring altogether.[12] However, many critics feel that unless key corporations and government bureaus stop hiring people on the basis of the university attended, the system will continue in one form or another. Whether one is a critic or a fan of the examination system, few Japanese (even those who believe that schools do a good job) are likely to agree that the scores on the tests are an indication of the high quality of the schools. There are too many other factors involved to attribute scores to the work of the schools alone.

Finally, it is somewhat misleading to compare the performance of Japanese and American high school students because the systems work in different ways. For the Japanese student the high school is a time of intense pressure and rigorous study. Although this is also the case for some students in the United States, many do not begin to take schooling seriously until they enter a college or university. In Japan, however, the university is known to be a reasonably relaxing period in a student's career. The important thing is to get in. My own impression is that the graduate programs in Japan are generally underdeveloped, a fact which probably helps to account for the asymmetry in the flow of graduate students between the two countries. Even if we were to accept the view that the test scores tell us something about the efficiency of the Japanese and American high schools, we must also realize that they do not tell us much about the productivity of the system as a whole. At a very minimum we would need to know something about the scores at the point at which the representative student exited from the system. Yet this kind of measure would give to the tests more credit than they deserve. As Hidaka, a noted Japanese critic, observes:

If students graduating from my university were to take the . . . University Entrance Examination without prior preparation, their average scores would be far lower than those of candidates sitting for the exam. Indeed, I even doubt whether the teaching staff at national and other public universities would do as well as candidates if they were to take the same exam. This alone indicates the absurdity of the National Standard Entrance Examination.[13]

The assault on equality

Although *A Nation at Risk* speaks of an act of unilateral educational disarmament, it neglects to identify a reason for this act. The report issued by the Twentieth Century Fund Task Force, *Making the Grade*, is more explicit. It believes that it is the emphasis on equality that has led to a decline in quality.[14] Although the report does not propose that efforts on behalf of educational equality be discontinued, its recommendations, including one that would curtail the scope of bilingual programs, give the strong impression that equality and diversity have gone too far.

A few years ago, the authors of any proposal that linked programs undertaken on behalf of minority populations with a decline in educational quality would have felt compelled to offer some evidence to support their claim. It is indicative of the present climate that this report provides no such evidence. Rather, the observation feeds into a popularly held belief that the educational and financial costs of recent programs enacted for the benefit of minority populations have been too high. Having provided fuel for this belief, the recommendation that the commitment to equality be continued appears to be little more than a begrudging concession to convention.

The ideological slant of this report becomes apparent when one looks at the two different parts of the document. The first part is the actual report of the task force. Although it is clearly the most prominent feature of the report, it takes up only the first twenty-two pages of the document. The second part is a much longer background research paper written by Paul Peterson which follows the part written by the task force. This paper was used by the task force members in writing their report, and, as one would expect, there are recognizable similarities between the two. Yet the tone, balance, and rhetoric are different. For example, whereas the task force endorses the view of the National Commission that there is a serious crisis in education and speaks of avoiding the "threatened disaster," the author of the background paper writes that "the crisis in education is greatly exaggerated."[15] And, whereas Peterson agrees fully with the task force that there must be a renewed federal commitment to educational quality, he observes, but the task force does not, that "it cannot be said that nationwide school integration has been put forward with undue haste. According to one account the degree of segregation in public schools was greater in 1980 than in 1970."[16] In contrast to Peterson's cautious words about the slow pace of integration, the task force lists the goal of dissolving racial divisiveness as one of the items placed under the general subheading "Excessive Burdens." Under the same heading the task force also mentions maintaining ethnic distinctiveness, thus suggesting that the two goals are incompatible and that schools cannot be expected to meet them both. There is no argument provided, however, that integration must take place at the expense of cultural integrity, but the task force later builds upon this insinuated conflict in its suggestion that funds for bilingual programs be diverted. Peterson, however, again provides a more balanced view. In reviewing the rather mixed evaluations that have been given regarding the academic effectiveness of bilingual programs, Peterson notes the studies that show their effectiveness in reducing the dropout rate significantly and concludes, "Even if bilingual education programs do nothing more than increase the number of Spanish-speaking school staff members, that may be sufficient reason for many Hispanics to support these programs."[17] Finally, whereas the report lays much of the blame for the perceived decline in standards on teacher unions, Peterson identifies the fall in teacher salaries as one of the problems that has inflicted education in recent years.[18] The task force does not mention this as a factor which has motivated teachers to join unions. Rather, it decries the spread of the trade union mentality in education. Although the shift in tone from the background paper to the report is not radical, it is sufficient to tilt the substance of the report away from recent concerns to use education to empower minority groups. In so many words, the report lets us know that it is in the attempt to meet the demands of Latinos, Blacks, and other groups that the federal government has let its commitment to quality slip.

The assault on equality is subtle. Equality of opportunity is accepted by all of the reports as a proper goal of schooling, which, of course, it must be if a proposal is to attain any credibility. Rather, the assault is on particular interpretations of equality, which in *Making the Grade* is evidenced by the begrudging acknowledgment given to affirmative action programs. The task force notes that "even affirmative action programs registered some success, although most were hampered by excessive federal manipulation."[19] The nature of this manipulation is not stated, but the comment fits well with the declining commitment to such programs that we have witnessed on the federal level in recent years.

Although traditional formulations of equality of opportunity are not challenged by the report, there is an indirect challenge made to developing interpretations of this principle. Two related interpretations are important in understanding the force of this report. However, because they are only implied by the document, they require some explicit explanation.

The first is a view of equality that argues the appropriateness of judging inequality on a group as well as an individual basis. The implication of this argument is that some kind of quota system may be appropriate in applying affirmative action guidelines. The appropriateness of this interpretation is implicitly rejected by the report in its oblique reference to the federal manipulation of affirmative action. Since the word *quota* is left for the reader to insert into the text, the report provides no argument against the use of quota, nor does it provide any discussion about the way in which quotas have actually been used by the federal government. There is not even a discussion about the extent of their use. Nevertheless, the intended message is clear. The use has been excessive.

The second interpretation of equality that is implicitly rejected is signaled by the attack on bilingual programs. This interpretation involves the right of different minority groups to help determine their own educational agenda. Again, the report does not spell out the reason for its objection to bilingual programs, but its excessive anxiety about the effects of bilingual programs seems to reflect a much deeper anxiety about the power of minority groups to conceive of and affect changes in the schools.

Of course, the two interpretations of equality are related. If students who cannot read, write, or speak English cannot be taught in their native language, then all of their other skills will suffer. By not allowing intergroup inequality to count as prima facie evidence of unjust discrimination, we will have little choice but to explain the performance deficiencies that will probably arise as signs of inferior ability or as the result of a cultural deficiency fostered by the home. Here, the dissenting comment in the report by task force member Carlos Hortas is an instructive footnote to the committee's recommendation. In it Professor Hortas shows that the committee was informed of the underlying social purpose of bilingual programs and of their actual practices. Although it is fortunate that the task force preserved individual dissent in footnotes to its document, there is no evidence that Hortas's comments were incorporated into the report. He writes:

No bilingual program in the United States promotes another language as a *substitute for English*. In fact, intensive English instruction is a part of every bilingual program. Bilingual programs attempt to show that English is not, in and of itself, a superior or richer language than the student's native language. There is a greater social benefit in promoting and encouraging linguistic diversity than in calling for specious uniformity.[20]

The italics are in the original and refer to a comment made in the main document characterizing bilingual education as a substitute for English teaching and warning against a multiplicity of specific language programs in each community. It is precisely the linguistic diversity that Hortas would encourage that the larger committee fears.

All of this is not to deny that there is a real concern among the authors of the various reports about the ability of the schools to produce higher-level scientists and engineers. However, the actual growth in jobs in these areas will be relatively small when compared with the growth in jobs at the lower levels of the economy,[21] and the problems of structural unemployment have not been solved, although the tolerance for higher levels may be increasing. The concern about bilingual education and affirmative action and the nervous lobbying for the recognition of English as the national language[22] are expressions of a general anxiety about the empowerment of minority groups. In other words, they represent a curtailment of what the Trilateral Commission has referred to as the excesses of democracy that developed in the 1960s and 1970s.

Education for a unified culture

Some nostalgics believe that there was once a time when people in the United States shared a common culture: a time when the masses and the elite were bound together by a common belief in the Bible and when the elites were clearly recognizable and legitimated by their ability to read the classical texts in the original Latin or Greek. I don't know when or whether this time existed, but there are some who believe it can be recaptured, even if in a different form. My own belief is that any common heritage will have to be found in the struggles by which different peoples confront existing institutions and in the changes that result, both to the people and the institutions, in the course of this struggle.

The Paideia Proposal,[23] written by Mortimer Adler on behalf of the Paideia Group, is an attempt to assert the idea of a unified culture built not on the Bible but on a curriculum that reflects a unified cultural experience. Adler believes that there is a series of objectives and courses which should be prescribed for all primary and secondary school children, and he further believes that students should be allowed to take only these courses. (*The Paideia Proposal* actually comprises the first of three volumes. Although it is the most publicized of the three, the third volume, *The Paideia Program*, with specific essays on pedagogy by members of the Paideia Group, is actually the most useful.)[24]

Adler argues that all elective courses should be eliminated from the school curriculum and that vocational and specialized subjects should be undertaken only after a student graduates from high school. He believes that each student should undergo the same general program, one which reflects the basic goals of a liberal education. The subject matter that he proposes fits into three groups: language, literature, and the fine arts constitute the first; mathematics and natural science constitute the second; geography and social studies constitute the third.[25] These are selected presumably because they relate most directly to the three goals of education which Adler identifies—individual growth, citizenship, and a vague category that he calls the development of "the basic skills that are common to all work in a society such as ours."[26]

Adler has presented similar proposals in the past, but the present climate is especially receptive and his work is receiving considerable publicity. The proposal is endorsed by a group of twenty-two leading educators[27] who call themselves the Paideia Group, and there have been reports of individual schools establishing a curriculum along the lines suggested in the proposal. Adler's work has also been strongly criticized by a number of professional educators, often on the grounds that is does not take into account individual differences.[28] The actual substance of Adler's proposal does not, in fact, warrant the severe criticism that it has received, nor does it deserve the enthusiastic support that a number of admirers have granted it.

The *Proposal* itself contains very few useful guidelines for directing the educational process. It gives the appearance of specificity but not the substance. For example, there is the appearance of a rational argument for the elimination of vocational training, but there is nothing which tells us what is to count as vocational training. We have no way of knowing whether a course that uses the automobile to teach certain principles of physics would count as a science course or as a course in automobile mechanics. We do not know whether it would make a difference if students worked on a real car or if they only looked at pictures of an engine to illustrate the principles. We are told that students are to be spared specialized courses. However, we do not know whether a course in black history from 1800 to 1950 would be seen as too specialized–or, if so, whether a course in American history from 1800 to 1950 would be seen in the same way. The fact is that Adler provides no answers to questions like these because he confuses the label of a course with its substance. The difficult questions are not whether history or literature should be taught; it is whose history or whose litera-ture. It is amazing that after the curriculum debates that have been raging for the past twenty years, Adler thinks that he can pluck a label out of the air and thereby provide the substance of a curriculum.

Adler's document has political significance because it provides rhetori-cal support for the belief that American society rests on a unified set of cul-tural themes which are known by some and can be taught by others. Adler does not offer a pedagogy; he creates a mood whereby education rides calmly over the political fracas secure in the understanding that it rests on an expertly sanctioned body of knowledge. The intensity of the debate over Adler's work is interesting only because there is nothing offensive in the substance of Adler's proposal.[29]

The alternatives

One of the striking features about the documents discussed so far is that they are not based on any observations of actual schools, but rather draw their conclusions either from an analysis of statistical data about school per-formance or, as is the case with Adler, from some timeless ideals that have been pasted onto the present situation. This analysis is in sharp contrast to other evaluations which rely in varying degrees on direct classroom obser-vation to fill in the details that a priori and survey methods must inevitably overlook. Three works in this genre include in impressively detailed study of the American school by John Goodlad[30] as well as two other works of substance. The first is a composite impression of the American high school drawn by Theodore Sizer.[31] The second, which like Goodlad's uses both survey and observational techniques, is a report written by Ernest Boyer for the Carnegie Foundation for the Achievement of Teaching.[32]

There are a number of common features to these three works. First, all of them view schools in a much less alarmist fashion than does *A Nation at Risk* or *Making the Grade*. Second, all argue that the upgrading of the teaching profession requires not just the development of some form of career ladder for teachers, but also more autonomy for the local school. Third, although all advocate some form of core curriculum, they each have an interest in improving more than the academic side of school life. All three authors believe that the school has an important responsibility for developing a sense of community among its students. Even though all are in favor of a core curriculum, their recommendations are sensitive to the pedagogical problem of relating the curriculum to the interests of the student. In contrast to the earlier documents, there is a diminished emphasis on declining test scores and a warning that we should not assume that the decline in such scores necessarily indicates a decline in educational quality. In addition, there is a strong concern about the vast differences in quality and opportunities that are presented by different high schools.

However, many of the specific issues that have occupied the public's attention in recent years are missing from these accounts. There is no discussion of busing, for example, and one does not find in the index to either Goodlad's or Boyer's book (Sizer did not include an index) a reference to either sexism or racism. Goodlad explains this shift in emphasis by noting that although the struggle for equal access to education is not over, we have entered a new era in that struggle, one in which greater attention will be paid to what and how students learn in school.[33] Although I would agree with the observation, I would want to emphasize that social class and racial and sexual differences in access to high-quality education remain a major educational problem.

The analyses presented in these three books benefit when contrasted to *A Nation at Risk*. They are less doctrinaire than the report of the National Commission, and they have a more balanced view of the problems and purposes of schooling. There is even some gentle sparring with a few points made by the National Commission. For example, Boyer, without naming his opponent, chides some reformers for neglecting the well-being of the individual in their concern for the national interest.[34] He also places considerably less emphasis on the school's role in developing scientists and engineers and considerably more on the need that future citizens will have to understand the social impact of science and technology.

There are, of course, differences among the reports, and one could take exception to any of a series of recommendations. One could argue with Sizer for deemphasizing foreign language and physical education. We could quibble with Boyer about his suggestion that voluntary community service be made a compulsory part of the curriculum. And many people would take strong exception to Goodlad's proposal that tracking be eliminated. Yet all of these proposals arise from a fuller understanding and a more sensitive treatment of schooling than those that we looked at earlier, and in doing so they provide balance to the recent string of pedagogical proposals. However, the situation is more complex when it comes to assessing the ideological place of these documents.

The gentle turn

If the documents under discussion place less emphasis on the relationship between education and national defense than, say, *A Nation at Risk*, they also reflect a tilt away from a more radical mode of educational analysis—one which sought to understand the mechanisms whereby schools help to reproduce an unequal social order. The tilt is gentle because the authors maintain much of the sensitivity to injustice and discrimination that inspired the more radical criticisms of schooling. For example, Theodore Sizer, in his book, *Horace's Compromise*, notes that after visits to a number of schools serving different social classes, "It got so that I could say with some justification to school principals, 'Tell me about the incomes of your students' families and I'll describe to you your school.'"[35] Nevertheless, although the sensitivity remains, the tilt is serving to blunt the kind of political and social analysis which the radical critique would use to explain why these inequalities persist.

The point of that critique is that a society which has large-scale inequalities built into its basic economic structure will also have a mechanism to reproduce that inequality across generations. For a variety of reasons, it is argued that the schools have often served this function in modern industrial capitalist societies. Moreover, some of the problems found in schools may arise out of a need on the part of students or parents to resist the forces of reproduction. To the extent that this analysis is accurate, it means that educational reforms are likely to be implemented in such a way as to reflect in the classroom the unequal relations that exist outside the schools. Thus, for example, we are likely to find that certain kinds of curriculum reform, say those that emphasize strict behavior discipline, rule following, and lower-order memorization, will more often find their way into schools with children from the lower socioeconomic class, and reforms that emphasize creativity or higher-order conceptual skills will be more likely incorporated into schools with children from higher socioeconomic groups.

The analysis clearly needs refinement. Inequalities may persist above and beyond those that are required by the economic system, periods of rapid economic expansion may facilitate new instruction modes that are not simply reflective of existing economic relationships, and structural inequality may not require intergenerational inequality. Moreover, it has been too easy for critics to take this kind of analysis as a pessimistic appraisal, one suggesting that no efforts at school reform can ever be successful even on an individual level. (Were this the intended implication of the critical analyses, they would be as silly as the suggestion that the quality of training makes no difference in developing a professional pianist.) It is more appropriate to view such criticism as an attempt to understand the many factors, both inside and outside the school, which must be taken into account if successful, large-scale change is to be achieved. A full understanding of classroom inequalities requires an analysis of school-society relations. It is one thing to show that inequalities exist. It is quite another to show why they continue to exist in the way that they do.

Of all the reform proposals, only Goodlad's acknowledges that a critical literature on this subject exists, but even Goodlad is unable to engage this literature or to incorporate its insights into his analysis and recommendations. He observes that the division of high school programs into a vocational and an academic track supports a two-class system and blocks opportunities for minority students.[36] He reports, without substantive criticism, on research which suggests that the benefits distributed by schools must, short of radical social change, reflect the benefits distributed by the larger economic and social order[37] and he concludes that the children in his survey had "quite different opportunities to gain access to knowledge during their years of schooling."[38] However, instead of pursuing the question as to the extent to which school inequality is a function of work inequalities, the argument is deflected into a discussion of the great difficulty that schools have in modifying the advantages and disadvantages provided by the home[39] and leads to a suggestion that tracking be eliminated and a core curriculum instituted.

The suggestions themselves are worth considering on their own account, and Goodlad is certainly right to point out that "accepting the need for society to have more typists, better automobile drivers and a steady supply of health workers does not necessarily justify . . . the development of programs in stenographic skills, driver training, and practical nursing in the nation's secondary schools."[40] Although it is correct, the observation does not address the main point raised by the critical tradition: the reproduction of the relations of production depends much less upon the specific course label than upon the patterns of behavior that are encouraged and rewarded in the classroom. Even the elimination of tracking, a proposal which should be given much more serious attention than it is likely to receive, is, by itself, unlikely to overcome the differences that are reflected on a large scale in unequal economic relations. Goodlad deflects the discussion of economic inequality by viewing the home as the major source of advantages and disadvantages, thereby suggesting that the school can have only a modest effect on changing these inequalities.[41] By deflecting the analysis in this way and by looking at the reproductive process only in terms of the family, he misses an important opportunity to understand the ecology of schooling. In other words, the advantages and disadvantages passed on by the family must, themselves, be understood in a context of work and schooling. To isolate the analysis of schooling and of the family from an analysis of the character of work is to fail to understand the important economic function that schools serve.

The difficulty is not with Goodlad's proposals. Indeed, many of his organizational and curriculum suggestions are constructive and, given the right setting, could improve the educational situation in many schools. Rather, the problem is with the limitations of the analytic tools that he uses to understand the direction of school reform. Schools are, among other things, reproductive mechanisms, and it is important to understand the nature of the product that they are reproducing.

The difficulties that this limitation presents are more apparent with Boyer's treatment of schools than with Goodlad's. Boyer, along with Goodlad and Sizer, has been an articulate spokesperson for improving the working conditions of teachers. Among his recommendations is a proposal that would significantly improve the salaries of the teaching profession.[42] Unlike Goodlad, however, Boyer does not even acknowledge the significance of a critical educational tradition, and this oversight contributes to recommendations which are likely to reduce, rather than enhance, the independence of the public school.

Boyer makes a number of recommendations to improve the condition of the teaching profession. In addition to recommending a substantial increase in salaries, his proposals include such things as sabbaticals, time off for study, and exchange programs. The problem arises when the cost of implementing these and other proposals is considered. If schools are having difficulty meeting their present budget, they will certainly have trouble supporting Boyer's plan. Although Boyer does not provide any detailed suggestions about how his proposals will be financed, he clearly has the problem of funding in mind and makes a few suggestions which are intended to relieve the financial burden. The most significant of these is a proposal to increase the involvement of business and industrial support through direct grants to individual schools. To illustrate his idea, he singles out for special commendation the "Adopt a School Program," which has arisen in some communities. In this program, a partnership is formed between a local industry and a school. Boyer mentions, as especially noteworthy, the good works in certain communities of energy utilities, oil companies, chemical manufacturers, and candy companies.

This proposal raises some serious issues. For example, it does not address the real structural problem with school finance and the implications of the fact that school revenue is one of the few areas where citizens have a direct say over their level of taxation. Since citizens have little opportunity to vote on other taxes, such as those used for defense or highways, the school tax remains the one area where frustration can be voiced. This arrangement is one of the reasons it is so difficult in many areas to increase the education budget. Boyer's proposal does nothing to address this problem and leaves the fate of the school to the goodwill of the businesses in the community. Since public schools have not developed an independent intellectual tradition, this arrangement would increase the influence of special interest groups and would make the reproduction process more direct.

There is a related problem with Boyer's suggestion. All of the reports decry the lack of academic rigor in the schools, but only a few decry the lack of intellectual rigor as well. Goodlad is sensitive to the flat intellectual tone of many schools, and Sizer captures the intellectual deficiency best in one of the anecdotes that he uses to indicate the flavor of a school. In a casual conversation with a senior boy, Sizer raises the question of registration for the draft: "Did it come up in school when registration was first required by the federal government? No. Did any of the guys decide not to register? No, but some of them may have forgotten to. Did any of the teachers raise the issue, perhaps in social studies classes? No. . . . We don't talk about things like that."[43]

There is no indication that this particular school was in partnership with a business enterprise or that it had been adopted by some corporation seeking to improve its image by doing good works. This is probably a reasonably typical situation. High schools are not generally intellectually active institutions, and that is unfortunate. However, some high schools do have intellectually active teachers, and these people already have enough hurdles to jump. For the teacher who might want to develop a unit on the effects of sugar on health or on the problems of hazardous waste or industrial accidents, Boyer's proposal would require special care not to offend the school's industrial sponsor. Although it is unfortunate that a tradition of free and open inquiry has not flourished in public education, a company school is not quite the remedy that is needed.

Conclusion

Reform documents are not all equal. *A Nation at Risk* is a slim manuscript, but page for page it is clearly the most influential of the recent proposals. It has set the tone for the discussion about education, and, because the character of that tone is harsh and one-sided, I have an appreciation for those authors who moderate their criticism of schooling, avoiding the unfortunate national chauvinism that marks the commission's report. Although I object to Boyer's failure to see the entanglements that he is endorsing for the schools, I agree with many of his suggestions for rejuvenating the teaching profession. Although I can criticize Sizer for not probing the causes of the inequalities that he identifies, I can appreciate the sensitivities that his observations display. And although I do not believe that Goodlad's analysis goes far enough in analyzing the effects that the nature of work has on the nature of education, I can appreciate the fact that, in the present climate, it has gone as far as it has. Indeed, given the present political climate, I am doubtful whether one could go much further in critically analyzing the schools than Sizer and Goodlad have done without being dismissed as an irresponsible critic. Nevertheless, it is important to recognize when a compromise has been struck between influence and insight.

Although there has been a lot of nonsense packaged under the heading of this or that national commission or this or that foundation report, the fact still remains that there are problems with the young that schools have not been able to address. The high illiteracy rate mentioned by a number of the reports is clearly one of them. However, the resolution of this problem will need an effort that goes far beyond the traditional practices of schools and will require far more understanding of cultural and linguistic diversity than even present bilingual programs have provided.

There is another problem too that is important to mention, but which has been neglected by all of the reports. It is the inability of the school, either through lack of will or lack of awareness, to provide students with the understanding that they need in order to critically reflect upon the political and cultural values that are being thrust upon them. For example, a decision to enter military service ought to be taken very seriously after a searching understanding of the causes that one might be asked to kill or to die for. At this state in our history, any youngster thinking of making such a commitment ought to know a great deal about our continuing relationship with Central America and the various techniques, from overt invasion, to covert economic sabotage, that we have used to overthrow indigenous, popular regimes. There should be an awareness of various interpretations of this relationship, both those which are available in the conservative and liberal presses and those which are not. These would range from interpretations which, like the Reagan administration, view our action as a struggle for freedom over slavery, to interpretations that see the government acting to protect the economic interests of a relatively few American corporations. Although it would be important to allow youngsters to decide which of the various interpretations is most appropriate, critical reflection would require that they be informed of various possibilities and that they be encouraged to think through the implications of each of them for their own personal choice. It is, of course, difficult to say whether such an informed group would result in a stronger or a weaker military, but it would clearly contribute to a more adequately educated youth population.

At the present time the situation is not encouraging. Many youngsters, unable to find a decent job and inadequately prepared by their high school education to interpret this situation, have found that the military recruiting office presents an attractive alternative to unemployment. Some seem quite pleased to have the opportunity to defend their country's honor, hoping only that we do it right this time—in Nicaragua. They want to help their president make them say "uncle."

This situation is fed by a culture machine which most schools have been both unwilling and unable to challenge. This summer, *Rambo* has been playing to packed audiences and, I am told, has often received standing ovations. I have been wondering whether educators could counter the impact of this cultural product by commissioning a film about a small, courageous group of Palestinians who, with great daring, offer their lives in a clandestine attack on the United States in order to release Sirhan Sirhan from prison. If the project mirrored Rambo, however, it would be too obnoxious to be educational. Yet the idea highlights the enormously difficult job that schools would have if they were to undertake the development of critical reflection in a serious way.

My own concern about educational reform is whether a sufficient intellectual and moral tradition can be established within the public, secondary schools to interrupt the reproduction process and whether the public schools could provide the intellectual climate that would enable young people to critically reflect upon the situation into which they have been thrust. The issue is not whether we should do our best to establish an academic climate in the high school. The question is whether we can do so in an intellectually honest and a politically open context.

Curriculum in the Closed Society

Philip Wexler

Insofar as there is any public life among American academic intellectuals, some small part of its limited attention is now drawn to the curriculum of schooling. Without disturbing too much the routine work of specialized knowledge production, a general cultural interest is being asserted. This interest is one of reaction against a society that is portrayed as flattened by cultural relativism, a society become too open, where "openness has driven out the local deities" (Bloom, 1987, p. 56). The general cultural interest asserted is one of restoring "the Great Books," "the Tradition," the culture of "the West" to college, and then to all school curricula.

The view of educational curriculum that embeds knowledge in experience and in practice, in the relation between teacher and student, is dismissed as "educational formalism" (Hirsch, 1987). The educational process is not curriculum. On the hypothesis that attention to the relationship between the student and teacher has been the cause of contemporary ignorance, Hirsch argues that "cultural literacy" requires a curriculum of "traditional culture" and "commonly shared information." "The culprit," according to a commission of the National Endowment for the Humanities (Cheney, 1987, p. 11), "is 'process.'" Curriculum should be the content that transmits cultural memory through school subjects. Despite, or maybe even because of, this prophetic tone, as well as because of the government sponsorship of such statements, curriculum is now more a public topic, issue, and concern than it has been since Soviet science scared education to curriculum reform in the late nineteen-fifties.

Attention to school curriculum is not limited, however, to polemical government reports or the popular commercial success of jeremiads about the state of intellectual ruin among American youth and their teachers. Social scientists have already argued for some time now that too little interest has been paid to what is being taught in school, and to how such curricula may affect individual lives and the organization of society. Within social science establishments, both sides – the engaged critics and the value-free scientists (neither term is accurate, I think) – are agreed that there is too little understanding of the character, structure, and consequences of knowledge in schools.

Perhaps the earliest modern analytic social interest in the content of education was in the work of the 'new sociology', particularly in England. Young wrote (1973, p. 339): "The almost total neglect of how knowledge is selected, organized, and assessed in educational institutions (or anywhere else for that matter) hardly needs documenting." New sociologists like Whitty remain unconvinced that there has been adequate social study of school curriculum (1987, p. 110): "Even its limited success in reorienting sociology of education towards curriculum issues was relatively shortlived."

The same emphasis on the content of schooling exists in the less overtly political, recent quantitative research of American sociologists of education. The reconceptualization of school effects as better understood through the stratification of learning opportunities (Sorensen and Hallinan, 1977) has encouraged empirical interest in studying curriculum differentiation as a cause of differences in students' achievements (Alexander and Cook, 1982). As with the new sociologists, the learning-opportunities researchers aim to correct the earlier paradigms' neglect of variation in the internal processes of school organization, especially the neglect of curriculum or the content of school knowledge as a primary determinant of student learning achievement.

Dreeben and Barr, in their research in which "curriculum as an organizational phenomenon represents an agenda of work," observe the following of the earlier paradigms (1987, p. 14): "None of these considerations draws much attention to the schools' conventional tasks of transmitting through instruction the knowledge contained in the curriculum." Supporting this emphasis on curriculum content, Gamoran concludes, in research arguing for the importance of within-school influences (1987, pp. 152, 153): "But variation in student experiences within schools has important effects on achievement. Most of the significant within-school differences are tied to differential coursetaking . . . Curricular programs – a feature of school structure – are the basis for the differentiation of opportunity within schools."

The same emphasis on the importance of curriculum content is echoed by educational researchers studying teaching. Referring to the "missing paradigm problem," Shulman (1986) asks, "Where did the subject matter go?" Lacking either the polemical interest in a cultural restoration or the sociologists' structural and multivariate interest in a social specification of the educational process, Shulman emphasizes curriculum content from an interest in pedagogy, in the practice of teaching. In reviewing studies of teaching, he writes (1986, p. 6): "In their necessary simplification of the complexities of classroom teaching, investigators ignored one central aspect of classroom life: the subject matter . . . Even those who studied teacher cognition . . . investigated . . . with little concern for the organization of content knowledge in the minds of teachers."

Culture, social relations, history

During this period, social theorists rediscovered 'culture' as a topic and as a resource in explanation. Here too, as with the emphasis on curriculum content, all sides agree that cultural understanding is underdeveloped. The avant-garde proponents of the linguistic and structuralist revolutions and beyond are pushing culture in on social science from literature and philosophy on the platform that everything is a 'text'. The Parsonian restoration in professional sociology reaches back to Durkheim for a reawakened sense that society should be studied as a moral, symbolic order. The second wave of academic theoretical Marxism is openly cultural.

Curriculum is a cultural question. To understand curriculum culturally, however, means more than to simply assert cultural value preferences or to apply general cultural theory. To understand curriculum culturally is to place school curriculum in relation to the dynamics of a particular culture, to show the ambiguous movement of the structure of that culture, and to proceed beyond commonsense categories, especially those of the most apparent cultural oppositions and contradictions.

I am going to suggest that the dynamic oppositions within the wider culture that shapes the curriculum are false. Culture is getting to be a closed book. That is why *text* (despite qualifying claims about its openness) may be just the right word, the historically suitable sign with which to classify a closed culture.

A way to open the book of culture, it seems, is to contextualize it, to place it within social relations. Texts are dead without the living pragmatics of social relations, the human interactions of social institutions. The effort to contextualize, pragmatize, and socialize the culture text promises an opening to the complex dynamics of institutional life and practices that can vivify culture, and curriculum.

Here too, however, the opposition between closed culture and an open context of social relations is false. The institutional context that nurtures the informal beneath the official, active personal agency alongside the anonymous reproduction of organizational structure, identity and self against position and institution – that social context is a falsely promising ideology of progress and openness. Instead, identity and institution are joined in social relations. The social road out of a dead-end cultural text is itself narrowing and closing. No less in the school than in the corporation, the fusion of identity and institution stabilizes the context.

I want to describe these particular dynamics and statics of culture and social relations as a way to understand schooling, especially curriculum. With few exceptions, the explanation of curriculum as part of a larger cultural text that is placed within the social relational context of school has been closed to an historical understanding. Yet it is an historical understanding of the formation of culture, social relations, and curriculum that points to what is open in this society, and to the process of opening.

I'm going to suggest, specifically, that the current historical point of opening—ironically in the culture of scientism—is scientific practice. As science becomes practically demystified and deconstructed, its antitextualism and inherent revisionism offer an alternative to the closure of contemporary culture and society. The question will become how to understand such a 'new science' and how to use it to produce a self-generative permanent revolution in curriculum.

Culture: Scientism and postmodernism

"In the most general sense of progressive thought, the Enlightenment has always aimed at liberating men from fear and establishing their sovereignty. Yet the fully enlightened earth radiates disaster triumphant." These words are from Horkheimer and Adorno's theoretical assaults on modern culture (1972:3). Their target is a cultural dynamic in which reason and science degenerate to ritual and myth. The "factual mentality," the reduction of ideas to "abstract quantities" that erase dissimilarities, the leveling domination of objectified, machinelike thought, are their early characterizations of the culture of scientism.

In a more recent critique of culture, Lyotard (1984) argues that culture is encased in narratives of legitimation. Reason and science are included along with the philosophies of humanity and spirit as the grand narratives of legitimation. Lyotard may seem to demur and even dissent from Horkheimer and Adorno's critique of scientism when he observes (1984, p. 29), "This is not the place to chart the recurrence of the narrative in the scientific." But in fact he too sees the degeneracy of science to scientism, effected through its incorporation in the social relations of capital. For Lyotard also (1984, pp. 45–47), "science becomes a force of production, in other words, a moment in the circulation of capital. 'Science' falls under the control of another language game." That game is the "discourse of power," "performativity," or, simply, the triumph of the law of "the best possible input/output equation." Science becomes scientism. Its criterion of validity is not found in the grand narratives of idealism and humanism, but in operational logic, in efficient performance. This is the language of the new "realm of terror" in which knowledge gives way to information, and the grand narratives are destroyed by the operational power of efficient performance.

The scientific, in its degenerative abstract form, has replaced the older legitimating, culture-binding narratives of humanity, spirit, and reason. It is science, not human emancipation, not is it, as the Restorationist critics correctly perceive, the "classical Tradition of the West and its Great Books memories," which provides the most pervasive popular material for the deep structure of the official story.

The victory of scientism over humanism is not, however, simply a secret of deep cultural structure. It has been the organizing cultural practice of schooling for more than a half century. Callahan's (1962) seminal research describes in detail precisely how scientific management became what we might call the "practical grand narrative" of American education. Schools were organized like factories. The merging of ideology and practice in structuring everyday school life toward a Taylorist social form is a pervasive example of Horkheimer and Adorno's view that a formalist culture of scientism would reinforce a rationalized and alienating daily social life (1972, p. 30): "The derivation of thought from logic ratifies in the lecture room the reification of man in the factory and the office." The redefinition of knowledge as skill and information, which the Restorationist cultural critics deplore while they do not see its social basis, is how scientism works its way through the curriculum. This general conversion of science and knowledge to power and performance is what Lyotard describes as "the route of data storage and accessibility, and the operativity of information."

Such a culture of scientism in school and curriculum is the critical target of a new generation of educational critics. Apple (1982) has pointed to the commodity form of school curricula packages. Giroux (1983) has attacked the instrumentalism of educational discourse and practice. Popkewitz (1987) has described a "psychologization of curriculum" as the particular educational infrastructure of a broader movement for social efficiency. Whitson (1987) has argued that the current curriculum discourses of "effectiveness and choice" serve ideological censorship and exclusionary educational practices. Still, with terms like *resistance, agency, contestation,* and *dialogical,* the critics seek to define alternatives, to find and help create the oppositional force to a narrativized culture of scientism, and to the curriculum that performs it.

The oppositional force appears to already be on the scene. Neither science nor philosophy, but literature, according to Rorty (1982), is the "presiding discipline." If literary modernism's theme was that of a heroic aesthetic self struggling against the bourgeois philistinism of industrial culture, then postmodernism is ironic rather than heroic, antisubjective rather than self-centered, and discursive as opposed to psychological. Indeed, as Newman (1985:10) argues, "The Post-Modern is above all characterized by the *inflation of discourse*, manifesting itself in literature through the illusion that technique can remove itself from history by attacking a concept of objective reality which has already faded from the world, and in criticism by the development of secondary languages which presumably 'demystify' reality, but actually tend to further obscure it."

The renewed cultural preeminence of literature, at least in the academy and as critical theories about language and literature, rather than Great Books of Literature, is only one act in postmodernism's scene. The migration of poststructuralism particularly—which I see as postmodernism's most formal theory—but also literary theory in general, is reflected in social science's current "interpretive turn." Geertz's (1980) effort is to infuse social science theory with the guiding metaphors of literary-oriented cultural theory. But the decenteredness, the linguistic distancing from objective referents, the replacement of the serious struggle of self against society with a bemused play of words on the page as writing, all of which characterize poststructuralism, are not the only aspects of postmodernism. Poststructuralism is only postmodernism's literary face.

The ethos and practice of postmodernism are quotidian. Newman's characterization of postmodern literature as an "inflation of discourse" is seen by Baudrillard (1981) as a characteristic of the culture as a whole. The displacement of the referent by the sign in literary theory is only an element in the wider culture's organization according to a logic of consumption in which meaning is "entirely independent of objects themselves and exclusively a function of the logic of significations." The environment, for Baudrillard, has become "semanticized." The culture ruled by consumption according to the logic of signs is one of "total functionality, total semiurgy," a culture in which there is such a "passion for the code" that it finally "abolish(es) the cardinal reference to the individual" (pp. 67, 86).

Postmodernism is antireferential, antiindividual, antinarrative. Postmodernism as a cultural theory and cultural practice appears to be the antidote to the instrumental realism of the culture of scientism. Postmodernism is disruptive, playful, compositional, superficial, and ironic. It appears, in theory and practice, to be running against the grain of a narrativized and scientized instrumental culture. The rupturing of the bond between sign and object described by poststructuralism and the 'blurring of genres' that results from the infusion of literary theory into social science are also practices of everyday life in postmodern culture. Television is postmodernism's machine.

The blurring of genres is, in television's daily practice, the blurring of a differentiated cultural structure. It is antipositivism with a vengeance. Meyerowitz (1985, pp. 7, 6) argues that "electronic media have undermined the traditional relationship between physical setting and social situation . . . By bringing many different types of people to the same 'place', electronic media have fostered a blurring of many formerly distinct social roles." Television is central in what Luke (1986, p. 71) calls the "spectacular system," where "signs and signing displace discourse." The function of print media has changed within a postmodern culture. Trow's (1980) interpretation of *People* magazine as all foreground without frame is an indicator of a cultural text that uses celebrities for focus in the face of changing ad hoc contexts. His magazine interpretations could well stand for a larger cultural diagnosis: "a thousand small figures moving in confusion against a shifting background."

Postmodernism seems to be the antithesis of scientism. It opposes the narrative linear structure of scientism with deliberate antinarratives of language as polymorphous. It opposes objective instrumentalism with nonreferential playfulness. It certainly raises the possibility of openness, otherness, and the perpetual reflexive underlining that things could be otherwise. Postmodernism should be the basis for challenging the cultural text of scientism, in culture and in curriculum. It is a cultural resource for the pluralist attitude toward culture that is needed to rectify class, race, and gender exclusions in education. It opens the discursive field to a Bakhtinian sense of alterity (Gunn, 1987) and curriculum as dialogue (Whitson, 1987). At least, it should be the discourse and practice that keep the culture vibrant by the very fact of its clear difference from the prevailing scientistic narrative.

The difference between the cultures of scientism and postmodernism is a false surface difference that is dissolved in the deeper structure of commodity culture. Narrative and antinarrative, ideals of science or of language, are really pre-texts for another dynamic cultural text which unites them. Television's "blurring" of difference is not individual freedom. In the age of exposure, Meyerowitz observes (1985, p. 311), television finally exposes the same "ordinariness" of everyone. This flattening of difference is not, however, the result of a culture of pluralism gone relativist, as Bloom argued. The closing of culture is not the effect of an impoverished curriculum in school and college.

The cultural text closes, and scientism and postmodernism merge under the unifying sign of the commodity. The incorporation of science in the performative efficiency of capital production analyzed by Lyotard and

Horkheimer and Adorno is true also for the ironic revolts of postmodernism. Culture is incorporated in the market and in the distributional apparatus rather than in traditional sites of scientized production. Production and market together, united by the commodity, close the culture.

The apparent autonomy of literary postmodernism is revealed to be, in Newman's term (1985, pp. 192, 196, emphasis added), a "calculated evanescence": "In short, what began as a discontinuous aggregate of forms and processes which appeared to be independent, ended up as a blinding succession of temporary cultures, disseminated by increasingly *centralized agencies*, in which the economic calculus of profitability was the only criterion . . . In any event, Post-Modern ended, as all aesthetic movements must, when it could provide no values as an alternative to the marketplace." Newman's observation about the current unification of academic and mass cultures, despite their differences, applies equally to the unification of scientism and postmodernism (1985, p. 135, emphasis added): "In both cases the *mode of transmission, the market-maker*, becomes the dominant reality. The culture becomes defined solely by markets for culture." In this sense, it is the 'context', the pragmatics of the text, that blocks the creative potential of dynamic tensions which inhere in the current cultural text. It is the context of the social relations of education that determines whether the curriculum is open or closed.

Social relations: Institution and identity

It was the hope of curricularists that interpersonal relations could overturn the dominance of a static culture embedded in curriculum. *Hidden curriculum* meant to show that whatever the syllabus, the relations between teacher and student, and among students themselves, would filter and modify the dead cultural labor of formal curriculum. The same hope in the power of social relations to reverse culture resurfaced among the new sociologists. *Resistance* was meant to signal the durability of extraschool subcultures and their power to transform the meaning and impact of the official messages of the school's curriculum channel. The narrative of curriculum might represent the larger culture of scientism. But the hidden curriculum and student resistance, like the culture of postmodernism, could disrupt and recode the official school story in the crucible of concrete social relations.

The opposition between the formal and the informal, culture and subculture, the reproductive and the resistant in school life as the dynamic of change proves as illusory as the hope of dynamism and openness in the opposition between the degenerate forms of science and language in the cultures of scientism and postmodernism. The ironic finding of Willis's (1977) case study was that resistance confirmed the status quo.

The belief that the social relations of schooling could overturn its culture embedded in curriculum was premised on a macrosocial understanding of class conflict and social change. What the faith in social relations missed, in this leap from curriculum to the application of macrosocial theories of change, was that the social relations of the school are not unmediated class relations. The school is a social institution. Social relations are institutionally patterned. The analytical attempt to transcend the cultural limits of curriculum by emphasizing wider social relations has had the unintended effect of ignoring the *social*, institutional character of school life.

In an analysis of "education as an institution," Meyer observes (1977, p. 74), "Operating at the institutional level as an authoritative theory of personnel and knowledge in society, the schools constitute a crucial ritual system: a system of initiation ceremonies (personnel) and of classifications of information (knowledge)." The power of social relations to regulate and transform culture in education is not through the subversion of subcultural resistance. Rather, the social power of schooling is in its institutional legitimacy, both in everyday school life and in the currency which education has in the larger society. Authority, not resistance, is where the lever of the social relations of education over the culture of curriculum resides. This lever is in practice a ritual and collective one within schools, as Lesko (1987) shows in her recent case study of the social in school organization. As Meyer puts it (1987, p. 169): "The power of education, we have argued above, lies in the *institutional* rules that give it widespread meaning and binding authority over the future of students. The implied contrast here is with education as a system of organized interaction, interpersonal meaning and immediately relevant content." The product of this institutional process is to authorize or legitimate categories and types of knowledge and personnel in society. In this sense, I suggest that the social relations of schooling produce collective social identities.

If the curriculum is regulated by social relations, and if the most powerful aspects of its sociality are of the authority of the institution to define legitimate knowledge and personnel, is there no opposition within the institution? Are the conflicts and contradictions of social relations smoothed over by students' awareness of institutional power? My answer, though less ironic than Willis', is in a comparative study of the social life of students in four high schools (Wexler, 1987). To say it baldly, the informal social lives of students support the institutional production of stratified identities.

There are students who actively oppose the social rules and rites of the school. Yet each form of student opposition is paired with a pattern of student affirmation. Together, the paired identities follow an overarching institutional class form of the school. They are differences within a sameness, although the institutional sameness is variable, across schools, depending on the schools' location in the social-class structure. I have described in some detail the complex interactions through which the split identities are unified under the class character of the institution as 'symbolic economies of identity'.

These economies each have an institutional definition, whether it is school as factory, welfare agency, country club, or corporation. Within each institutional form, the institutional process revolves around the regulatory solution of a particular class problem, whether that problem is the regulation of physical movement and the body, social derogation, organizational incorporation, or achievement. Within each of these institutional forms, contradictory structures or patterns of social relation become the locus for the organization of personal identity. In the factory form, for example, structured social relations of discipline or warmth organize the personally appropriated identities of 'losers' or 'good kids'. These personally appropriated, paired identities – the 'somebody' who each student is – including the forms which disaffection takes in each educational organization, are enacted within a specific class institutional definition of the institution.

The formal and the informal, the reproductive and the resistant, are joined binary aspects of the institutional process of identity production. Informal social life, in its patterned dynamic – symbolic economy of identity – is a work site of the institution. The informal is the infrastructure of the formal. Identity formation, even in its negative oppositional instances, is an integral part of the institutional process and definition.

Social relations is not the context which opens a curriculum text taken from the closed cultural book of unified scientism and postmodernism. Rather, the appearance of opposition and difference within the context of school social relations is also unified. Identity is fused with institution, the individual with the social. Social relations in the schools I studied are not without internal contradiction and conflict, but they work toward self-replicative insularity and closure.

History: Science and culture

We have seen a negative dialectic of culture, but not of science. Culture, Marcuse argued (1968), even in its most affirmative idealist forms, offers the hope of transcendance, the possibility of negating the present and imagining something different. Science, for the cultural critics, is only degenerative. It becomes absorbed in the logic of production, loses its critical potential to subvert taken-for-granted understanding, and winds up a servant of power as it instrumentalizes culture. Against this view, I suggest the possibility of a deconstructed and historicized science, a 'new science' which in its contextual specificity offers the revolutionary openness denied by contemporary culture and social relations—especially in school and in curriculum.

The new science, and what it implies for an open curriculum, demands an antipathy to the grand narratives. The antipathy to narrative is not only to the classical grand or 'meta' narratives of humanity and spirit, but also to the narratives of science and history. Instead, a new science finds in the *specificity* of history and scientific practice the opening promised by a failed oppositional culture and the institutional apparatus of social relations. Science specified, historically and contextually, offers an alternative to what Schwab (1978), in his essay on science education and civil discourse, called the "rhetoric only of conclusions."

There are, I think, a number of pathways that lead to a new science and toward its educational practice as a revisionary curriculum. First, there is the scholarship that restates school curriculum into its historical formation. The importance of curriculum history studies, exemplified by Goodson's (1987) work, goes beyond the intention to show how curriculum interest groups determine school subjects. The unanticipated value of this work is that, in the process of linking the establishment of school subjects with the history of academic disciplines, the current hegemony of science in the university is made more salient than popular curriculum critics appear to acknowledge. The tie between university and school, in the present historical context, points ineluctably to the centrality of science as determinant of curriculum form as well as content.

The second path toward a reconstructed scientific practice that works against the closed society is a less historical, but nonetheless contextualist, sociology of science. In contradistinction to both the internalist and macrosocial historical and sociological studies of science, constructivists offer microsocial, ethnographic accounts of the production of scientific facts and theories. Their empirical microstudies, which to some degree seem to be "critiques" of science, can also be read as renovations of narrative science in favor of a new scientific practice. Knorr-Cetina and Mulkay (1983, p. 123), for example, summarize the findings of some of the microresearches: "It is perhaps the single most consistent result of laboratory studies to point to the indeterminacy inherent in scientific operations, and to demonstrate the *locally situated, occasioned* character of laboratory selections."

Latour's (1983, pp. 139–169) research aims "to study the *very content* of what is being done inside the laboratories." Scientific content is deconstructed to the specific practices, including the linguistic, which function as "inscription devices" through which knowledge is produced. Science, including its content, its curriculum as it were, is understood as a set of contingent, instrumental, and linguistic practices. Content is the outcome of practice. The deconstruction of science to scientific practice is also described at a more macrosocial, historical, and organizational level in the work of Elias, Martins, and Whitley (1982) and of others, like Rip, who writes of "looking at science as productive labor. Scientific work is, as is work in general, concerned with transforming objects with tools for some goal" (1982, p. 220). In the United States, Mendelsohn, Weingart, and Whitley (1977, p. 7) express a related view in their criticism of Kuhn for "an almost total independence of the shape of the cognitive structures, or the content of the concepts, from either the institutional structures or the broader societal processes and structures."

Emphasis on the contextual specificity of the labor of scientific practice as the basis of the content of knowledge is what leads toward science as an opening practice, against culture's and scientism's closure at the hands of the market and the operational apparatus of production. It is a contingent practice that opens because it is true to what Schwab (1978, p. 134) called the "revisionary character of scientific knowledge." Lave (1984) takes this practical view of knowledge to the most fixed point in the school curriculum: mathematics. From her research on arithmetic practices in grocery shopping (Lave, Murtaugh, and de la Rocha, 1984), she shows how what we take as the necessarily given knowledge of curriculum can be understood as contextually contingent practical activity. Her research on a contextually transposed curriculum—arithmetic in the supermarket—puts in still deeper question the view of curriculum as a cultural object shaped by social context. Lave has reversed the 'recontextualization' of knowledge described by Bernstein's (1987) pedagogic device: from schooled pedagogy back to the context of production. Knowledge for Lave, Knorr-Cetina, Elias, and others is integrally and internally produced in contextual practical activity, not shaped by an external 'context.'

Lyotard (1984) finds the deconstructed contextualism of a local and specific scientific practice, a practice which by its indexicality and contingency is inimical to cultural closure, in the dialectic of science. From traditional, narrativized science subservient to the discourse of power, there develops at this historical moment within scientific research a new search for instabilities, for powers that destabilize and a desire for the unknown, that Lyotard calls "paralogy." Paralogy is a "move . . . played in the pragmatics of knowledge." It aims toward producing not the known, but the unknown. Lyotard finds this "new scientific spirit" in examples from modern physical science that require attention to instabilities, discontinuities, and local states of processes. The legitimation of paralogy is not efficiency, but its capacity to produce openness, as Lyotard writes, "to generate ideas . . . new statements." Prigogine and Stengers develop a similar physical science interest in open systems, and a science that does not press for stability. "The key words," for them (1984, p. 13), are "nonlinearity, instability, fluctuations."

If the current hegemony of science – either from the curriculum of the university or out of scientism within production – can support a "new scientific spirit," then constructivism and paralogy will not be false alternatives, functioning like postmodernism does in culture. There is no guarantee that it can. But the promise of revisionary contextual scientific practice is that it is opposed to the closure of curriculum and culture by its very definition of what knowledge is. Whether such a definition of knowledge, one which directly implies a revisionary curriculum – a curriculum of practical activity rather than merely the transmission of great books – can be realized is itself a practical question. The goal of a practical, historical, contextual, revisionary approach to curriculum will depend, I think, on the future of science in both education and production.

The dialectic of science is not ultimately closed for Horkheimer and Adorno, those severe critics of the instrumental culture of scientism. Whether or not the open revolutionary ethos of science can reemerge from the cocoon of scientism is a historical and practical question (1972, p. 9): "But the situation cannot be changed by purely theoretical insight, any more than the ideological function of science can be. Only a change in the real conditions for science within the historical process can win such a victory."

Practical Teacher Education and the Avant-Garde

Richard Smith
Anna Zantiotis

The concern with what teacher education is ultimately about has been resuscitated in recent years. On the one hand, there are the various apologists for current economic regimes and conditions in the West whose reports and research prefigure a kind of programing of instructors who will transmit knowledge of standarized forms. They represent teacher education courses as narrowly focusing on a specific kind of individualization, technocratic effectiveness, and coordination of schooling to fit the requirements of an emergent economic order. The general effect of this trend is to make teaching an instrumental activity, and teacher education programs that are implicated in it lose sight of the nexus of value, purpose, and procedure that constitute education and social conditions (Popkewitz, Pitman, and Barry, 1986; Whitty, Pollard, and Barton, 1987). The discourse of this contemporary settlement in education may be labeled as "dominant."[1]

On the other hand, there is another tradition which is of major concern for the purposes of this paper. That tradition is visionary and is anchored in a genre of discourse that privileges the concepts of emancipation, liberation, and democracy. Its avowed intention is to neutralize and exclude dominant teacher education discourse and to replace it with a language of possibility and hope. Teacher education in this tradition has the task of reconstructing educational institutions as a macrosocial prerequisite for the extension of public domains of debate, dialogue, and individual freedom and sociality. We refer to this counterdominant discourse as the "avant-garde."[2]

The recent spate of educational policy documents in Australia and elsewhere (see Australian Government, 1985; Apple, 1986a; Marginson, 1986; National Task Force, 1986; Queensland Board of Teacher Education, 1987) provide some examples of what we mean by a dominant discourse. On the surface these documents address visible symptoms of fundamental changes, particularly youth unemployment, that are under way in the world, national, and state postindustrial or corporatist economies (Panitch, 1977; Dow, Clegg, and Boreham, 1984).

Such symptoms are indexes of other changes, such as the transformation of capitalism from within. In Australia, spectacular corporate takeovers in recent years are examples of the relative insignificance of private property and the obsolescence of the notion of free enterprise in today's world. Instead, economic power is located in corporations and private and public bureaucracies, and coordinated by the state. The use of information technologies such as computers and communications compound the real loss of jobs that occurs in such conditions and reflect a progressive deskilling of the work force as machines are substituted for skilled labor and an increase in the range of low-paid unskilled work. Moreover, the reports neglect the nature of the dominant consumerist social ethic, so that the addiction to ownership of mass-produced objects and images is left untouched (Lasch, 1986). Finally, elements of the cultural restoration movement sparked by religious fundamentalist attacks on modernity and shading off into the economic and social agendas of the New Right are implicitly incorporated as the language of efficiency, competence, competition, and productivity and become taken for granted in public and private life.

These documents then produce an educational discourse in which there are implicit assumptions that transnational capital and an international division of labor determine the economic direction of even the most powerful nations; that schools need to serve an emergent economy by providing "flexible" workers; that "education" at all levels should concentrate on human "software" so that workers can be continuously reskilled for unpredictable conditions; and that information technology will provide a mechanism for reducing costs in a restructured economy by capital-labor substitution. Primary and secondary schools are being reorganized everywhere to account for such imperatives. In the teaching work force, curriculum knowledge is now readily discernible as hierarchically packaged structures that produce different kinds of students and that contain historicized and reified "facts." There are pressures to reduce teaching to scientific methods and technology and to make student progress more "efficient," to scientize assessment and selection procedures, evaluation, and pupil "progress." The bureaucratic workload of teachers has sharply increased as more time is demanded for the normalizing functions of schools (Apple, 1986b; Freedman, Jackson, and Boles, 1983). In short, education itself is constituted as a commodity, and the logic of the new marketplace, including deregulation and privatization, applies to all levels of the system. Under corporatism, according to Wexler (1986), the social relations of the school are altered. The curriculum comes to mean skills. The student-teacher relationship is made into lists of individual basic competencies.

Dominant and avant-garde discourse in teacher education

Under the dominant discourse, schooling and education cannot be seen as relatively autonomous in the sense of being distant and simply affected by economic, cultural, and social "factors." The so-called context of schooling is the relationship between knowledge production and an emergent social order. Let us be clear about what we mean by this. The claim is not that schools are irrevocably determined by economic or any other forces so that everything that is done or thought about is in the interests of capital or some other monolithic category. Neither do we wish to argue that the changes noted previously are necessarily reactionary. Instead, we prefer to think about the discourses and practices of education as composing a field in which there are preferred claims to truth about depictions of the objects and events to which the field is directed and how they are actualized. At one level, the field can be abstracted as policy statements of a highly rhetorical kind that, in turn, are transformed into functional requisites clothed in the constraints of education system bureaucracies. At another level, the field is teacher education lecturers, student-teachers, and students who are positioned within the discourses and practices of an educational institution, be it university, college, or school, and what they individually and collectively do.

Clearly there are potentials for movement on the part of teachers, students, and administrators within such a field, and the actuality is that people can, and do, passively accept, negotiate, and oppose what is said and done (Morley, 1980; Hall, 1983). In addition, the discourses that make up the field of education, which are many, are in a constant state of interplay and transformation. Nevertheless, if teacher education is thought of as a social space, the field is a constraint that can be depicted in Foucault's (1980) terms: "Each society has its regime of truth, its 'general politics' of truth: that is, the types of discourse which it accepts and makes function as true; the mechanisms and instances which enbale one to distinguish true and false statements, the means by which each is sanctioned; the techniques and procedures accorded value in the acquisition of truth; the status of those who are charged with saying what counts as true." (p. 131).

What counts as true in teacher education is produced within the discursive complex adumbrated above. By this we mean that 'teacher education' consists of a number of overlapping and often contradictory practices of knowledge production. Practices such as curriculum studies or educational psychology or teaching studies contain their own internal rules that systematize and regulate what can be said and done, as well as how contradictions and inconsistencies are resolved. In addition, each is articulated with the other so that there is always room for concepts, metaphors, and models to be imported, which allows for novelty (Henriques et al., 1984; Laclau and Mouffe, 1985; Frow, 1986; Bernstein, 1986). In addition, all such practices are informed by normative assumptions that are produced from the interdependence of the social theory that educators use and the practices of schools. Hence the social (school) world is commonsensically represented in dominant teacher education discourse as consisting of pupils, individuals, classes, teachers, processes, and so on. The regime of truth of teacher education then can be characterized as a dispersion of regulated competing claims and agreements centered on the production of knowledge and practices in and about schools and teaching. It is organized in the departments of teacher education in universities and other teacher preparation institutions and in state and private school systems, and is coordinated by the state to serve educational markets (Wexler, 1986).

The dominant discourse of teacher education is not then a unified and logically coherent whole consisting of a finite set of elements. As Terdiman (1985, p. 57) proposes, there is no empirical "proof" of the existence of the dominant discourse because it consists of a "moving and flowing network of practices and assumptions." In teacher education it appears as a series of instances and traditions that have a relationship with each other and that contest the form and content of teacher education while depicting it as eternal and inevitable in its objects and interests.

One such tradition is what we refer to as the realist genre,[3] which is concerned with valorizing teacher work and knowledge so that teachers will be better prepared to act professionally. Professionalism in this context is essentially centered on teachers making their own decisions about curriculum and pedagogy. Teacher preparation of this genre is therefore directed by a complex pastiche of eclectic ideas about expertise gained in the transmission of knowledge in teacher education programs and in the milieu of schools. School-based experience is a necessary tenet of this tradition. We return to the realist tradition shortly.

Like all concepts and classifications, the contrasting of dominant, realist, and avant-garde conceals the overlaps and contradictions that occur in teacher education institutions and theorizing. We use the concepts analytically, but not simply in the sense of describing a particular style of teacher education or a mere difference over definitions. Instead, we generalize Volosinov's (1973, p. 23) insights to indicate what we intend. Volosinov argues that different classes use the same language, but that signs become an arena for class struggle because "differently oriented accents intersect in every ideological sign." Human communities then use words not in contemplation but in competition (Terdiman, 1985, p. 38; Foucault, 1980, p. 114). Our distinctions are those of power and the struggle over it.

There are two issues here. The first is that the dominant discourse is the taken-for-granted, the "normal," and the established, whereas the avant-garde has a relativizing and estranging effect, is subversive of normality, and is heterodox. The latter strives to be sovereign, but in fact takes on alien elements of the dominant in its attempt to overcome them, to impose on them silence or radical meaning. Similarly, the dominant has to expend energy on absorbing or extinguishing the avant-garde — or on simply doing nothing, thus confirming dominance. Whatever the dynamics, the dominant and the avant-garde, the normal and the heterodox, are symbiotic.

The second issue is the correlation of the discourse and practices of teacher education with the emergence of a new economic order, social life, and culture, the postindustrial, semiotic, or corporatist society. The concepts of dominant and avant-garde may be read as having a periodizing function such that dominant and avant-garde may be seen as different responses to these conditions. We subscribe to Wexler's (1986) view that realist theory and practice are better characterized as a transitional stage, developed as they were from the socio-cultural-political upheavals of the 1960s and 1970s and the reformulation of social theory in that period. Nevertheless, we will argue that the practices and theory of realist teacher education, reflecting the dynamics of the symbiosis between the dominant and the avant-garde noted earlier, have been rapidly incorporated into the dominant field. Its central tenet, school-based experience, is now in our view the critical motor for dominant teacher education forms and content.

There are some immediately apparent ambiguities facing teaching education in such a scenario. They turn first on the relationships between the production of knowledge in teacher education institutions, and their object of interest, schooling (teachers, students, and so on). Second, they profoundly affect the organization of courses and the kinds of knowledge they purport to produce. Central to both issues is the understanding that teacher education practices are involved in the production of schooling, and indeed, the production of society, as R. Connell et al. (1982) point out, including the kinds of social conditions we enumerated earlier. The work of teacher educators should then be apprehended as a form of cultural politics in which "truth" about schools and teaching is produced and contested; they have political and economic as well as educational roles to play. Critics of schooling as "quasi-reproductive" institutions and of teacher education as an homologous set of practices would agree (See Wood, 1984).

What we wish to underscore, however, is that the outcomes of teacher education practices are both intentional and unintentional in the sense that programs are implemented which address some of the "real" issues mentioned earlier and which endeavor to create reflective and critical teachers. At the same time, such programs produce the kind of knowledge that allows for managing the easy transition of cohorts of new teachers into the already existing but changing schools for a corporatist order. We begin this task with a discussion of the concept of 'practicality', a central tenet of dominant teacher education practice.

The discourse of 'practicality'

The discourse of practicality does not exhaust what might be said about teacher education, teaching, or teachers, nor is it an internally coherent, uncontested, consistent depiction of what teachers or teacher educators do. Rather, it is, in our view, an important signifying practice that functions metonymically to cue teacher education subjects to the already known and to mobilize a sense of the past associated with teaching for teacher educators. Our purpose in drawing attention to it, though, is to show how the discourse of practicality delimits what can be said about teaching and teachers while providing the dialogic space for making other kinds of statements drawn from other discourses.

'Practicality' privileges teacher work in the labor process of teaching. A host of papers have identified the major elements of teacher work as those concerned with the immediate, the particular, the concrete conditions and events in classrooms. In this perspective, teachers are primarily involved in routinized and typical, if unpredictable, events. There are two sides to the teacher's 'problematic'. One is captured by metaphors such as *survival strategy, practicality ethic,* and *public servant role.* These metaphors construct teaching as constrained by always already exigencies of organizational structures such as time, teacher/pupil ratio, and the need for control. It is then a relatively short step to the conclusion that teacher's work is determined, whether mediated or not, by the peculiarites of the segmented labor market of teaching, by the political and economic structures of which education is a component. Practicality in this representation of teaching and teachers is evidence that teacher work is framed so that the theories of reproduction work and that education fulfills the functions of an ideological state apparatus. The other side of the teacher's problematic is the proposal that although frames indeed "define an operational space for planning and subsequent actions taken by teachers and students," the uses of that space depend on ideas about teaching and knowledge, perceptions of constraints, and possible courses of action (Kallos and Lundgren, 1979, p. 32). Teachers are thus invested with the freedom to act autonomously, and the focus is placed on the complexity of what teachers do (see, for example, R. Connell, 1983). But the routines and practicalities of dealing with the complexity take on a new meaning. The strategies of coping are redefined as a proactive resource and a technology (Pollard, 1980). Classroom work becomes a skilled management of insoluble dilemmas by teachers whose roles are those of brokers of contradictory interests (Lampert, 1985). Teachers' personal practical knowledge is lit up as a special form of expertise, the recognition of which is seen as a way of enhancing the professional status of teaching (Clandinin, 1985). Moreover, the production and use of such knowledge is located theoretically in the objective relations of teaching rather than in the discourses about teaching that characterize the scholarly journals, curriculum guides, and especially teacher education programs (see Westbury, 1983). Olsen (1984, p. 31 and 35) proposes that teachers know how to do teaching and what they know is "embedded in their know how." The routines of teaching thus become the "highest expression" of what teachers know how to do. Teacher practice, teaching, becomes what teachers do, and the truth claim is that the judgements about that practice are internal to the practicality of doing classroom work. Thus, practicality is an attempt to redeem the work of teachers in itself and as a site for contesting the oppression of the social and political order and the imposition of experts.

The contradictions of practicality

The discourse of practicality raises a number of difficulties for teacher education programs as they are presently organized in relation to what they do and their relationships with schools.[4] In brief, the argument is simple. By redeeming teacher work and by privileging practicality as the foundation on which teacher education programs are authorized, the discourse simultaneously deauthorizes teacher education as a practice and "professionalizes" teacher culture within social theory. Some trends in teacher education practices signal this phenomenon. We discuss two of these before drawing some conclusions.

The first difficulty we wish to highlight as fundamental is what might be called the "reality effect" (Hall, 1985). This is the presupposition that the discourse and practices of teacher education are ineluctably directed by the "real" practices and processes of schools, and ought to be. For many teacher educators such an assumption carries the weight of common sense. What is wrong with this kind of claim is that it fails to account for the ways in which "reality" itself is produced by the regime of truth that is constructed by the discursive practices of teacher educators, researchers, and teachers. In other words, the materiality of teaching is not in question: what we query are the ways in which researchers and teacher educators produce knowledge about teaching and act in accord with it.

Consider the characteristic elements of practicality briefly sketched earlier, and the use made of them by teacher educators. Preservice and inservice programs typically strive for authenticity by undertaking "realistic" activities that increase a teacher's repertoire; that are "craft-legitimate" for practitioners; that require a minimum of back-up resources; that have rapid payoff in the classroom; and so on (See Huberman, 1985). All of these reference the already known, what everybody commonsensically knows. In addition, the "real" world of classrooms and teacher work, defined by the practices of teachers, is articulated with a theoretical discourse about the importance, centrality, or inescapability of those activities, significantly referred to as being "realist." The general point is that the mutual effects of the already known and the discourses about it are such that "reality" is now the previously established effects between them, rather than a pregiven entity that exists beyond the discourses of either teacher education or teachers. This is not to argue that the concept of practicality causes teachers to be practical, but to point to the symbiotic productive relationship between campus and schools that creates what teacher educators then refer to, and act in accord with, as real.

An important effect of discourse about the real is the differentiation between appropriate and inappropriate conceptions of teaching that seems obvious on the basis of an appeal to the "truth" and credibility of practicality. 'Practicality' is of course always open to disarticulation and transformation by other conceptions of teaching and teacher work. Nevertheless, the 'practicality' concept draws its legitimacy from a collective professional belief in its value. Like the conventional meaning of art, practicality "would be nothing without the whole tradition . . . and without the universe of celebrants and believers who give it meaning and value in terms of that tradition" (Bourdieu, 1986, p. 137).

The reality effect profoundly shapes on-campus teacher education "teaching" programs by calling into question the very point of on-campus courses about teaching. Teacher education programs are in principle motivated by an anticipated later effect – "good" teaching or some variant on that theme – and on-campus courses and simulations are directed at that end. For instructors, usually former teachers, important elements of their personal identity are tied to expertise in the folklore of teaching and their charisma as (former) school practitioners. But they are left with reinventing a sense of the past, with plagiarizing older plots and narratives to tell stories about teaching, by the realization that 'teaching' has already been invented (Jameson, 1985) by the discourse of practicality. *Teaching* on campus becomes a metaphor of reality in schools (Smith, 1979), and as such, crucially gets by without the referents associated with consumerism and the corporatist society, while sustaining them: that is, beyond history.

A good deal of theory about teaching reinforces this tendency. During the 1970s interpretive and hermeneutic social theory was articulated with elements of anthropological culturalism in an attempt to displace the dominance of positivistic psychological models of teaching and learning. The success of that movement and the consequent interest in the ecology of teaching and learning reinforce the discourse of practicality and the (un)reality of on-campus courses about teaching whose referents and unity lie in a temporal and spatially distant site, schools. Under these circumstances it is not surprising that student-teachers, whose subjectivities are progressively reproduced by course work that normalizes practicality, and by school "experience" during practicums, recognize and are frustrated by courses about teaching which are the image of an image (Jameson, 1985) of practicality.

The second major difficulty is that the discourse of practicality, curiously, deemphasizes pedagogical work as productive. We illustrate what we mean by returning to Olsen's work cited earlier. We do not criticize his work for its internal consistency or for misrepresenting the "facts." Rather we argue that it is representative of a genre of storytelling about teaching that is bound by the reality effect as constituted by the regime of truth about teaching.[5] It will be recalled that Olsen aruges that teachers' teaching strategies are embedded in their know-how. He also argues that "if we want to study teacher practice – what teachers know how to do, we have to observe what they do"; and "not 'thinking' about teaching does not stop teachers from efficient practice." (p. 37). These statements are made in the course of a critique of technocratic information-processing models of teaching, and we agree with their intent. Nevertheless, we have serious reservations about them.

In the first place, we have argued that the concept of practicality is part of the definition of what it means to be practical. The discourse of practicality demarcates other discourses so that what counts as being intelligible in that discourse becomes the criterion for judging other claims. Olsen's position lends weight to the idea that what teachers do is "teaching," and the criteria for judging the doing are internal to the practices. His notion of efficient practice then begs the question of what might constitute it, because the criteria for determining efficient (good, etc.) teaching are already set in what teachers do. There is little to be gained by laboring the point that the political implications of this position force opposing views to establish their intelligibility according to the criteria that favor the dominant (natural) claim (Henriques et al., 1984). Moreover, the position as an exemplar of the kinds of mechanisms described earlier in which teaching-cum-practicality becomes a timeless image cut off from the contemporary associations that produce its meaning now. Teacher practice, teaching, becomes what teachers do, and the truth claim is that judgements about that practice are internal to the practicality of doing classroom work. The real danger is that pedagogy is undervalued in favor of instrumental teaching procedures that "work," regardless of their known effects. The social (schooling) is postponed as an object of interest on the grounds of more pressing needs.

In the second place, by emphasizing the apparent producer of teaching, the teacher, as especially important (the interpretive and hermeneutic turn in social theory), Olsen's view suppresses the issue of what authorizes the producer (Bourdieu, 1986, p. 133). We have argued that the coarticulated discourses and practices of teacher education and teacher work accomplish this task. In contrast, Olsen's practicality perspective leaves open the possibility of misrecognizing teaching practices as the production by an individual teacher rather than as an effect of the system of objective relations which constitute teaching, the struggles of which it is the site, and the form of capital that is generated there (see Bourdieu, 1986). In this respect, the kind of "thinking" about teaching that is available in the discourses of teachers is not inconsequential if it remains ignorant of, unfeeling about, or accepting of the political outcomes of teaching practices. It is again but a short step to a view of teaching that is instrumental and technique centered, and in which the signifying practices of schooling remain transparent. Teaching would then be apprehended as a kind of *a priori* set of activities which teachers do in order to distribute knowledge. Of course student (pupil) subjectivities are important in such a scenario, but only as adjuncts to teaching, as hurdles to be cleared if learning (that is, transmission) is to occur. Pedagogy as the engagement of learner, teacher, and knowledge is assumed, but its productivity is denied. Donald (1985, p. 245), discussing hierarchically ordered forms of knowledge that are made available in schools, puts it thus:

This symbolic organization also generates a network of subject positions in relation to these hierarchies—it defines what it is to be educated, cultivated, discriminating, clever, literate and so forth. It therefore differentiates not only between forms of knowledge but also between people. And it also makes it possible for this system of differentiation to be presented not in terms of social conflict and antagonism, but as the natural consequence of the psychological and intellectual attitudes of the people who occupy those subject positions.

Finally, the discourse of practicality, so commonsensically self-evident and eternal, is inherently political because, in staking a claim to truth to which all other claims must subscribe if they are to be credible, it extinguishes heresies. To this extent, the struggle around what schooling and teacher education are about, like that over literacy (Giroux, in press), is part of a wider struggle for control over the knowledge, values, and social practices of an emergent society. But in doing so it largely fails to recognize the changed circumstances of its theory and practice. In particular, the very theoretical insights that informed the school-based movement and much action research in teaching, devised in the defense of teachers against the domination of "experts," have not become a device to redefine knowledge production and consumption in teacher education. Interpretive and hermeneutic theory has helped to shape the representation of preservice teacher education so that campus inputs have been absorbed into the schools and the former consist of little more than supervisory and administrative functions that facilitate the credentialing of teachers. This, together with the collapse of history into the present and the redefinition of reality into images in the discourse of practicality, leaves power-knowledge relationships unrecognized. Thus, by establishing the limits of the sayable, the discourse of practicality allows the imperatives of the public policy to remain as "the unsaid to be said without being uttered," that is, without the speakers of it (teachers, school administrators, teacher educators, etc.) "taking responsibility, for the enunciation of the message" (Frow, 1986, p. 78). Teaching is consequently profoundly deracinated as it becomes more intense. The discourse of practicality is to this extent an effect, a symptom, of the post-industrial society that ignores the political, economic, and social implications of schooling and the part played by teacher education as a site of knowledge production in that field.

The avant-garde agenda

The collective belief in maintaining schooling as it is provides both the strength of discourses on teacher education and the field of struggle over alternative visions of what teaching is as a concept. The most interesting counterdominant ideas of avant-garde work turn on the notion of 'transformation'. This concept centers on the relationships between public schools, culture, and society in the present and the ambivalent situations in which schools, students, teachers, and teacher educators find themselves. Transformation is both a visionary project and praxis. The intent of the concept is to register the conviction that schooling ought, and can be, part of an ongoing struggle for the restoration and maintenance of "public spheres" and democracy (Giroux, 1985). To this end, transformation focuses on the purposes of schooling and the self- and social empowerment of individuals and groups.

What the avant-garde have in mind is that public education has lost sight of the responsibility to shape and reflect democratic social forms and the production of an active, critical citizenry. Their critiques of education expose the policy shifts in public education in recent years that have displaced a concern for equity and social justice in favor of schools modeled on the "company store," instrumentally linked with economic modes of production (Giroux and McLaren, 1986). Their analyses point to the dominant orthodoxies of educational practice in the 1980s–technicism, standardization, competency, and narrow performance skills–that have well-documented effects such as systematic marginalization of large numbers of students; intensification and deskilling of teacher work; centralization of control over curriculum; and increased bureaucratic control and surveillance of teachers and students. In short, the avant-garde provides penetrating insights into the processes of schooling for a corporatist society.

In contrast to the profession which defines teaching as what teachers do and which defends the logic of constrained practical action and its outcomes, the avant-garde is concerned with reconstructing schooling for a different set of future ends. First, schooling should take a clear moral and ethical stand, and this is usually tied to the standpoint of the victims of any society as the starting point for the critique of that society. Teacher education in this perspective should be concerned with "which educational, moral and political commitments ought to guide our work in the field rather than with the practice of merely dwelling on which procedures and organizational arrangements will most effectively help us realize tacit and often unexamined ends" (Zeichner, 1983, p. 8). Second, teacher education programs should be based on a form of "cultural politics" that uses social, cultural, political, and economic dimensions as the "primary categories" for understanding contemporary schooling (Giroux and McLaren, 1986, p. 229). The intent of such a curriculum is to make explicit the "socio-cultural dimension of the schooling forces," including the productive role of language in defining a way of life, the relationships between power and knowledge, the empowerment of students, the study of student cultures and history, and alternative teaching practices. Significantly, there is a far greater emphasis on pedagogy as a category than on teaching, to which we return in a subsequent part of this paper. A critical element cutting across all of these is the rearticulation of the language of domination into a language of possibility, vision, and hope (Aronowitz and Giroux, 1987). In short, the agenda is that of preparing teachers who are willing and able (Zeichner and Liston, 1987) to fight against repression on the basis of their own expertise, and who are "free from unwarranted control of unjustified beliefs, unsupportable attitudes, and the paucity of abilities which prevent that person from completely taking charge of his or her life" (Siegel, cited in Zeichner and Liston, 1987, pp. 23–24). Such a teacher, capable of intelligent reflection on the social and knowledge and the self, and attentive to the possibilities of human agency, is designated a transformative or resisting intellectual (Wexler, 1985; Giroux, 1986; Aronowitz and Giroux, 1987).

There are many criticisms that have been made of the avant-garde (McNeil, 1981; Sharp, 1982), and more that can be made. There is a strong tendency in this work to confuse discourse about convictions for the future with strategies for proceeding in the present. We do not wish to dwell on these, but instead take up the possibility that student-teachers might indeed be prepared so that they possess the visions of the avant-garde. Let us then assume closure on the avant-garde agenda as contesting the discourse of practicality and concentrate on what it might mean for teacher education programs.

Changing consciousness and constructing affinities: An avant-garde prerequisite

We begin this task with Clandinin's (1985) reporting of a teacher's image of her classroom as a "home" and its emotional and moral dimensions. Stephanie's moral views, Clandinin reports, were not neutral, but provided a "judgemental standard for her practices." For Stephanie, a classroom "should be like a home and both a classroom and a home should have certain features."[6] Similarly, Veenman (1984) reviews research that shows that "progressive" young teachers, despite having difficulties with their superiors, with their colleagues, and in the classroom, exhibited more long-standing innovative attitudes than their more "conservative" peers. Both these progressive teachers and Stephanie, in other words, possess representations with which they are able, contra Olsen, to think about what they do and which override the exigencies which are routinely said to shape teachers' practices. We cite these instances simply to underscore the fact that the orthodox research literature already contains examples of how teachers use knowledge positions that are political in their effects and to make the point that potentially counterdominant practice is not all that rare. Yet this is the single element of teachers' practice that is typically denied in teacher education. The professional discourses that constitute objectivity and that define the political as "bias," or more usually for liberals, as "emotive," leave student-teachers "free" to individually decide what the texts of schooling and course work mean (see Henriques et al., 1984; Richards, 1986). Where, as we have argued, the dominant regime of truth is that of practicality and the emphasis is often directed at the "problems" of beginning teachers, the overlapping texts set formidable (but not insurmountable) limits to what can be read from them. In our view, it is the knowledge position, the moral and ethical bases for doing teaching at all, that teacher educators need to be clear about. A serious implication of this position is that it necessitates the active autoethnography of teacher education in the contemporary world and an intentional focus on why it is like it is, rather than on how it can better fit what is apparently there today.

The root assumption of this possibility is that avant-garde teacher education programs are uncompromising in their intent that beginning teachers recognize themselves as resisting intellectuals in both new discourses about schooling which lay claim to knowledge and in alternative practices. Given what has been said so far in this paper, such knowledge and practice must intend to produce challenges to dominant definitions, explanations, and practices in the consciousness of student-teachers. The ontology of such tranformative work lies in the cultural materials students bring to teaching and the experiences *sui generis* which enable them to recognize themselves in what Alberoni (1984, pp. 20–21) calls an "alternative interpretation of reality" or the nascent state: "*The nascent state is an exploration of the limits of the possible within a given type of social system, in order to maximize the portion of experiences and solidarity which is realizable for oneself and for others at a specific historical moment* (italics in the original)." Alberoni argues that the nascent state emerges because of the coincidence of certain complex structural preconditions and can be provoked by the deliberate intervention of "missionaries, agents, or agitators." Structural preconditions constitute those circumstances where single persons and collectivities experience authentic contradictions and discontinuities between everyday and institutional life (schools, for instance) and what they desire, so that the former become intolerable. "What is a rebel? . . . what does he mean by saying 'no'? He means, for instance, that 'this has been going on too long,' 'so far but no further,' 'you are going too far,' or again 'there are certain limits beyond which you shall not go.' In other words, his 'no' affirms the existence of a borderline" (Camus, cited in Alberoni, 1984: 53). This is the "fundamental experience," in which it is likely that regions of subjectivity are changed so that previously disconnected elements of knowledge and emotions are resynthesized and some existing connections disintegrate. The restructuring of fields of experience oriented to new ends–liberation, enlightenment, self-determination–is the basis for a shared affinity on the part of participants and that which sets them apart. But the concept of the nascent state captures "the *direct experience* of transcending everyday existence" (Alberoni, 1984, p. 31, emphasis added) rather than the utopian sense of only believing in the future perfectibility of institutions.

In Alberoni's view, the nascent state is more likely to occur in persons and groups whose social location lies between the privileged and the exploited, a position sometimes attributed to teachers. In any case, the nascent state provides an analogue and a necessary prerequisite for the intentions of the educational avant-garde. If the concept is to contribute to the visionary agenda of the avant-garde in teacher education, it brings with it a number of implications, which we briefly explore.

Hope and transformative practice: The need for a new settlement

The achievement of the nascent state in teacher education is heavily dependent on creating the threshold conditions for it, and pedagogical strategies are central to those conditions. By this we mean that the teacher education discourses of the avant-garde are by definition produced in criticism of existing social conditions, in social theories that appropriate the status of "truth" for their knowledge, and in the ways teaching is conducted and learning is actualized. Those discourses, though, need to be more than *about* critical issues or critical pedagogy, or indeed about possibilities. They need to shape and critically inform the knowledge position that is being used in them while enabling student-teachers to engage with their own and their students' subject positions and schooling. For the avant-garde (and we suspect for many mainstream teacher educators), the essential problem is one of the adequacy of theorizing teaching, learning, and so forth in general "without a consciousness of the conditions which produce, negotiate, transform, realise and return it *in practice*" (Lusted, 1986, p. 3). This is why so much of dominant practice is caught in a history which it is unable to interpret, and why teacher education is a strategic site: its potential for liberationary educational work has not yet been fulfilled.

There are, in our view, two starting points for the development of a progressive pedagogy in teacher education that draw on Alberoni's insights and provide substance for an avant-garde agenda. The first are the cultural materials that students bring with them, their multiple subjectivities. In order to provide an example of the kinds of cultural materials we have in mind, we can identify science and mathematics graduates in particular (Smith and Sachs, in press) as recognizing themselves in discourses that implicitly rank knowledge in hierarchical order, although it would be a mistake to limit this observation to them alone or to their discipline knowledge. Concomitantly, many teacher education students frequently have a strong instrumental understanding of education and what it means to be taught and to teach, so that undergoing a teacher education program is *"on condition* that it does not undermine or weaken or challenge the boundaries between 'private' and 'public' subjectivity" (Richards, 1986, p. 75, emphasis in the original). Williamson (1985, p. 92), discussing the effects of prior education on students, takes up the point in these terms: "Many of them have experienced their entire education hitherto as some kind of external structure which makes either less or more assault on them, and which in almost *every* case, had made them feel that 'ideas' and 'complexities' and 'abstractions' are somehow weapons used *against* them, not tools for their own use." This student identity issue can be evaluated pedagogically as a problem of ill-informed students that must be corrected or as evidence that students have different combinations of class, gender, race, age, and biography. Some combinations are more sensitive to scrutiny by teachers or lecturers (Lusted, 1986, p. 6), and in teacher education programs, Williamson's prognosis is likely, give the liminal nature of the student-teacher status (Smith, 1979).

The second starting point is an awareness of the mode, tenor, and content of *specific* teacher education programs. Conventional arrangements are frequently divisive in the sense that they fragment knowledge, replicate existing school social relations in their form (they look and feel like school programs), and provide little in the way of structural or intellectual coherence. Although it is true that student knowledge is produced in the mutual interaction of teacher, knowledge, and student, rather than in the intentions of instructors, the conditions in which it is produced in teacher education programs affect the possibilities for transformative work. In particular, as Connell (1983) has pointed out, work in a radical enclave, such as a social foundations subject within an unsympathetic structure, is unlikely to provide the conditions for the tranformation of student consciousness and action. Indeed, such enclaves may work in reverse, reinforcing and reproducing the very beliefs and practices that they critique because their institutional status is pregiven in the discourse of practicality. The "voice" of a teacher education program, namely, its preferred messages, then needs to be generative, rather than merely supportive of, a critical and adventurous pedagogy and politics. We see little room for compromise on this issue.

The doing of avant-garde teacher education is a pedagogical problem that has two main objectives, namely, recontextualizing the reality of schooling, and realizing a counterdominant practice.

The first objective is captured by Terdiman's (1985, p. 68) interdependent concepts of 're/citation', surrounding the dominant discourse in order to "neutralize or explode it," and 'de/citation', excluding or expunging the dominant discourse. Central to the first concept is the relativizing of personal experience in schools. The object is to recover, make explicit, what is constitutive of personal and group representations of schooling that student-teachers have in order to question what is thought of as boundaries between the individual and the social. Both the representations and their attributed sources are thus made available for analysis by those who have produced them.

The task should be extended into the cultures of the school students, parents, and teachers so that further comparisons between representations are established. The use of structured ethnographic-like field experiences make available narratives from a variety of voices that make up culture as a field of struggle for the production of knowledge, including, of course, the discourses of education. The face-to-face investment of social self in such exercises is an important source of insight into one's own and others' presuppositions and is a part of the continuing process of identity making.

The kind of analysis of such cultural materials that is undertaken is crucial. We take Lusted's (1986, pp. 9–10) point that is essential to avoid closing the analysis around an assumption that people are manipulated and "inevitably positioned" by the practices of schools discerned by school critics, that there is a simple correspondence between a particular type of discourse and an extradiscursive reality (Belsey, 1980). Such a course, Lusted argues, "neither brooks dissent nor appeals to the possibility of debate within it." Instead he recommends "open ended and specific pedagogies" that account for context and difference, the social position of the group and the individuals within it.

Nevertheless, the kind of social theory that is adequate (that facilitates the avant-garde agenda) is not infinitely open-ended because the agenda, to reiterate, contests the discourse of practicality and requires moral and ethical judgements. Such theory, discursively produced in the process of conflict between discourses, must lead *in principle* to understandings about the concepts being used and the representations they imply or evoke about themselves and other representations. Fundamentally they must provide the provisional *means to think with* (Richards, 1986, p. 77) that simultaneously enhances the "this has been going on too long" syndrome while providing a range of acceptable and possible options. This would seem to be the major prerequisite of Terdiman's second concept, expunging the dominant discourse and creating the conditions for an alternative reality.

There is a necessary second condition about which the avant-garde literature seems curiously silent, but which is central to the direct experience component of the nascent state. It is the concern with curriculum content and teaching strategies of the conventional teacher education field, glossed as "curriculum" or "teaching" studies. If the avant-garde is to expunge the dominant discourse of practicality with its instrumental recipes and techniques of teaching, then it too needs an alternative curriculum and teaching *practice* that is consistent with its social critiques and that transcends the reality of the discourse of practicality.[7]

The modes of resistance used by student-teachers to mystifying "theory," and to domination by "irrelevant" (foundations) courses include a desire for immediate resolutions to the problems and a wish to commence teaching. Although such resistance is a symptom of the dominant discourse of practicality, experiences in a revamped teacher education program and racial theorizing alone are unlikely to expunge such a tradition.

An avant-garde teacher education program, then, requires an organic relationship with schools and teachers, but on its *own* terms.[8] It needs to incorporate "curriculum" studies on campus and provide school-based exemplars of practice that embody the same principles that underlie the program, the direct experience of transcending everyday school life. Only then can avant-garde teacher education produce its stories of hope on the experiential basis of hope-full teaching in hope-filled classrooms, of which there are many. The expectation of student-teachers in this vision of the practicality ethic would be to explore the "normal" alternative of professional work provided by the school-campus link.

As a teacher educator and a schoolteacher, the authors can think of a no more subversive move in the present teacher education scene because it would unify the mission of teacher education programs and dissolve the differences between avant-garde theoretical enclaves and work in schools. There seems little likelihood of such an eventuality without a struggle to forge links with the teaching profession and to reformulate policy at the institutional level. The centrality of educational policy studies and teacher education as political practice is thus confirmed.

PART THREE

Schooling, Ideology, and the Politics of Student Voice

Schooling as a Form of Cultural Politics: Toward a Pedagogy of and for Difference

Henry A. Giroux

Within the last fifteen years, the relationship between culture and power has become a central concern of radical social theory. Moving beyond the reductionist classical Marxist position in which culture is viewed merely as a reflex of the economy, leftist theorists have begun to explore in great depth the implications of Marx's claim that "it is always necessary to distinguish between the material transformation of the economic conditions of production, which can be determined with the precision of natural science, and the legal, political, and religious, artistic or philosophic–in short, ideological forms in which men(*sic*) become conscious of this conflict and fight it out."[1]

Drawing upon the work of Gramsci, E. P. Thompson, Raymond Williams, and others, leftist theorists have begun to reconstruct a view of social theory that has refashioned the ways in which cultural questions become the starting point for analyzing traditionally separate spheres such as the economic, political, and psychological. This is particularly clear in the emergence of such fields as literary studies, cultural studies, feminist studies, and various forms of postmodernism and poststructuralism.[2] Each of these areas has offered new insights into the study of culture and power. Three of these major insights are particularly relevent for illuminating the political project that has shaped discourses that have linked culture and power. First, the concept of culture has been intimately connected with the question of how social relations are structured within class, sexual, and

125

age formations that produce forms of dependency and oppression. Rejecting the subordination of cultural issues to class analyses, more recent radical social theory has analyzed gender, racial, and ethnic social relations as irreducible forms of domination that have parallel dynamic cultural forms, each of which needs to be studied in its own right and in its particular relations to other forms of domination.[3] Second, culture is analyzed in these perspectives not simply as a way of life, but also as a form of production that always involves asymmetrical relations of power, and through which different groups in their dominant and subordinate positions struggle to both define and realize their aspirations. Third, culture is viewed as a field of struggle and social difference in which the production, legitimation, and circulation of particular forms of meaning and experience are central areas of conflict and battle.[4]

Within the newly emerging interdisciplinary studies, two major approaches have dominated recent attempts to restructure the discourse of culture and power. In the first instance, there has been a focus on the issues of everyday life and the insistence that "cultures" must be analyzed in their particular, concrete, historical, and social forms. The emphasis here has been on forms of consciousness, experience, and the subjective side of human relations. Power in this case has been linked to culture through the ways in which particular social and class formations are either constrained or enabled to produce their own experiences and histories around emancipatory goals. There is a strong emphasis in this approach, as indicated in the more recent writings in the field of social and cultural anthropology, to challenge the discourse and universalizing historicism used to both constitute and legitimate existing configurations of power and domination.[5] In this view, there is an attempt to uncover and reconstitute the suppressed histories and voices of subordinate groups in order to restore and affirm the legacy and unrealized potential of the forms of subjectivity, agency, and experience characteristic of such groups. Central to this project has been the attempt to uncover how the suppression of difference is implicated in various expressions of power and domination, how a theory of resistance can be reconceptualized within the constraints of powerfully hegemonic social contexts, and how experience can be reconstructed as part of a language of contestation and struggle. In the second instance, the emphasis shifts to the notion that subjectivities are produced and therefore must be analyzed as the effect of wider social "forms." Meaning is derived in this approach less in the consciousness of social actions than in the forms of language, narrative, and other sign systems that position subjects within specific webs of possibility. This position has been dominated by the discourses of poststructuralism and postmodernism. Central to this approach has been a si-multaneous rejection of the humanist notion of the unified subject and an attempt to retheorize subjectivity as a site of multiple and often contradic-tory subject positions; a rejection of all forms of truth defined and legiti-mated through a language characterized in neutral or objective terms; and an attempt to define language and other forms of representation as both constitutive and expressive of particular relations of knowledge and power.[6]

More recently there has been an attempt by social theorists such as Stan-ley Aronowitz, Richard Johnson, Stuart Hall, and others to break down the opposition between these two approaches and to view them as part of the various processes of circulation that link overall forms of cultural pro-duction.[7] In this case, structure and agency are not sealed against each other but are seen as interrelated aspects of what Francis Mulhern calls the "cul-tural field." Mulhern's notion of the cultural field is important because it not only points to significant theoretical elements of cultural analyses, but it also suggests form of inquiry and broad areas of cultural practice that can be taken up productively by radical educators. He is worth quoting at length on this subject:

The cultural field is constituted by the complex unity of (1) all those practices whose principal function is signification, (2) the institutions that organize them and (3) the agents that operate them. It is this contradictory ensemble that forms the dis-tinctive object of cultural analysis and cultural struggle. The main forms of cultural struggle correspond directly to three components of the definition. The first entails challenges to particular representations or orders of representation. The second would encompass such issues as the internal organization of an institution, the con-ditions of work in it, its relationship with the State or with capital. The third has to do principally with questions such as the differential accessibility of means of cul-tural production, or the institutions supporting them, to (say) women, ethnic minorities, trade unionists.[8]

Mulhern's categories point to a range of possible political interventions that have and might continue to characterize the field of cultural politics: there is the struggle over how language, representation, and symbolism are produced, sustained, and legitimated in an effort to reproduce, challenge, or create particular ways of life; there is the struggle for control over institu-tions which produce and legitimate culture—this includes in the most ob-vious sense education, media, arts, popular culture, and other agencies of cultural formation; in addition, there is the urgent need to make cultural struggle a central aspect of larger political and social movements. In this case, the primacy of the cultural as a political practice would reaffirm the importance of linking political struggle to the dynamics of everyday life, it would revitalize the attempt to understand how people individually invest both intellectually and emotionally in particular ideologies and social practices, it would analyze how they learn to either accept or refuse the practices of dominant social forms, and it would redefine the role that intellectuals play as central actors in various areas of cultural and political practice. I have spent some time elaborating some of the more general theoretical elements and social practices that have become an object of analysis with the broader debate taking place around the issues of culture and power because this debate points to some important understandings that critical educators might pursue in theorizing a cultural politics for a radical theory of education. Moreover, it is against such understandings that I first want to examine some of the theoretical gains made by radical educators in the last decade, particularly by those educators who have attempted to use political and cultural analyses to further develop how schools mediate and reproduce their relations to the dominant society.

Radical educational theory and the language of critique

Radical pedagogy emerged in full strength as part of the new sociology of education in England and the United States over a decade ago as a critical response to what can be loosely termed the "ideology of traditional educational theory and practice."[9] Preoccupied with the imperative to challenge the dominant assumption that schools are the major mechanism for the development of a democratic and egalitarian social order, radical educational theory set itself the task of uncovering how the logic of domination and oppression was reproduced within the various mechanisms of schooling. Rather than accepting the notion that schools were vehicles of democracy and social mobility, radical educational critics made such an assumption problematic. In doing so, their major ideological and political task has been one of trying to unravel how schools reproduce the logic of capital through the ideological and material forms of privilege and domination that structure the lives of students from various class, gender, racial, and ethnic groupings.

Radical critics, for the most part, agreed that educational traditionalists generally refused to question the political nature of public schooling. In fact, traditionalists eluded the issue through the paradoxical attempt to depoliticize the language of schooling while reproducing and legitimating capitalist ideologies. The most obvious expression of this approach could be seen in an instrumental discourse that took as its most important concerns the mastery of pedagogical techniques and the transmission of knowledge functional to the existing society.[10] In the traditional world view, schools were seen almost exclusively as instructional sites. That schools were equally influential as cultural and political sites was largely ignored (until the late 1980s), as was the notion that they represented areas of contestation among differentially empowered cultural and economic groups.

In the discourse of the radical educational theorists, traditional educational theory suppressed important questions regarding the relations among knowledge, power, and domination. Furthermore, out of this criticism emerged a new theoretical language and mode of criticism which argued that schools did not provide opportunities in the broad Western humanist tradition for self- and social empowerment in the society at large. In opposition to the traditionalist position, leftist critics provided theoretical arguments and empirical evidence to suggest that schools were, in fact, agencies of social, economic, and cultural reproduction.[11] At best, public schooling offered limited individual mobility to members of the working class and other oppressed groups, but, in the final analysis, there were powerful instruments for the reproduction of capitalist relations of production and the dominant legitimating ideologies of ruling groups.

Radical critics of education provided a variety of useful models of analysis and research to challenge traditional educational ideology. Against the conservative claim that schools transmitted objective knowledge, radical critics developed theories of the hidden curriculum as well as theories of ideology that identified the specific interests underlying different knowledge forms.[12] Rather than viewing school knowledge as objective, as something to be merely transmitted to students, radical theorists argued that school knowledge was a particular representation of the dominant culture, a privileged discourse that was constructed through a selective process of emphases and exclusions.[13] Against the claim that schools were only instructional sites, radical critics pointed to the transmission and reproduction of a dominant culture in schools. Far from being neutral, the dominant culture of the school was characterized by a selective ordering and legitimating of privileged language forms, modes of reasoning, social relations, and lived experiences. In this view, culture was linked to power and to the imposition of a specific set of ruling-class codes and experiences.[14] But school culture, it was claimed, functioned not only to confirm and privilege students from the dominant classes; it also functioned through exclusion and insult to disconfirm the histories, experiences, and dreams of subordinate groups. Finally, against the claim by traditional educators that schools were apolitical institutions, radical educators illuminated the ways in which the state, through its selective grants, certification policies, and legal powers, influenced school practice in the interest of particular dominant ideologies.

But in spite of its insightful theoretical and political analyses of schooling, radical educational theory suffered from some serious flaws, the most significant being its failure to move beyond the language of critique and domination. Radical educators remained mired in a language that linked schools primarily to the ideologies and practices of domination. In this view, schools were seen almost exclusively as agencies of social reproduction, producing obedient workers for industrial capital, school knowledge was generally dismissed as a form of bourgeois ideology, and teachers were often portrayed as being trapped in an apparatus of domination that worked with all the certainty of a Swiss watch.

Although it is true that the reproductive model of schooling became increasingly more sophisticated theoretically as it explored the role schools played in the process of capital accumulation, ideological legitimation, and the production of knowledge necessary to carry on the increasing demands of a changing capitalist society, the underlying logic that informed this position did not change. This model of analysis rigidly operated within and in reponse to the logic of capital. This is basically a reactive mode of analysis, one that repeatedly oversimplifies the complexity of social and cultural life and ultimately ignores creating a theoretical discourse that transcends the imperatives of possibility within existing capitalist configurations of power. The major failure of this position has been that it prevents leftist educators from developing a programmatic language in which they can theorize *for* schools. Instead, radical educators have theorized primarily *about* schools as agencies of domination, and, as such, they have seldom concerned themselves with the possibility of constructing new, alternative approaches to school organization, curricula, and classroom social relations.

Radical educators have abandoned the language of possibility for the language of critique. By viewing schools as primarily reproductive sites, they have not been able to develop a theory of schooling that offers a viable possibility for counterhegemonic struggle and ideological contestation. Within this discourse, schools, teachers, and students have often been written off as merely extensions of the logic of capital. Instead of viewing schools as sites of contestation, negotiation, and conflict, radical educators tend to articulate an oversimplified version of domination that suggests that schools cannot be seen as sites of political intervention. Since schools are often viewed in radical educational theories as ideologically and politically overburdened by the dominant society, the moral and political necessity for developing a programmatic discourse for working within schools is either seen as unproblematic or simply ignored. Thus, the role that teachers, students, parents, and community people might play in waging a political struggle regarding the public schools is rarely explored as a viable strategy.

Radical educational theory has been burdened by more than the language of critique; it has also failed to explore and develop a number of important concerns that I believe are central to a critical theory of schooling. First, it has failed to develop a public philosophy that integrates the issues of power, politics, and possibility around the role that schools might play as democratic public spheres. Radical educational theorists have been so caught up in describing the reality of *existing* schools that they have failed to raise questions of purpose and meaning around what it is that schools *should* be. Lacking any substantive vision, radical theorists have ignored the task of developing the foundation of a progressive public philosophy as a referent for reconstructing schools as democratic public spheres. In this case, such educators have failed to construct a programmatic discourse for providing students with the knowledge, skills, and values they will need to exercise the civic courage, compassion, and leadership necessary to find their own voices while learning how to both understand and connect such voices to the exercise of social responsibility and civic courage. For example, radical educators have not been able to articulate a vision of schooling that begins by linking public education to the imperatives of democracy rather than to the narrow demands of the marketplace; that is, there is an absence in this discourse regarding how the meaning and nature of public education can be situated within the broader context of what it means to view schools as primary to the formation of a critical and engaged citizenry, as social sites from which to organize the energies of a moral vision in order to challenge the sterile instrumentalism, selfishness, and contempt for democratic community that has become the hallmark of the Reagan era.

Second, radical educational theorists have virtually ignored any attempt to develop a theory of ethics in order to provide a referent for justifying either their own language or for legitimating the social practices necessary for defending a particular vision of what schools might become. Caught within the paradox of exhibiting moral indignation without the benefit of a well-defined theory of ethics and morality, radical educators have been unable to move from a posture of criticism to one of substantive vision.

Third, radical educational theory has been unable to develop forms of analyses that interrogate schooling as a site that actively produces and legitimates privileged forms of subjectivity and ways of life. There is no sense in this language of how subjectivities are schooled, how power organizes space, time, and the body, how language is used to both legitimate and marginalize different subject-positions, how knowledge not only mystifies, but also functions to produce identities, desires, and needs.[15] In effect, as Philip Corrigan has pointed out, there is no moral and political discourse in radical education theory that interrogates how existing social forms encourage, disrupt, cripple, dilute, marginalize, make possible, or sustain differentiated human capacities that extend the possibilities that humans have for living in a truly democratic and life-affirming society and world.[16]

Fourth, radical educational theory has vastly underplayed the importance of redefining the actual roles that teachers might play as engaged critics and intellectuals in both the classroom and as part of a wider movement for social change. On the one hand, teachers have been worked on but not included as self-determining agents of political and pedagogical change; on the other hand, little has been done by radical educational theorists to address the role that teachers might play in alliance with parents and other members of the wider community in order to address the issues of policy formation and change as part of a wider educational and sociopolitical movement. Examples of such alliances between teachers and the parents of black, Latino, and low-income white children have been widespread during the Reagan era. For example, in Chicago parents joined with teachers in creating the Parent Equalizers of Chicago, headed by Dorothy Tillman. As a result of this movement, hundreds of parents were educated about the workings of the school system, how to actually get actively involved in the schools, and how to get elected to various levels of policy-making boards. These parents got rid of the Mastery Learning Reading Program, created Local School Improvement Councils, and have played an active role in promoting school criticism and active reform.

The political and strategic inadequacy of much of what constitutes radical educational theory is also evident in its overall refusal to engage the theoretical gains that have come to characterize the fields of literary studies, feminist theory, poststructuralism, postmodernism, and democratic theory. Theoretically isolated from the many innovations taking place in the large world of social theory, many radical educational theorists have removed themselves from critically engaging the limitations of the political projects implicit in their own work and have resorted instead to preaching the importance of the language of simplicity and the privileging of practice over theory. The call to writing in a language that is touted as clear and accessible has become the political and ideological equivalent of a moral and political vision that increasingly collapses under the weight of its own anti-intellectualism. Similarly, theory is now dissolved into practice under the vote-catching call for the importance of focusing on the concrete as the all-embracing sphere of educational strategy and relevance. To aruge against these concerns is not meant as a clever exercise intent on merely reversing the relevance of the categories so that theory is prioritized over practice, or abstract language over the language of popcorn imagery. Nor am I merely suggesting that critical educators mount an equally reductionist argument against the use of clear language or the importance of practice. At issue here is the need to both question and reject the reductionism and exclusions that characterize the binary oppositions that inform these overly pragmatic sentiments. Let me pose an alternative argument.

Language is always constructed with respect to the specificity of the audience it addresses and should be judged not only in pragmatic terms but also with regard to the theoretical and political viability of the project it articulates. It is not the complexity of language which is at issue but the viability of the theoretical framework it constitutes and promotes. Moreover, the relationship between theory and practice is multifaceted and complex. Simply put, theory in some instances directly informs practice, whereas in others, practice restructures theory as a primary force for change, and in some cases theory (in the more limited sense of the practice of producing narrative and rhetoric) provides the refuge to think beyond current forms of practice so as to envision that which is "not yet." Privileging practice without due consideration of the complex interactions that mark the totality of theory-practice and language-meaning relationships is not simply reductionistic but also a form of theoretical tyranny. Theory, in this sense, becomes a form of practice that ignores the political value of "theoretical discourse" within a specific historical conjuncture: that is, rather than examining the language of theory as part of a wider historical moment of self-examination, the language and politics of theory are merely reduced to an unproblematic concern with clarity rather than with the problematizing of certainty itself. The intimacy of the dialectic between theory and practice is reduced to an opposition between theory and complexity, on the one hand, and practice and clarity on the other. This is the mark of a vapid, pragmatic, anti-intellectualism whose leveling tendency occludes the role of language in constructing theory as a historical specific practice that makes politics and praxis possible as part of an engagement with the particularities and problems of a given time and place.

Within the present historical conjuncture, with its appeal to universality, its totalitarian view of history, its ethnocentric embrace of culture, and its celebration of greed and individualism, the questions to be asked about language and theory might begin with the conditions necessary to develop forms of theoretical practice capable of retrieving history as the discourse of the other, reclaiming democracy as a site of struggle within a wider socialist vision, and developing a radical ethic that rejects finality and consensus for the voice of difference and dialogue. At the present time, theory offers the opportunity for a discursive practice whose identity and political value can only be understood in particular circumstances, informed by the historical conjuncture that gives it meaning. As Bruce Robbins has so brilliantly stated, the real debate over theory is about both the specific ideological content of various theoretical discourses *and* the "circumstances that give these ideas their limits and their cogency."[17] At issue here is whether the language of theory works in the interest of making the familiar strange, acknowledging difference as the basis for a public philosophy that rejects totalizing theories that view the other as a deficit, and providing the basis for raising questions the dominant culture finds too dangerous to raise. What many "radical" educators forget is that the importance of language as a theoretical practice derives from its power as a critical and subversive discourse. To judge theory next to the simple yardstick of clarity more often than not represents a specific theoretical discourse incapable of reflecting on its *own* practice within the present historical conjuncture, a practice that has more to do with a defense of the status quo than it does with a viable politics of theory, language, and schooling.

It is worth reemphasizing that although radical educators have linked culture to the issue of power, they have not done so in ways that extend the full implications of such analyses. The notion that culture is a real site of contestation has been undermined by an often lifeless determination that increasingly retreats into a political project marked less by its insight than by its bad faith. The major problem that I want to analyze is, How is it possible to develop a radical pedagogy located in a discourse that acknowledges the spaces, tensions, and possibilities for struggle within the day-to-day workings of schools? Underlying this issue is a theoretical and political attempt to generate a set of categories that provide new modes of critical analyses and point to more viable ways in which the interconnection between culture and power can function within a language of possibility, one that points to alternative strategies and social relations around which educators at all levels of schooling can redefine the nature of intellectual work and inquiry.

Culture and the crisis of the intellectual

One of Antonio Gramsci's most important formulations regarding the political nature of culture was the central role intellectuals played in the production and reproduction of social life.[18] For Gramsci, the emerging role of intellectuals as a primary political force in maintaining the ideological rule of dominant groups signaled an important shift in the relationship between such central elements of cultural struggle as language, knowledge, and social relations, on the one hand, and the dynamics of control and power on the other. In this case, intellectuals became producers of cultural capital, which as a deliberate analogue to material capital signifies the transformation of social relations from a fundamental reliance on the primacy of the policing function of the state to more subtle modes of control organized around forms of knowledge that name and construct everyday experience in accord with the logic of domination. Of course, Gramsci's emphasis on cultural hegemony and the role of intellectuals has been developed by a host of social theorists such as Nicos Poulantzaz, Regis Debray, Alvin Gouldner, George Konrad and Ivan Szelnyi, Rudolf Bahro, and Russell Jacoby.[19] But in my mind none of these theorists have substantially furthered Gramsci's project of viewing intellectuals as not only elaborators of dominant culture but also as a vital fundamental social and political force in any counter-hegemonic struggle.

Since I have elaborated in other places on the many ways in which cultural domination is played out within the different mechanisms and levels of schooling, I do not want to repeat that position here. Instead, I want to develop a theory of schooling around a wider notion of cultural politics and in doing so further elaborate the role that teachers might play as producers of cultural forms and discourses that point to specific notions of authority and pedagogical practice whose underlying logic is consistent with a radical theory of ethics. In other words, I want to redefine the role of teachers as intellectuals around the view of authority that points to the importance of specific forms of intellectual work and practice in any programmatic discourse for developing alternative forms of schooling. Such a stance is important because it posits a view of intellectual practice born of commitment, struggle, and a substantive ethical vision. Furthermore, it provides a referent for analyzing and criticizing those intellectuals who have been transformed into either a technical intelligentsia performing a wide variety of the overly specialized functions in late capitalist society or who have become hegemonic intellectuals by actively working to produce and sustain ideological and cultural relations that legitimize the dominant society and existing configurations of power. In the Age of Reagan, right-wing hegemonic intellectuals have assumed a high visibility. Some of the more obvious examples include Nathan Glazer, the editor of *The Public Interest*; Hilton Kramer, the editor of *The New Criterion*; Norman Podhoretz, the editor of the influential magazine *Commentary*; Diane Ravitch, writer and educator; Allan Bloom, writer and educator; and John Silber, president of Boston University.

Authority and intellectuals: Toward a cultural politics

It is important for educators to develop a dialectical view of authority, for a number of reasons.[20] First, the issue of authority serves as both an important referent and an ideal for public schooling: that is, as a form of legitimation and practice necessary to the ongoing ideological and material production and renewal of society, the concept of authority provokes educators to take a critically pragmatic stance regarding the purpose and function that schooling is to play in any given society. As a form of legitimation, authority is inextricably related to a particular vision of what schools should be as part of a wider community and society. In other words, authority makes both visible and problematic the presuppositions that give meaning to the officially sanctioned languages and values that legitimate what Foucault has called particular "material, historical conditions of possibility [along with] their governing systems of order, appropriation, and exclusion."[21]

Second, the concept of authority raises issues about the ethical and political basis of schooling: that is, it calls into serious question the role that school administrators and teachers play as intellectuals in both elaborating and implementing their particular views or rationality. In other words, such a concept defines what *school* authority means as a particular set of ideas and practice within a historically defined context. In short, the category of authority reinserts back into the language of schooling the primacy of the political. It does so by highlighting the social and political function that educators serve in elaborating and enforcing a particular view of school authority, one that legitimates a particular form of life.

Third, the concept of authority provides the theoretical leverage to analyze the relationship between domination and power by both raising and questioning the difference between the shared meanings that teachers elaborate in order to justify their view of authority and the effects of their actions at the level of actualized pedagogical practices. In this case, authority provides both the referent and the critique against which to analyze the difference between the legitimating claims for a particular form of authority and the way such claims are actually expressed in daily classroom life.

If the concept of authority is to provide a theoretical referent for rethinking the purpose and meaning of public education and radical pedagogy, it must be rooted in a view of community life in which the moral quality of everyday existence is linked to the notion of critical democracy.[22] Authority in this view becomes a mediating referent for the ideal of democracy and its expression as a set of educational practices designed to empower students to be critical and active citizens. In other words, the purpose of schooling now becomes fashioned around two central questions: What kind of society do educators want to live in? and What kind of teachers and pedagogy can be both informed and legitimated by a view of authority that takes critical democracy and active citizenship seriously? Such a view of authority points to a theory of democracy that includes the principles of representative democracy, workers' democracy, and civil and human rights. It is, in Benjamin Barber's terms, a view of authority rooted in "strong democracy," and is characterized by a citizenry capable of genuine public thinking, political judgement, and social action.[23] Such a view of authority endorses a concept of the citizen as more than a simple "bearer of abstract rights, privileges, and immunities"; it sees the citizen as a member of any one of a diverse number of public spheres that provides a sense of communal vision and civic courage. Sheldon Wolin's discussion of political power speaks to the connected and engaged nature of critical citizenship.

A political being is not to be defined as . . . an abstract, disconnected bearer of rights, privileges, and immunities, but as a person whose existence is located in a particular place and draws its sustenance from circumscribed relationships: family, friends, church, neighborhood, workplace, community, town, city. These relationships are the sources from which political beings draw power—symbolic, material, and psychological—and that enable them to act together. For true political power involves not only acting so as to effect decisive changes; it also means the capacity to receive power, to be acted upon, to change, and be changed. From a democratic perspective, power is not simply force that is generated; it is experience, sensibility, wisdom, even melancholy, distilled from the diverse relations and circles we move within.[24]

The notion of authority is important, in Wolin's case, because it implies a connection between the purpose of schooling and the imperatives of a critical democracy; it also provides a basis from which to argue for schools as democratic public spheres. In other words, schools need to be understood and constructed within a model of authority in which they are legitimated as places where students learn and collectively struggle for the economic, political, and social preconditions that make individual freedom and social empowerment possible. Within this emancipatory model of authority, a discourse can be fashioned which provides educators with the ideological tools that can struggle against a right-wing view of authority in which the purpose of schooling is linked to a truncated view of patriotism and patriarchy that functions as a veil for a suffocating chauvinism. In its emancipatory form, authority exists as a terrain of struggle and as such reveals rather than hides the dialectical nature of its interests and possibilities; moreover, it offers a rationale for viewing schools as public spheres inextricably connected to ongoing wider movements and struggles for democracy. For radical educators and others working in oppositional social movements, the dominant meaning of authority must be redefined to include the concepts of freedom, equality, and democracy.[25] Furthermore, the more specific concept of emancipatory authority needs to be seen as the central category around which to construct a rationale for defining teachers as transformative intellectuals and teacher work as a form of intellectual practice related to the issues, problems, concerns, and experiences that link classroom life to the daily concerns of the wider community and society. It is important here to stress the threefold nature of the emancipatory model of authority which I am presenting. On the one hand, it provides a basis for linking the purpose of schooling to the imperatives of a critical democracy. On the other hand, it establishes theoretical support for analyzing teaching as a form of intellectual practice; moreover, it provides the ontological grounding for teachers who are willing to assume the role of transformative intellectuals.

The concept of emancipatory authority suggests that teachers are bearers of critical knowledge, rules, and values through which they consciously articulate and problematize their relationship to each other, to students, to subject matter, and to the wider community. Such a view of authority challenges the dominant view of teachers as primarily technicians or public servants, whose role is primarily to implement rather than conceptualize pedagogical practice. The category of emancipatory authority dignifies teacher work by viewing it as a form of intellectual practice. Within this discourse, teacher work is viewed as a form of intellectual labor that interrelates conception and practice, thinking and doing, and producing and implementing as integrated activities that give teaching its dialectical meaning. The concept of the teacher as an intellectual carries with it the imperative to judge, critique, and reject those approaches to authority that reinforce a technical and social division of labor that often silences and disempowers both teachers and students. In other words, emancipatory authority establishes as a central principle the need for teachers and others to critically engage the ideological and practical conditions which allow them to mediate, legitimate, and function in their capacity as authority-minded intellectuals.

Emancipatory authority also provides the theoretical scaffolding for educators to define themselves not simply as intellectuals, but in a more committed fashion as transformative intellectuals. This means that such educators are not merely concerned with forms of empowerment that promote individual achievement and traditional forms of academic success. Instead, they are also concerned in their teaching with linking empowerment—the ability to think and act critically—to the concept of social engagement and transformation: that is, teaching for social transformation means educating students to take risks and to struggle within ongoing relations of power in order to be able to envision and promote those unrealized possibilities in the wider society that point to a more humane and democratic future. Acting as a transformative intellectual means helping students acquire critical knowledge about basic societal structures, such as the economy, the state, the workplace, and mass culture, so that such institutions can be open to potential transformation. Doug White, the Australian educator, is instructive on this issue:

In the broadest sense it is education – the bringing of knowledge into social life – which is central to a project which can turn possibilities into actualities. Radical teachers have not made a mistake in being too radical, but in not being radical enough. The task is for teachers, with others, to begin a project in which the forms of social institutions and work are considered and transformed, so that the notion of culture may come to include the development of social structures. The true nature of curriculum . . . is the development of that knowledge, thought and practice which is required by young people to enable them to take part in the production and reproduction of social life and to come to know the character of these processes.[26]

As transformative intellectuals, teachers need to make clear the nature of the appeals to authority they are using to legitimate their pedagogical practices. In other words, radical educators need to be reflective about the political and moral referents for the authority they assume in teaching particular forms of knowledge, taking a stand against forms of oppression, and treating students as if they ought also to be concerned about the issues of social justice and political action. In my view, the most important referent for this particular view of authority rests in a commitment that addresses the many instances of suffering that are both a growing and threatening part of everyday life in America and abroad. Central to this position is a notion of commitment grounded in an affirmative view of liberation which acknowledges that the notion of 'truth' does not reside in abstract definitions of principle, but is, in part, the outcome of particular power struggles that cannot be removed from either history or existing networks of social and political control. This position suggests that one's beliefs are always subject to a critical analysis and that the process of learning how to learn is always contingent upon the recognition that one's perspective can be both challenged and transformed. The politics of such a skepticism is firmly rooted in a view of authority that is deeply forged in "a creation of a politics of truth that defines the true as that which liberates and furthers specific processes of liberation."[27]

The pedagogical rationality at work here is one that believes that teachers have an important and historic opportunity in the upcoming decade of the 1990s to reclaim the language of democracy, citizenship, and social responsibility. Instead of weaving dreams limited to the private imperatives of material success, teachers as transformative intellectuals can work to become part of a collective effort to build and revitalize a democratic culture.

Such teachers can work collectively to reject the role of the disconnected expert, specialist, or careerist and adopt in its place that of the practice of the engaged intellectual.[28] This is not a call for educators to become wedded to some abstract ideal that removes them from everyday life or turns them into prophets of perfection and certainty.[29] As engaged and transformative intellectuals, teachers can undertake social criticism not as outsiders but as individuals who address the most important social and political issues of their community and nation, as persons who have intimate knowledge of the workings of daily life as it bears down on and shapes the voices of the students with whom they work, and as people who make organic connections with the historical traditions that shape the communities and collective memories that provide students with a voice, history, and sense of belonging. Teachers need to find new ways to get involved with the communities in which they live and teach, to make a difference, or, as Rene Du Bois wrote, to think globally and act locally. The notion of teachers as transformative intellectuals and engaged critics is not one that simply argues for tolerance. Rather, it is an ideological referent infused by a passion and commitment for justice, joy, and collective struggle. It is also a social practice marked by a moral courage and respect for criticism that does not require teachers to step back from society as a whole, but only to distance themselves from being implicated in power relations that subjugate, corrupt, or infantalize. As engaged critics, transformative intellectuals practice what Michael Walzer has called "criticism from within."[30] In part, this means telling stories that speak to the voices of those who have been silenced, enabling those who have been excluded and marginalized to speak. As engaged critics, transformative intellectuals place themselves in history rather than attempt to step outside of it. This criticism also means developing one's own voice in the interest of a utopian vision dedicated to creating a public culture capable of animating the spirit and practices of a critical democracy.[31]

I have spent some time developing the rationale that teachers might use for legitimating a form of authority that both defines and endorses their role as transformative intellectuals. Of course, developing a legitimating basis for a form of emancipatory authority does not guarantee that a transformative pedagogy will follow. But it does provide the principles for making such a transformation possible. Furthermore, it establishes the criteria for organizing curricula and classroom social relations around goals designed to prepare students to relate, understand, and value the relation between an existentially lived public space and their own practical learning. I now want to turn to some of the theoretical elements presented at the beginning of this paper. In doing so, I attempt to reconstruct and extend the notion of schooling as a form of cultural politics through the development of what I call a "pedagogy of and for difference."

Schooling and Cultural politics: Toward a pedagogy of and for difference

To view schooling as a form of cultural politics suggests that teachers can both elaborate and implement empowering pedagogical practices, and it is to this issue that I will now turn. The search for a radical pedagogy informed by a cultural politics involves the task of creating theoretical models that provide a critical discourse for analyzing schools as socially constructed sites of contestation actively involved in the production of knowledge, skills, and lived experiences. Central to this approach is the need to understand how pedagogical practice represents a particular politics of experience, or, in more exact terms, a cultural field where knowledge, discourse, and power intersect so as to produce historically specific modes of authority and forms of moral and social regulation.

Such an approach makes central the need to analyze how human experiences are produced, contested, and legitimated within the dynamics of everyday classroom life. The theoretical importance of this type of analysis is linked directly to the need for teachers to fashion a language in which a comprehensive politics of culture, voice, and experience can be developed. At issue here is the recognition that schools are historical and cultural institutions that always embody ideological and political interests and that signify reality in ways that are often actively named and contested by various individuals and groups. Schools in this sense are ideological and political spheres in which more often than not the dominant culture attempts to produce knowledge and subjectivities consistent with its own interests; but it is important to stress that schools cannot be reduced to a mirror image of the dominant society. They are also places where dominant and subordinate groups define and constrain each other through an ongoing battle and exchange in response to the sociohistorical conditions "carried" in the institutional, textual, and lived practices that define school culture and teacher and student experience within a particular specificity of time, space, and place. In other words, schools are anything but ideologically innocent; nor are they simply reproductive of dominant social relations and interests. At the same time, as previously mentioned, schools do exercise forms of political and moral regulation intimately connected with technologies of power that "produce asymmetries in the abilities of individuals and groups to define and realize their needs."[32] More specifically, schools establish the conditions under which some individuals and groups define the terms by which others live, resist, affirm, and participate in the construction of their own identities and subjectivities. Central to recognizing the insight that schools are agencies of moral and political regulation is the notion that power is productive of knowledge, meaning, and values. But, as Teresa de Lauretis points out, "We have to make distinctions between the positive effects and the oppressive effects of such production."[33] In pedagogical terms, this means being able to identify the ways in which the complex associations of habits, relations, meanings, desires, representations, and self-images are organized around the construction of gender, race, class, ethnicity, and age considerations in the production of different forms of subjectivity and ways of life. Again, as Lauretis argues, it is imperative that educators and others come to understand how subjectivity, experience, and desire interrelate within specific technologies of power that name and legitimate differences that both enable and limit or punish differentially empowered groups in this society.

Lauretis's work suggests the need to develop what I will call a *pedagogy of difference* and a *pedagogy for difference*. In the first instance, it is important that educators come to understand theoretically how difference is constructed through various representations and practices that name, legitimate, marginalize, and exclude the cultural capital and voices of various groups in American society; similarly, a pedagogy *of* difference needs to address the important question of how the representations and practices of difference are actively learned, internalized, challenged, or transformed. For it is only through such an understanding that teachers can develop a pedagogy *for* difference, one which is characterized by "an ongoing effort to create new spaces of discourse, to rewrite cultural narratives, and to define the terms of another perspective—a view from 'elsewhere.'"[34] This suggests a critical pedagogy in which there is a critical interrogation of the silences and tensions that exist between the master narratives and hegemonic discourses that make up the official curriculum of the school and the self-representations of subordinate groups as they might appear in "forgotten" histories, texts, memories, experiences, and community narratives. A pedagogy *for* difference not only seeks to understand how difference is constructed in the intersection of the official curriculum of the school and the various voices of students from subordinate groups; it also brings into play all of the contradictions within the multiple subject positions that characterize the subjectivities of the students themselves. The voices that characterize various groups of students are not of one piece, reducible merely to the categories of class, race, or gender; they are produced within cultural formations that create historically constituted subject-positions which are often shifting and multiple. These subject-positions are constructed within horizons of meaning, habit, and practice that are available in ways both determined and limited by the discourse, cultural context, and historically specific relations that constitute the conditions and parameters of student voice. Not only do these historically specific associations and positions construct students in gendered, racial, and class-specific terms, but they also provide the basis for making the practices of subjectification problematic and the object of political and theoretical reflection.

A pedagogy of and for difference does not merely illuminate the welter of conflicting ideologies and social relations that operate within the public and private spheres of students' lives; it also attempts to have students engage their experiences through "political, theoretical, self analyzing practice by which the relations of the subject in social reality can be rearticulated from the historical experience of women [or from the historical experiences of blacks, Latinos, poor working-class males, etc.]."[35] This approach to the related issues of subjectivity and difference further suggests that the issues of language and experience need to become central categories in a theory of schooling as a form of cultural politics. It is to these issues that I will now turn.

By defining schools as sites of contestation and cultural production, it becomes possible to engage forms of self- and social representations, along with the practices and interests they articulate, as historically specific cultural practices that construct as well as block the exercise of human agency among students. This becomes clearer by recognizing that one of the most important elements at work in the construction of experience and subjectivity in schools is language. In this case, language intersects with power in the way particular linguistic forms structure and legitimate the ideologies of specific groups. Intimately related to power, language functions to both position and constitute the way that teachers and students define, mediate, and understand their relation to each other, school knowledge, the institution of schooling, and the larger society.[36] The notion that meaning is constituted in language is a crucial insight, but it is equally important to recognize that what is actually chosen as meaningful within a range of historically constituted meanings is what gives cultural and political substance to the pedagogical practice of agency and identity formation. Students make choices, not as autonomous, free-floating "subjects" in the manner argued by liberal humanism, but within a range of historically constituted conditions and discursive boundaries. However, it needs to be stressed that students are not merely positioned into discovering meanings; they also actively construct meaning by analyzing the "real practices and events" that constitute their everyday lives. The main point here is that although language constitutes meaning, it is not, as Linda Alcoff points out, "the sole source and locus of meaning, [and] that habits and practices are crucial to the construction of meaning, and that through self-analyzing practices we can rearticulate . . . [the] matrix of habits, practices, and discourses" that constitute our subjectivity.[37] In this case, language *and* practice provide the intersecting constructions that make the notion of 'choice' an element of lived experience that both constitutes the basis for theorizing a notion of subjectivity and simultaneously makes it the object of pedagogical inquiry. As part of a wider pedagogical task, this suggests making the notion of subjectivity not merely problematic but also the point of a political inquiry regarding how the particulars of human will, identity formation, investments of meaning, and desire are implicated and constructed regarding how people learn to consent, resist, negotiate, and live out their lives within a wide range of signifying practices and meanings.

As a form of cultural politics, a radical pedagogy must insist upon analyzing language as a central force in carrying the historical weight of already constituted meanings as well as a major force in the production of meanings that are constantly being generated as part of the discourse of opposition and affirmation. Discourse in this sense is not merely a meaning system over which one struggles, that is, not simply a system of signification whose real meanings need to be uncovered and demystified. Such an approach to language is important but insufficient for a radical pedagogy. Foucault illuminates a broader approach in his claim that "discourse in not simply that which expresses struggles or systems of domination, but that for which, and by which one struggles; it is the power which one is striving to seize."[38] In this sense, the relationship between language and power is not reduced solely to its oppressive, hegemonic functions. On the contrary, language is viewed more dialectically to include its productive, positive moments as part of the wider issue of voice, as a discourse that produces and confirms particular ways of life. This position represents one of the most important pedagogical tenets of a cultural politics: the necessity for teachers to work with the knowledge that students actually use to give meaning to the truth of their often difficult lives, to construct meaning out of their own narratives: in other words, knowledge that is often derived within the context of the intersection of mass and popular cultures, neighborhood life, family experiences, and the historical memories and contradictory narratives that define one's sense of identity and place.

With the above theoretical assumptions in mind, I want to argue in more specific terms for the development of curricula that embody a form of cultural politics. In effect, I want to present the case for constructing a pedagogy of cultural politics around a critically affirmative language that allows teachers to understand how subjectivities are produced within those social forms in which people move but which are often only partially understood. Such a pedagogy makes problematic how teachers and students sustain, resist, or accommodate those languages, ideologies, social processes, and myths that position them within existing relations of power and dependency. Moreover, it points to the need to develop a theory of politics and culture that analyzes discourse and voice as a continually shifting balance of resources and practices in the struggle for privileging specific ways of naming, organizing, and experiencing social reality. Discourse in this case can be recognized as a form of cultural production, linking "agency" and "structure" through the ways in which public and private representations are concretely organized and mediated within schools. Furthermore, discourse can be acknowledged as a diverse and fractured set of experiences that are lived, enjoyed, and suffered by individuals and groups within specific contexts and settings. In this perspective, the relationship between language and experience is governed by social practices and power relations operating within historically specific contexts. As Chris Weedon points out:

Experience is not something which language reflects. In so far as it is meaningful experience it is constituted in language. Language offers a range of ways of interpreting our lives which imply different versions of experience. In the process of interacting with the world, we give meaning to things by learning the linguistic processes of thought and speech, drawing on the ways of understanding the world to which we have access. Yet it is possible to transform the meaning of experience by bringing a different set of assumptions to bear on it . . . The recognition that experience is open to contradictory and conflicting interpretations puts into question the ideas that language is transparent and expresses already fixed meanings.[39]

In this view the concept of experience is linked to the broader issue of how subjectivities are inscribed and taken up within cultural processes and power relations that develop with regard to the social and cultural dynamics of production, transformation, and struggle. Understood in these terms, a pedagogy of cultural politics presents a twofold task for teachers. First, they need to analyze how cultural production is organized, within asymmetrical relations of power, through the knowledge, codes, competencies, values, and social relations that constitute the totality of schooling as a lived experience. Second, teachers need to construct political strategies for participating both in and out of schools in social struggles designed to fight for schools as democratic public spheres, that is, as places where students are educated to be active, critical citizens willing to struggle for the imperatives and principles of a meaningful and substantive democracy.

In order to make these tasks realizable, it is necessary to understand classroom social relations as historically constructed cultural forms that produce and legitimate particular experiences that should be the object of inquiry rather than merely the starting points for a theory of schooling. For example, teachers need to be able to examine critically how subjectivities are schooled and what the codes are that govern and give meaning to specific forms of moral and political regulation. But teachers need to do more than provide a critical reading of the cultural forms that structure classroom life; they also need to admit social relations and classroom practices in which needs and ideologies can be experienced and subjectively felt and that legitimate progressive values and democratic forms of sociality. In this case, knowledge, power, and desire provide central categories for understanding how experiences are constructed and reconstructed across social relations that embody varying forms of inequality, dependence, and resistance. As mentioned previously, I take as a starting point here a view of cultural politics that first confirms the lived experience and cultural capital of students so that the latter can then be analyzed more critically as part of a wider set of cultural processes. In this case, student experience has to first be understood and recognized as the accumulation of collective memories and stories that provide students with a sense of familiarity, identity, and practical knowledge. Furthermore, it is imperative to extend the possibilities of such cultural capital both by making it the object of critical inquiry and by appropriating in a similarly critical fashion the codes and knowledge that constitute broader and less familiar historical and cultural traditions. To empower students means more than simply affirming and analyzing the stories, histories, and experiences that are in place in their neighborhoods, that provide an organic connection to the web of relations that immediately shape their lives; it also means making them citizens of a much wider community. A critical pedagogy in this case addresses, affirms, and critically analyzes the experiences, histories, and categories of meaning that shape the immediate reality of students' lives, but it does not limit itself to these categories.

Radical pedagogy and the discourse of student experience

In order to develop a critical pedagogy as a form of cultural politics, it is imperative that modes of analysis be developed that do not assume that lived experiences can be inferred automatically from structural determinations: that is to say, the complexity of human behavior cannot be reduced to merely identifying the determinants, whether they be economic modes of production or systems of textual signification, in which such behavior is shaped and against which it constitutes itself. The way in which individuals and groups both mediate and inhabit the cultural forms presented by such structural forces is in itself a form of production and needs to be made problematic through related but different modes of analyses. In order to develop this point, I want to briefly present the nature and pedagogical implications of what I call the "discourse of student experience."

Central to this view is the need to develop an analysis of how teachers and students give meaning to their lives through the complex historical, cultural, and political forms they both embody and produce. This suggests the need for incorporating into a critical theory of schooling an analysis of those social practices that both organize systems of inequality and that assign meaning to individuals through the self- and social representations that define the dominant categories for ordering social life in any given society. Developing a theory of schooling as a form of cultural politics means analyzing how social power organizes the basic categories of class, race, gender, and ethnicity as a set of ideologies and practices that constitute specific configurations of power and politics. This points to the need for teachers to develop a deconstructive practice that uncovers rather than suppresses the complex histories, interests, and experiences that make up the diverse voices that construct student subject positions. This is not merely a discourse of pluralism; it is a discourse of irruption, one that pushes history against the grain by challenging those forces within existing configurations of power that sustain themselves by a spurious appeal to objectivity, science, truth, universality, and the suppression of difference. The discourse of student experience is not respectful of abstract, universal claims to the truth. On the contrary, it is a discourse premised on the assumption that

what has been presented in our social-political and our intellectual traditions as knowledge, truth, objectivity, and reason are actually merely the effects of a particular form of social power, the victory of a particular way of representing the world that then presents itself as beyond mere interpretation, as truth itself . . . [The discourse of experience] wants to challenge reason on its own ground and demonstrate that what gets called reason and knowledge is simply a particular way of organizing perception and communication, a way of organizing and categorizing experience that is social and contingent but whose socially constructed nature and contingency have been suppressed.[40]

The discourse of student experience supports a view of pedagogy and empowerment that allows students to draw upon their own experiences and cultural resources and that also enables them to play a self-consciously active role as producers of knowledge within the teaching and learning process. This is a pedagogy in which students get the knowledge and skills that allow them to ascertain how the multiple interests that constitute their individual and collective voices are implicated, produced, affirmed, or marginalized within the texts, institutional practices, and social structures that both shape and give meaning to their lives. Such a pedagogical practice would draw attention to the processes through which knowledge is produced within the ongoing relations in which teachers, students, and texts and knowledge interact. Within these relations teachers and students produce knowledge through their own particular readings of the codes that structure and give meaning to texts.

The type of pedagogy for which I am arguing is not concerned simply with creating classroom knowledge produced through individual oppositional readings of a text, but also with a recognition of the importance of understanding the various ways in which teachers and students produce different forms of knowledge through the complex patterns of exchange they have in their interactions with each other over what constitutes dialogue, meaning, and learning itself. In other words, pedagogy itself represents an act of production. For example, both teachers and students produce knowledge in their interaction with a text by attempting to understand and reproduce the codes and assumptions that inform an author's particular writing; knowledge is also produced in an interpretative practice that reads texts as part of a wider set of cultural and historical experiences and thus produces knowledge that goes beyond the said, stated, and obvious. Finally, any reading of a text can produce what Robert Scholes calls "a text against a text," that is, a reading which challenges and refuses the basic assumptions and codes that shape the values that shape the text.[41] Of course, all of these readings are not produced with equal levels of sophistication or skill, but I would argue that they do exist in various stages of development and operation, and although it is the task of a critical teacher to provide the skills unique to each form of reading, students generally exhibit these skills in rudimentary form in their interactions with teachers and school knowledge. Viewed as an act of production, pedagogy can also be better understood as a historical construction related to economic, social, and political practices as they are produced within particular sets of social relations. David Lusted is very helpful on this issue.

It enables us . . . to ask under what conditions and through what means we 'come to know'. How one teaches is therefore of central interest but, through the prism of pedagogy, it becomes inseparable from what is being taught and, crucially, how one learns . . . What pedagogy addresses is the process of production and exchange in this cycle, the transformation of consciousness that takes place in the interaction of three agencies–the teacher, the learner, and the knowledge they produce together."[42]

Within this perspective, pedagogy is about how teachers and students operate within historically defined contexts to produce particular notions of high-status knowledge, specific views of authority, and selected representations of self- and collective identity. Pedagogy in this sense is both a cultural and political practice. As Roger Simon and I have stated elsewhere, "Pedagogy is simultanously about the practices that students and teachers might engage in together and the cultural politics such practices support. It is in this sense that to propose a pedagogy is to construct a political vision."[43]

A pedagogy of student experience must also be linked to the notion of learning for empowerment: that is, curriculum practices must be developed that draw upon student experience as both a narrative for agency and a referent for critique. This suggests curriculum policies and modes of pedagogy that both confirm and critically engage the knowledge and experience through which students authorize their own voices and social identities. In effect, it suggests taking seriously, as an aspect of learning, the knowledge and experiences that constitute the individual and collective voices by which students identify and give meaning to themselves and others. It is crucial to reemphasize that such a pedagogy is not meant to imply that student experience should be romantically celebrated; on the contrary, as I have mentioned previously, it means developing a critically affirmative language that works both with and on the experiences that students bring to the classroom. Although this approach valorizes the language forms, modes of reasoning, dispositions, and histories that students use in defining themselves and their relation to the larger society, it also subjects such experiences and ideologies to the discourse of suspicion and skepticism, to forms of analysis that attempt to understand how they are structured by cultural and symbolic codes inscribed within particular configurations of history and power. Similarly, this means teaching students how to identify, unravel, and critically appropriate the codes, vocabularies, and deep grammar of different cultural, social, historical, and collective traditions. The pedagogical goal here is not to have students exercise rigorous analytical skills in order to arrive at the right answer, but to better exercise reasoned choice through a critical understanding of what the codes are that organize different meanings and interests into particular configurations of knowledge and power.

At issue here is the development of a pedagogy that provides the foundation for developing curriculum models that replace the authoritative language of recitation and imposition with an approach that allows students to speak from their own histories and voices while simultaneously challenging the very grounds on which knowledge and power are constructed and legitimated. Such a pedagogy makes possible a variety of human capacities which expand the range of social identities that students may become.[44] Such a pedagogy articulates not only a respect for a diversity of student voices; it also provides a fundamental referent for legitimizing the principle of democratic tolerance as an essential condition for forms of solidarity rooted in the virtues of trust, sharing, and a commitment to improving the quality of human life. Schools need to incorporate the diverse and contradictory stories that construct the interplay of experience, identity, and possibility that students bring to the classroom. For too many students, schools are places of "dead time," that is, holding centers that have little or nothing to do with either their lives or their dreams. Reversing that experience for students must be a central issue in reconstructing a theory of schooling as a form of cultural politics.

In more general terms, the language of student experience not only repesents an acknowledgement of the political and pedagogical processes at work in the construction of forms of authorship and voice within the process of schooling, but it also constitutes a critical attack on the horizontal ordering of reality inherent in the unjust practices that are actively at work in the wider society. To redress some of the problems which I have sketched out in the preceding pages, I believe that schools need to be reconstructed around a cultural politics and pedagogy that demonstrate a strong commitment to engaging the views and problems that deeply concern students in their everyday lives. Equally important is the need for schools to cultivate a spirit of critique and a respect for human dignity that is capable of linking personal and social issues to the pedagogical project of helping students to become critical and active citizens.

In conclusion, I have attempted in this essay to construct a radical pedagogy within forms of cultural analyses that point to the importance of combining the language of critique with the language of possibility around a set of categories that provide some important starting points for developing a programmatic discourse for radical educators. My underlying project has been to explore how the categories of authority, transformative intellectuals, language, and voice contribute to a politics of practical learning and to move beyond the anti-utopianism that is characteristic of so much of the current writing on radical pedagogy. A cultural politics has to be organized around a learned hope, a pedagogy forged amidst the realization of risks, struggles, and possibilities. At risk is not only the future of our children, but the very fate of democracy itself.

Silencing and Nurturing Voice in an Improbable Context: Urban Adolescents in Public School

Michelle Fine

> *October 1986 national conference on education*: Phyllis
> Schafly demands that elementary, junior, and senior
> high school courses on child abuse and incest be
> banned as "terrorizing tactics against children."
>
> *Later that same month*: Judge Thomas Gray Hull of the
> Federal District Court in Greeneville, Tennessee,
> upholds Fundamentalist parents' right to remove their
> children from public school classes in which offending
> books, including *The Wizard of Oz* and *Diary of a
> Young Girl*, are taught.

One might wish to imagine that demands for silencing in public schools resonate exclusively from the conservative New Right. In this article I will argue that Schafly and these Fundamentalist parents merely caricature what is standard educational practice—the silencing of student and community voices.

Silencing signifies a terror of words, a fear of talk. This essay examines such practices as they echoed throughout a comprehensive public high school in New York City, in words and in their absence; these practices emanated from the New York City Board of Education, textbook publishers, corporate "benefactors," religious institutions, administrators, teach-

152

ers, parents, and even students themselves. The essay explores what doesn't get talked about in schools: how "undesirable talk" by students, teachers, parents, and community members is subverted, appropriated, and exported, and how educational policies and procedures obscure the very social, economic, and therefore experiential conditions of students' daily lives while they expel critical "talk" about these conditions from written, oral, and nonverbal expression.

In the odd study of *what's not said* in school, it is crucial to analyze (1) whom silencing protects; (2) the practices by which silencing is institutionalized in contexts of asymmetric power relations; (3) how muting students and their communities systematically undermines a project of educational empowerment (Freire, 1985; Giroux, 1983; Schor, 1980); and (4) how understanding the practices of silencing can make possible a public education which gives voice to students and their communities.

Why silencing in urban public schools? If we believe that city schools are public spheres which promise mobility, equal opportunity, and a forum for participatory democracy (Giroux and McLaren, 1986), indeed one of few such sites instituted on the grounds of equal access (Carnoy and Levin, 1985); if we recognize the extent to which these institutions nonetheless participate in the very reproduction of class, race, and gender inequities; and if we appreciate that educators working within these schools share a commitment to the former and suffer a disillusionment by the latter, then it can be assumed that the practices of silencing in public schools do the following:

1. Preserve the ideology of equal opportunity and access while obscuring the unequal distribution of resources and outcomes
2. Create within a system of severe asymmetric power relations the impression of democracy and collaboration among "peers" (e.g., between white, middle-income school administrators and low-income black and Hispanic parents or guardians)
3. Quiet student voices of difference and dissent so that such voices, when they burst forth, are rendered deviant and dangerous
4. Remove from public discourse the tensions between: (a) *promises* of mobility and the material *realities* of students' lives; (b) explicit claims to democracy and implicit reinforcement of power asymme ries; (c) schools as an ostensibly *public* sphere and the pollution wrought on them by *private* interests; and (d) the dominant language of equal educational opportunity versus the undeniable evidence of failure as a majority experience for low-income adolescents

Silencing removes any documentation that all is not well with the workings of the U. S. economy, race and gender relations, and public schooling as the route to class mobility. Let us take a single piece of empirical data provided by the U. S. Department of Labor to understand why urban schools might be motivated to silence.

In 1983 the U. S. Department of Labor published evidence that a high school diploma brings with it quite discrepant opportunities based on one's social class, race, and gender, and further, that the absence of such a diploma ensures quite disparate costs based on the same demographics. Although public rhetoric has assured that dropping out of high school promotes unemployment, poverty, and dependence on crime or welfare, the national data present a story far more complex. Indeed, only 15 percent of white male dropouts (age twenty-two to thirty-four) live below the poverty line, compared with 28 percent of white females, 37 percent of black males, and 62 percent of black females (U. S. Department of Labor, 1983). Further, in a city like New York, dropouts from the wealthiest neighborhoods are more likely to be employed than high school graduates from the poorest neighborhoods (Tobier, 1984). Although having a degree corresponds to employment and poverty levels, this relationship is severely mediated by race, class, and gender stratification.

In the face of these social realities, principals and teachers nevertheless continue to preach, without qualification, to black and Hispanic students and parents a rhetoric of equal opportunity and outcomes, the predictive guarantees of a high school diploma, and the invariant economic penalties of dropping out. Although I am no advocate of dropping out of high school, it is clear that silencing, which constitutes the practices by which contradictory evidence, ideologies, and experiences find themselves buried, camouflaged, and discredited, oppresses and insults adolescents and their kin who already "know better."

The press for silencing disproportionately characterizes low-income, minority urban schooling. In these schools, the centralization of the public school administration diminishes community involvement; texts are dated (often ten to fifteen years old) and alienating, in omission and commission; curricula and pedagogies are disempowering, often for students and teachers; strategies for discipline more often than not result in extensive suspension and expulsion rates; and calls for parental involvement often invite bake sale ladies and expel "troublemakers" or advocates. These practices constitute the very means by which schools silence. Self-proclaimed as fortresses against students' communities, city schools offer themselves as "the only way out of Harlem" rather than in partnership with the people, voices, and resources of that community.

Silencing more intimately shapes low-income, public schools than relatively privileged ones. In such contexts there is more to hide and control, and indeed a greater discrepancy between pronounced ideologies and lived experiences. Further, the luxury of examining the contradictory evidence of social mobility may only be available to those who continue to benefit from existing social arrangements, not those who daily pay the price of social stratification. The dangers inherent in questioning from "above" are minor relative to the dangers presumed inherent in questioning from "below." In low-income schools then, the process of inquiring into students' lived experience is assumed, a priori, unsafe territory for teachers and administrators. Silencing permeates classroom life so primitively as to render irrelevant the lived experiences, passions, concerns, communities, and biographies of low-income, minority students. In the process the very voices of these students and their communities, which public education claims to enrich, shut down.

This essay focuses on silencing primarily at the level of classroom and school talk in a low-income, "low-skill" school. Surely there are corporate, governmental, military, and bureaucratic mandates from which demands for silencing derive. But in the present analysis, these structural demands are assumed, not analyzed. Located primarily within classrooms and with individual teachers, this analysis does not aim to place blame on teachers, but only to retrieve from these interactions the raw material for a critical examination of silencing. The data derive from a yearlong ethnography of a high school in Manhattan, attended by 3,200 students, predominantly low-income blacks and Hispanics from Central Harlem and run primarily by black paraprofessionals and aides, white administrators and teachers, and some Hispanic paraprofessionals and teachers (see Fine, 1985, 1986).

An analysis of silencing seems important for two reasons. First, substantial evidence has been accumulated which suggests that many students in this school, considered low in skill, income, and motivation, were quite eager to choreograph their own learning, to generate a curriculum of lived experience, and to engage in a participatory pedagogy (Rosen, 1986). Every effort by teachers and administrators which undermined such educational autobiographizing violated one opportunity, and probably preempted others, to create dialogue and community–that is, to educate–with students, their kin, and their neighborhoods (Bastian et al., 1985; Connell et al., 1982; Lightfoot, 1978). Those administrators, teachers, and paraprofessionals who were sufficiently interested and patient did generate classrooms of relatively "alive" participants. More overwhelming to the observer, however, was the silencing that engulfed life inside most classrooms and administrative offices.

Second, this loss of connection has most significant consequences for low-income, minority students. These adolescents are fundamentally ambivalent about the educational process and appropriately cynical about the "guarantees" of an educational credential (Carnoy and Levin, 1985). The linear correspondence of years of education to income does not conform to their reflections on community life. Most were confident that "you can't get nowhere without a diploma." But most were also mindful that "the richest man in my neighborhood didn't graduate but from eighth grade." And in their lives, both "truths" are defensible. It is precisely by camouflaging such contradictions that educators advance adolescents' cynicism about schooling and credentials, thereby eroding any beliefs in social mobility, community organizing, or the pleasures of intellectual enlightenment.

The silencing process is but one aspect of what is often, for low-income students, an impoverished educational tradition. Infiltrating administrative "talk," curriculum development, and pedagogical technique, the means of silencing establish impenetrable barriers between the worlds of school and community life. To unearth the possibility of reclaiming students', teachers', and communities' voices, the practices of silencing must be unpacked.

The impulse to silence as it shaped educational research

> Lying is done with words and also with silence.
> —Adrienne Rich, *On Lies, Secrets and Silence*

In June of 1984 I began to lay the groundwork for what I hoped would be an ethnography of a public high school in New York City, to being the fall of 1984 (see Fine, 1985, 1986).[1] To my request for entry to his school, the principal greeted me as follows:

Field Note: June 1984

MR. STEIN: Sure you can do your research on dropouts at this school. With one provision. You cannot mention the words *dropping out* to the students.
MF: Why not?
STEIN: If you say it, you encourage them to do it.

Even the research began with a warning to silence me, and the imaginations of these adolescents. My field notes continue: "When he said this, I thought, adults should be so lucky, that adolescents wait for us to name the words *dropping out*, or *sex*, for them to do it." From September through June, witnessing daily life inside the classrooms, deans' and nurses' offices, the attendance room and the lunchroom, I was repeatedly bewildered that this principal actually believed that adult talk could compel adolescent compliance.

The year progressed. Field notes mounted. What became apparent was a systemic fear of *naming*. Naming involves those practices which facilitate critical conversation about social and economic arrangements, particularly about inequitable distributions of power and resources by which these students and their kin suffer disproportionately. The practices of administration, the relationships between school and community, and the forms of pedagogy and curriculum applied were all scarred by the fear of naming, provoking the move to silence.

The white noise created by administrative silencing

Field Note: September 1984

We are proud to say that 80 percent of our high school graduates go on to college.
— Principal, Parents' Association meeting,
September 1984

At the first Parents' Association meeting, Mr. Stein, the principal, boasted an 80 percent "college-bound" rate. Almost all graduates of this inner-city high school head for college: a comforting claim oft repeated by urban school administrators in the 1980s. Although accurate, this pronouncement masked the fact that in this school, as in other comprehensive city high schools, only 20 percent of incoming ninth-graders *ever* graduate. In other words, only 16 percent of the 1,220 ninth-graders of 1978–1979 were headed for college by 1985. The "white noise" of the administration reverberated silence in the audience. Not named, and therefore not problematized, was the substantial issue of low retention rates.

Not naming is an administrative craft. The New York City Board of Education, for example, has refused to monitor retention, promotion, and educational achievement statistics by race and ethnicity for fear of "appearing racist" (personal communication, 1984).[2] Huge discrepancies in educational advancement, by race and ethnicity, thereby remain undocumented in board publications. Likewise, dropout estimates include students on the register when they have not been seen for months; they also presume that students who enroll in GED programs are not dropouts, and that those who produce "working papers" are actually about to embark on careers (which involves a letter, for example, from a Chicken Delight clerk assuring that Jose has a job so that he can leave school at sixteen.) Such procedures contribute to *not naming* the density of the dropout problem.

Although administrative silencing is unfortunately almost a redundancy, the concerns of this essay are primarily focused on classroom- and school-based activities of silencing. By no means universal, the fear of naming was nevertheless commonplace, applied at this school by conservative and liberal educators alike. Conservative administrators and teachers viewed most of their students as unteachable. It was believed, following the logic of social studies teacher Mr. Rosaldo, that "If we save 20 percent, that's a miracle. Most of these kids don't have a chance." For these educators, naming social and economic inequities in their classrooms would only expose circumstances they believed to be self-imposed. Perhaps these teachers themselves had been silenced over time. It is worth noting that correlational evidence (Fine, 1983) suggests that educators who feel most disempowered in their institutions are most likely to believe that "these kids can't be helped" and that those who feel relatively empowered are likely to believe that they "can make a difference in the lives of these youths."

Disempowered and alienated themselves, such educators see an enormous and inherent distance between "them" and "us," a distance, whether assumed biologic or social, which could not be bridged by the mechanics of public schooling. So when I presented "dropout data" to these faculty members, and suggested that the level of involuntary "discharges" processed through this school would never be tolerated in the schools attended by their children, I was rapidly chastised: "That's an absurd comparison. The schools my kids go to are nothing like this – the comparison is sensationalist!" The social distance between them and us are reified and naturalized. Naming would only be inciting.

The more liberal position of other educators, for whom not naming was also routine, involved their loyalty to belief in a color- and class-neutral meritocracy. These educators dismissed the very empirical data which would have informed the naming process. Here they followed the logic of science teacher Ms. Tannenbaum: "If these students work hard, they can really become something. Especially today with Affirmative Action." They rejected counterevidence: for example, that black high school graduates living in Harlem are still far less likely to be employed than white high school dropouts living in more elite sections of New York (Tobier, 1984), for fear that such data would "discourage students from hard work and dreams." Enormous energy must be required to sustain beliefs in equal opportunity and the color-blind power of credentials, and to silence nagging losses of faith when evidence to the contrary compels on a daily basis. Naming in such a case would only unmask realities, fundamentally disrupting or contradicting educators' and presumably students' belief systems.

Still other educators actively engaged their students in lively, critical discourse about the complexities and inequities of prevailing economic and social relations. Often importing politics from other spheres of their lives, the feminist English teacher, the community activist who taught grammar, or the Marxist historian wove critical analysis into their class-rooms, with little effort. These offices and classrooms were permeated with the openness of naming, free of the musty tension which derives from conversations-not-had.

Most educators at this school, however, seemed to survive by not nam-ing or analyzing social problems. They administered and taught in ways that established the school as a fortress for mobility *out* of the students' communities. They taught with curricular and pedagogical techniques they hoped would sooth students, and smooth social contradictions. Many would probably have not considered conversation about social class, gen-der, or race politics relevant to their courses, or easily integrated into their curricula. Some would argue that inclusion of these topics would be "po-litical"–whereas exclusion was not. One could have assumed that they be-nignly neglected these topics.

But evidence of educators' *fear*, rather than *neglect*, grew apparent when students (activated by curiosity and rebellion) initiated conversations of cri-tique which were rapidly dismissed. A systemic expulsion of dangerous topics permeated these classrooms. For educators to examine the very con-ditions which contribute to social class, racial, ethnic, and gender stratifica-tion in the United States, when they are relatively privileged by class usually and race often, seemed to introduce fantasies of danger, a pedagogy which would threaten, rather than protect, teacher control. Such conversations would *problematize* what seem like "natural" social distinctions, potentially eroding teachers' authority. If not by conscious choice, then, some teachers and administrators actively engaged in pedagogical strategies which pre-empted, detoured, or ghettoized such conversations. *Not naming*, as a par-ticular form of silencing, was accomplished creatively. Often with good in-tentions, the practice bore devastating consequences.

Naming indeed subverts or complicates those beliefs which public schools aim to promote. It is for this very reason essential that naming be inherent in the educational process, in the creation of an empowered and critical constituency of citizens (Aronowitz and Giroux, 1985). It was ironic to note that pedagogic and curricular attempts to not name or to actively avoid such conversation indeed cost teachers control over their classrooms. Efforts to shut down such conversations were usually followed by the counting of money by males, the application of mascara or lipstick by females, and the laying down of heads on desks by students of both genders: the loss of control over the classroom.

To *not name* bears consequences for all students, but most dramatically for low-income, minority youths. To not name systematically alienates, cuts off from home, from heritage, and from lived experience and ultimately severs these students from their educational process. The pedagogical and curricular strategies employed in *not naming* are examined critically below.

Pedagogical and curricular muting of students' voices

Constructing taboo voices: Conversations never had

A mechanistic view of teachers terrorized by naming, and students passively accommodating, could not be further from the daily realities of life inside a public high school. Many teachers name and critique, although most don't. Some students passively shut down, although most remain alive and even resistant. Classrooms are filled with students wearing walkmen, conversing among themselves and with friends in the halls, and some even persistently challenging the experiences and expertise of their teachers. But the typical classroom still values silence, control, and quiet, as John Goodlad (1984), Theodore Sizer (1985), Jean Anyon (1983), and others have documented. The insidious push toward silence in low-income schools became most clear sometime after my interview with Eartha, a sixteen-year-old high school dropout.

Field Note: January 14

> MF: Eartha, when you were a kid, did you participate a lot in school?
> EARTHA: Not me, I was a good kid. Made no trouble.

I asked this question of fifty-five high school dropouts. After the third responded as Eartha did, I realized that for me, participation was encouraged, delighted in, and a measure of the "good student." Yet for these adolescents, given their histories of schooling, participation meant poor discipline and rude classroom behavior.

Students learn the dangers of talk, the codes of participating and not, and they learn, in more nuanced ways, which conversations are never to be had. In Philadelphia, a young high school student explained to me: "We are not allowed to talk about abortion. They tell us we can't discuss it no way." When I asked a School District Administrator about this policy, she qualified: "It's not that they can't *talk* about it. If the topic is raised by a student, the teacher can define abortion, just not discuss it beyond that." The distinction between defining and discussing makes sense only if learning assumes teacher authority, if pedagogy requires single truths and if classroom control implies silence. Perhaps this is why classroom control often feels so fragile. Control through omission *is* fragile. Fully contingent on students' willingness to collude, such "control" betrays a plea for student compliance.

Silencing in public schools comes in many forms. Conversations can be closed by teachers, or forestalled by student collusion. But other conversations are expressly withheld, never had. Such a policy of enforced silencing was applied to information about the severe economic and social consequences of dropping out of high school. This information was systematically withheld from students who were being discharged. Few, as a consequence, ever entertained second thoughts.

When students are discharged in New York State, they are guaranteed an exit interview, which, in most cases, involved an attendance officer who asked students what they planned to do, and then requested a meeting with the parent or guardian to sign official documents. The officer handed the student a list of GED and outreach programs. The student left, often eager to find work, get a GED, go to a private business school, or join the military. Informed conversations about the consequences of the students' "decision" were not legally mandated. As they left, these adolescents *did not learn* the following:

• Over 50 percent of black high school dropouts suffer unemployment in cities like New York City (U. S. Commission on Civil Rights, 1982).
• Forty-eight percent of New Yorkers who sit for the Graduate Equivalency Diploma test fail (New York State Department of Education, 1985).
• Private trade schools, including cosmetology, beautician, and business schools, have been charged with unethical recruitment practices, exploitation of students, earning more from students who drop out than those who stay, not providing promised jobs, and having, on average, a 70 percent dropout rate (see Fine, 1986).
• The military, during "peacetime," refuses to accept females with no high school degree, and only reluctantly accepts males, who suffer an extreme less-than-honorable discharge rate within six months of enlistment (Militarism Resource Project, 1985).

Students who left high school prior to graduation were thereby denied informed consent. Conversations-not-had nurtured powerful folk beliefs among adolescents: that "the GED is no sweat, a piece of cake"; that "you can get jobs, they promise, after goin' to Sutton or ABI"; or that "in the Army I can get me a GED, skills, travel, benefits." Such is a powerful form of silencing.

Closing down conversations

Field Note: October 17, Business Class

> WHITE TEACHER: What's EOE?
> BLACK MALE STUDENT: Equal over time.
> WHITE TEACHER: Not quite. Anyone else?

BLACK FEMALE STUDENT: Equal Opportunity Employer.
TEACHER: That's right.
BLACK MALE STUDENT (2): What does that mean?
TEACHER: That means that an employer can't discriminate on the basis of sex, age, marital status or race.
BLACK MALE STUDENT (2): But wait, sometimes white people only hire white people.
TEACHER: No, they're not supposed to if they say EOE in their ads. Now take out your homework.

Later that day:

MF (to teacher): Why don't you discuss racism in your class?
TEACHER: It would demoralize the students, they need to feel positive and optimistic—like they have a chance. Racism is just an excuse they use to not try harder.

What enables some teachers to act as if students benefit from such smoothing over (Wexler, 1983)? For whose good are the roots, the scars, and the structures of class, race, and gender inequity obscured by teachers, texts, and tests (Anyon, 1983)? Are not the "fears of demoralizing" a projection by teachers of their own silenced loss of faith in public education, and their own fears of unmasking or freeing a conversation about social inequities?

At the level of curriculum, texts, and conversation in classrooms, school talk and knowledge were radically severed from the daily realities of adolescents' lives and more systematically aligned with the lives of teachers (McNeil, 1981). Routinely discouraged from critically examining the conditions of their lives, dissuaded from creating their own curriculum, built of what they know, students were often encouraged to disparage the circumstances in which they live, warned by their teachers: "You act like that, and you'll end up on welfare!" (Most were or had been surviving on some form of federal, state, or city assistance.)

"Good students" therefore managed these dual/duel worlds by learning to speak standard English dialect, whether they originally spoke Black English, Spanish, or Creole. More poignant still, they trained themselves to produce two voices. One's "own" voice alternated with an "academic" voice. The latter denied class, gender, and race conflict; repeated the words of hard work, success, and their "natural" sequence; and stifled any desire to disrupt.

In a study conducted in 1981, it was found that the group of South Bronx students who were "successes"—those who remained in high school—when compared with dropouts, were significantly MORE depressed, LESS politically aware, LESS likely to be assertive in the classroom if they were undergraded, and MORE conformist (Fine, 1983). A moderate level of depression, an absence of political awareness, a persistence of self-blame, low assertiveness, and high conformity may tragically have constituted the "good" urban student at this high school. They learned not to raise, and indeed to help shut down, "dangerous" conversation. The price of "success" may have been muting one's own voice.

Other students from the school in Manhattan resolved the "two voices" tension with creative, if ultimately self-defeating, strategies. Cheray reflected on the hegemonic academic voice after she dropped out: "In school we learned Columbus Avenue stuff and I had to translate it into Harlem. They think livin' up here is unsafe and our lives are so bad. That we should want to move out and get away. That's what you're supposed to learn."[3] Tony thoroughly challenged the academic voice as ineffective pedagogy: "I never got math when I was in school. Then I started sellin' dope and runnin' numbers and I picked it up right away. They should teach the way it matters." Alicia accepted the academic voice as the standard, while disparaging with faint praise her own voice: "I'm *wise*, but not *smart*. There's a difference. I can walk into a room and I know what people be thinkin' and what's goin' down. But not what he be talkin' about in history."

Finally, many saw the academic voice as the exclusively legitimate, if inaccessible, mode of social discourse. Monique, after two months out of school, admitted: "I'm scared to go out lookin' for a job. They be usin' words in the interview like in school. Words I don't know. I can't be askin' them for a dictionary. It's like in school. You ask and you feel like a dummy."

By segregating the academic voice from students' own voice, public schools do not only linguistic violence (Zorn, 1982). The intellectual, social, and emotional substance which constitutes minority students' lives in this school was routinely treated as irrelevant, to be displaced and silenced. Their responses, spanning acquiescence to resistance, bore serious consequences.

Contradictions folded: Excluding "redundant" voices

If "lived talk" was actively expelled on the basis of content, contradictory talk was basically rendered impossible. Social contradictions were folded into dichotomous choices. What does this obscure, and whom does this accommodate? The creation of such dichotomies and the reification of single truths may bolster educators' authority, reinforcing the distance between those who *know* and those who *don't*, discrediting often those who *think* in complexity (McNeil, 1981).

To illustrate: In early Spring, a social studies teacher structured an in-class debate on Bernard Goetz—New York City's "subway vigilante." She invited "those students who agree with Goetz to sit on one side of the room, and those who think he was wrong to sit on the other side." To the large residual group who remained midroom the teacher remarked, "Don't be lazy. You have to make a decision. Like at work, you can't be passive." A few wandered over to the "pro-Goetz" side. About six remained in the center. Somewhat angry, the teacher continued: "OK, first we'll hear the pro-Goetz side and then the anti-Goetz side. Those of you who have no opinions, who haven't even thought about the issue, you won't get to talk unless we have time."

Deidre, a black senior, bright and always quick to raise contradictions otherwise obscured, advocated the legitimacy of the middle group. "It's not that I have no opinions. I don't like Goetz shootin' up people who look like my brother, but I don't like feelin' unsafe in the projects or in my neighborhood either. I got lots of opinions. I ain't bein' quiet cause I can't decide if he's right or wrong. I'm talkin'." Deidre's comment legitimized for herself and others the right to hold complex, perhaps even contradictory positions on a complex situation. Such legitimacy was rarely granted by faculty—with clear and important exceptions, including activist faculty and those paraprofessionals who lived in Central Harlem with the kids, who understood and respected much about their lives.

Among the chorus of voices heard within this high school, then, lay little room for Gramsci's (1971) contradictory consciousness. Artificial di-chotomies were delivered as natural: right and wrong answers, appropriate and inappropriate behavior, moral and immoral people, dumb and smart students, responsible and irresponsible parents, good and bad neighbor-hoods. Contradiction and ambivalence, forced underground, were experi-enced often, if expressed rarely.

I asked Ronald, a student in remedial reading class, why he stayed in school. He responded with sophistication and complexity: "Reason I stay in school is 'cause every time I get on the subway I see this drunk and I think 'not me.' But then I think 'bet he has a high school degree.'" The power of his statement lies in its honesty, as well as the infrequency with which such comments were voiced. Ronald explained that he expected sup-port for this position neither in school nor on the street. School talk prom-ised what few believed, but many repeated: that hard work and education breed success and a guarantee against welfare. Street talk belied another real-ity, described by Shondra: "They be sayin', 'What you doin' in school? Could be out here scramblin' [selling drugs] and makin' money now. That de-gree ain't gonna get you nothing better.'"

When black adolescent high school graduates, in the October following graduation, suffered a 56 percent unemployment rate and black adolescent high school dropouts suffered a 70 percent unemployment rate, the very contradictions which were amplified in the minds and worries of these young men and women remained unspoken within school (Young, 1983).

Conversations psychologized: Splitting the personal and the social voice

Some conversations within schools were closed; others were dichotomized. Yet a few conversations, indeed those most relevant to inequitable social arrangements, remained psychologized: managed as personal problems inside the offices of school psychologists or counselors. The lived experiences of *all* adolescents, and particularly those surviving city life in poverty, place their physical and mental well-being as well as that of their kin in constant jeopardy. And yet conversations about these very conditions of life, about alcoholism, drug abuse, domestic violence, environmental hazards, gentrification, and poor health – to the extent that they happened at all – remained confined to individual sessions with counselors (for those lucky enough to gain hearing with a counselor in the 800:1 ratio, and gutsy enough to raise the issue) or, if made academic, were raised in hygiene class (for those fortunate enough to have made it to twelfth grade, when hygiene was offered). A biology teacher, one of the few black teachers in the school, actually integrated creative writing assignments such as "My life as an alcoholic" and "My life as a child of an alcoholic" into her biology class curriculum. Her department chairman reprimanded her severely for introducing "extraneous materials." Teachers too were silenced.

The marginalizing of the health and social problems experienced by these adolescents exemplified the systematic unwillingness to address these concerns academically, in social studies, science, English, or even math. A harsh resistance to name the lived experiences of these teens paralleled the unwillingness to integrate these experiences as the substance of learning. Issues to be avoided at all costs, they were addressed psychologically, individually, and in isolation, and even then only after they pierced the life of the adolescent seeking help.

The offices of school psychologists or counselors therefore became the primary sites for addressing what were indeed social concerns, should have been academic concerns, and were most likely to be managed as personal and private concerns. The privatizing and psychologizing of public and political issues served to reinforce the alienation of students' lives from their educational experience.

Democracy and discipline: Maintaining silence by appropriating and exporting dissent

The means of maintaining silences and ensuring no dangerous disruptions know few bounds. If silence masks asymmetric power relations, it also ensures the impression of democracy for parents and students by appropriating and exporting dissent. This strategy has gained popularity in the fashionable times of "empowerment."

At this school the Parents' Association executive board was composed of ten parents: eight black women, one black man, and one white woman. Eight no longer had children attending the school. At about midyear teachers were demanding smaller class size. So too was the president of the Parents' Association at this executive meeting with the principal.

PRESIDENT: I'm concerned about class size. Carol Bellamy (City Council President) notified us that you received monies earmarked to reduce class size and yet what have you done?

MR. STEIN: Quinones (Schools Chancellor) promised no high school class greater than 34 by Feb. That's impossible! What he is asking I can't guarantee unless, *you* tell me what to do. If I reduce class size, I must eliminate all specialized classes, all electives. Even then I can't guarantee. To accede to Quinones, that classes be less than 34, we must eliminate the elective in English, in Social Studies, all art classes, 11th-year Math, Physics, accounting, word processing. We were going to offer a Haitian Patois Bilingual program, fourth-year French, a Museums program, Bio-Pre-Med, Health Careers, Coop and Pre-Coop, Choreography and Advanced Ballet. The nature of the school will be changed fundamentally.

We won't be able to call this an academic high school, only a program for slow learners.

WOMAN (1): Those are very important classes.

STEIN: I am willing to keep these classes. Parents want me to keep these classes. That's where I'm at.

WOMAN (2): What is the average?

STEIN: 33.

WOMAN (1): Are any classes over 40?

STEIN: No, except if it's a *Singleton* class—the only one offered. If these courses weren't important, we wouldn't keep them. You know we always work together. If it's your feeling we should not eliminate all electives, and maintain things. OK! Any comments?

WOMAN (1): I think continue. Youngsters aren't getting enough now. And the teachers will not any more.

WOMAN (3): You have our unanimous consent and support.

STEIN: When I talk to the Board of Education, I'll say I'm talking for the parents.

WOMAN (4): I think it's impossible to teach 40.
STEIN: We have a space problem. Any other issues?

An equally conciliatory student council was constituted to decide on student activities, prom arrangements, and student fees. They were largely pleased to meet in the principal's office. At the level of critique, silence was guaranteed by the selection and then the invited "democratic participation" of these parents and students.

If dissent was appropriated through mechanisms of democracy, it was exported through mechanisms of discipline. The most effective procedure for silencing was to banish the source of dissent, tallied in the school's dropout rate. As indicated by the South Bronx study referred to above (Fine, 1983) and the research of others (Elliott, Voss, and Wendling, 1966; Felice, 1981; Fine and Rosenberg, 1983), it is often the academic critic resisting the intellectual and verbal girdles of schooling who "drops out" or is pushed out of low-income schools. Extraordinary rates of suspensions, expulsions, and discharges experienced by black and Hispanic youths speak to this form of silencing (Advocates for Children, 1985). Estimates of urban dropout rates range from approximately 42 percent from New York City, Boston, and Chicago boards of education to 68 to 80 percent from Aspira, an educational advocacy organization (1983).

At the school which served as the site for this ethnographic research, a 66 percent dropout rate was calculated. Two-thirds of the students who began ninth grade in 1978–1979 did not receive diplomas or degrees by June 1985. I presented these findings to a collection of deans, advisors, counselors, administrators, and teachers, many of whom were the sponsors and executors of the discharge process. At first I met with total silence. A dean then explained, "These kids need to be out. It's unfair to the rest. My job is like a pilot on a hijacked plane. My job is to throw the hijacker overboard." The one black woman in the room, a guidance counselor, followed: "What Michelle is saying is true. We do throw students out of here and deny them their education. Black kids especially." Two white male administrators interrupted, chiding what they called the "liberal tendencies" of guidance counselors, who "don't see how really dangerous these kids are." The meeting ended.

Dissent was institutionally "democraticized," exported, trivialized, or bureaucratized. These mechanisms made it unlikely for change or challenge to be given a serious hearing.

Whispers of resistance: The silenced speak

In low-income public high schools organized around control through silence, the student, parent, teacher, or paraprofessional who talks, tells, or who wants to speak transforms rapidly into the subversive, the trouble-maker. Students, unless they spoke in an honors class or affected the academic mode of introducing nondangerous topics and benign words, if not protected by wealth, influential parents, or an unusual capacity to be critics *and* good students, emerged as provocateurs. Depending on school, circumstances, and style, students' response to such silencing varied. Maria buried herself in mute isolation. Steven organized students against many of his teachers. Most of these youths, for complex reasons, ultimately fled prior to graduation. Some then sought "alternative contexts" in which their strengths, competencies, and voices could flourish on their own terms:

Hector's a subway graffiti artist: "It's like an experience you never get. You're on the subway tracks. It's 3 a.m., dark, cold and scary. You're trying to create your best. The cops can come to bust you, or you could fall on the electric third rail. My friend died when he dropped his spray paint on that rail. It exploded. He died and I watched. It's awesome, intense. A peak moment when you can't concentrate on nothin', no problems, just creation. And it's like a family. When Michael Stewart [graffiti artist] was killed by cops, you know he was a graffiti man, we all came out of retirement to mourn him. Even me, I stopped 'cause my girl said it was dangerous. We came out and painted funeral scenes and cemeteries on the LL #1 and the N [subway lines]. For Michael. We know each other, you know an artist when you see him. It's a family. Belonging. They want me in, not out like at school."

Carmen pursued the Job Corps when she left school: "You ever try plastering, Michelle? It's great. You see holes in walls. You see a problem and you fix it. Job Corps lost its money when I was in it, in Albany. I had to come home, back to Harlem. I felt better there than ever in my school. Now I do nothin'. It's a shame. Never felt as good as then."

Monique got pregnant and then dropped out: "I wasn't never good at nothing. In school I felt stupid and older than the rest. But I'm a great mother to Chita. Catholic schools for my baby, and maybe a house in New Jersey."

Carlos, who left school at age twenty, after five frustrating years since he and his parents exiled illegally from Mexico, hopes to join the military: "I don't want to kill nobody. Just, you know how they advertise, the Marines. I never been one of a Few and the Proud. I'm always 'shamed of myself. So I'd like to try it."

In an uninviting economy, these adolescents responded to the silences transmitted through public schooling by pursuing what they considered to be creative alternatives. But let us understand that for such low-income youths, these alternatives generally *replace* formal schooling. Creative alternatives for middle-class adolescents, an after-school art class or music lessons privately afforded by parents, generally *supplement* formal schooling.

Whereas school-imposed silence may be *an initiation* to adulthood for the middle-class adolescent about to embark on a life of participation and agency, school-imposed silence more typically represents *the orientation* to adulthood for the low-income or working-class adolescent about to embark on a life of work at McDonalds, in a factory, as a domestic or clerical, and/ or on AFDC. For the low-income student, the imposed silences of high school cannot be ignored as a necessary means to an end. They are the present *and* they are likely to be the future (Ogbu, 1978).

Some teachers, paraprofessionals, parents, and students expressly devoted their time, energy, and classes to exposing silences institutionally imposed. One reading teacher prepared original grammar worksheets, including items such as "Most women in Puerto Rico (is, are) oppressed." A history teacher dramatically presented his autobiography to his class, woven with details on the life of Paul Robeson. An English teacher formed a writers' collective of her multilingual "remedial" writing students. A paraprofessional spoke openly with students who decided not to report the prime suspect in a local murder to the police, but to clergy instead. She recognized that their lives would be in jeopardy, despite "what the administrators who go home to the suburbs preach." But these voices of naming were weak, individual, and isolated.

What if these voices, along with the chorus of dropouts, were allowed expression? If they were not whispered, isolated, or drowned out in disparagement, what would happen if these stories were solicited, celebrated, and woven into a curriculum? What if the history of schooling were written by those high school critics who remained in school and those who dropped out? What if the "dropout problem" were studied in social studies as a collective critique by consumers of public education?

Dropping out, or other forms of critique, are viewed instead by educators, policy makers, teachers, and often students as individual acts, expressions of incompetence or self-sabotage. As alive, motivated, and critical as they were at age seventeen, most of the interviewed dropouts were silenced, withdrawn, and depressed by age twenty-two. They had tried the private trade schools, been in and out of the military, failed the GED exam once or more, had too many children to care for, too many bills to pay, and only self-blaming regrets, seeking private solutions to public problems. Muting, by the larger society, had ultimately succeeded, even for those who fled initially with resistance, energy, and vision (Apple, 1982).

I'll end with an image which occurred throughout the year, repeated across classrooms and across urban public high schools. As familiar as it is haunting, the portrait most dramatically captures the physical embodiment of silencing in urban schools.

Field Note: February 16

Patrice is a young Black female, in eleventh grade. She says nothing all day in school. She sits perfectly mute. No need to coerce her into silence. She often wears her coat in class. Sometimes she lays her head on her desk. She never disrupts. Never disobeys. Never speaks. And is never identified as a problem. Is she the student who couldn't develop two voices and so silenced both? Is she so filled with anger, she fears to speak? Or so filled with depression she knows not what to say?

Whose problem is Patrice?

Nurturing the possibility of voice in an improbable context

To pose a critique of silencing requires a parallel commitment to exploring the possibility of voice in public schools. For if we are to abandon all hopes that much can be done inside the public school system, we have surely and irretrievably sealed and silenced the fates of children and adolescents like those described in this manuscript. And so the responsibility to unearth possibility lies with the critic of educational institutions (Aronowitz and Giroux, 1985).

Indeed, after a year at this public school I left with little but optimism about these youngsters, and little but pessimism about public high schools as currently structured. And yet it would be inauthentic not to note the repeated ways in which students, communities, and parents were, and the more numerous ways in which they could be, granted voice inside schools. Those teachers who imported politics from elsewhere, who recognized that educational work is political work, that to talk about or not to talk about economic arrangements is to do political work, took as their individual and collective responsibility a curriculum which included critical examination of social and economic issues, and a pedagogy that attended to the multiple perspectives and ideas inside their classrooms. In vocational education class, Ms. Rodriquez invited students to discuss the conditions of their lives, the relationship of labor market opportunities to their own and their families' survival, and the consequences of giving up, being discouraged, or making trouble at work. Although a thoroughgoing critique of workplace management was not undertaken, a surface analysis was begun and trust was enabled. Likewise, in hygiene, Ms. Wasserman continually probed the lived experiences and diversity among the students. She integrated writing assignments with curricular and social issues, inviting students to author letters to their mothers—alive or dead—about questions "you wish you could or did ask her about sexuality, marriage and romance." A social studies teacher created a class assignment in which students investigated their communities, conducting oral histories with neighbors, shop owners, and local organizers to map community life historically and currently.

But of course much more could be done if all educators saw politics as inherent, and the giving of voice as essential, to the task of education. To *not* mention racism is as political a stance as is a thoroughgoing discussion of its dynamics; to *not* examine domestic violence bears consequences for the numerous youths who have witnessed abuse at home and feel alone, alienated in their experience, unable to concentrate, so that the effects of the violence permeate the classroom even–or particularly–if not named.

I am not asking teachers to undertake therapy in the classroom, nor to present only one political view, but instead to interrogate the very conditions of students' lives and the very thoughts that they entertain as the "stuff" of schooling.

For each possibility, new dilemmas and paradoxes arise.

*With a pedagogy which empowers multiple views, it is often difficult to manage the truly racist, sexist, elitist, or homophobic student without privileging some positions over others, thereby subtly silencing.

*With a curriculum which engages the lived experiences of students, there will undoubtedly be moments in which the "personal" pours into the classroom, disrupting (or liberating) the traditional, rational classroom discourse. Teachers must be equipped to handle such conversation (although current disruptions, which I would argue derive from not allowing the "personal" to pour in, are now numerous and overwhelming to many teachers).

*With a set of democratic structures which invite parents, community activists, and students, educational administrators need to facilitate the giving up of their autocratic power. Questions will emerge about "who's accountable?" Contexts need to be generated within which school and community can be partners, and not competitors for hegemonic influence over youngsters. Indeed, once a commitment to community involvement is forged, the thin line between involvement and surveillance, as the Fundamentalist parents remind us too poignantly, needs to be considered critically.

*And with a set of procedures that facilitate discipline rather than discharges, schools must generate explicit, nonracist criteria for suspension, expulsion, and other in-school punishments. Further, schools must consider the arbitrary ways in which "sad," "bad," and "mad" youths are now classified, and reconsider how peer counseling, advocacy, community-based services, and guidance counseling can best be allocated for large numbers of adolescents in need.

The good news is that students in public high schools, as thoroughly silenced as they may be, retain the energy, persistence, and even resistance which fuel a willingness to keep trying to get a hearing. They probe teachers they don't agree with, challenge the lived experiences of these authorities,

and actively spoof the class and race biases which routinely structure classroom activities:

Field Note: September 18

SOCIAL STUDIES TEACHER: A few years ago a journalist went through Kissinger's
garbage and learned a lot about his life. Let's make believe we are all sanitationmen
going through rich people's and poor people's garbage. What would we find in rich
people's garbage?

Students call out: Golf club! Polo stick! Empty bottle of Halston! Champagne
bottle! Alimony statements! Leftover caviar! Receipts from Saks, Barnies, Bloomies!
Old business and love letters! Rarely worn shoes–They love to spend money! Bills
from the plastic surgeon–for a tummy tuck! Things that are useful that they just
throw out cause they don't like it! Rich people got ulcers, so they have lots of medicine bottles!

TEACHER: Now, the poor man's garbage. What would you find?

STUDENT (1): Not much, we're using it.

STUDENT (2): Holey shoes.

OTHERS: Tuna cans! Bread bags!

STUDENT (3): That's right, we eat a lot of bread!

OTHERS: USDA cheese boxes! Empty no frills cans! Woolworth receipts! Re-
used items from rich man's garbage! *Daily News!*

STUDENT (3): *Daily News* from week before.

OTHERS: Old appliances! Rusty toasters!

STUDENT (4): Yeah, we eat lots of burned toast.

STUDENT (5): You know, poor people aren't unhappy. We like being poor.

TEACHER: Let's not get into value judgements now. There are people who are
eccentric and don't have these things, and poor people who have luxuries, so it is
hard to make generalizations.

STUDENT (6): That's why we're poor!

Despite the teacher's attempts to halt the conversation of critique,
these students initiated and persisted. The room for possibility lies with the
energy of these adolescents, and with those educators who are creative and
gutsy enough to see as their job, their passion, and their responsibility the
political work of educating toward a voice.

Postscript on research as exposing the practices of silencing

The process of conducting research within schools to identify words that
could have been said, talk that should have been nurtured, and information
that needed to be announced suffers from voyeurism and perhaps the worst
of post hoc academic arrogance. The researcher's sadistic pleasure in spot-
ting another teacher's collapsed contradiction, aborted analysis, or silencing

sentence was moderated only by the everpresent knowledge that similar analytic surgery could easily be performed on my own classes.

And yet it is the very naturalness of not naming, of shutting down or marginalizing conversations for the "sake of getting on with learning" that demands educators' attention, particularly so for low-income youths highly ambivalent about the worth of a diploma, desperately desirous of and at the same time discouraged from its achievement. If the process of education is to allow children, adolescents, and adults their voices—to read, write, create, critique, and transform—how can we justify the institutionalizing of silence at the level of policies which obscure systemic problems behind a rhetoric of "excellence" and "progress"; a curriculum bereft of the lived experiences of students themselves; a pedagogy organized around control and not conversation; and a thoroughgoing psychologizing of social issues which enables Patrice to bury herself in silence and not be noticed? A self-critical analysis of the fundamental ways in which we teach children to betray their own voices is crucial.

On Ideology and Education: Critical Pedagogy and the Cultural Politics of Resistance

Peter L. McLaren

In this essay I propose to develop a theory of ideology which attempts to expand the theoretical advances of both orthodox Marxists and post-Marxists alike. In doing so, I shall privilege the terrain of the body as an ideological site. Understanding how ideology is constituted through competing discourses that play themselves out on the terrain of the flesh can, I trust, better enable educational theorists to understand the multiple dimensions of student resistance. The politics of resistance has its corporeal dimensions, which include, among others, the gendered and racial structuring of social relations. I argue that pedagogical approaches aspiring to be critical must be attentive to these various dimensions of resistance in order to effect a politics of classroom change.

Attempts by Marxists and non-Marxists alike to fully delineate a theory of *ideology* has, over the years, produced a voluminous body of work, the vast sweep of which has so far failed to grasp adequately this often diffuse and impalpable term. Few concepts in social theory are as pervasive and durable, yet few continue to provoke such a cleavage of opinion among theorists. What makes such an ephemeral concept so tenacious is difficult to ascertain, since it continues to exercise scholars of various theoretical stripe and disciplinary affiliation. The major theoretical traditions have ranged from the work of French rationalists, to Anglo-Saxon empiricists, to German idealists. The most that scholars have been able to achieve—admittedly no small feat in itself—has been to produce a temporary theoretical truce around contesting definitions of the term.

Over the last decade especially, there has been a steady proliferation of studies attempting both to pry loose some determinate meaning from this historically stubborn concept and to register a new set of analytic claims regarding how it should be defined and employed in critical research.[1] In the first part of this essay, I propose to sketch the contours of some of these new analytic claims in order to specify some problems with existing conceptions of ideology and its critique and attempt to move beyond them. In the second part I will bring my discussion to bear on a concrete public sphere—schooling—in order to illustrate how some of these perspectives on ideology can be rethought in analyzing student resistance and developing a critical pedagogy. A portion of this section will draw from a recent ethnographic research project which I undertook in a Catholic junior high school in Toronto, Canada.

Analyzing the orthodox Marxian position on ideology means widening the discussion of ideology in order to question some of its underlying theoretical assumptions and premises. Although there always exists the possibility of overgeneralizing some of the assumptions of orthodox theorists by addressing issues which they imply but do not directly pose, it nevertheless remains necessary to tap the broader ideological currents of their thought. In a concerted attempt to avoid what Stuart Hall refers to as "epistemological heavy warfare," I shall refrain from taking all the connotations or contextual factors or consequences of this position into consideration. My purpose in drawing attention to this work is to show how the orthodox position on ideology is marred by a number of theoretical shortcomings which characterize its basic assumptions. The theoretical tension between the orthodox Marxist conception of ideology and alternative radical interpretations will be examined, including what have sometimes been referred to as "post-Marxian" formulations.

Ideology and the correspondence theory of truth: The case for multiple subjectivities

Since limitations of space preclude a lengthy sojourn into the volatile and contentious history of ideology, I shall begin by offering a direct rejoinder to one of the mainsprings of the orthodox position, namely, its indebtedness to a correspondence theory of truth. Here the question of ideology becomes yoked to the materialist and epistemological question of what can be proven subversive of empirical truth. The correspondence theory of truth presumes an achieved system of equivalence between ideas, beliefs, and reality, and resonates with Popper's criterion that a proposition must be subject to falsifiability, refutation, and empirical test. It is explicitly concerned with the problem of demarcation between science and nonscience. From this perspective, the concept of ideology must be defended as something to be logically unveiled according to a defensible criterion rooted in objective reality. This places the individual knower in a complicitous relationship with scientific knowledge and the real world. Such a view asserts that reliable knowledge about the world is objective only when it exists independently of an observer. Here we must ask if one can actually search for knowledge without a knowing subject, or if logic can stand outside of human will or volition or the system of differences we use to semiotically construct the world. Unfortunately, such a position betrays little theoretical acquaintance with the idea that the "real" world within which social construction takes place never stands still but necessarily remains fluid and unfinished.

To adhere to a correspondence theory of truth is to ignore the serious crisis in analytic and referential discourse. Conspicuously absent from this orthodox position is an understanding of ideology as a form of cultural production. Or, in terms we have come to associate with the late Michel Foucault, this position ignores recent poststructuralist formulations which call for the primacy of *discursive formations* in understanding the rudiments of ideological production. In other words, the orthodox position fails to consider the *positivity* of ideology.[2] For all of the theoretical frenzy and epistemic turmoil created by the development of discourse theory, it has at the very least proven an undeniable corrective to simple 'action theory' in sociological analysis, which assumes the subject as the unproblematic author of choice and agency. Discourses, as any modern scholar of poststructuralism knows, articulate concepts through a system of signs, and these signs always signify by means of their relationship to each other rather than to objective entities in the world. The world, in this view, becomes a simulacrum that is itself constructed in language. This poststructuralist perspective dramatically conflicts with the classical realist position on the status of truth, exposing it to be tautological insofar as language always mediates the world by positioning us in particular discursive alignments within distinctive social formations.[3] Of significance here is that the ideological codes correlating signifiers and signifieds are never natural, immutable, or unproblematic but are, instead, historically and culturally inscribed. From this standpoint, we cannot know the nature of the world or its 'truth' in the same way that we can hold up for interrogation the discursive order inscribed in particular truth claims. This is similar to asserting, along with Foucault, that we can only discover the 'truth effects' of particular discourses and never the 'whole truth'.

Foucault's understanding of knowledge does not entail a notion of ideas corresponding either to a 'reality' independent of knowledge or a notion of truth separate from the conditions of its production.[4] Foucault understands power as *immanent in the morphology of discourse*, a factor which permits various discursive subject positions to be distributed within a field of asymmetrical relations. In this way, discourses are not simply related to contradictions at the level of production. Notwithstanding Foucault's tendency to essentialize natural history by reducing social relations to discursive formations,[5] his approach delivers a formidable blow to the correspondence theory of truth, adding to the growing disillusionment with scientific Marxism.[6]

The failure of orthodox Marxists to link ideology to a Foucauldian conception of power lets slip an opportunity to analyze the productive aspects of ideology, that is, its positive relation to truth, or the 'effects' of truth that is produces. From Foucault's genealogical perspective, ideology does not work to distort and mystify the truth as much as to produce and legitimate a particular regime of truth – a process which in many ways is more dangerous to its victims. The truth, in this view, is not freedom from ideological constraint but rather the result of particular power-knowledge constellations.[7] Power-knowledge regimes of truth govern social relations not by producing coherent subjects with fixed identities but through discursive practices that produce subject positions, which are always potentially contradictory. According to Foucault, the relationship between Marxism's theoretical project and its methodological defense as a science has more to do with the various epistemologies Marxism *unwittingly suppresses* than with the question of truth value.[8]

The danger, of course, is that Marxism's pursuit of the scientificity of its theory has unwittingly become an exercise in domination because it has become synonymous with an acceptance of the institutions and effects of power that invest scientific discourse with legitimacy and credibilty.[9] The important idea here is that discursive "rules of formation" – the governing rules under which specific types of statements are consistently produced and distributed within a discursive field – are *not* determined solely or mainly by modes of economic production so much as by historical conditions (*some* of which may be economic) which are as various as they are complex. Foucault's position, therefore, necessarily raises some fundamental questions in relation to the orthodox position. Are mental categories, the laws of thought, and criteria of judgement *extra discursive* or are they inscribed in a symbolic order? If they are, indeed, inscribed in the symbolic order, is this order preconstituted by modes of economic production? Are human agents encysted in an ideological matrix that can only reiterate patterns of signification which have been irremediably inscribed according to the logic of capital accumulation and the social relations of production?

Viewed from the orthodox perspective, however, the ideological subject is advanced as being de facto constituted by capital; all too cavalierly discredited is the notion that ideologies are not symptomatic of some prior cause but rather constitute both the medium and the outcome of a recursive generation of representations and social practices, all of which coalesce simultaneously in the ideological 'event'. For poststructuralist theorists, the constitution or "positioning" of the subject constitutes *only one* predetermining element in the functioning of ideological discourses. What is not addressed adequately within the orthodox canon is how individuals can inhabit contradictory ideological positions or how ideologies are often provisionally secured by their contingency upon features other than modes of economic production (such as social ascription according to race, class, and gender) or by their relation to other discourses, institutions, and social formations.

The poverty of the orthodox perspective is revealed most fully in what it ignores. Rarely, if ever, does it take up or even cursorily consider the concept of ideology as the production of multiple subjectivities, a position which permits educators especially to theorize beyond the traditional individual-society dualism when attempting to understand how schools and everyday life locate students within multiple subject positions.[10]

A point worth emphasizing is that consciousness, rather than conceived as false, can be better conceived as a 'text'. In other words, ideologies are best "read" as socially constructed relations which constitute the products of numerous histories, institutions, processes of inscription, and traditions of mediation. Ideology is not, in a word, a domain of pure ideality. In this context, Bakhtin's demolition of the concept of the autonomous self and his theory of language as a kind of ideology-brought-into-speech further exposes the theoretical debility of the classical Marxian approach, helping to put it even further under erasure.

To assert, as may poststructuralists do, that ideologies are inscribed in signifying practices which constitute various representations of reality is not the same thing as asserting that these representations are false. For example, underlying the work of various theorists such as Raymond Williams, Henry Giroux, and Philip Wexler is a common understanding of ideology as forms of representation central to the organization of experiences and subjectivities. Wexler rightly insists that ideology must be studied "not as a collection of entities, ideas, but as itself a production, a set of practices, structures, or methods which make meaning."[11] Such an understanding of ideology as an imbricated intertextuality constitutes a significant theoretical advance over the vulgar Marxian conception of materialist epistemology based on the concept of false consciousness. The point to consider is that consciousness is not all of one piece, a seamless web of either truth or distortion.

The reluctance of orthodox theorists to appropriate new developments in discourse theory and their failure to theorize adequately on these issues contribute, in part, to their inability to address ideology as a discourse of production. In order to move beyond the strangulated silence of their position, orthodox theorists would have to refute adequately the idea that knowledge does not reflect an objective or pristine ontological reality but instead constitutes a particular ordering and organization of a world constituted by our experience and social relations. Both these positions have a combative history.[12]

Ideology, essentialism, and the contingency of the social

One of the major problems with the orthodox theory of ideology is that it fails to seriously question the idea that perhaps the terms *true* and *false* are themselves theoretically problematic and involve contentious epistemological issues. An assignment of the features of truth and falsity to an empirical status presupposes the very notions of validation, logical consistency, and verifiability. And in an attempt to defend the claims of science to universality, scientificity, and normativity, orthodox theorists unwittingly fall victim to a position dangerously close to a naive essentialism, thus undercutting their argument in two ways: by leaving themselves open to a discursive skepticism regarding their assumption of social totality; and by rendering vulnerable the ontological security that results from taking refuge in a correspondence theory of truth.[13] By attempting to restore ideology within a correspondence theory of truth, orthodox theorists actually empty ideology of its presumed ability to position subjects within a multiplicity of discursive formations (which I argue are not directly–or mainly–mediated by the reflex of capital).

The question of multiple discursive formations becomes an important focus in the work of Ernesto Laclau. His recent work has attempted to combine poststructuralist discourse theory with a neo-Gramscian, nonreductionist concept of hegemony by advancing a politics of signification around the way in which ideologies produce subjects through the articulation and disarticulation of discourses. In his development of Althusser's concept of interpellation and its discursive and ideological function, Laclau has significantly weakened the orthodox position, which is predicated upon a base-superstructure model and the concept of false consciousness. Laclau argues that both of these criteria for a restricted conception of ideology are grounded in an *essentialist* conception of society and social agency.[14] The validity of the conception of false consciousness presupposes a concept of human agency which possesses "an ultimate essential homogeneity whose misrecognition was postulated as the source of 'ideology.'"[15] Similarly, the validity of the base-superstructure model rests on a conception of society as "an intelligible totality, itself conceived as the structure upon which its partial elements and processes are founded."[16]

Against recognizing the essence of the social order behind the empirical variations at the surface of social life, Laclau argues for accepting "the *infinitude of the social*, that is, the fact that any structural system is always surrounded by an 'excess of meaning' which it is unable to master and that, consequently, 'society' as a unitary and intelligible object which grounds its own partial processes is an impossibility" (italics original).[17] This perspective highlights the relational character of identity and at the same time clearly renounces the fixation of these identities in a system. Instead, Laclau links the social with *an infinite play of discursive differences*. Thus, the meaning of the social becomes impossible to fix because it no longer takes the form of an underlying essence. The order—or structure—which we call "society" is really an attempt to *hegemonize* the social. The 'totality' does not establish the limits of the social by transforming it into a determinate object (e.g., society). Laclau argues that "each social formation has its own forms of determination and relative autonomy, which are always instituted through a complex process of overdetermination and therefore cannot be established *a priori*. With this insight, the base/superstructure distinction falls and, along with it, the conception of ideology as a necessary level of every social formation."[18] Along the same line of attack, the concept of ideology as "false consciousness" also proves exceedingly vulnerable to Laclau's criticisms. The notion of class consciousness only makes sense if the identity of the social agent (in our case, the student) is fixed. This means, according to Laclau, that identity must be positive and noncontradictory. Only on the basis of recognizing true identity can it be asserted that the consciousness of the subject is indeed false.

Against the position put forward by Laclau, orthodox Marxists are often propelled by a dubious will to totality which is conceptually limiting precisely because it fails to credit sufficiently the concept of shifting discourses, the multiple play of differences, and the precarious discursive nature of any positivity. It also assumes a monolithic concept of ideology and of the ruling class which articulates class interests in a noncontradictory and unambiguous way. Laclau's position is that particular ideological elements do not have a pregiven class location. Of course, we must be careful not to endorse without qualification Laclau's position by detotalizing the social order in such a fashion that we effectively lose the concept of the social formation as centrally directed by relations of oppression (a predicament which constitutes some of the self-contradictions of post-Marxian theorists). Whereas arguments put forward by orthodox theorists do little to free social relations from the burden of scientific Marxism and the scientism of the Second International, contemporary poststructuralists such as Laclau tend to essentialize and eliminate political economy and natural history from their revolutionary text by effectively reducing social relations solely to discursive formations.[19] To break free from both these extremes means recognizing Laclau's concept of the contingency of the social while keeping in mind that determinate forces of various stripe do exert a hegemonizing influence – *but only within historically specific moments and on the basis of particular cultural configurations.*

It is difficult to see where in the orthodox canon on ideology there is room for a politics of signification. We require a poststructuralist theory of subjectivity where ideology is not conceptualized as false consciousness but as an effort to make sense in a world of contradictory information and indeterminacies, "a way of holding at bay a randomness incongruent with consciousness."[20]

Science, ideology, and context

Capital logicians within the classical Marxist tradition demand an empirical science that works within a prescribed rationality whose range of possibilities is narrowly tied to formal criteria of prediction, linear causality (the effect is proportional to the cause), and lineal (straight line) causality. The work of Stanley Aronowitz is worth noting as a worthy rejoinder to the failure of many orthodox theorists to problematize the cohabitation of science and ideology. Aronowitz's position on the relationship between ideology and science can be summarized in remarks he made during a critical reading of Kurt Hubner's classic work, *Critique of Scientific Reason:* "Every historical period produces precepts that govern what counts as a scientific fact. Facts . . . are generated, not merely discovered; they cannot be understood separately from the theoretical framework that gives them meaning."[21] What Hubner and Aronowitz appear to be saying is that empirical verification is in some sense meaningless because raw data only begin to function when they have already entered theory: that is, there exists no facts-in-the-world which are positioned outside of theory from which a refutation can appeal. From this perspective, science relinquishes the immediate privilege to discover sovereign truth.[22]

Drawing upon early attempts by Frankfurt School theorists to collapse natural and social science, Aronowitz has demonstrated the essentially metaphoric nature of science. This position is understandably difficult for classical Marxists, who consider scientific observations to be isomorphic to reality and who hold to the nineteenth-century version of science as the natural arbiter of social questions. But it is a position which makes sense whether or not reality is understood in the "picture sense" described by Wittgenstein or in Lenin's "approximate" connotation model. Aronowitz argues (rightly, in my opinion) that the problem is not that of a materialist world that is historically and epistemologically prior to and independent of human cognition, *but whether the external world is independent of the social character of knowing.*[23]

In Aronowitz's view, knowledge gathered in the cool sanctuaries of science cannot be objectively "true" insofar as it can never exist independently of the social processes which generate it. Thus, "doing science" (e.g., the procedures and conditions of scientific inquiry itself) necessarily alters the world by constituting an intervention.[24] The very notion of scientific neutrality that is celebrated by orthodox theorists is, from Aronowitz's perspective, blatantly ideological. In actuality, there exists no sovereign referent—no uncontaminated or interpretationless backcloth—from which to assess the validity of scientific observation that isn't subject to an infinite regress of decentering, as poststructuralists and deconstructionists have taken great pains to show us. Aronowitz actually claims that there is no longer a normal science, only normal technological research.[25] A normal science which presupposes a neutral science contradicts itself because all science is configured by social relations and is in itself a form of social knowledge (and therefore ideological). This position does not imply that there is no reality outside of the 'text' or that the external world is somehow a relativistic projection of our collective mentality. But it does deny the existence of some 'pristine other', a privileged referent which scientific law is supposed to have as its backcloth.

Aronowitz goes so far as to argue that the very notion of the material object is itself a metaphor which can be historically situated inside a specific problematic within the capitalist mode of production. Although he does concede that the realist theory of truth is in some sense tenable as a kind of article of faith, comparable to Althusser's economic determination in the last instance, he nevertheless claims that this perspective has no practical significance with respect to understanding the nature of scientific inquiry itself.[26] How to escape the relativistic notion of the socially constituted nature of scientific discovery remains a problem, but simply to recycle the myth of the neutrality of science and the separation of science and ideology certainly constitutes a step backwards, especially in this post-Gramscian era of bourgeois late capitalism, when we are compelled to pay close attention to the social relations of signification and to the corporate marketing battle over the sign.

In order to escape the conceptual conundrum of their own position, exponents of the classical Marxian theory of ideology must demonstrate preexisting concepts which constitute a neutral nomenclature existing independently of the contingency of social practices. To fail to do so precludes the opportunity of challenging with sufficient credibility the impossibility of securing aseptic grounds – beyond the social practice of "doing science" – with which to judge the truth and falsity of theoretical propositions. In short, the orthodox position appears to assert that science occupies the privileged sphere of the *transhistorical*. It is to insist wrongly on the transparency of normative practices such as establishing criteria for empirical validity and an ontological guarantee of truth. Science, in this view, becomes self-justifying: that is, it becomes a self-referential simulacrum.

Foucault, like Aronowitz, rejects the distinction between scientific truth and ideological distortion. Instead of trying to discern the epistemological basis of the 'really real', Foucault undertakes a historical analysis of how the 'effects of truth' are produced within discourses that are neither true nor false. He wishes to prevent the history of knowledge from being colonized by epistemological categories. In other words, Foucault never forgets that knowledges are social practices. As Veronica Beechey and James Donald point out, Foucault refuses to engage with epistemological questions, being more concerned with how truth is produced in discourse and how 'regimes of truth' are empowered and deployed in everyday social practices.[27] To explore the various factors which constitute truth's regulating gaze appears to me to be an eminently more worthwhile challenge for radical theorists to undertake than the impossible task of arguing how the ideological superstructure "corresponds to" the economic base or how a particular ideology distorts the real truth of the world.

Nevertheless, there is a danger lurking in current attempts to deconstruct Marxian science which abandons the categories of history and class altogether. In such cases, we can find ourselves saddled with little more than a new empiricism. Therefore, it is important that the concept of truth be defended *within a specific system of rationality*, and not as 'discovered laws' that somehow correspond with the 'really real'. Speaking to this issue, Aronowitz provides us with an excellent definition of truth as "the critical exposition of the relations of humans to nature within a developing, historically mediated, context."[28] Truth, in other words, *must always be understood in its historical and discursive specificity.*

Ideology and the reflex of capital

Giving pride of place to the productive moment, orthodox theorists privilege the vaunted mechanistic base–superstructure model. From this vantage point, the signified (or that which is represented) is relegated to a derivative status and correspondence and identity are posited as central axioms of epistemology. There is no inherent problem with a loose application of the base-superstructure model so long as it is not followed by a blithe exclamation that all forms of human practice can be explained in the last instance by reference to an economic 'base'. As Terry Eagleton points out, the term *superstructure* "does not designate an ontological 'realm,' a fixed determinate, and unequivocal set of functions or structures; it invites us instead to contextualize a certain piece of practice or discourse in a particular way, without the slightest guarantee that this is always and everywhere the most appropriate contest for it."[29]

It is highly questionable whether the traditional base-superstructural model is capable of dealing with Eagleton's interdependence of shifting discursive formations or not. It is also doubtful that such a quasi-physicalist model can allow for the relatively autonomous nature of the social relations of signification. Gramsci's theory of hegemony, which conceptualizes ideologies as more than the effluxes of the prevailing economic infrastructure, but rather as entities possessing a logic of their own,[30] is often used by Marxist theorists to counter the insularity of the base-superstructure model. In the orthodox view, the individual subject becomes simply a bearer of social roles (in an Althusserian sense) as they are mediated by economic structures or relations of production. Here we must be cautious of mechanistic formulations. Ideology does not simply constitute the linear arrangement of ideas, domino-fashion, with the economic as an unalloyed *primum mobile* at one end, presumably acting as a generator of history. Neither can ideology be adequately explained by theories of expressive causality, homology, or overdetermination, although Fredric Jameson's development of the idea of structural causality constitutes a major advance over most Marxian theories of causality.[31] Orthodox theories of ideology have difficulty accounting for the development of different interpretive communities within society, with their often antagonistic goals and strategies. In the final instance, it becomes a futile exercise to argue that the economic sphere alone is capable of explaining how men and women are ideologically positioned within asymmetrical relations of power. It is equally as difficult from this position to render intelligible the variety of subject positions and wide range of discourses in which we are all constructed. As Paul Hirst reminds us: "Conducts are *constructed*. They are not mere 'subjective registers' of economic relations—which are somehow more 'real' or 'objective'" (italics original).[32]

It is not surprising that claims of economic determinism such as those made within the orthodox tradition have been found lacking even among scholars who appropriate many of the theoretical categories of traditional Marxism. If we have difficulty tracing a causal link from the economic base to ideologies in the superstructure, it is possibly because, as Ernst Bloch informs us, the superstructure *is not dualistically separate from the base*;[33] hence, ideologies can be seen in the details and forms of the organization of everyday life. Bloch claims that there exists both bad ideology (false consciousness) and good ideology (*true* false consciousness). The latter category cannot simply be reduced to false consciousness. Although the primary site of ideology is the superstructure, there always exists a cultural "surplus" which outlasts the society and social strata in which it develops.[34] There exists, for instance, social strata which are not contemporaneous with the dominant mode of production. This cultural surplus, when freed from the negative sense of false consciousness and the illusory reconciliation of contradiction, possesses an incipient utopian dimension.[35] It is precisely this utopian dimension that provides both the freedom from restraint and the autonomy of purpose for self- and social transformation. Bloch insisted that the individual, the natural world, and history all have the fundamental character of not-yet being. Bloch's work can be summarized in the slogan "The subject is not yet the predicate."[36]

The incipient epistemological materialism of the orthodox Marxian view, according to which the objective realm independent of agency constitutes the object of social knowledge, has been refuted by numerous theorists, such as Derrida, Laclau, Mouffe, and Hirst. That these theorists have argued so convincingly that all objects are constituted discursively as "language games" (as Wittgenstein so presciently put it) undermines, to say the least, the orthodox Marxian distinction between the base and superstructure which implies hierarchy of both determination and historical priority.[37]

Although particular discourses considered in isolation may indeed be structured in dominance within capitalist productive relations, nevertheless through particular intersections, forms of reversal, and combinations with other discourses they may also be mutually informing, self-constituting, and capable of generating forms of knowledge which effectively escape assimilation into the dominated contents of capital accumulation. In other words, ideology considered as the production of meaning, the positioning of the subject, and the investment of affectivity can exist relatively independent of the logic of the economy. Addressing the problem of economic determination, Stuart Hall offers a different conception of determinacy from that generated by the usual "causal determinism" or "expressive totality" ways of conceiving relations between practices within social formations. From Hall's standpoint, relations between different levels are seen as *mutually determining* rather than flowing unidirectionally from the base upward; consequently, the economy cannot effect a final closure on the domain of ideology.[38]

Radical education and the production of meaning

Now I intend to link the concept of ideology more directly to the issue of how it has been theorized by radical educators in their various analyses of schooling. Radical pedagogy has certainly not remained immune to the profusion of debates surrounding theories of ideology. But here, as elsewhere, orthodox Marxists engage in theoretical combat with structuralists and their heirs and successors. The disagreement over how to define ideology has grown increasingly more fierce in recent years through attempts by some Marxian educational theorists to promote—perhaps "resuscitate" is more appropriate—a restricted definition of ideology. Radical theorists who assail such measures contend that an orthodox "straightjacketing" of the term can only impede the progress of radical pedagogy toward developing a programmatic discourse of hope and social transformation. In other words, it is felt that the creeping orthodoxy surrounding the term harbors its own unrecognized ideological assumptions which strip the term of its heuristic and critical potential.[39]

A recent attempt by Marxist educator Michael Dale to develop a conception of ideology for employment in educational research offers a fitting example of the orthodox position. Dale argues that ideology should be restricted only to those beliefs and ideas that (1) are false, (2) that contribute to the reproduction of production relations and class domination, and (3) that are determined and explained by the production relations.[40] Clearly, Dale's materialist, realist reading of ideology advances the general but important claim that ideas, beliefs, and values which are duplicitous and distortive can best be explained by comprehending the material forces that remain hidden from consciousness.[41] Dale's conception of ideology covers roughly the same ground as the classical Marxist theory of ideology, which argues that specific forms of consciousness produced by signifying practices—music, art, literature, religion, and so on—are at least partially determined by the social relations that inform the organization of economic production in any given social order. Yet although this praiseworthy position serves as an effective counterweight to the idealist who regards consciousness as primarily self-determining, Dale unwittingly sides with a theory of ideology that contributes to its own devaluation.

In its attempt to examine schooling as a state-regulated *social form* as against the process of knowledge transmission, the work of Henry Giroux sets forth an approach to ideology that differs significantly from those articulated by orthodox theorists. In Giroux's view, a failure to understand classroom pedagogy as a form of ideological production prevents both teachers and students from recognizing the centrality of their own epistemological claims for truth. Giroux's conception of ideology is *fundamentally grounded in a theory of interest:* that is, Giroux takes seriously which particular interests are embodied in various discursive formations and power-knowledge relations, both in schools and the wider society.

Although I do not have enough space to do justice to the range and scope of Giroux's work, I will attempt to summarize why Giroux's approach to ideology bodes well for the development of an emancipatory politics of education. In Giroux's terms, not only does ideology work "on and through individuals to secure their consent to the basic ethos and practices of the dominant society,"[42] but it also functions "in the interest of social transformation."[43]

The view of ideology as a double-sided process has been articulated by Douglas Kellner, who writes that "the concept [of ideology] commonly refers both to those ideas, images, and theories that mystify social reality and block social change, and to those programs of social reconstruction that mobilize people for social activism."[44] In a similar vein, Gibson Winter writes that

ideology . . . faces in two directions. It is a Janus-like phenomenon. Ideology may be primarily oriented to preserving and legitimating the established powers in a society. It may also face primarily toward the future and project a utopian model for a more just society. In either case, ideology draws upon the symbolic powers that generate a people's identity whether to legitimate powers that be or to authorize proposals for transformation.[45]

The view of ideology expressed by Stuart Hall and James Donald bears a striking similarity to that of Giroux. They define ideology as "the frameworks of thought which are used in society to explain, figure out, makes sense of or give meaning to the social and political world . . . Without these frameworks, we could not make sense of the world at all. But with them, our perceptions are inevitably structured in a particular direction by the very concepts we are using."[46] Ideology in this view possesses both positive and negative functions coexisting at any one moment. For instance, the *positive function* of ideology is to "provide the concepts, categories, images, and ideas by means of which people make sense of their social and political world, form projects, come to a certain consiousness of their place in the world and act in it."[47] The *negative function* of ideology "refers to the fact that all such perspectives are inevitably selective. This perspective positively organizes the 'facts of the case' in *this* and makes sense because it inevitably excludes *that* way of putting things."[48] According to John Thompson, ideology as a negative function works through four different modes: legitimation, dissimulation, fragmentation, and reification. *Legitimation* occurs when a system of domination is sustained by being represented as legitimate or as eminently just and worthy of respect. *Dissimulation* results when relations of domination are concealed, denied, or obscured in various ways, that is, when social processes are described in such a way that they conceal the interests and practices which inform them. *Fragmentation* occurs when relations of domination are sustained by the production of meanings in a way which fragments groups and places them in opposition with one another, such as in the classic case of "divide and rule." *Reification* results when transitory historical states of affairs are presented as permanent, natural, and commonsensical, as if they existed outside of time.[49] From the perspectives just sketched, the question of understanding ideology becomes one of investigating *which* concepts, values, and meanings mystify our understanding of the social world and our place within the networks of power-knowledge relations, and which clarify such an understanding. The self- and socially transformative aspect of ideology involves the issue of "how ideology creates the terrain for self-reflection and transformative action."[50] For Giroux, ideology is conceptualized both as "a set of representations produced and inscribed in human consciousness and behavior, in discourse, and in lived experiences"[51] and as "concretized in . . . various 'texts', material practices, and material forms."[52]

More specifically, Giroux defines ideology as generic with

the production, consumption, and representation of ideas and behavior, which can either distort or illuminate the nature of reality. As a set of meanings and ideas, ideologies can be either coherent or contradictory; they can function within the spheres of both consciousness and unconsciousness; and, finally, they can exist at the level of critical discourse as well as within the sphere of taken-for-granted lived experience and practical behavior.[53]

When linked to the concepts of struggle and critique, the notion of ideology can be employed to address critical relationships among discursivity, meaning, and interest. For instance, when the concept of ideology is linked to that of social struggle, it also illuminates the inseparability of knowledge as power. Therefore, when viewed in its historical specificity, ideology can be linked not only to the discursive formations and the social relations they structure, but also to the interests that they further.[54] In this way it is important to understand ideology as both *the medium and outcome of human experiences*, including the discourses and institutions which anchor and legitimate them. In this way, ideology functions not only to limit human action but also to enable it. Given Giroux's conception, the term *ideology* (being a noun which we take to have a single referent) could be more frutifully appropriated if it were employed as a verb: that is, its usefulness for critical pedagogy resides in its *operational field*.

Considered as such, ideology is involved in the production of multiple subjectivities; it operates with individual experience in the sphere of the unconscious and through the structure of needs, the realm of common sense, and the sphere of critical consciousness.[55] Individuals inhabit an "ideological universe" in which contradictions exist within and between dominant and subordinate cultures. Meaning must not therefore be reduced simply to the domain of the individual but "has to be understood in its articulation with ideological and material forces as they circulate and constitute the wider society."[56]

Giroux maintains that in their attempt to grasp the relations between agency and structure, educators working within the critical tradition should support a theory of ideology that is "also capable of comprehending the way in which meaning is constructed and materialized within 'texts', or cultural forms such as films, books, curriculum packages, fashion styles, etc."[57] In short, Giroux considers the critique of ideology to consist of the material manipulation of signs as well as the hidden manifestations of subjectivity and behavior.

By clearly embracing a fully fledged dialectic approach to ideology, Giroux is able to reveal how individuals are more than just the reflexes of capital and social texts, in that they mediate representations and material practices through their own histories and class- or gender-related subjectivities. These relations are distinct, if not disparate, in their specificity and concrete historicity. In addition, it is to Giroux's credit that he takes seriously both the affective power of ideological production, which is organized around the body, and the individual's affective investment in systems of signification and discursive practices. It is precisely Giroux's uncompromisingly dialectical approach to ideology that permits conceptual access to the relations that characterize the interface among ideology, culture, and schooling. By emphasizing ideology as the production and mobilization of meaning, Giroux is able to uncover those aspects of the dominating culture that shape student subjectivities within asymmetrical relations of power.

Consequently, Giroux is able to uncover moments of *self-production* for the purposes of both critique and the construction of emancipatory pedagogical practices. In this way, an understanding of the productive aspects of ideology *can help radical teachers to link more effectively school practices to student experiences.*

It is clear that opposition to the dominant sociocultural order exists not only because language cannot fully formulate unconscious desire, as Kristeva, Lacan, and others have pointed out, but because people actively suffer the materiality of the pain of oppression. Ideology can never "fix" us as dependent, coherent, and stable subjects, fully positioned in an iron-clad, pregiven relationship to the productive relations of capital. Consequently, resistances to domination can never be manifested as merely "attendant" features of ideologies, as some Marxists would argue, but rather serve as *mutually constitutive aspects* of the very process of ideology itself. With this formulation, theorists such as Aronowitz and Giroux have managed in their discussion of resistance to restore some conceptual half-tones to the depressingly dark picture of total domination.[58]

Ideology as ritual performance

In my ethnographic study of resistant student populations, I have adopted a perspective of ritual which attempts to take seriously the concepts of ideology and power and which addresses ritual as a cultural production constructed as a collective reference to the symbolic and situated experience of a group's social class. Following Aronowitz's critique of historical materialism,[59] I would argue that the categories of ritual and the symbolic must compete with those of the economic sphere and class if we are to understand present-day domination and resistance. Such a position is reinforced by MacCannell's pronouncement that in modern societies cultural productions supersede economic productions as a basis of shared values, lifestyles, and world views.[60] Not only do social forces give rise to symbolic expressions (as Durkheim has shown us), but symbols and rituals are now in the process of creating social groups.[61]

My emphasis on analyzing ideology and schooling from the standpoint of ritual performance attempts to uncover the importance of the sundry and the ordinary in social life—the liturgy of the everyday, so to speak—from the full range of symbolic acts running from ritualization behavior in animals, through interaction ritual, to highly differentiated religious liturgies and civil ceremonies. My specific interest lies with the practical and the mundane and how these domains become sanctified inside schools.

One of the crucial categories often overlooked by theorists of ideology is that of the body and the manner in which it becomes inscribed in the geography of desire through ritual. Related to this is how our affective or visceral investments in the world provide a sense of unity and totality to the "ritualized" creation of multiple subject positions within discursive formations. Ideology has to be seen not simply as the property of the text, in which human agency is denied an active role, but rather *as a process of production* in which pleasure and pain are produced by individuals in gestural engagement with their surroundings.[62] Rarely considered in the debates over ideology is the notion that ideology is *performatively constituted*. It is, in a word, discourse given sentience. The way we ritualize our lives is culture somaticized – culture incarnated in and through our bodily acts and gestures. Ensconced in the framework of both private and institutional life, rituals become part of the socially conditioned, historically acquired, and biologically constituted *rhythms and metaphors of human agency*.

I have given the term *ritual knowledge* to that aspect of ideological production which emphasizes affective investment or bodily knowing as distinct from ideational or semantic competency. *Ritual*, as I have defined the term, is the gestural embodiment of metaphors and symbols; that is, they are symbols or metaphors somaticized or "bodied forth."[63] Ideology cannot be theorized in purely cognitive terms so that false beliefs constitute inadequate information or distorted communication. Ideology is fundamentally related to the politics of pleasure and the body. Ideology, in this perspective, lies in the motional world; it "thematizes" its milieu through mindful bodily gesture. As a form of ideology, ritual has a tendency to become self-effacing since it often assumes the second nature of habits: that is, it completes its work by disguising its own activity.

According to MacCannell, "ritual codes are the most arbitrary and the most authoritarian areas of social life"; in fact, he claims that, empirically, they constitute *political tracts on practical lines of action that can be written with the body*.[64] MacCannell locates ritual within the debates between Derrida and Lévi-Strauss, maintaining that ritual is a *forbidden form of writing*, a type of practice that Umberto Eco refers to as "rhetorical over coding," one which blocks undesired readings of events while substituting other concerns.[65] Ritual, as a form of arche-writing with the entire body, does not establish a particular interpretation of social action as much as it establishes a difference between itself and practical behavior.[66] Rituals, in this sense, are undeniably ideological because "each time you gloss your behavior with a ritual overlay, you are reinforcing a particular structural relationship or suspending it: i.e., somehow rewriting it. Ritual as a form of political arche-writing is . . . performance aimed at dominating another's thought, of forcing, suppressing particular interpretations of behavior."[67]

The schooled body: The ritualized regimentation
of desire and the domestication of subjectivity

Within the framework sketched above, the pedagogical encounter between teachers and students can be understood as a ritual performance consisting of ideologically coded gestures. Students react to and often resist pedagogical instruction, which is itself a form of ritual knowledge. Ritual knowledge possesses an incarnate character; it is acquired noetically and inheres in the "erotics of knowing."[68] It is both reflective and prereflective.[69] Students acquire and react to information viscerally, depending upon both the symbols and metaphors available during the pedagogical encounter and the morphology of the instruction itself; that is, *students make affective investments in certain kinds of knowledge*. In so doing, the distinction between the symbols they employ and their actions often becomes nominal: the student becomes both the means and the end of the ritualizing act. Thus, to speak of students creating classroom rituals is somewhat misleading. It is better to say that rituals both create and are created by their participants "ideologically." Rituals provide and legitimate the gestural metaphors and rhythms through which students engage the world. Ritual knowledge is not something to be "understood"; it is always, whether understood or not, something which is felt and responded to somatically.

Ritual knowledge is epistemologically disparate from traditional conceptions of school knowledge. Research which I undertook in a working-class Catholic school revealed a distinction between streetcorner knowledge and knowledge acquired in classroom settings. Knowledge acquired in the streets was "lived" and mediated through discursive alignments and affective investments not found in the school. It was mediated by a different symbol and ritual system in which what mattered was always somehow "felt," whereas school knowledge was often sullied by an inflated rationalism. In the streets, students made use of more bodily engagement and organic symbols. In the classroom, knowledge was more symbolically sophisticated, but because such knowledge was discarnate and not a lived engagement, it remained distant, isolated, abstract. Students chose not to invest affectively in this kind of knowledge. Students whose subjectivities were "decentered" in school could reclaim their sense of subjective continuity through affective investment in street life. Students battled daily to reconcile the disjunction between the lived meaning of the streets and the thing-oriented, digital approach to learning in the classroom. An inordinate emphasis was placed in school on knowledge *about*, or the digital dimension of learning (univocality, precision, logic) as opposed to knowledge *of*, or the analogic dimension (equivocation, ambiguity, description) experienced by students in the street.[70] Classroom instruction constituted what Everhart calls "reified knowledge"–knowledge that is given, linear, relatively unproblematic, and which places students in the role of passive recipients.[71] Resistance to this type of knowledge in the classroom mirrored student behavior in the street, and constituted a ritualized attempt to bring the street into the school. In Everhart's terminology, the type of knowledge gathered through resistance of this sort becomes a form of "regenerative knowledge" which asserts creative control over the knowledge production process.[72] This type of knowledge, which I refer to as "ritual knowledge," is interpretive and does not draw upon assumed categories. Furthermore, it is established to resist the role that students occupy in the labor process of the school.[73]

The distinction between bodily knowledge and classroom knowledge is complex. Bodily or ritual knowledge learned in the streets offers students a connectedness and relational context–a "lived meaning"–while negotiating their day-to-day existence. Lauren B. Resnick has recently offered an analysis of the different ways learning takes place inside and outisde the classroom which reflects a striking similarity to my own research. Resnick writes that schooling generally focuses on individual, isolated activites and on the individual's performance, whereas out-of-school mental work is often socially shared. Schooling cultivates symbolic thinking in which symbols are all too often detached from their referents, whereas mental activity outside school is more directly linked to objects and situations. The decontextualized learning in schools constructs forms of learning much different from those found in learning situations outside of schools. Resnick found that when school programs designed to teach higher-order cognitive skills have features characteristic of out-of-school learning styles, students fare much better.[74] Learning outside school appealed more to the students in my own study because it was contextually embedded in a shared culture.

Instructional rituals became useful adjuncts in the ideological positioning of students as subjects within various discursive alignments and institutionalized regimes of power and in the ingraining–both bodily and cognitively–of certain acceptable dispositions and dimensions which were linked to the cultural capital of the dominant culture. Students reacted against the eros-denying quality of school life in which students became manipulable objects, discarnate beings unsullied by the taint of living flesh. Intellectual labor had little affective currency because it was removed from any celebration of the body as a locus of meaning. This brings us to the idea that ideological hegemony is not realized solely through the discursive mediations of the sociocultural order but through the enfleshment of unequal relationships of power. Hegemony is manifest intercorporeally through the actualizations of the flesh and imbedded in incarnate experience.

Student gestures had become reified into intercorporeal manifestations of hegemony and could be described, in the words of David Michael Levin, as a "hostile, calculative, reductively mechanistic re-presentation of the body."[75] By observing the cramped, defensive posturing of students and the brusque, authoritative gestures of the teachers, one could see how relations of power were grafted onto the medium of living flesh and marrow like a type of second biology. Power and privilege became somaticized. Ritual, in this sense, is the context of the body turned into ideology.

Every social practice, including that of being schooled, calls forth the body. And every body is burdened by history's way of seeing it. As R.W. Connell says: "The body is never outside history and history never free of bodily presence and effects on the body. The traditional dichotomies underlying reductionism now have to be replaced by a more adequate and complex account of the social relations in which this incorporation and interplay occur."[76] Every body carries a history of oppression, a residue of domination preserved in stratum upon stratum of breathing tissue. The bodies of the students in my study were ideologically swollen with meaning; they were pervaded by symbols which were infolded in the musculature, pressed into the tendons and encased in the meshwork of bone and sinew. Symbols, claims Dixon, are part of human physiology.[77] Hegemony, which is inscribed in the physiognomic symbols of the student's bodies and compressed into gesture, is an act of corporeity. In my study of Catholic schooling, hegemony was revealed to be ideologically laminated over the students' skeletal and muscular structures. The structuration of students' subjectivities begins with their subordination to a field of cultural desire born of the symbols and narratives of the street and the classroom and also related to the organization of their bodies. In other words, subjectivity is produced corporeally as well as discursively, beginning with the regimes of truth governing desire and movement. The positionalities of ideology become the intersections at which symbols and metaphors are inscripted into the body and absorbed or reabsorbed by the flesh. Resistance to school instruction among the students was a resolve not to be ritually dissimulated in the face of oppression, a fight against the erasure of their streetcorner gestures and symbols. It was, furthermore, an attempt to ritually construct a transitional world that could erase the past and deconstruct present psychosocial adaptations in order to forge new self-presentations (resurrected bodies) of greater potency. Accordingly, the bodies of the students became sites of struggle in which dominant symbols and metaphors designed to regulate the body were resisted much the same way a transplanted organ by a foreign donor is often rejected by a body's tissues. Resistance also became a way of gaining power, celebrating pleasure, and fighting oppression in the lived historicity of the moment and the concrete materiality of the classroom. To resist meant to fight against the monitoring of passion and desire and the capitalist symbolization of the flesh. It became a fight against the privatized body correlated with the interpersonal relations of market ideology (the body as a "self-serve" commodity). Resistance became a rejection of the human subject reformulated as a docile object when spontaneity is repressed for efficiency and productivity, in compliance with the grammar of capitalist domination. It was a reaction against the purging of the body of its ability to produce pleasure in favor of a disembodied ideal of what consitutes "proper" learning and behavior.

It is important to recognize that students both have bodies and are bodies.[78] They have possession of their bodies but do not necessarily have ownership (and this is particularly true of women, whose bodies have become alienated by the sexual division of labor).[79] When understood in these terms, student resistance can be seen as transgressive behavior in the form of a *corporeal unlearning*: dismantling the language of the body which had become sedimented into habits through years of schooling practices. In addition, resistance is a protest against the trammels of ideology, which assume a form of tyranny against the students' own play of subjectivity, their own relational cognitive and gestural style.

As a celebratory splintering of subject positions which solicit the body as if it were merely an appendage of the mind, resistance became an irruption of the social distribution of pleasure. Every social practice calls forth the body and concomitantly history's burden on the body in terms of the social definitions which bring it into being. Student resistance meant resisting "subjection" (i.e., their historical role as bodily subjects) and instead seeking out identities as active bodily agents.[80] Students acting as agents not only resisted the historical definitions of their bodies in terms of how they could represent and express their felt pleasure but attempted to actively reshape their own technologies of desire.

At times students used their bodies to savage classroom culture as a medium of decorum and civility. Sexual gestures would accompany school prayer, machismo-style swaggering would follow polite questioning from the teacher. The image of the body as an instrument of toil and mental labor (which had gained increasing legitimacy in the classroom) was recontextualized by resisters into a regressive image of machismo and physical pleasure. Female resisters were defined within the ideological lineaments of patriarchal discourse by being repositioned as sexually active subjects: "sluts" (females that have been conquered) or "decent ones" (women still to be conquered).

Subventing the institutionalized networks of ideology and power became for the students subjective responses to feelings of powerlessness resulting in a form of pleasure which Roland Barthes called *jouissance* (which he distinguished from *plaisir*). *Plaisir* occurs when the culture's codes "speak" the subject. *Jouissance* results when the subject intentionally fractures or ruptures the dominant cultural codes which both constitute discourse and shape the governance of the body. Paul Smith describes this distinction as follows: "Whereas *plaisir* relies upon the fixity of the 'subject' within the codes and conventions it inhabits, *jouissance* is specifically transgressive and it marks the crossing by the human agent of the symbolic codes which attempt to keep us in place as one 'subject'."[81] *Plaisir*, therefore, is the pleasure one gains from identifying with the *law*; whereas *jouissance* constitutes the bliss felt when the codes that fix the subject as a unitary subject are transgressed. According to Smith, "Codes . . . never allow us to speak our desire; they are intrinsically totalitarian in that respect, since they take our place and speak *for* us."[82] Since subjects cannot be abstracted from their object of knowledge, it may be said that classroom knowledge presents itself fully codified *for* the student who serves as a "receptor" for such knowledge, whereas streetcorner knowledge is actively produced by the student by drawing on the informal codes of street culture. Resistant students seek to reestablish the boundaries set up by the teachers demarcating streetcorner knowledge and school knowledge. Such boundaries in themselves offer an incitement to transgression and a provocation to acts of an oppositional nature, especially for those students anxious to play a role in generating the type of knowledge that can secure for them a subject position for affirming their desire. Understood in these terms, resistance constitutes the unfreezing of the subject, promoting different contexts for group identification. As such, resistance narrativizes the body and historicizes student subjectivity in wholly different ways than are possible in the confines of the classroom: by writing across one's body and establishing a field of *jouissance* and by constructing momentary options for alternative forms of subjectivity and the exercise of collective voice. Students make affective investments in these options, which promise students the ability to relativize existing discourses of subjection.

Cultural politics and resistance

I want to stress that a cultural politics of resistance on the part of students does not always manifest itself as a form of oppositional *praxis*, as an overt or innovative political statement and activity in which the invisible forces of domination are probed and contested for their unsaid propositions. As such, resistance does not always serve as a form of lived critique. Rosalind

O'Hanlon makes the important point that the very dichotomy between domination and resistance "bears all the marks of dominant discourse, in its insistence that resistance itself should necessarily take the virile form of a deliberate and violent onslaught."[83] She writes:

Rejecting [the view of resistance as deliberate political opposition], we should look for resistances of a different kind: dispersed in fields we do not conventionally associate with the political; residing sometimes in the evasion of norms or the failure to respect ruling standards of conscience and responsibility; sometimes in the furious effort to resolve in ideal or metaphysical terms the contradictions of the subaltern's existence, without addressing their source; sometimes in what looks only like cultural difference. From this perspective, even withdrawal from or simple indifference to the legitimating structures of the political, with their demand for recognition of the values and meanings which they incessantly manufacture, can be construed as a form of resistance.[84]

Resistance occurs as part of the very process of hegemony: *not* in reaction to it. Resistance is part of the process of negotiation, which works through the ideology-shaping characteristics of the school, and is often the means by which hegemony is secured. Thus, what might look like idiosyncracy, passivity, and indifference among students really "marks the point where our own political project runs into the subaltern's fundamental otherness, which may render his consciousness of the political in forms alien or even antipathetic to us."[85] Of course, this does not condemn the subaltern to a cultural politics that exists outside moments of revolutionary heroism, but suggests that there exist less visible operations of resistance that do not necessarily fit dominant conceptions of active, political struggle.[86] The concept of resistance prompts us to ask in what ways oppositional acts signal and inform the contradictions between the human capacities that schools profess to nurture and promote and the institutional and pedagogical forms in which schooling actually occurs. Occasionally, resistance can take the form of what Richard Brown calls "dialectical irony":[87] the enactment of a subterranean irony in which, to quote Terry Eagleton, "any signified may become a signifier, any discourse may be without warning rapped over the knuckles by some meta-discourse which may then suffer such rapping in its turn."[88] Dialectical ironists such as the class clown or the critical pedagogue reveal the tenuousness and arbitrariness of the social codes that keep social practices from spinning away from the centrifugal pull of normative social rules and codes. Rather than engaging in the "defanged" and "digested" forms of resistance through a symbolic inversion redolent of the rock music industry—a "ritual of co-option masked as dissent"—resistance as dialectical or free irony holds forth the promise of self-reflexive action.

Unlike "pure" irony, which undercuts the potency of every value and discredits all ideas, the concept of 'free irony' has much to offer students and educators attempting to ground resistance in a political project. According to Brown, dialectical or free irony forms the basis of public and personal life.[89] When reconstituted as a form of dialectical irony, resistance can not only help us recognize the contradictions and ambiguities in classroom and streetcorner life, but can assist us in realigning them with humane values and liberating political action.

Dialectical irony derealizes existing teaching practices and school-society relations as self-sufficient explanations where the "ostensibly apolitical value neutrality of rule-following honesty is revealed to be politically and morally inauthentic. Its small truth becomes a larger lie."[90] Dialectical irony also recognizes the contradictions inherent in the way the gendered body has been constructed and how the body learns.

It is important to emphasize, when discussing the role of corporeal learning or unlearning, that within the mainstream social theory, bodies are constructed as objects of research by modes of inquiry that produce a "fiction" of gendered identity. Within such a fiction, identity is manufactured after the image of the male, according to the dominant logic of opposition which sees women's bodies as deviations from the male norm. In other words, mainstream research often reflects the homogenizing logic reflected in the phallicism of dominant social theorizing. It is important not to underwrite a view of gender which privileges a phallocentric economy of the flesh and which rules out women's specificity. Consequently, my account of resistance needs to be submitted to an investigation of how gender-differentiated subject positions are solicited by technologies of power and how the meaning effects of such technologies are absorbed into the flesh.

Given what has been emphasized in the preceding pages, it would appear wrong to limit our understanding of ideology to the production of signs within particular discursive alignments and at specific historical junctures. Rather, we should give consideration to the affective power invested in particular ideologies and the body's sensuous relationship to the popular and everyday. Lawrence Grossberg understands this relationship as the "totalizing power of ideology." He writes that

in order to understand the relation of this totalized subject to reality it is necessary to recognize that the world is affectively as well as semantically structured. I am using the term affect to refer to the intensity or desire with which we invest the world and our relations to it . . . this process of affective investment (through which the body is inserted into its physical and social environment) results in the very possibility of a totalized sense of reality.[91]

Though not unproblematic, Grossberg's work is important since it allows for the recognition that discursive fields are organized affectively (within a "politics of feeling") as well as semantically. According to Grossberg, affect is a resource that can be mobilized, although he is quick to point out that affective economies ("mattering maps") are not equivalent to discourses of pleasure which function as the alibi for sexual deployment.[92] Nor are affective formations, which deal with structures of feelings and the texture of lived experience, confined to cultural activities such as leisure or romance. Rather, all affective relations, according to Grossberg, are shaped by the materiality and negativity of everyday life. What has not been made clear in Grossberg's work, and what must be theorized, is the notion that men and women invest differently in discourses and social practices in which there exists a differential solicitation or interpellation of male and female subjects.[93]

Ideology: A matter of truth or praxis?

Rather than adhering to a restricted notion of a definition of ideology as set forth by the orthodox tradition, it makes more pedagogical sense to ascertain the ways in which social relations and social practices represent various degrees of an emancipatory or dominating logic. This should not be undertaken by employing empirical criteria but by advocating a set of core ethical principles. Our central concern should not simply hinge upon whether or not the subjective "moment" of ideological production is subservient to, or dominated by, material and objective forces. What really matters is *the political project around which the concept of ideology can be put into practice.*

At this point I would assert that it matters less that any test for the 'truth' of an idea is incontrovertible than that the idea can be linked to a praxis of emancipation. Although political praxis cannot be the criterion for theoretical truth, it is politics, not philosophy or science, which seems the more appropriate site for understanding the rules of justice and social transformation.[94] From this perspective, it is wrong to argue that political considerations are generally irrelevant to the issue of correctly conceptualizing ideology within explanatory theories, since the fundamental question that should be put to any theory of ideology must deal with the inherent political project underpinning the theory. Speaking to this issue, Giroux writes the following:

Radical theory in its first instance should be valued for its political project, its socially relevant criticism, its estranging quality. In other words, it should be valued for the extent to which it can provide potentially liberating forms of critique and the theoretical basis for new forms of social relations. The underlying value of radical educational theory cannot be reduced to the deadening and politically harmless issue of consistency and reliability, a peculiar obsession of dominant social theory; on the contrary, its value should be assessed against the ability of forms of radical educational theory to confront the discourse and social practices of oppression with what Benjamin once called "potentially liberating images of freedom."[95]

All theories are privileged around particular interests and theories of ideology are by no means exempt. The choice that orthodox educational theorists offer is not one based on how subjectivities are constructed, but on a choice between a realism, with its attendant monism, and a radical relativism. The real choice to be made, of course, is far removed from either of these extremes.

Somewhere between the essentialism of the orthodox position and the voluntarism of ultrarelativists, a common ground for discussing ideology must be sought by both Marxists and non-Marxists alike. The importance of understanding ideology as the production of experience cannot be underscored enough, since such a viewpoint is fundamental to developing a project of possibility. It is from this standpoint that orthodox Marxian accounts of ideology fail to recognize or acknowledge the positivity of ideology, which includes forms of representations central to the organization of experiences and subjectivity. This failure only emphasizes the politically strategic need to enlist ideological struggles in the development of a public language rooted in the traditions, histories, and experiences of the marginalized, displaced, and dispossessed.[96]

Clearly, critical pedagogy must displace questions of ideology from the procrustean bed of economic determination and false consciousness; rather, it must seek other ways of mapping the terrain of ideology. Needed is an approach to ideology in which the emphasis is not simply on capital accumulation or the primary determinants of distortion and false consciousness, but on the means whereby the ruling elite manufactures and mediates the relations between the material and symbolic needs of the dominant culture and the productive, lived, and embodied symbols of subordinate groups. In other words, a move needs to be made away from criteriologies such as those laid out in orthodox Marxian accounts, which attempt to categorize the formal properties of ideology, in favor of a critical examination of the concrete ideological practices that are constituted and "bodied forth" in the rituals of schooling and everyday life.

In short, needed is a conception of ideology that neither rejects Marxist theory as false nor forecloses on the ability to speak to praxis and ideology in a manner that takes the Marxist problematic seriously. At the same time, it is necessary to break through the theoretical limitations of the classical Marxian approach. Although the search for a theory of ideology must steer wide of the restricted orthodox position, it must be careful not to abandon the important categories of class and history (or else we run the danger of falling prey to new postmodernist or post-Marxian manifestations of positivism). Instead of dichotomizing ideology into authentic reflections or distortions of reality, a critical pedagogy should conceive of reality–most importantly classroom reality–as a multiplicity of social relations, embodied metaphors, and social structures which cohere and contradict, some of them oppressive and some of them liberating.

An understanding of the body as a cultural site where ideology does its work can help teachers understand how schools implant students in discursive, nondiscursive, and material hegemony. The concept of the gendered body helps raise the important question: What are the social relations of the body legitimated in the school that contribute to a hegemonic masculinity and patriarchal violence? We must remain aware that the construction of gender (as distinct from biological sexuality) is both the product and the process of representation and self-representation.[97] And we must remain attentive to how the social construction of the body is absorbed subjectively by students and teachers so that it becomes part of everyday consciousness. Thus, the gendered body must be seen by teachers as constituted not by sexual difference but through and within language and representation, and in the experience of race, class, and sexual relations. How do males and females invest differently in different and similar ideological configurations? These and other questions must be raised by critical educators who wish to take student experience seriously in furthering the project of liberation and social transformation.

Of course, the very term "body" itself is problematic, ranging from being understood as a warehouse of archaic instinctual drives, to a cauldron of libidinal impulses, to a fiction of discourse. It is better if educational theorists begin to conceive of the body as a "body/subject", as a site of embodied or enfleshed subjectivity which reflects the weight of social structures pressed upon it or gridded into it. This means that the body itself is expressive of a multiplicity of social relations and intra-textual determinations. Intentionality or desire is rarely manufactured in innocence or in a relationship of unmediated transparency to its object. The meaning of human action both in and on the world functions at the level of the body within a discursively ordered set of relations produced within specifiable institutional conditions at certain historical junctures. We cannot peel away the flesh to yield an unobstructed view to some irreducible urge or desire since intentionality is always produced within historically and culturally specific forms. The challenge for critical educators is to begin to excavate those forms and to eventually access them in the interests of a more liberating human community. If the capitalist economy requires the body to be incorporated into the sign as a form of inner control, how can bodies turn themselves into political instruments by becoming symbols? In other words, how can the power *of* the body resist the power *over* the body? How can the body as symbol resist the body as sign?

The study of ideology charted out in this essay has tried to help teachers develop a critical pedagogy that is attentive to what Foucault refers to as "the technology of the self."[98] The technology of the self, which refers to the discarded and valued images of the self created throughout history in order to understand the self, works to provide students and teachers alike with public definitions of who they are. These definitions help to solicit how student bodies are positioned within schools; furthermore, the classifications and social practices governing the body help to determine consciousness and the possibilities for experience. Such positions are "always already" gendered positions and must be understood as such by teachers who wish to develop new forms of social practices that enable rather than constrain human liberation.

In the final analysis, the concept of ideology must not be reduced into a brute, intractable articulation, nor allowed to remain so broad that it loses any conceptual utility in a theoretical sense. The more pressing challenge for scholars of ideology is to provide the concept with enough determinate meaning that it works heuristically within a well-defined political project. Especially at a time when dominant ideologies and social practices are shifting us precariously closer to the Right, where, as Brecht said, "gangsters strut around like statesmen on the stage of history," the Left more than ever must formulate a vision of critical hope.

PART FOUR

Popular Culture, Text, and Critical Pedagogy

11

Children's Literature as an Ideological Text

Joel Taxel

The sociology of school knowledge

Critical curriculum scholarship has dramatically increased our understanding of the many and complex dimensions of the process of schooling. Whereas the dominant thrust of work in the curriculum field for much of the century had been directed toward "creating the *most efficient method* of doing curriculum work" (Apple, 1982, p. 12, emphasis in original), critically oriented researchers suggested that the knowledge accorded legitimacy by schools, rather than being neutral, actually represented "the ideological configurations of the dominant interests in a society" (Apple, 1982, pp. 12, 19).

Sociologists of school knowledge have sought to understand how both the formal and hidden curricula of schools contribute to the reproduction of a social order divided by race, class, and gender. Studies of textbooks (e.g., Anyon, 1979; Council on Interracial Books for Children, 1977), literature, (e.g., Christian-Smith, 1984; Dixon, 1977a, 1977b; Taxel, 1981, 1984; Wald, 1981), other curriculum materials (e.g., Beyer, 1983), as well as the social relations of the classroom (e.g., Anyon, 1981; Everhart, 1983; Sharp and Green, 1975) have provided chilling evidence of the extent to which classrooms are dominated by the world views and ideological perspectives of those occupying positions of socioeconomic and political pre-eminence in society.

Raymond Williams (1977) refers to this dominating set of perspectives and world views as a "selective tradition" and argues that the intentionally selective transmission of the knowledge, history, and culture of only certain groups or classes from the larger universe of possible knowledge, history, and culture is central to the process of social and cultural definition and identification. The selective tradition provides historical and cultural ratification of the social order and is a vital element of the "hegemonic" culture which pervades the "whole process living." This "lived system of meaning and values" becomes, according to Williams (1977, p. 110), "reality for most people in a society."

The concept of a hegemonic selective tradition has provided a powerful theoretical lens through which to view the numerous studies of school knowledge. Wexler (1982, p. 279) notes the following: "This new sociology of school knowledge and curriculum demonstrates that social power is culturally represented, and that knowledge and culture are essential moments in the process of social domination . . . The selective transmission of class culture as common culture silences the cultures of the oppressed, and legitimates the present order as natural and external." Wexler's (1982, pp. 279–280) essay seeks to move reproduction theory beyond its initial formulation and exemplifies the willingness of sociologists of school knowledge to engage in self-criticism. Like Wexler, Apple (1982, 1986) and Giroux (1983) argue against mechanistic correspondence theories of reproduction which suggest that the economy or economic form determines, in a straightforward fashion, the form and content of schooling, literature, and other aspects of culture. Also implicit in correspondence theories is the suggestion that there is little in either corpus school knowledge, or the culture at large, which contradicts or opposes the ideology and world views of the dominant social groups, and that this imposed tradition is passively internalized by students.

Aronowitz and Giroux (1987, p. 14) note the crucial importance of "Marx's statement that the ruling ideas of any society *are* the ideas of the ruling class" to radical critics of schooling. They view studies of school knowledge as part of an attempt to "de-mystify" ruling ideas "through relentless critique." School knowledge is conceptualized as "an instance of bourgeois ideology . . . an instrument of ruling class power." Although providing a fruitful analytic framework, this viewpoint also leads to what Aronowitz and Giroux (pp. 14–15) see as a "debilitating problem."

> School knowledge is viewed negatively as an instrument of domination; therefore, given the structural limits imposed by bourgeois hegemony, the chance for genuine education through schooling is virtually nil. Almost nowhere in Marxist educational theory and critique can one find a discussion of *counterhegemony* . . . Marxist education theorists have spent little time discovering the internal contradictions within prevailing school knowledge, disruptions that could provide a basis for a real educational movement.

In this chapter, I attempt to shed light on the notion that children's literature is an ideological text governed by a selective tradition and thus deeply implicated in the process of social domination and reproduction. In examining some of the recent research in children's literature, I will explore the relation between it and some of the issues raised by Aronowitz and Giroux and will suggest that an adequate understanding of the role of children's literature in the maintenance of hegemony must admit to far more complexity, even contradiction, than many, including myself, had initially allowed.

The selective tradition in children's literature

R. Gordon Kelley (1984, p. 86) has argued that attempts to "formulate a pure or rigorous (i.e., literary) approach to children's literature" are "doomed from the start." "So-called literary approaches," he insists, are "specific cultural allegiances wrapped in the mantle of art and labeled 'handle with reverence.'" My view, which builds on that of Kelley (1970, 1974), is that authors of books for children, consciously or not, are engaged in a process of socializing children into specific "cultural allegiances," values, beliefs, world views, and so forth. Children's literature is viewed as an important symbolic form through which a society attempts to communicate to its young central elements of the culture, as well as what Zipes (1983) calls "discourses on socialization," and which I have labeled "models of social action" (Taxel, 1984, 1986). Clearly, the elements of the culture legitimated by children's literature do not reflect a random and unbiased selection from the richly diverse cultures of America's citizenry. In short, despite the existence of important "oppositional" elements, the canon of children's literature has been governed by a selective tradition.

Some of the best-known studies of children's literature have investigated its content and documented the ways women and racial minorities, such as blacks, have been represented in the literature. These studies have revealed that the selective tradition historically has functioned by both underrepresenting or excluding these groups and by presenting them in stereotypic, often distorted roles (Taxel, 1981). Undoubtedly, socially conscious researchers and educators are aware of these problems and are deeply concerned about their possible effects on children (e.g., Campbell and Wirtenberg, 1980; Klein, 1985; Zimet, 1976). Sociologists of school knowledge (e.g., Apple, 1979; Taxel, 1981) have argued that these and similar analyses substantiate one of their basic claims: that there is a direct relation between social and political power and the ability of certain groups to define *their* knowledge, history, and culture as "official" knowledge, history, and culture.

The initial preoccupation of sociologists of school knowledge with literary *content* has eventually given way to a growing awareness that "the true bearers of ideology in art are the very forms rather than the abstractable content of the work itself" (Lukacs, quoted by Eagleton, 1976, p. 24). Bourdieu (1971, p. 1255), suggests that cultural artifacts such as literature contain a "symbolic representation of the social world adjusted to the structure of the socioeconomic relationships." Because the relationships are received as "natural," Bourdieu argues that they make a vital contribution to the "symbolic buttressing of the existing balance of forces." Willis (1977, p. 74) makes a similar point when he states that it is at the "cultural level that aspects of the real structural relationships of a society are transformed into conceptual relationships and back again."

My study (Taxel, 1984) of the content and form (or narrative structure) of a sample of thirty-two novels about the American Revolution published between 1899 and 1976 seeks to take into account these important theoretical concerns. I have endeavored to document the changing ways that authors writing over a seventy-seven-year period recreated the Revolution as a historical event (the "content" of the novels), and to describe how they structured their novels in terms of characterization, action, conflict presentation and resolution, and so forth (the narrative structure of the novels). Following Wright (1975, p. 193), I argue that the novels communicate a model of social action, a "paradigm for making sense of life." The evolution of these complex and interrelated elements is examined in relation to historical developments and changes in the socioeconomic structure of American society.

The American revolution in children's fiction

A major conclusion of this study is that authors of revolutionary war fiction have selectively drawn from the available interpretations of this pivotal event in American history. Despite some extremely significant changes in tone and emphasis in the most recent books, and one important exception, the sample is dominated by a simplistic and conservative explanation of the Revolution. Missing from the overwhelming majority of books is any discussion of either the economic dimensions of the Revolution or the conflict among the anti-British forces over the nature of the society to be established *after* independence was attained. This issue of "who should rule at home" was central to the interpretation of the progressive historians and remains the concern of the revisionist historians today.

The image of the Revolution which dominates the sample, and especially the first two periods into which it was divided (1899–1930; 1937–1953), reflects the interpretation of the "Whig" historians and their less pedantic and moralistic descendents, the "Consensus" historians. For the Whigs, the Revolution was a divinely inspired, life-and-death struggle against a tyrannical king bent on destroying the cherished rights and liberties of the valiant American colonists. In Crownfield's *Freedom's Daughter* (1930), for example, the novel's heroine speaks repeatedly of risking war to gain independence for her "oppressed land" and of the determination of the colonists "to resist further oppression." Gilbert Westwood, the hero of the novel, is similarly resolved to resist "sinful oppression and wicked tyranny that violate the God given right of humankind" (pp. 10, 19).

This theme of the Revolution as a struggle for political rights and liberty is central to Forbes's *Johnny Tremain* (1943), a novel said to encapsulate the dominant view of the American Revolution in American culture (Kammen, 1978, p. 206). That Forbes conceived of the Revolution as an ideologically motivated struggle is made clear in an impassioned speech by James Otis to the Sons of Liberty. Otis speaks of "fighting for rights such as . . . will be enjoyed a hundred years from now. There shall be no more tyranny . . . We give all we have . . . we fight, we die for a simple thing. Only that a man can stand up" (pp. 189–190, 192). This theme is repeated in virtually all of the books published through the mid 1950s and is reinforced by significant aspects of plot and character, what I have referred to as "narrative structure."

The configuration that dominates the books written in the first two periods finds a good, relatively weak protagonist living in a home dominated by a male who is strong, good, and devoted to the ideals of the Revolution. This initial, youthful weakness and dependence of the protagonists is critical in that their eventual, longed-for involvement in the conflict results in their transformation into stronger, more independent individuals. In essence, this experience constitutes a "rite of passage" for these characters and is the basis of the unity of novel content and structure in that it is a metaphor for the experience of the nation itself. Much like the heroes and heroines of the novels, the nation itself was undergoing a transformative passage from weak, colonial dependence to independent nationhood.

A crucially important dimension of the novels concerns the way "goodness" and "badness" are related to commitment to the Revolution. Reba Stanhope of *Freedom's Daughter* (1930), for example, is good not only because she is a warm and caring person, but also because she works tirelessly for the "life and death struggle for high principle" (Crownfield, 1930, p. 66). In contrast, Richard Skinner is a man with a "cold and selfish nature" (p. 77) who hides his activities for the Crown behind a pretense of neutrality. "An ambitious and unscrupulous man," Skinner is "determined to wrest every iota from his country's crisis that it could be made to yield" (p. 35). Skinner is evil, however, not simply because he sides with the British, but because he does so for materialistic reasons, a fact made evident through the character of Henry Skinner, his father. Henry is representative of a number of Tories who are "good" because their allegiance to the King stems from their loyalty to the Crown. In short, the content and structure of the novels written during Periods I and II offer what Cooke (1973, p. 93) has referred to as a "flattering explanation of a complicated story," one which "satisfies our insatiable hunger for good guys and bad guys."

Coming of age for the heroes and heroines in Periods I and II requires that they demonstrate the worth and readiness needed to enter the world of responsible adulthood. Since the values of adults and the ideals of the Revolution are unquestioned, the conflict simply provides the terrain on which they prove their worth and readiness. Thus, the model of social action in these books suggests that duty, commitment, persistence, and obedience will ultimately lead to success and acceptance into the adult world. As we shall see, there is a significant shift in the model in a number of books published in Period IV.

Another striking aspect of Period I and II books is their treatment of the issue of race (Taxel, 1981). Historian Edmund Morgan (1976) describes the fact that the revolutionary movement for liberty and independence occurred at the very time slavery was being institutionalized in many colonies as the "central paradox of American history." Although many authors simply exclude black characters from their stories, others are condescendingly paternalistic. Most shocking is the delight many authors seem to derive from their denigration of blacks, who are described repeatedly as "niggers," "Sambo," and in other vulgar ways. Indeed, many of the most ardent champions of freedom and liberty are themselves slaveholders. The father of Jack Jouett, for example, is described as a man ill-disposed to submit to "oppression and injustice," yet he is a slaveholder (Hawthorne, 1937, p. 5).

Caudill's *Tree of Freedom* (1949) is the only book written between 1899 and 1953 to manifest an awareness of the paradox mentioned above. It speaks pointedly of those who fled the oppressions of Europe and "began enslaving others as soon as they found a refuge in [the] new world" (p. 87). The nineteenth book in the sample, *Tree of Freedom* is the first to explicitly denounce slavery and to caution against making "any deal with slavery of any sort" (p. 142).

Although the books written after *Tree of Freedom* are free of the vicious stereotyping found in the books that preceded it, the paucity of black characters and discussion of the "black issue" in Periods III and IV (1959–1961; 1967–1976) suggests that authors were either unwilling or unable to deal with the contradictions posed by the black presence. This is especially surprising given the extent to which civil rights dominated the news during this time.

The one truly oppositional or counterhegemonic book in the sample is the *only* one which places the contradictions posed by the black presence in America at center stage as well as the only book to draw on the progressive/revisionist interpretation with its emphasis on economic factors and the internal dimensions of the conflict. Sally Edwards's *When the World's on Fire* (1972) paints a poignant picture of the tragic dilemma faced by many blacks during the Revolution. Could they trust either the British or the Americans, both of whom understood the vital role which black soldiers could play and who, accordingly, made promises they either couldn't or wouldn't keep? The essence of this tragic dilemma is noted by Maum Kate, who bitterly points out that although "the Americans babble about liberty . . . it is only their liberty they dream of, not ours." Likewise, the British "promise freedom only to enslave the slaves. We lose either way" (p. 101). Edwards's narrative shows blacks engaged in bold and decisive action on behalf of their own freedom, a portrait which stands in marked contrast to the apathy which characterizes black attitudes toward their condition in other novels. Again, it is Maum Kate who gets to the heart of the matter when she delivers the sample's only affirmation of black strength and humanity: "We are too easily fooled by so much talk of liberty. Yet we have our own strength, our own spirit. And someday this spirit will shine so bright the sun will seem a feeble candle" (p. 102).

Previously (Taxel, 1984), I noted that, despite some important changes in characterization, tone, and emphasis, the image of the Revolution in a majority of the novels written during Period III and IV (1959–1961; 1967–1976) is consistent with the earlier novels: that is, they continue to emphasize British violations of colonial rights and liberties as the root cause of the conflict. Among the most striking changes in the Period III and IV novels is the lessening of the impassioned, often simplistic rhetoric about freedom and liberty that charaterized many of the earlier novels. Books like Fritz's *Early Thunder* (1967) and Finlayson's *Redcoat in Boston* (1971) manifest an awareness of the complexity of the issues that separated Britain and the American colonies. Although both novels view the Revolution as a struggle for political rights and liberty, they *do not* see the American side as having an exclusive claim to virtue and decency. The issues are presented more evenhandedly. Since the Revolution is no longer reduced to a struggle of "good guys" against "bad guys," there also is increased complexity and realism in the development of characters. Thus, we rarely find the venal, avaricious Tories who were so important in defining the "goodness" of the earlier, idealistic Patriots. In fact, the distinction between good and bad now has little to do with a character's commitment to the Revolution but instead is solely a function of his or her qualities as a person. Fathers, who previously were towers of strength and virtue, are, in a number of important instances, weak. Some are even Tories. Perhaps most significant is that a number of Period IV protagonists lack the sense of commitment to revolutionary ideals and ideology that was so central to the characterization of their predecessors, who, above all, desired to play a role in the conflict. That several protagonists end up *rejecting* the ideals of the Revolution is a development that would have been unthinkable in the moral universe of Period I and II.

Collier and Collier's *My Brother Sam is Dead* (1974) is perhaps the best example of a novel in which revolutionary ideology proves insufficient to motivate a character to go to war. After tragically losing both his father and brother to, respectively, the British and American sides, Tim Meeker concludes that they are equally self-serving and hypocritical. Tim's disdain for revolutionary ideology and his ultimate decision to sit out the war are astounding in light of the way revolutionary ideals and ideology are exalted in the first two periods.

Equally astonishing is the image of the Revolution contained in *Freelon Starbird*. Richard Snow's (1976) novel with the protagonist boldly declaring his intention to put to rest "brave and nonsensical stories about the American colonies" (p. 1). Freelon's anything-but-glorious account reveals that rather than enlisting out of passionate attachment to revolutionary ideals, he does so "accidentally," in the midst of a drunken stupor. Even George Washington, that paragon of virtues, fails to escape the bitter barbs of a narrator who, lamentably, fails to provide a meaningful explanation of what the Revolution was all about. Avi's (1984) *The Fighting Ground* is another book short on interpretation, focusing instead on grimly portraying the horrors of war. Published after the completion of the study, this book makes the antiwar theme which is so important to many of the Vietnam-era books (those published in Period IV) *the* central theme. By providing an appendix containing a verbatim translation of the German spoken by the seemingly evil Hessian mercenaries who are the captors of the protagonist, the author compels us to abruptly switch viewpoints and to thus learn that in the present instance it is the "Patriots," not the Hessians, who are guilty of senseless brutality.

The shift in key elements in many of the Period IV books contributes to a markedly different model of social action than was found in the first two periods. Although passage to adulthood remains the central concern of the contemporary novels, there is now a preoccupation with each individual's perception of reality and a questioning of the notion that the initiates must accept the dictates of adult authority. Because many no longer do so, they engage in an often painful struggle to decide precisely what is, and is not, worth fighting for. Thus, an implicit message of many of the Period IV novels is that values and ideals are suspect and to be viewed with suspicion. The unreliability of adult counsel and the insufficiency of revolutionary ideology lead to the elevation of personal experience and feelings to the status held previously by the family and the values and ideals of the Revolution. Consequently, it is only through an often painful "testing of the waters" that many of the contemporary protagonists decide on a suitable course of action.

Space does not permit a full explanation of this startling shift from a view of the Revolution as a divinely ordained struggle that resulted in the creation of a near-perfect society based on liberty and freedom to one where causes are ill-defined, if defined at all, where senseless brutality abounds, and where confidence in the future is noticeably lacking. It is clear, for example, that books like *Johnny Tremain* (1943) and *Battle Lanterns* (Allen, 1949), which emphasize the ideological issues surrounding the Revolution and the notion of a "just war," are reflective of the confidence in America and American institutions that were a product, first, of America's crucial role in the Second World War and, later, its role as "defender of the free world" during the initial states of the "Cold War." Similarly, it seems evident that the antiwar sentiment of books like *My Brother Sam is Dead* (1974) and *Freelon Starbird* (1976) is a product of the profound sense of disillusionment engendered by the Vietnam War.

This apparent relation between historical events and the content of literature does not, however, justify the conclusion that there is a direct causal linkage between them. Historical events such as wars obviously help to shape the sociopolitical climate, which, in turn, shapes and affects literary creation. However, the dangers of simplistic, reductive attempts to explain the presence, or absence, of particular ideas in narrative forms like children's literature are immediately apparent when one considers how little impact so important a phenomenon as the civil rights movement appears to have had on authors of the books in the sample writing during the sixties and seventies (Taxel, 1984, pp. 28–30).

More difficult to understand and explain are the changes in the narrative structure of the novels. The problems, and dangers, attendant on explicating the dramatic shifts in the coding of characters, the decline in the authority of the father, and the diminished efficacy of the ideals of the Revolution as motivators of action are, in fact, quite similar to those involved in explaining the relation between changes in the structure of the economy and changes in the form of schooling. Drawing on the theoretical work of Eagleton (1976), and on Wright's (1975) study of the evolution of the narrative structure of western films, I have suggested that these changes were, at least in part, a product of profoundly important changes in the economy. Thus, I suggest that the changes in the character coding and narrative structure across the sample (i.e., from Periods I and II to Periods III and IV) and the parallel shift from the "classical" to the "professional" western in the films studied by Wright, are reflective of the ideological changes marking the transition from a market to a corporate economy (Taxel, 1984, pp. 30–41). I argue that such changes in "concrete social relations" (i.e., the economic organization of a society) affect, in ways that are still not entirely understood, "forms of perception" or "particular ways of seeing the world" such as literature (Eagleton, 1976, p. 6).

Clearly, a more complete examination of the complex process of cultural creation, one which will avoid the debilitating pitfalls of reductive, mechanistic correspondence theories, must take into account the intentions of authors and editors, include investigations of the political economy of publishing (e.g., Apple, 1986), and perhaps most significantly, determine whether the meanings ascribed to literary works by researchers do, in fact, "superimpose themselves automatically and finally onto the consciousness or behavior of all audiences at all times" (Gitlin, 1979, p. 253).

Recognizing the very exceedingly complex nature of the processes of cultural creation and consumption in no way invalidates the claim that cultural artifacts such as children's literature are, in fact, "ideological texts." What *is* open to challenge is the claim that belief in the existence of a selective tradition compels us to view the ideology contained in either individual, or groups of, literary works as mere instances of bourgeois ideology or as instruments of ruling-class power. My analysis of the novels in Period IV leads to the conclusion that at least some contemporary authors of historical fiction for children are no longer willing to offer young people simplistic explanations for complicated, often contradictory, historical events. Whether publishers are willing to continue publishing such books, whether librarians, parents, and teachers will purchase and use them in ways that take full advantage of the critical, even emancipatory potential within them are questions beyond the scope of this chapter. It does seem apparent, however, that the selective tradition which has historically dominated children's revolutionary war fiction is, at present, in the process of being reshaped and redefined.

Learning to cope with racism: Two perspectives

Few themes in children's literature have proven to be more contentious than the black experience in the United States. As was noted earlier, the black experience has been subject to a selective tradition which simultaneously excluded and vilified Afro-Americans. Although there have been some determined efforts to counter this insidious tradition (e.g., Harris, 1986), it was not until the sixties and the "creation" of a market for books about black children and the emergence of a group of "culturally conscious" writers that a really effective challenge was mounted (Sims, 1982). Despite the appearance of substantially more books containing black characters, controversy about the more subtle forms of stereotyping which began to appear in the early sixties continued to rage. A discussion of one instance of this sort of controversy will clarify an important, contemporary struggle over the selective tradition as well as point again to the potential of children's literature to foster critical thinking.

Ouida Sebestyen's *Words by Heart* (1979) received the prestigious Children's Book Award of the International Reading Association in 1980. Set at the turn of the century, the novel is told from the point of view of Lena Sills, a bright and spunky young black child who is compelled to come to grips with racism in the previously all-white town to which her family has moved. Lena's relationship with her father, Ben, occupies center stage in the novel, and it is his counsel that she heeds in learning to cope with racism and violence. It is through the words and actions of Ben that Sebestyen, who is white, develops the model of social action which has elicited the ire of more socially and politically conscious critics such as Rudine Sims (1980).

Ben has moved his family from Scattercreek, an all-black community in the Deep South, out west to Bethel Springs. Although Ben's motives in making the move are not entirely clear, we do know that although "it was easier there," he "wasn't proud" of himself (Sebestyen, 1979, p. 25). In addition to this apparent antipathy to life in an all-black town, Ben's attitude toward black history is similarly negative. He purposefully withholds "forty years of history that belong to" Lena, claiming, "They're past and ought to be put out of our memory to give room for better things" (pp. 23, 17). When Ben finally informs Lena of the often bitter history of her people, his account not only is marked by a tone of shame and despair, but is also rife with factual inaccuracies (Sims, 1980).

Perhaps the most controversial aspect of *Words By Heart* relates to Ben Sills's reaction to the hatred, threats, and violence directed toward himself and his family. It is this response, and in the example that Ben sets for Lena, that the novel's model of social action is developed. Sims (1980, p. 14) argues that the "cumulative picture of Ben Sills is the prototype of the good Negro—hard working, Bible-quoting, understanding, passive, loving and forgiving toward whites, and willing to 'wait on the Lord' until whites are ready to accept his family." This assessment is immediately apparent when the family returns from Lena's unexpected victory in a Bible recitation contest and finds a knife thrust menacingly through a freshly made loaf of bread. Lena's suggestion that the act is the work of Tater Haney, the son of a drunken bigot whose job as a hired hand for the eccentric Mrs. Chism is being assumed by the industrious and dependable Ben, is dismissed by her father as "nothing," the act of "some kid" on a dare. Ben responds similarly to the untimely death of the family's dog and insists that it is God, not Lena, who is to judge people (Sebestyen, 1979, pp. 15, 27).

This pattern of defending those who threaten him and his family is repeated throughout the novel and justified by reference to scripture. Ben believes, as he tells his wife Claudie, that the "Lord meant it when He said to love your enemies and turn the other cheek to those who hurt you" (p. 29). His philosophy of passivity and nonviolence is most clearly illustrated in the shattering conclusion of the novel. After reluctantly agreeing to repair some fences for Mrs. Chism, Ben is pursued and shot by Tater. Besides mortally wounding Ben, the shot spooks Tater's horse and he is seriously hurt after being dragged through some rough underbrush. Sensing danger, Lena arrives on the scene and finds Ben tending to his assailant. As he dies, Ben pleads with Lena to help and forgive Tater. "Every nerve and muscle said I can't. I won't . . . She knew with a heavy sinking, how Papa would answer, whom he would quote. Love thy enemies and do good to those who hate you. Give to him that asketh thee" (pp. 123–124). Lena later refuses to identify Tater as the murderer of her father, stating, "I have to let God handle it. That's all" (p. 129). Clearly, she has taken the words and actions of her father to heart and decided that the evil of racism can be combatted with love, forgiveness, and trust in God.

On the surface, Mildred Taylor's *Roll of Thunder, Hear My Cry* is remarkably similar to *Words by Heart*. It too received a prestigious literary award (the Newbery Medal), and is told from the point of view of a spunky and intelligent young black girl. Like Lena, Cassie Logan's naiveté about the world is shattered by events she is unable to control. Here too, it is the father who is most instrumental in teaching the child to cope with and respond to racial hatred and violence. However, these similarities prove to be superficial as close scrutiny reveals that the novel, written by a black author, differs in some fundamental and profoundly important ways from the one just discussed.

To begin, the Logans are influential and respected members of a closely knit black community in rural Mississippi. Because they own a four-hundred-acre tract of land, they are insulated from the oppressive sharecropping system which binds their neighbors to the whims and fancies of white landowners. The Logans are actively involved in church and community affairs, and it is because of their pride and sense of civic responsibility that Mary Logan instigates and organizes a boycott of the store owned by the Wallaces. This action not only puts their land in jeopardy; it sets off a chain of events that have tragic consequences.

In addition to their strong sense of community, the Logans take pride in the history of their family and people. There are numerous instances in which history is recalled in order to illuminate some present-day occurrence. When the "night riders" are out terrorizing the community, for example, Mr. Morrison recalls how his parents "had fought them demons out of hell" and died fighting (Taylor, 1976, p. 113). Mary Logan's insistence that the truth about slavery be taught leads to her firing as a teacher. Rather than being something to be shamefully hidden, history in *Roll of Thunder* provides a means to establish continuity between past struggles against oppression and those of the present.

Ownership of the land and the sheltering love of strong-willed parents afford Cassie and her brothers a measure of protection from the crushing impact of the racist caste system that governed social relations in Mississippi in the 1930s. However, a series of events make it impossible even for Mary and David Logan to withhold from them the bitter truth of what it means to be black. The most significant of these incidents occurs when Cassie accompanies her grandmother to Strawberry. "No day, in all my life," she recalls, "had ever been as cruel as this one" (p. 87). It is in their efforts to lessen the pain and humiliation Cassie endures at the hands of Charlie and Lillian Jean Simms that we come to understand the novel's model of social action, one which is radically different from that contained in *Words by Heart*.

Mary Logan perceives immediately the traumatic impact of the day's events on Cassie. Her explanation of Lillian Jean and Charlie Simms's belief in white superiority and black inferiority leads her to trace its historical roots in attempts to justify slavery. Mary notes that slavery was also rationalized "because it taught us to be good Christians—like the white people." She is quick to add, however, that religion was not meant "to save our souls, but to teach us obedience . . . But even teaching us Christianity didn't make us stop wanting to be free, and many slaves ran away" (p. 96).

Although the words and deeds of the Logans certainly qualify them as good Christians, their religious philosophy is quite different from that of Ben Sills, something that becomes readily apparent when David Logan speaks to Cassie about the Strawberry incident and her plan to "repay" Lillian Jean. David begins by recalling his bitterness toward John Anderson, a white man who decimated a much-loved stand of trees on Logan property. Referring to the bibilical injunction to turn the other cheek, David explains: "But the way I see it, the bible didn't mean for you to be no fool. Now one day, maybe I can forgive John Anderson for what he done . . . but I ain't gonna forget it. I figure forgiving is not letting something nag at you—rotting you out" (p. 133). David tells Cassie that he suppressed his desire to give Charlie Simms " a good thrashing" after considering "the hurt of what happened" to her, with "what could've happened if I went after him." David's advice is that Cassie weigh carefully the consequences of her response to Lillian Jean and to the fact that "Lillian Jean probably won't be the last white person to treat you this way." He does, however, make one thing perfectly clear: "There are other things . . . that if I'd let be, they'd eat away and destroy me in the end. And it's the same with you, baby. There are things you can't back down on, things you gotta take a stand on. You have to demand respect in the world, ain't just gonna hand it to you . . . Ain't nobody's respect worth more than your own." (p. 134).

The remainder of *Roll of Thunder, Hear My Cry* is a demonstration of how Cassie, Mary, David, and the other Logans put this philosophy into practice in the fact of the escalating danger and violence precipitated by the boycott of the Wallace store initiated by Mary. Although the Logans suffer injury, hardship, and economic loss, they act with a courage born of a conviction about what is just and fair. Others are less fortunate, and the tragic fate of the troublesome T. J. undercuts, for many readers, the confidence they feel for Cassie and her future. This confidence stems from the obvious fact that the teachings of her parents have provided her with the strength, determination, and self-respect she will need to overcome the trials sure to come. Despite the optimism afforded by this knowledge, we are also cognizant that the irrational, deeply rooted bigotry and hatred that Cassie and her family endured persists to this day. Nevertheless, the novel's suggestion that racism be forthrightly confronted by groups of individuals who have carefully assessed the situation and considered the possible implications and consequences of their actions sounds very much like the strategy successfully used during the civil rights movement.

It is difficult for many readers of *Word by Heart* to be similarly optimistic about the prospects of Lena Sills. One wonders about her change from the spirited girl who challenges and defeats the heretofore invincible Winslow

Starnes in the recitation contest, to one who is willing to allow her father's murderer to escape justice. Although her refusal to name her father's assassin can perhaps be said to follow her decision to honor his last wish, it is less easy to explain Lena's transformation into one who, in the words of her stepmother, will "know how to knuckle under" to the likes of Mrs. Chism (Sebestyen, 1979, p. 133). Illustrator George Ford, for example, rejects the notion that *Words by Heart* is "a tribute to the human spirit," and sees it instead as a book which "mindlessly celebrates the gradual disintegration of a spirit." Lena, concludes Ford, "will forsake her drive for success – not because she is weak – but because she is Black" (quoted in Sims, 1980, p. 17).

Also troublesome is the novel's rather facile equation of justice and revenge. Is it really the case that for Lena to have "named" Tater would have meant that she was seeking revenge? Sims (1980, p. 27) has decried the fact that in *Words by Heart* the "responsibility for loving, forgiving and overcoming evil with good lies solely with the book's Black characters." She similarly rejects the implication that "white people should be understood and forgiven, even for violent racist acts." The notion that social change will occur when racism's victims show sufficient patience and faith in the Lord is a profoundly conservative one. Indeed, it can be argued that had the leaders of the civil rights movement adopted this strategy, as opposed to the one implicit in *Roll of Thunder*, black Americans would still be riding on the back of the bus.

Finally, in assessing the actions of Ben Sills, one is reminded of David Logan's remark that "the bible didn't mean for you to be no fool." Ben Sills's adamant refusal to respond to the threats made to his family, his decision to sacrifice his life for the bigoted youth who has shot him when he knows that this action will leave his children fatherless, if perhaps not the actions of a fool, are, for many, simply too fantastic to accept. In short, the actions of the novel's pivotal character lack credibility.

Conclusions

The issues raised by this comparative analysis are many and complex. One of the most significant is how one balances concern for the sociopolitical values contained in a literary work and its aesthetic values. In a more comprehensive discussion of these books (Taxel, 1986), I suggest a mode of analysis that is sensitive to both vital concerns. In the case of *Words by Heart*, for example, I argue that its problematic model of social action is related, at least in part, to the deeply flawed character of Ben Sills.

The fact that the more politically progressive of the two books was written by a black author raises interesting questions about the way certain kinds of background and experiences contribute to particular kinds of perspectives and viewpoints. Sims (1982) offers a compelling case for her claim that it is only in the writings of a group of socially conscious black writers— those she refers to as "image makers"—that it is possible for young readers to encounter a realistic glimpse of the black experience in America. In other words, it appears that most, if not all, of the works that counter or oppose the selective tradition about the black experience are written by those who have actually lived the experience being recounted. It is also the case that the controversy precipitated in *Words by Heart* is but one of many which have resulted from "a non-Black author trying to create a fictional story about growing up in the bosom of a Black American family, told from the perspective of someone at the center of that family" (Sims, 1984, p. 155).

In this chapter I have argued that although, over the expanse of its history, children's literature *has* been dominated by a selective tradition that has reflected and legitimated the interests of dominant social groups, this tradition, at present, has little in common with the sort found in countries like for example, the Soviet Union, where literature is centrally controlled by the state (O'Dell, 1978). Although contemporary writers of children's literature are significantly influenced by the conservative climate of our day and increasingly by the imperatives of a publishing industry undergoing consolidation—and thus more and more subject to the dictates of the "bottom line" ("is it profitable?")—they have retained considerable autonomy in terms of their freedom to select subjects and themes, and to treat them in whatever manner they see fit. Although we would be foolish, in the extreme, to underestimate the threat posed to these freedoms by the forces of reaction which the Reagan administration has done so much to encourage, it is useful to keep in mind Raymond Williams's (1977, p. 117) reminder that struggles against selective traditions have always been "a major part of all contemporary cultural activity."

The revolutionary war novels written during Period IV and the works of writers like Mildred Taylor are simply not compatible with neat and tidy theories suggesting that children's literature is little more than an instrument of domination and bourgeois hegemony. My experience reading and discussing with students various kinds of literary works in an open ended fashion (Taxel, 1987) has affirmed my belief in literature's perhaps unique power to facilitate dialogue on a number of critical issues. The first pertains to the existence of a selective tradition. By asking students to reflect on their experiences with literature and by reading books which contain some of the more insidious dimensions of the selective tradition (e.g., racism and sexism), students begin to develop awareness not only of the existence of the selective tradition, but the ways in which it has contributed to their attitudes toward race, gender, as well as their outlooks of life and living. By reading and discussing some of the books discussed in this chapter, we are also able to see the potential of literature to raise critical issues too often ignored by textbooks which seek to avoid controversy and create an impression of a society free of conflict and ruled by consensus (e.g., Fitzgerald, 1979). Taylor's book, for example, makes it possible to lay bare the glaring contradiction between our country's cherished ideology of liberty and justice for all and the relentless denial of these "rights" to our black citizens. Indeed, Sally Edwards's (1972) book makes it clear that this contradiction was inherent to the Revolution that led to the founding of our country.

The belief that selective traditions are continuously being shaped, reshaped, and contested is, finally, consistent with theories of resistance which have been so important in the recent work of sociologists of school knowledge (e.g., Apple, 1982; Giroux, 1983). These theories have restored to us the theoretical possibility of "agency," the belief in our ability to influence and shape our lives, indeed our history, that was effectively denied by early formulations of reproduction theory. Resistance theory also bears a striking resemblance to theories of reader response (e.g., Agee and Galda, 1983; Rosenblatt, 1978) which conceive of the reader as an active, dynamic maker of meaning whose response to literary works can simply not be assumed or predicted by even the most sophisticated forms of textual analysis. An important role of critical scholarship in children's literature must be to make clear the nature of the contemporary struggle to fashion and define the tradition we seek to pass on to our children. Working in concert with those who work daily with children, we can hopefully empower children to make this struggle their own.

Reading Rock'n'Roll in the Classroom: A Critical Pedagogy

David R. Shumway

Several years ago at a meeting of the Popular Culture Association, I gave a paper entitled "Rock as a Way of Knowing." The paper addressed claims by rock'n'roll lyrics and criticism that the experience of rock'n'roll is radically and positively transformative.[1] My point was that, although such claims were grossly inflated, rock'n'roll might be a means by which one's general understanding of the world could be altered, but this would be true only for those whose experience of the form was both emotionally deep and intellectually complex. I don't know if I would put it this strongly today, but that is irrelevant, for I bring this paper up only to provide a context for one of the responses to it. Remember that the setting is a convention of academics who spend at least some of their professional lives writing and thinking about things like the soap operas, outdoor decks, and clothing store mannequins. One of these people, after listening to my paper, remarked that he didn't see how rock'n'roll could have anything to do with knowing, since it was often openly anti-intellectual and since, like television, the mindless repetition of it deadens the intellect and displaces more worthwhile objects of attention. This view is, I believe, quite common—it received audible murmurs of approval from the audience at that session—and it leads one to believe that the last thing one would want to do is to bring rock'n'roll into the classroom. What I will argue here, however, is that even if my critic's point of view were true without qualification, as a teacher one would still want to address rock'n'roll. In fact, a critical pedagogy would require that it be addressed all the more under those circumstances. But I will also argue here that, like all cultural forms, rock'n'roll contains elements which both support and undermine the dominant ideology.

My task in what follows is thus both to show why one should undertake a critical pedagogy of rock'n'roll and what such a project might look like. To explain why rock'n'roll should be taught, I will need to address in some detail various conceptions of the form's cultural significance. My argument will be that the purpose in bringing rock'n'roll into the classroom is to provide students with a critical understanding of a cultural form that often plays a significant part in their lives. Furthermore, there are emancipatory and oppositional aspects of the form which the larger project of a critical pedagogy can draw upon. In describing the critical pedagogy, the following points will be developed: (1) teaching rock'n'roll and other materials from popular culture differs from most other subjects in that it involves bringing into a school situation material with which students often strongly identify and upon which they have already placed strong interpretations; (2) rock'n'roll cannot be treated merely as a kind of music, but must be understood as a cultural form that involves different codes and conventions, including those of stage behavior, videos and films, cover art, and so forth.

There are two attitudes toward rock'n'roll and other forms of mass culture that come out of the tradition of critical theory. The more influential of the two positions, at least within the Frankfurt school, was the one articulated by Adorno in his attacks on jazz and popular music (1941, 1967) and, by Horkheimer (1972), on mass cultural generally.[2] In these critiques it is argued that culture under capitalism has been turned into an object produced by the "culture industry." Previously, culture "always . . . raised a protest against petrified relations" under which humans live (Adorno, 1975, p. 13). Now, however, critical thought itself has become impossible. Culture has lost whatever oppositional character it once had. The opposing view comes from Walter Benjamin (1969). He argues that the ability to produce art by means of mechanical reproduction offers the possibility for the masses to experience much art for the first time. Thus, for Benjamin, the same technological innovations which for Adorno result only in standardizing culture under capitalism so that oppositional perspectives are never taken becomes the potential for the masses to make art their own and not the sole property of the ruling class.

Both the Adorno and the Benjamin positions have their equivalents in political positions to their right. Adorno's position is echoed in those claims one so often hears about television and rock'n'roll turning our youth into mindless sponges. Allan Bloom (1987), for example, in his best-selling book *The Closing of the American Mind*, argues that rock'n'roll depicts life as "a nonstop commercial prepackaged masturbational fantasy."[3] Bloom's specific charge against rock'n'roll—and popular culture in general—is that it has caused the minds and souls of our youth to atrophy. This is almost precisely Adorno's complaint, but Bloom certainly isn't upset by a lack of opposition. In fact, the oppositional politics of the sixties are a major part of the problem. Bloom is applying to intellectual life the right-wing position which holds that what is lacking in our culture is labor. Mindless pursuit of sex and other pleasures has made workers of all kinds undisciplined. Mass culture is thus partially responsible for the decline in productivity, shrinking profits, increasing trade deficit, and an undisciplined work force. It is interesting that a phenomenon considered by Adorno as wholly complicitous in the ideology of capitalism and the rationalization of all aspects of human existence appears to the Right to do virtually the opposite.

The Benjamin position's equivalent is the populism which holds that a mass cultural form can be the genuine expression of various subcultures (Belz, 1972; Frith, 1981; Grossberg, 1984; Hebdige, 1979; Marsh, 1979). Populism thus treats rock'n'roll as a kind of folk culture, a status it does not as often accord to film or television, and for obvious reasons: although the production of feature films and most television programs is highly centralized and controlled by large corporations, the making of records is to some extent decentralized and in the hands of independent producers. This distribution and marketing of these records, however, remains nearly as concentrated within the entertainment conglomerates as is television or film production. In spite of the control of production by these conglomerates, the populist position still holds that a variety of authentic cultural and political perspectives are presented in popular recordings. For example, they point to British working-class forms such as punk or black forms such as rap and hip hop. Although these forms *are* politically significant, to treat them as folk culture is to misunderstand the way that they are produced and consumed under capitalism. Furthermore, the populist position tends to deny the notion that there is any hegemony over popular music by arguing that such music derives its identity and power from its popularity. Popularity is thus equated with success, and the populist critic falls into the trap of judging records as record company executives do, by their ranking on the charts.

None of the four positions I have described here is adequate to support a critical pedagogy of rock'n'roll. Each fails to take a genuinely dialectical stance toward its object. The Frankfurt school and conservative positions each assume that consumers of rock'n'roll are mindlessly in the thrall of the music to which they listen. Their assumption is that the music acts as a simple influence on the listener without any interpretive activity on the latter's

part. Any class discussion of a song or album will be sufficient to demonstrate that even devoted fans of a particular performer or genre interpret
it differently. On the other hand, the position associated with Benjamin
and the populists assumes a freedom for the consumers that permits them
to control their use of the product and be entirely aware of its meaning.
Therefore, self-reports are taken at face value and the potential effects of the
listener's unconscious or of unexamined assumptions of a dominant ideology are ruled out in advance. It is harder to demonstrate the existence of
meanings that the listener is not aware of than it is to show the existence
of diverse interpretations of rock'n'roll; we are less likely to know when a
student realizes that part of the appeal of a record has stemmed from its
repetition of patterns of thought that are integral to racism, patriarchy, and
economic domination. But most of us have recognized this moment in our
own lives. The effects and meaning of any cultural form must be understood in terms of a play of awareness and its lack. The music is interpreted
by listeners, but not from a position of complete freedom.

There has been an insufficiently dialectical conception of the artist's
role as well. The populist position claims that the freedom exists to allow
all kinds of music to be played and all beliefs and perspectives to be expressed. This position denies the power of the entertainment conglomerates to shape and limit what gets distributed and played. The Adornian position, on the other hand, denies that there is any significant diversity at all
in popular music, or indeed in any of the products of the culture industry.
Here again, neither position is sufficiently dialectical. In fact, the products
of the culture industry are remarkably diverse, but such diversity is itself
a function of, not a challenge to, capitalism. Here we need to pay attention
to the surface of culture, where products have neither repressive nor liberating meanings, but have differences required to stimulate continued demand. This is one of the major differences between the products of mass
culture, which always claim to be "new" even as they continually recycle
old formulas, and folk cultures, where cultural forms such as music, crafts,
or oral literature are valued precisely because they are traditional. Nevertheless, the fact that differences in mass culture are generated in the service of
increasing the sale of commodities does not render those differences necessarily meaningless or politically repressive.

There is one thing upon which all of these positions agree: that rock'n'roll
and other forms of mass culture are a powerful force in the lives of today's
young people. Thus it might be argued from any one of these positions
that rock'n'roll should be addressed in the schools. The right shrinks from
this conclusion on the grounds that to bring rock'n'roll into the classroom
is to lend it legitimacy. This point is true but trivial, since there is little

schools can add to the legitimacy rock'n'roll already has among youth. The Adornian might teach the music only to expose its pernicious effects, a position which at least has the virtue of recognizing that the radical educator must address dominant elements of a culture, for to ignore them is to simply accept the current hegemony. Thus, whether one likes rock'n'roll or whether one regards it as repressive, a critical pedagogy of it remains necessary. Students need to be able to read the social meanings of mass cultural products, and this ability does not develop naturally from exposure to them. On the other hand, rock'n'roll is not neutral territory for most students. To take the Adornian position as the basis for one's treatment of rock'n'roll is to put oneself in the same moralizing role that the Right has taken since the fifties. Not only will this destroy one's credibility as a teacher of this material, but it will also prohibit one from making this subject an occasion for encouraging emancipatory hopes and developing emancipatory strategies.

Rock'n'roll should be brought into schooling precisely because it can challenge some of what is most repressive about schooling itself. Although Bloom and other critics complain about the up-front sexuality of rock'n'roll, this characteristic can also be viewed positively. Sexuality is part of rock'n'roll's larger preoccupation with the body, the name *rock'n'roll* itself being a pun that refers to both having sex and dancing. Thus, as in Chuck Berry's "School Days," songs often oppose time spent in school with the desire to dance. Such an opposition is not merely a matter of representing what are undoubtedly common daydreams, but of challenging the fundamental restrictions which schooling puts on the body. Such restrictions are certainly a part of the hidden curriculum, which teaches students to be the docile, dependable workers needed by industry and other business. But even more fundamentally, they are part of a broader system of strategies and technologies that Foucault (1977) has called "discipline." Foucault argues that discipline is a new form of control which came into dominance in the nineteenth century. Unlike earlier forms of control, which relied on making a spectacle of the body of a criminal in order to inspire terror or teach a lesson, discipline works directly on the body to produce aptitude. It treats the body as a machine and uses it more productively than did earlier forms of control.

The modern school is made possible by such disciplinary strategies as the classroom, with its neat ranks of desks under the surveillance of the teacher they face; the timetable, with its careful measurement of time allocated to a repeatable sequence of activities; and the examination, by which students are observed, ranked, and measured against a norm. All of these procedures are of relatively recent historical origin, and all of them to a greater or lesser extent restrict the body. The regime of discipline is so pervasive that it cannot simply be abandoned. But its effects can be noted, and in so doing some distance can be established between the person and the "individual" defined by the norms and hierarchies of discipline. Rock'n'roll can help us do this by presenting the body as a site of fun and pleasure, of the pure energy of movement freed from disciplinary aptitude. No school, of course, could allow this to be the only way the body is understood, and none will. The point is not to change the school into a disco, but to provide a counterpoint to the monodimensional way the body is figured and formed in schools. Rock'n'roll can do this because it already does it, but only outside. To bring the opposition into the classroom is to make it possible to treat it dialectically, to allow each to be a perspective on the other.

The body for Foucault is not a euphemism for the sexual, and desexualizing is only one aspect of the way the body is constructed in schooling. The body is used by Foucault to indicate the fact that disciplinary controls are not merely memorized or acccepted, but actually form the body itself. One could say that they are habits in the sense that they work without the conscious choice of an individual but are ingrained in the very posture and musculature of the body. Thus when we say that rock'n'roll presents another body, it is not just a pleasurable body, but a body that refuses these habits; it is a rebellious body. Thus rock'n'roll is a form that already recognizes itself as a site of struggle, that already speaks of the need for emancipation, that already offers the hope of liberation. As we will see later, sometimes the emancipatory project of rock'n'roll is clearly related to particular injustices and oppressions; often, however, the project seems vague and apolitical. But this is precisely why rock'n'roll needs to be the subject of critical pedagogy: the elements of the emancipatory and the elements of the dominant are not easily separated. The ability to separate them is a principal skill which any critical pedagogy must teach (Giroux, 1983).

But how can teachers draw on the oppositional character and the emancipatory project of rock'n'roll while at the same time treating it critically? It is this dilemma which troubles all attempts to treat cultural forms dialectically, but it is especially difficult when the attempt is made with regard to popular culture, since part of its emancipatory potential lies in its audience's identification with it and rejection of more dominant institutions. Lawrence Grossberg has argued in his important essay, "Teaching the Popular," that the construction and sound of songs cannot be directly interpreted to explain the effects of the music (1986, p. 181). Nor, one might add, can they be interpreted to yield the social meaning of rock'n'roll as a cultural practice. The rock'n'roll text is thus elusive, not only in the sense that poststructuralism has shown us that all texts are elusive, but also in that the experience of rock'n'roll cannot be centered in any of its many sign systems. Grossberg's experience teaching courses in the history of rock'n'roll and youth cultures has led him to another sense in which the rock'n'roll song seems to refuse to be interpreted. He reports that "the students in his course could neither hear nor see meaning that seemed obvious to me, both as a critic and member of a different generation of the rock'n'roll culture. Even when they acceded to my readings, this had little impact on their responses to the music" (1986, p. 181). Grossberg attributes the lack of impact of his interpretations to the fact that listeners don't just respond to the songs, but to the larger structures, the sign systems mentioned above, in which the songs are situated.

Grossberg's experience parallels my own, but his analysis of it does not. This is largely a function of his own focus on his students' *response* to rock'n'roll. Grossberg's goal in thinking about this cultural form is to understand its power and its popularity, and the terms of this project confine him to thinking about the effects of the form on its listeners—its power—and the responses of the listeners to the form—its popularity. No wonder, then, that his interpretations of songs should prove to be irrelevant. Their relevance could only stem from their duplication of his students' interpretations, but such duplication would be unlikely given not only the generational difference, but more importantly, Grossberg's training as an academic critic. Grossberg's solution is essentially that we abandon the project of critical reading, and instead direct our "analysis toward the ways in which rock'n'roll is empowered by and empowers particular fractions of its audience" (1986, p. 182). Although Grossberg denies that this project involves asking people about their responses to the form, there is no other means by which the data needed to perform such an analysis can be obtained. Thus Grossberg's goals would seem to require the kind of ethnographic research that Janice Radway (1984) has done on the popular romance, with the classroom itself becoming the laboratory where the research is conducted. Ethnographic research is valuable in that it serves as a corrective to those who see only the oppressive aspects of popular forms. On the other hand, it does tend to cause researchers to discard the critique of ideology altogether, as it very nearly does in *Reading the Romance*.

Grossberg's attribution of his students' failure to see or hear his readings to the fact that rock'n'roll songs are not self-sufficient texts represents a significant flaw in his argument. If this explanation were correct, the problem would stem from Grossberg's own practice and could be remedied by interpreting not songs, but the entire cultural form. But the resistance to new interpretations is common even in classes where the texts are traditional literary ones, and all the more so when the students come to a course with significant personal experience of a form, as they often do when popular materials are the subject matter. The purpose of teaching popular materials is not to get students to change their responses to them, but to teach them how to read both the materials and their responses critically. This requires that the teacher attempt to separate response from interpretation, to attempt to maintain a dialectic of pleasurable involvement and critical distance.

That this is easier said than done is obvious, but it also points to more likely sources of the students' resistance to Grossberg's interpretations. To offer the kind of academic, critical reading that Grossberg himself would find pleasurable would already be to divorce the text from the students' narcissistic involvement with it, and this for two reasons. Not only is the critic's discourse distinctly *other* than the students' discourse, but it wounds the students' narcissism because it claims to be a superior discourse and seeks therefore to deprive the students of their previous claim on the music. But students resist not only because their identification with rock'n'roll is threatened by the teacher's interpretations, but also by the character of the student-teacher relationship itself. As Felman (1982) and Penley (1986) suggest, the classroom, like the psychoanalyst's office, is the scene of transference and resistance. Students will tend to resist all imposition by the teacher upon that part of their world they have not previously ceded to the school. The limited transference that establishes the teacher's authority also restricts that authority.

The particular problem this raises for an explicitly critical pedagogy is multiplied when one is dealing with material that has an oppositional character. Insofar as the texts are experienced as oppositional, they will tend to encourage resistance on the part of the students to the teacher's critical readings, since the teacher is for students a representative of the dominant. On the other hand, by merely bringing rock'n'roll into the classroom one may be compromising the oppositional status of the experience or texts by giving them the imprimatur of curricular status. Students define themselves both by their school experience and against it, and rock'n'roll is often explicitly associated with the out-of-school self. Thus the oppositional character of the form itself increases the likelihood that students will not easily accept the teacher's interpretations. Paradoxically, however, this problem may be addressed by taking seriously the critique of schooling as a cultural practice presented in rock'n'roll which I described earlier, and by foregrounding the experience of rock'n'roll fans. The latter involves two distinct moments, one of which is the exploration of the oppositional feelings and attitudes experienced by fans. For example, various forms of rock'n'roll—heavy metal, punk, and others—include styles of dress and behavior which are designed to shock and which constitute a rejection of bourgeois styles and behavior. Although students are not likely to interpret the forms in this explicitly political way, they do experience these forms as a rejection of the norm and often as the expression of anger and frustration. These oppositional sentiments do not usually occur without a corresponding expression of the possibilities of power and liberation. Again, these sentiments are not usually expressed in political terms; indeed, they may often be expressed only in "power" chords, buzz saw guitar solos, and the loud volume at which the music is played. Nevertheless, the realization that lack of power is an issue can be derived from students' own experience. By treating fans of punk or heavy metal as oppositional groups, one can valorize the fans' experience without acceding to their limited interpretation of it.

The second moment in the treatment of rock'n'roll fandom tries to show how the role of fan is one structured by the system of production that is responsible for rock'n'roll performers. A critical pedagogy requires that we teach students to deal with popular culture not as fans—they already know how to do that—but as social, moral, and intellectual beings capable to some extent of separating their emotions and their tastes from their analysis and interpretation. Part of that education is learning that in being fans we are not simply choosing to like this or that performer, but are acting in socially defined and economically significant ways. In this second moment, what we as teachers have to offer them are discourses which cannot but alter the experience of popular forms. Our job is to make these discourses available to students, whether they find it pleasurable to use them or not. Obviously, however, it is more likely that they will use them if they do take pleasure in it, so showing how interpretation and analysis can be pleasurable is an important corollary. There are no secret methods for accomplishing these tasks. Teaching critical reading is no easier than teaching algebra or chemistry, and, although it makes different intellectual demands upon students, they are not in principle easier demands. The rewards of learning these skills may be more apparent to students if they also learn what critical pedagogy must also teach: how their own interests are served or frustrated.

Thus, although semiotics may seem like a complex theory suited only for graduate students, it can in fact serve as the basis for an approach to rock'n'roll which can be used with students at all levels. In the sense that I will invoke it here, semiotics does not involve an elaborate set of terms or procedures, but rather some assumptions about how sign systems work.

One of the assumptions necessary for a critical pedagogy of rock'n'roll is that its potentially liberating and potentially repressive elements are not determined either by the judgements of listeners or by the intent of the producers. A semiotic approach allows one to distance the analysis of rock'n'roll from either of these poles. Semiotics does not assume that signs are a medium by which the consciousnesses of individual subjects reach each other. Its assumption is rather that signs are entities in which subject, object, and interpretation are fused (MacCannell and MacCannell, 1982). Furthermore, semiotics is well suited to the analysis of rock'n'roll because it can take into account the different simultaneous discourses which make up this form. Not only is rock'n'roll the obvious combination of music and lyrics in songs, but it also involves sign systems such as stage behavior and design, dress, films, videos, visual art in album covers and posters, and so on. Semiotics reads each of these sign systems in terms of its own codes and thus allows one to foreground the diverse and contradictory meanings available in the experience of rock'n'roll.

In classical music, the score is the primary text. Even an opera, which like rock'n'roll is a combination of media and sign systems, has a clearly identifiable "text," its libretto and score. This text can be interpreted in performance by different companies, but it can also be interpreted by critics apart from any particular performance. As Alan Durant has argued, however, rock'n'roll has "no single primary discourse or text" (1984, p. 169). He points out that to take the record as the primary "text" is to "neglect the way in which rock's musical forms have importantly diffused through a variety of technical means," including concerts, films, and videos (p. 168). Hence, if critics or teachers are to have something to interpret, they are forced to construct it themselves. A critical pedagogy should take as its object the "performing units," be they individuals like David Bowie or groups such as the Rolling Stones. Performing units are the locus of a large number of sign systems that include their music and lyrics but also their album covers, dress, films, videos, performing style, and concert staging. These sign systems cannot be understood as expressions of the performing individuals the way a poem or a painting is understood in romantic aesthetics as the expression of the poet or painter. An *auteur* theory is as much an oversimplification in rock criticism as it is in film criticism, since in both cases the final products are always the result of complex collaborative efforts. Thus performing units themselves should be treated as products of the various sign systems as well as producers of signs in those systems. The advantage of this system is that is sets aside the actual person who makes the music in favor of an explicit construct. In this way, public aspects of performers' lives can be analyzed without making any claims at all about the performer as a person. Furthermore, students who are fans can perhaps more easily take a critical attitude if they are not criticizing the "real" people they adore.

That performing units are sometimes produced is demonstrated by the very existence of the Monkees, a group which was created by the entertainment industry. The Monkees made a number of successful singles in the sixties and have experienced a recent revival. The point is not merely that it is possible to invent a rock band out of whole cloth and market it like soap or automobiles, but that it was done with so little resistance. If the Monkees are an extreme example, they are not fundamentally different even from Bob Dylan or Bruce Springsteen. These individuals are at best collaborators in their own creation as rock performers. This can be seen by looking at the changing personae Dylan and Springsteen have taken on during their careers. Dylan's changes are notorious not only because of their extremity but also because of one consistent feature of his different selves, their insistence on their own sincerity. David Bowie has appeared in at least as many forms as Dylan has, but Bowie has, until recently, not claimed any of them to be the real Bowie. Dylan, on the other hand, asks us to believe the folk, rock, country, and gospel are all genuine instances of self-expression, and to believe him when he tells us that "everybody must get stoned," that he has "tangled up in blue," that "a hard rain is gonna fall," and more recently that since "you gotta serve somebody" it ought to be Jesus. Sometimes one hears that Dylan has always presented himself as a prophet even though his message has changed. But even this is misleading. It's true that the prophet role adequately describes the Dylan of "Blowin' in the Wind" and of "You Gotta Serve Somebody," but it leaves out the aesthete of *Highway 61 Revisited*, with its liner notes that read like the most difficult modernist poetry and its references to Pound, Eliot, and Fitzgerald, and *Blond on Blond*, the down-home balladeer of *John Wesley Harding* and *Nashville Skyline* and the confessional poet of *Blood on the Tracks*. The point is not that Dylan is a hypocrite—it is inconceivable that anyone, even Dylan, could consciously invent Dylan the way Columbia Pictures invented the Monkees. Rather, each new role that Dylan has taken up has been written in advance not with the goal of marketing Bob Dylan but as part of a preexisting cultural system. Thus Dylan's initial role as folk singer, which began when Robert Zimmerman became Bob Dylan, was one already played by Woody Guthrie.

Bruce Springsteen's changes have been a good deal more subtle, but as the "Five Faces of Springsteen" series of photos from a 1985 *Newsweek* show, the Bruce of today signifies differently than the Bruces of 1973 or 1978 (Barol 1985). Springsteen was a bohemian of sorts at least through

1978 and the *Darkness on the Edge of Town* tour. During these years he plays Dylan in the jacket photos from *The Wild, the Innocent, and the E Street Shuffle* (contemporary with the first *Newsweek* photo), in *Born to Run*, and in the third of the *Newsweek* photos, which is contemporary with *Darkness*. The second of the five faces presents a different role entirely. Although *Newsweek* describes him as a near preppy in this shot, his black suit and white shirt are part of his costume for the 1978 tour, which featured the Miami horns and was clearly modeled on R & B concert formulas. The *Darkness* jacket itself presents a different Springsteen than the one in the contemporary photo. Glaring out at us in a leather jacket open to reveal a white undershirt and standing in front of closed blinds on which he casts a shadow, Springsteen resembles nothing so much as a character out of a soap opera, a role consistent with songs such as "Racing in the Streets" and the title track.

Between *Darkness* and *Born in the USA*, its not just Springsteen's clothes and hair which change, but also his body. His prominent muscles prompted *Newsweek* to identify him as a "bandannaed muscleman" and a "working class hero." Springsteen's appearance retains a subcultural edge in the first of the photos, as it does on the cover of *Live/1975–85*, although the subculture is distinctly working class rather than bohemian. Springsteen now looks like the characters he has been singing about since *Born to Run*. Springsteen's new body conveys more than just his identification with the working class, however; it signifies a sense of power and confidence that derives from that group rather than from the achievements of the individual which were celebrated in such songs as "Rosalita (Come Out Tonight)." This sense of power contrasts with the bleakness of Springsteen's treatment of working-class life in the album *Nebraska*. Songs such as "The River" and "My Hometown" are equally bleak, but they are also explicitly critical songs that attribute the causes of bad conditions to economic injustice. Thus Springsteen makes us aware of a working class becoming increasingly dispossessed under Reagan, as well as the moral strength and potential political power that also reside in that group. On the other hand, the last photo in the *Newsweek* sequence pictures Bruce in tee-shirt, blue jeans, baseball cap, and glove. Here Bruce is actually playing a role in the "Glory Days" video, and he looks like something to accompany Mom and apple pie. This corresponds to the use of the flag and to the title *Born in the USA*, and it is a Springsteen who seeks to represent rather than to reject mainstream American culture. This role clearly has helped to widen his audience and, perhaps not coincidentally, to add to the ambiguity of songs such as the title track, which both celebrates and criticizes America.

It is not the task of critical pedagogy to pin down the cultural meanings of performing units, or albums, or songs. Rather the task is to make the contradictions in those entities available to the students. No performing unit, no record, no video is devoid of the contradictions of the social system which produced them. It is thus important to identify both the emancipatory and oppressive implications of each of the objects one discusses. Springsteen's criticisms of American culture have been plainly articulated both in interviews and in his lyrics, but ambiguity remains because the contradictions of American culture cannot be eliminated. Furthermore, his well-publicized marriage to a model, his ownership of a mansion, and his status as a multimillionaire all contradict Springsteen's politically progressive statements and songs. These aspects of Springsteen as performing unit compromise his working-class identification in spite of whatever origins he claims. This contradiction belies the folk status Dave Marsh wants to accord Springsteen's music. Here a critical pedagogy would need to address the contradiction between, on the one hand, the fact that performers are commodified as stars, and, on the other, their persistent claims to being organically connected with a subculture that rejects this system.

One major aspect of the star's function is as an object of desire. The media portrayed Springsteen's marriage as an occasion for mourning by women all over the United States. Since romance and sex are the most frequent topics of rock'n'roll songs, a critical pedagogy should address sexual politics. In general, rock'n'roll tends to reflect the dominant ideology on this issue: it represents men and women in typical gender roles, is often misogynist, and usually sings in a male voice. The ideology of romance is commonly reflected in rock'n'roll songs which go beyond the male strutting of "cock rock." Yet even with regard to romance, some emancipatory moments may be found. Some of Springsteen's songs are explicitly critical of romance as an ideology, but the whole of Side 2 of *The River* can be taken as such a critique, each song presenting a different, contradictory phase of romance, from growth of desire to its satisfaction and inevitable loss, and *Tunnel of Love* is even more critical since it lacks the celebratory moment of *The River*. Madonna on one reading is simply a sex object, and some of her videos strongly support this reading. The star system encourages her to play this role and her audience to read her into it whether she plays it or not. But some of her songs, "Material Girl," for example, and her role in the film *Desperately Seeking Susan*, suggest a satire of that role. In that film, the contrast between her slightly pudgy body and the lacy lingerie worn as outerware seems more parody than prurient; furthermore, the character she plays in that film is an independent woman who emerges a heroine and yet remains independent.

In order to explain the contradictions found in the products of rock'n'-

roll, it is necessary for a critical pedagogy to discuss the system by which these performers and their performances come into being.[4] Students need to learn that rock'n'roll records and stars do not rise to popularity by the sheer force of their talent. Beyond the record companies themselves, MTV, radio, the rock press and other "news" media, and concert promoters all have some impact on the careers—and, hence, the records—of any successful performer. Even the most radical groups that make records are allowed to do so because they will make money for a large corporation, a fact which must serve to qualify the impact of radical lyrics. But even with this qualification, such lyrics are at least disseminated. The most common form of censorship of rock'n'roll is not the overt prohibition of recording particular ideas or beliefs, but the refusal to record what will not sell in large quantities. Since radical politics is currently not widely popular in the United States, even established stars such as Little Steven have had trouble finding a record company to give them a contract after recording explicitly political material.

As these considerations suggest, a critical pedagogy of rock'n'roll is not a simple task. It cannot be a matter of merely interpreting lyrics, but must address an entire cultural practice. This requires an historical conception of rock'n'roll itself, a knowledge of the economics and sociology of the entertainment industry, and the analysis of meaning produced by numerous distinct systems of signs. Even given this formidable background, the teacher is still faced with students who already have a claim on the material which they will be reluctant to give up in favor of the teacher's interpretation. The teacher may also be faced by administrators and colleagues who see this material as frivolous or inferior. These obstacles should not be regarded as prohibitive; there are many different occasions when teaching rock'n'roll can occur, many of which allow only for a very selective treatment of the topics I have suggested here. There is one very important requirement for those attempting to teach rock'n'roll: they must have some investment in and feeling for the form. Although those who lack these qualifications might be able to present an effective critique, they would find it difficult to deal with rock'n'roll's emancipatory moments. A critical pedagogy should always embody this dialectic, but in teaching popular materials, attention to the emancipatory is essential if the audience is not to be alienated.

Popular Culture and Critical Pedagogy: Everyday Life as a Basis for Curriculum Knowledge

Henry A. Giroux
Roger Simon

Within the last decade educational discourse in North America has focused primarily on two related issues. On the one hand, educational reform has been linked to the imperatives of big business. Schools in this perspective are training grounds for different sectors of the work force; they are seen as providing knowledge and occupational skills that are necessary for expanding both domestic production and foreign investment. This view links schooling to the demands of a technocratic and specialized literacy. Its offensive is less ideological than it is technicist and instrumental in nature. On the other hand, the late 1980s have witnessed the dramatic rise of the culturalist wing of the Far Right, especially in the United States. This ideological detour in the conservative offensive has been legitimated and sustained in the United States largely through the influence of William Bennett, President Reagan's secretary of education, since 1985. Bennett has broadened the conservatives' definition of schooling by reaffirming its primacy as a guardian of Western Civilization. Under the banner of excellence, Bennett has promoted a nineteenth-century brand of elitism by appealing to a narrowly defined "Western tradition" conveyed through a pedagogy unencumbered by the messy concerns of equity, social justice, or the need to educate a critical citizenry.

236

Bennett's redefinition of the purpose of education and the nature of teachers' work has set the stage for a number of ideological assaults against liberal and radical views of schooling. In this refurbished conservative discourse, the targets are modernity, democracy, difference, and above all, relativism. Classical Western traditions, in this view, are beset on all fronts by relativism. It is alleged to be running rampant in various academic disciplines; in the social protest movements of students; in the increasing cultural and ethnic diversity of the United States; and in the expanding sphere of popular culture, which is viewed as a tasteless and dangerous threat to the notions of civility and order.

Although these positions defend various aspects of the conservative agenda for schooling, they share a common ideological and political thread. They view schools as a particular way of life organized to produce and legitimate either the economic and political interests of business elites or the privileged cultural capital of ruling-class groups. More importantly, both positions represent an attack on the notion of culture as a public sphere where the basic principles and practices of democracy are learned amid struggle, difference, and dialogue. Similarly, both positions legitimate forms of pedagogy that deny the voices, experiences, and histories through which students give meaning to the world and in doing so often reduce learning to the dynamics of transmission and imposition.

We want to intervene in this debate by arguing for schools as sites of struggle and for pedagogy as a form of cultural politics. In both cases, we want to argue for schools as social forms that expand human capacities in order to enable people to intervene in the formation of their own subjectivities and to be able to exercise power in the interest of transforming the ideological and material conditions of domination into social practices which promote social empowerment and demonstrate democratic possibilities. We want to argue for a critical pedagogy that takes into consideration how the symbolic and material transactions of the everyday provide the basis for rethinking how people give meaning and ethical substance to their experiences and voices. This is not a call for a unifying ideology by which to construct a critical pedagogy; it is a call for a politics of difference and empowerment as the basis for developing a critical pedagogy through and for the voices of those who are often silenced. It is a call to recognize that, in schools, meaning is produced through the construction of forms of power, experiences, and identities that need to be analyzed for their wider political and cultural significance.

With these issues in mind, we want to emphasize the importance of critical pedagogy by analyzing its potentially transformative relations with the sphere of popular culture. In our view, popular culture represents not only a contradictory terrain of struggle, but also a significant pedagogical site that raises important questions about the elements that organize the basis of student subjectivity and experience.

At first glance, the relationship between popular culture and classroom pedagogy may seem remote. Popular culture is organized around pleasure and fun, whereas pedagogy is defined largely in instrumental terms. Popular culture is located in the terrain of the everyday, whereas pedagogy generally legitimates and transmits the language, codes, and values of the dominant culture. Popular culture is appropriated by students and helps authorize their voices and experiences, whereas pedagogy authorizes the voices of the adult world, the world of teachers and school administrators.

In addition to these differences, there is a fundamental similarity between popular culture and pedagogy that needs to be articulated. Both exist as subordinate discourses (Grossberg, 1986). For both liberals and radicals, pedagogy is often theorized as what is left after curriculum content is determined. It is what follows the selection of ideologically correct content, its legitimacy rooted in whether or not it represents the proper teaching style. In the dominant discourse, pedagogy is simply the measurable, accountable methodology used to transmit course content. It is not a mutually determining element in the construction of knowledge and learning, but an afterthought reduced to the status of the technical and instrumental. In a similar mode, in spite of the flourishing of cultural studies in the last decade, the dominant discourse still defines popular culture as whatever remains when high culture is subtracted from the overall totality of cultural practices. It is seen as the trivial and the insignificant of everyday life, and usually it is a form of popular taste deemed unworthy of either academic legitimation or high social affirmation.

The dominant discourse, in short, devalues pedagogy as a form of cultural production, and it likewise scorns popular culture. Needless to say, although popular culture is generally ignored in the schools, it is not an insignificant force in shaping how students view themselves and their own relations to various forms of pedagogy and learning. In fact, it is precisely in the relationship between pedagogy and popular culture that the important understanding arises of making the pedagogical more political and the political more pedagogical. Popular culture and pedagogy represent important terrains of cultural struggle which offer both subversive discourses and important theoretical elements through which it becomes possible to rethink schooling as a viable and important form of cultural politics.

Pedagogy and the production of knowledge

Pedagogy refers to a deliberate attempt to influence how and what knowledge and indentities are produced within and among particular sets of social relations. It can be understood as a practice through which people are incited to acquire a particular "moral character." As both a political and practical activity, it attempts to influence the occurrence and qualities of experiences. When one practices pedagogy, one acts with the intent of creating experiences that will organize and disorganize a variety of understandings of our natural and social world in particular ways. What we are emphasizing here is that pedagogy is a concept which draws attention to the processes through which knowledge is produced.

Such an emphasis does not at all diminish pedagogy's concern with "What's to be done?" As a complex and extensive term, *pedagogy's* concern includes the integration in practice of particular curriculum content and design, classroom strategies and techniques, a time and space for the practice of those strategies and techniques, and evaluation purposes and methods. All of these aspects of educational practice come together in the realities of what happens in classrooms.

But the discourse of pedagogy centers something more. It stresses that the realities of what happens in classrooms organize a view of how a teacher's work within an institutional context specifies a particular version of what knowledge is of most worth, in what direction we should desire, what it means to know something, and how we might construct representations of ourselves, others, and our physical and social environment. In other words, pedagogy is simultaneously about the practices students and teachers might engage in together *and* the cultural politics such practices support. It is in this sense that to propose a pedagogy is to construct a political vision.

The education organized by a critical pedagogy is one that must raise questions of how we can work for the reconstruction of social imagination in the service of human freedom. What notions of knowing and what forms of learning are required by such a project? Required is an education rooted in a view of human freedom as the understanding of necessity and the transformation of necessity. We need a pedagogy whose standards and achievement objectives are determined in relation to goals of critique and the enhancement of human capacities and social possibilities. This means that teaching and learning must be linked to the goals of educating students: to understand why things are the way the are and how they got to be that way; to make the familiar strange and the strange familiar (Clifford, 1981; Clifford and Marcus, 1986; McLaren, 198); to take risks and to struggle with ongoing relations of power from within a life-affirming moral culture; and to envisage a world which is "not yet" in order to enhance the conditions for improving the grounds upon which life is lived (Giroux, 1988; Simon, 1987).

Education and the popular

The development of cultural studies in the last two decades has produced an intense interest in the concept of 'popular culture' and, correspondingly, a number of important efforts to theorize the idea of 'the popular'. Given our specific concern with popular culture and its relation to pedagogy, it is important to recognize that well over a century ago those who controlled the developing agenda of state schooling were implicitly, if not explicitly, theorizing a notion of the popular that has dominated the practice of schooling ever since.

At the dawn of Canadian confederation (1860–1875), Egerton Ryerson, social architect, and, at that time, head of Ontario's emerging public school system, was writing and speaking against a particular form of 'the popular'. Addressing himself to educators, he warned against the "trashy and positively unwholesome literature which is so widely extended throughout the country in the shape of . . . novelette papers" (Ryerson, 1868, p. 72). He was convinced that reading such material would help undercut Canada's "connection with the mother country" and that officials at the U.S.–Canadian border should intercept the "obscene" and "filthy" publications "now so abundant in the States." Ryerson thought that "persons who read little or nothing besides the trashy novels of the day would do better not to read at all." He complained that "the most popular and best thumbed works in any of our common reading-rooms are invariably those which are the most worthless—we might say the most dangerous" (Ryerson, 1870, p. 53).

What Ryerson was talking about was not material analogous to contemporary pornography. He was referring to relatively inexpensive publications of short stories and novels filled with local vernacular expressions and "republican ideas." It was in a context such as this that, for instance, Ryerson criticized Mark Twain's *Tom Sawyer* (Morgan, 1987). What is at issue in positions such as Ryerson's is not simply an attempt at aesthetic definition—a matter, for instance, of articulating the distinguishing features between a "high" and a "low" or "popular" culture. Rather, given the current control over the social field by individuals who express ideas similar to Ryerson's, what is more fundamentally at issue is which set of cultural forms will be acknowledged as the legitimate substance of state-provided schooling. In other words, how will state schooling be used as an agency of moral regulation? The issue here is very basic; it is a matter of what vision of future social relations a public school system will support. Such visions have always been defined by a few for the many. Examining what has been excluded as well as required in official curricula clearly reveals, in country after country, that such decisions have been dialectically structured within inequitable and unjust relationships. Indeed, Ryerson's invective against the popular was asserted from the assumption of a superiority and natural dominance he associated with his class, gender, and race.

The popular has been consistently seen by educators as potentially disruptive of existing circuits of power. It has been seen as both threat and profane desire, that is, as both subversive in its capacity to reconstruct the investments of meaning and desire, and dangerous in its potential to provide a glimpse of social practices and popular forms that affirm both difference and different ways of life (Rockhill, 1987). The year 1988 is no exception. Allan Bloom's best-selling book in the United States, *The Closing of the American Mind*, argues that popular culture, especially rock music, has resulted in the atrophy of both nerve and intelligence in American youth. Rock music, and more generally popular culture, represent in Bloom's mind a barbaric appeal to a sexual desire. Not to be undone by this insight, Bloom further argues that since "young people know that rock has the beat of sexual intercourse" (Bloom, 1987, p. 73), popular culture is simply synonymous for turning "life . . . into a nonstop, commercially prepackaged masturbational fantasy" (p. 75). Of course Bloom's sentiments about popular culture in general and rock music in particular have been shaped by what he perceives as indices of a serious moral and intellectual decline among American youth. Specifically, he fears the challenge to authority formed from the student movements of the 1960s and the leveling ideology of democratic reform characteristic of the discourse of radical intellectuals. In effect, Bloom's book offers unsupported authoritarian ravings that appear to emulate the very convulsions he suggests characterize much popular culture.

The inevitable corollary of such sexual interest is rebellion against the parental authority that represses it. Selfishness thus becomes indignation and then transforms itself into morality. The sexual revolution must overthrow all the forces of domination, the enemies of nature and happiness. From love comes hate, masquerading as social reform. A worldview is balanced on the sexual fulcrum. What were once unconscious or halfconscious childish resentments become the new Scripture. And then comes the longing for the classless, prejudice-free, conflictless, universal society that necessarily results from liberated consciousness–"We Are the World," a pubescent version of *Alle Menschen werden Bruder*, the fulfillment of which has been inhibited by the political equivalents of Mom and Dad. These are the three great lyrical themes: sex, hate, and a smarmy, hypocritical version of brotherly love. Such polluted sources issue in a muddy stream where only monsters can swim. (Bloom, 1987, p. 74)

Of course, the monsters who inhabit this terrain are contemporary youth, subordinate groups, and all those others who refuse to take seriously the canonical status that Bloom wants to attribute to the Great Books that embody his revered notion of Western civilization. More specifically responsible for this version of contemporary madness are leftists, feminists, and anyone who uses a Walkman radio. Bloom's discourse is based on the myth of decline, and its attack on popular culture is inextricably linked to the call for the restoration of a so-called lost classical heritage. Rather than a sustained attack on popular culture, this is the all-encompassing discourse of totalitarianism using the veil of cultural restoration. Its enemies are democracy, utopianism, and the unrealized political possibilities contained in the cultures of "the other"–that is, those who are poor, black, female, and who share the common experience of powerlessness. Its goal is moral and social regulation in which the voice of tradition provides the ideological legitimation for a ministry of culture. Its echo is to be found in Hitler's Germany and Mussolini's Italy; its pedagogy is as profoundly reactionary as its ideology and can be summed up simply in the terms *transmission* and *imposition*.

In mentioning Ryerson and Bloom, we are stressing the rather straightforward point that, historically, state-regulated forms of schooling have viewed popular culture as a marginal and dangerous terrain, something to be inoculated against, or–at best–occasionally explored for the incidental motivational ploy that might enhance student interest in a particular lesson or subject. In other words, educators have traditionally viewed popular culture as a set of knowledges and pleasures which are distinguished from, properly subordinate to, and at times co-optable by, the agenda of schooling. And for our purposes, this traditional view cannot be completely dismissed. Despite all its repugnant aspects, it correctly places teachers' work at the center of its discourse: that is, useful notions of the concept of popular culture must be articulated to a particular notion of pedagogy.

Pedagogical relevance of popular culture
Our interest is not in aesthetic or formal qualities of popular cultures. Nor are we particularly concerned with the way in which various popular forms might be codified into subjects or themes for study in cultural studies pro-

grams. Rather we begin with more fundamental questions, including some that are raised by teachers: What relationship do my students see between the work we do in class and the lives they live outside of class? Is it possible to incorporate aspects of students' lived culture into the work of schooling without simply confirming what they already know? Can this be done without trivializing the objects and relationships important to students? And can it be done without singling out particular groups of students as marginal, exotic, and "other" within a hegemonic culture?

In asking these questions we have to assume that pedagogy never begins on empty ground. For this reason, a good starting point would be to consider popular culture as that terrain of images, knowledge forms, and affective investments which define the ground on which one's "voice" becomes possible within a pedagogical encounter (Giroux, 1988). In stating this it is apparent that we have a particular form of teaching and learning in mind. This form is a critical pedagogy that affirms the lived reality of difference and everyday life as the ground on which to pose questions of theory and practice (McLaren, in press). It is a form that claims the experience of lived difference as an agenda for discussion and as a central resource for a pedagogy of possibility (Simon, 1987).

Such a discussion of lived difference, if pedagogical, will take on a particular tension. It implies a struggle—a struggle over assigned meaning, a struggle over the direction in which to desire, a struggle over particular modes of expression, and ultimately a struggle over multiple and even contradictory versions of "self." It is this struggle that makes possible new investments and knowledge beyond individual experience and hence can redefine the possibilities we see both in the conditions of our daily lives and in those conditions which are "not yet." This is a struggle over the very notion of pedagogy itself, one which constantly makes problematic how teachers and students come to know both within wider cultural forms and in the exchanges that mark classroom life. It is a struggle that can never be won, or else pedagogy stops (Lewis and Simon, 1986).

This position does not require teachers to suppress or abandon what and how they know. Indeed, the pedagogical struggle is lessened without such resources. However, teachers and students must find forms within which a single discourse does not become the locus of certainty and certification. Rather, teachers must find ways of creating a space for mutual engagement of lived difference that does not require the silencing of a multiplicity of voices by a single dominant discourse; at the same time, teachers must develop forms of pedagogy informed by a substantive ethic that contests racism, sexism, and class exploitation as ideologies and social practices that disrupt and devalue public life. This is a pedagogy that refuses detachment, though it does not silence in the name of its own ideological fervor or correctness. A critical pedagogy examines with care and in dialogue how social injustices work through the discourses and experiences that constitute daily life and the subjectivities of the students who invest in them.

What might a teacher need to understand in order to engage in such a struggle? Though we will take this issue up in detail at the end of this chapter, we can suggest several questions that a teacher might pursue in the effort to develop a critical pedagogy. If we further define popular culture as both a site of struggle between dominant and subordinate groups (Hall, 1981) and a reference for understanding how experience is organized, produced, and legitimated within cultural forms grounded in the dynamics of everyday life, there are several questions a teacher might pursue. For instance, what are the historical conditions and material circumstances within which the practices of popular culture are pursued, organized, asserted, and regulated? Do such practices open up new notions of identities and possibilities? Do they exclude other identities and possibilities, and, if so, which ones? How are such practices articulated with the hegemonic forms of knowledge and pleasure? Whose interests and investments are served—and whose are critiqued and challenged—by a particular set of popular cultural practices? Finally, what are the moral and political commitments of such practices and how are these related to one's own commitments as a teacher? If there is a divergence between these two sets of commitments, what does this imply?

The importance of asking these questions is, in part, to remove the analysis of popular culture from simply a question of reading ideology into either commodity forms or forms of lived everyday relations. Rather, we are moving toward a position within which one could inquire into the popular as field of practices that constitute for Foucault an indissoluble triad of knowledge, power, and pleasure (Foucault, 1980a). In an important sense this is what the pedagogical struggle is all about: testing the ways we produce meaning and represent ourselves, our relations to others, and our relation to our environment. In doing so we consider what it is we have become, and what it is we no longer want to be. We also enable ourselves to recognize, and struggle for, possibilities not yet realized.

Some cautions on the way to rethinking the popular

Rethinking the notion of the popular is a difficult and hazardous task. Briefly, we wish to share our sense of some of these difficulties.

Popular cultural practices display a wide variety of differences which in part are organized by the struggles inherent in existing gender, class, racial and ethnic, age, and regional relations. As long as such differences are used to establish and maintain disadvantage and human suffering, we need in any discussion of pedagogy and popular culture to register the notion of difference clearly and loudly. Our preference then is to eliminate the singular and always speak about popular cultural *practices*. It is also important to stress that we view such practices as lived processes, as part of the way in which everyday life is experienced and responded to differently by different groups. Of course there is a danger here of reducing particular students to simple reflections of some putative characteristics of group membership. This is a path of classism, sexism, and racism. However, it is equally objectionable to avoid consideration of the social construction and regulation of both knowledge and desire.

We think it is important to retheorize the term *mass culture* in any analysis of popular culture. The agenda is not to simply assert the homogenization and domination of everyday life. We do not wish to conflate those forms which are mass-produced and distributed as products (toys, books, films, records, television programs) with popular culture. Of course, we are interested in those forms both as they offer and give form to (but not mechanically impose) the practices which organize and regulate acceptable styles and images of social activity and individual and collective identity. However, we think it is a mistake to reduce the discussion of popular culture to a discussion of products. If we want to sustain the notion of popular culture as a terrain of possibilities, not just of threat and profane desire, then we require other ways of conceptualizing the term. One alternative consistent with our emphasis on popular cultural practice is to consider commodities in their circuits of distribution as focusing on the commodity not as text but as event: in other words, to consider both the structured occasion of engaging a commodity and the ways in which a product is employed or taken up (Radway, 1984).

In making this suggestion we are stressing that popular culture is constituted not just by commodity forms but by practices which reflect a creative and sometimes innovative capacity of people. Popular culture may contain aspects of a collective imagination which make it possible for people to surpass received knowledge and tradition. In this sense, popular culture may inform aspects of a counterdiscourse which help to organize struggles against relations of domination. As Tony Bennett has written, "A cultural practice does not carry its politics with it, as if written upon its brow for ever and a day; rather, its political functioning depends on the network of social and ideological relations in which it is inscribed as a consequence of the ways in which, in a particular conjuncture, it is articulated to other practices" (Bennett, 1986, p. xvi).

This notion was recently illustrated for us in an essay written by a woman teacher participating in a masters of education course on the relation between pedagogy and popular culture. In this paper she was reflecting on her fondness of the persona of Marilyn Monroe as expressed in both Monroe's films and public imagery (Rowe, 1987). On the one hand, a given popular cultural practice (the event of watching Monroe's movies) may feed into existing forms of domination (in this case, patriarchy). However, at the same time such forms can be an acknowledgment of the nondeterministic subjective side of social relations in which human beings are characterized by an ideal or imaginary life, where will is cultivated, dreams dreamt, and categories developed. This teacher's paper showed that, for a young girl growing up amid the patriarchal relations of a traditional rural farm family, such forms can provide a type of counterdiscourse which is, in part, a promise of possibility. To ignore this possibility is to fail to understand that our material lives can never adequately reflect our imaginary lives. It is imagination itself that fuels our desire and provides us with the energy to reject relations of domination and embrace the promise of possibility (Fitting, 1987).

This view is not naively romantic. We cannot suppress those aspects of popular culture that we may see as regressive; rather we must face them for what they are and attempt to move beyond them. Fascism was and still is viable as a particular practice of popular culture. We must not forget that there will always be a moral project associated with particular cultural practices, and we need to understand and assess the relation of such practices to the commitments we hold as educators and citizens. It is important to reemphasize popular culture as a terrain of struggle infused with practices that are both pedagogical and political. Since consent has to be won for popular forms to be integrated into the dominant culture, popular culture is never free from the ideologies and practices of pedagogy. Similarly, popular forms have to be renegotiated and re-presented if they are to be appropriated in the service of self- and social empowerment. This suggests a critical pedagogy operating to disrupt the unity of popular culture in order to encourage the voice of dissent while simultaneously challenging the lived experiences and social relations of domination and exploitation. Adam Mills and Phil Rice capture the complexity of these issues and are worth quoting at length:

"Popular culture is always a threat": by always occupying the subordinate, illegitimate pole in the field of cultural relations the values embodied in the practices and representations there are antithetical to, what are by definition, the minority values of "elite" cultures. Of necessity those discourses and forms which originate in the dominant cultural institutions, as Stuart Hall suggests, must activate the "structural contradiction which arises whenever a dominant culture seeks to incorporate" and include, within its boundaries, the people. They must raise, in other words, even if it is only an attempt to neutralize, the spectre of oppression and subordination. That certain forms are popular must then require of analysis a recognition both of the means by which consent is won for those dominant discourses, and the way in which those discourses, by presenting themselves as popular, re-present yet connect with the lived practices and experience of subordinate social classes. This suggests that the popular is a site of political and ideological struggle, first and foremost over the formation of what is given as "popular," and beyond that over the formation of "the people." But more than this, it suggests that cultural forms can no longer be regarded as coherent, expressive unities, or even that popular forms are no more than one-dimensional commodities functioning as standardized and stupefying cultural narcotics for the masses. What is implied is that cultural forms comprise a contradictory and uneven balance of elements, both dominant and subordinate – those which connect with "popular" social life, and those dominant elements which attempt to close or constrain alternative meanings and which attempt to mute the voice of dissent. (Mills and Rice, 1982, pp. 24–25)

A pedagogy which engages popular culture in order to affirm rather than mute the voice of the student is not without its difficulties. Michel Foucault, in the first volume of *The History of Sexuality* (1980a), comments on "the pleasure of analysis": the pleasure of discovering and exposing the secrets of human pleasure. The teacher engaged in a pedagogy which requires some articulation of knowledge forms and pleasures integral to student everyday life is walking a dangerous road. Too easily, perhaps, encouraging student voice can become a form of voyeurism or a way to satisfy a form of ego expansionism constituted on the pleasures of understanding those who appear as "other" to us. This is why we must be clear on the nature of the pedagogy we pursue. Popular culture and social difference can be taken up by educators in either of two ways: as a pleasurable form of knowledge and power which allows for more effective individualizing and administration of forms of physical and moral regulation, or alternatively as the terrain on which we must meet our students in a pedagogical encounter that enables rather than disables human imagination and capacities in the service of individual joy, collective prosperity, and social justice. Dick Hebdige (1979) warns us when he reports the words of a young male member of a subculture he was studying: "You really hate an adult to understand you. That's the only thing you've got over them, the fact that you can mystify and worry them" (p. 117). Contemporary youth have cause to be wary of giving up their anonymity, of making their private and lived voices the object of public and pedagogical scrutiny.

There is yet one more caution to raise. We think it important to question the notion of what it means to put popular cultural practice into play in the context of a pedagogical encounter. Does it mean to make such practices topical as curriculum content, to put such practices "up" for discussion? Would doing so not fundamentally change their character? Iain Chambers (1985) has written quite explicitly about this question, and his admonition should be pondered:

High culture, with its cultivated tastes and formally imparted knowledge, calls for particular moments of concentration, separated out from the run of daily life. Popular culture, meanwhile, mobilizes the tactile, the incidental, the transitory, the visceral . . . It does not undertake an abstract aesthetic research amongst already privileged objects of cultural attention, but invokes mobile orders of sense, taste, and desire. Popular culture is not appropriated through the apparatus of contemplation but, as Walter Benjamin put it, through "distracted reception" . . . To attempt to explain fully . . . would be to pull back [popular culture] under the contemplative stare, to adopt the authority of the patronizing academic mind that seeks to explain an experience that is rarely his or hers. A role as Barthes has said that "makes every speaker a kind of policeman" . . . The vanity of such a presumed knowledge runs against the grain of the popular epistemology I have tried to suggest: an informal knowledge of the everyday, based on the sensory, the immediate, the concrete, the pleasurable . . . these [are] areas that formal knowledge and its culture continually repress. (Chambers, 1985, p. 5)

A practice of critical pedagogy

The issue, in this case, is, how does one make popular culture an object of pedagogical analysis without undermining its privileged appropriation as a form of resistance. How can popular culture become part of a critical pedagogy that does not ultimately function to police its content and forms?

A pedagogy which takes popular culture as an object of study must recognize that all educational work is at root contextual and conditional. Such a pedagogy can only be discussed from within a particular specific time and place and from within a particular theme. This points to a larger issue concerning the nature of critical pedagogy itself: doing critical pedagogy is a strategic, practical task, not a scientific one. It arises not against a background of psychological, sociological, or anthropological universals (as does much educational theory related to pedagogy), but from such questions as: How is human possibility being diminished here?

We are deliberately offering an expanded and politicized notion of pedagogy, one that recognizes its place in multiple forms of cultural production, and not just in those sites which have come to be labled "schools." Any practice which intentionally tries to influence the production of meaning is a pedagogical practice. This includes apsects of parenting, film making, theological work, social work, architecture, law, health work, advertising, and much else. These are all forms of cultural work. There are possibilities for pedagogy in any site: schools, families, churches, community associations, labor organizations, businesses, local media, and so forth. All work in such sites must begin with naming and problematizing the social relations, experiences, and ideologies constructed through popular forms that directly operate within such sites as well as those that emerge elsewhere but exercise an influence on those who work within them. A good part of the political work of pedagogy includes the articulation of practices not only within sites but also across them. Indeed, one of our long-term tasks as educators must be to define a framework that is helpful in articulating what critical pedagogies would be possible in a variety of sites of cultural work. This point is essential. The practical efficacy of our own commitments rests with the possibility of constructing an alliance among different forms of cultural work.

In what follows we want to bring our discussion to bear more directly on classroom reality by presenting a list of problems that have been raised by students and a diverse group of educators (elementary and secondary school teachers, university professors, literacy workers, health care professionals, artists and writers) in the process of sharing their own cultural work as well as their readings of various articles and books. In many ways, the questions and the issues they raise make clear that the journey from theory to pedagogical possibility is rarely easy or straightforward. At the same time, the problems being raised suggest new and alternative directions for rethinking pedagogy as a form of cultural politics supportive of a project of hope and possibility. Such problems are symptomatic of the fact that a critical pedagogy is never finished; its conditions of existence and possibility always remain in flux as part of its attempt to address that which is "not yet," that which is still possible and worth fighting for.

Curriculum practice

Of course, a critical pedagogy would be sensitive to forms of curriculum materials that might be implicated in the reproduction of existing unjust and inequitable social relations (e.g., sexism, racism, classism, heterosexism). But just what does this "sensitivity" imply? Does it lead to a legitimate form of censorship of material? The other side of censorship is the exclusionary choice we all make as to what set of materials we will use in our teaching during any particular period of time. What forms of authority can be invoked to make such choices? How should we make such choices? Can we employ reactionary material in the service of a progressive pedagogy? If one argues that we should include materials that (although reactionary) are integral to the dominant mythos of the community and hence "ripe" for critical analysis, in what ways would the material chosen for use be similar or different in the southern United States, in the northern United States, in English Canada, in French Canada, in England, in Australia, and so forth. What balance and integration should be given to the interrogation of global and regional social and cultural forms?

Critical pedagogy always strives to incorporate student experience as "official" curriculum content. Although articulating such experience can be both empowering and a form of critique against relations that silence, such experience is not an unproblematic form of knowledge. How can we avoid the conservatism inherent in simply celebrating personal experience and confirming that which people already know? In other words, how can we acknowledge previous experience as legitimate content and at the same time challenge it (Giroux, 1988)? How do we affirm student "voices" while simultaneously encouraging the interrogation of such voices (Giroux, 1988; McLaren, in press)?

Popular memories and "subjugated knowledges" (Foucault, 1980b) are often discussed as useful forms of critique of dominant ideologies. How can we draw on such knowledges in our pedagogy (Giroux, 1988)? Since, as we have suggested earlier, this means working with the knowledge embedded in the forms of sociality, communities of discourse, and the popular forms students invest with meaning, what should be done to avoid making students who live outside of dominant and ruling forms feel that they are being singled out as the marginal "other" when we take seriously the knowledge organized within the terms of their everyday lives? Furthermore, how do we confront forms of resistance by students to what they perceive as an invasion by the official discourse of the school into private and nonschool areas of their lives?

Cultural politics, social differences, and practice

In planning and enacting a pedagogy whose central purpose is directed at enhancing human possibility and establishing a just and caring community, how do we know that what we are doing is ethically and politically right? How can we keep from slipping from a vision of human possibility into a totalizing dogma?

Many teachers want to help students identify, comprehend, and produce useful knowledge—but what constitutes useful knowledge? Is it the same for all students no matter what their gender, class, race, ethnicity, age, or geographic region? If not, then how can I cope intellectually, emotionally, and practically with such diversity and social difference? What if the teacher's view of useful knowledge differs from what students and their families think? What should happen to the teacher's vision of education? How far can we go in doing critical pedagogy if people are not interested in our agenda or see it as suppressing theirs? Do democratic forms of curriculum making ensure a critical pedagogy?

What can we or should we know about the basis of the interest or disinterest in the topics and materials of our pedagogy? How can such knowledge make a difference to our practice? What would it mean to understand ignorance as a dynamic repression of information (Simon, 1984)? Is there a form of ignorance that is produced as a defense against hopelessness?

What does it mean to work with students in different class, racial, and gendered positions with regard to privilege? Why would those whose interests are served by forms of oppression want to change the situation? Is this structural conflict inevitable in our present society? Are there not issues and values that could mobilize broad interest in social transformations (e.g., ecology, peace, health)?

Guarding against hopelessness

Sometimes when students and teachers engage in a critique of existing social practices or forms of knowledge, a feeling of powerlessness comes over the group. Doing critical pedagogy can turn an educational setting into a "council of despair." How can we guard against the production of hopelessness when we take up an agenda of critique and social analysis? Given all the limitations of teaching and schooling, how can we effectively empower people (Aronowitz and Giroux, 1985; McLaren, 1986; Simon, 1987)?

Working with students to make clear the social contradictions in which we all live is an important aspect of critical pedagogical practice (Simon, 1987). However, will not raising contradictions in students' lives simply threaten them (Williamson, 1981–1982)? Will not pointing to social contradictions lead to cynicism and despair? Furthermore, if the value of understanding 'ideology' is to stress that what is often taken as natural and inevitable is historically constructed and morally regulated, will not ideology critique produce a destabilization of identity and a paralysis of action? If we start questioning the givens of everyday life, won't this simply be overwhelming?

The work of teaching

How can we understand the constraining effects of the administrative and economic contexts within which we work? How should we take into account the realities of state regulation and the limitations imposed by a corporate economy? Should these always be seen as limits?

For those of us who work within public education, why should a teacher act in a way that might be contrary to school board policy or directive? When would a teacher be justified in doing so? What would be the consequences? Should teachers be accountable to specific groups or an organized public sphere? In practice, how would or should this be done?

Given the fact that the practice of critical pedagogy requires a substantial personal investment of time and energy, does it require the near-abandonment of a teacher's "private" life? How can we cope with the moments of depression and emotional disruption that come from a continual concern with the extent of injustice and violence in the world? How can we develop forms of collegial association that might support our efforts?

Conclusion

Posing these questions should not suggest that they have not been addressed either historically or in contemporary forms of social and educational theory. In fact, much of our own work has developed in response to many of the issues and questions we have listed above. They are questions that emerge at different times from diverse voices under widely differing educational contexts, and need to be constantly reconstructed and addressed. The notion of critical pedagogy begins with a degree of indignation, a vision of possibility, and an uncertainty that demands that we constantly rethink and renew the work we have done as part of a wider theory of schooling as a form of cultural politics. Defining the connections between popular culture and critical pedagogy is only one part of this ongoing task, and our introductory comments on this issue have attempted to sketch our view of the work that lies ahead.

NOTES AND REFERENCES

Introduction

1. Andre Gorz, "Technology, Technicians, and Class Struggle," in Andre Gorz, ed., *The Labour Process and Class Struggle in Modern Capitalism* (Atlantic Highlands, NJ: Humanities Press, 1987), p. 180.

2. June Jordan, *On Call: Political Essays* (Boston: South End Press, 1987), p. 30.

3. See Henry A. Giroux, *Schooling and the Struggle for Public Life* (Minneapolis: University of Minnesota Press, 1988); Henry A. Giroux, *Teachers as Intellectuals* (South Hadley, Mass.: Bergin and Garvey Press, 1988); Peter McLaren, *Schooling as a Ritual Performance* (London: Routledge and Kegan Paul, 1986); and McLaren, *Life in Schools* (New York: Longman, Inc. 1988).

Chapter 1.

Notes

1. The Chinese community did better in this regard than the other two, but remained underdeveloped until the anti-Chinese laws in California were rescinded in the 1940s.

2. I call such resistance passive because it is not organized into a movement; rather, individuals from a particular community implicitly and individually refuse to accept the dominant-group ideology pertaining to them. As Sennett and Cobb (1972) and Willis (1977) have argued for the United States and Britain, this resistance is stimulated by strong peer pressure against acceptance of the dominant ideology, especially in school, where peers are fellow working-class or minority youth.

References

Althusser, Louis. 1971. "Ideology and Ideological State Apparatuses," in *Lenin and Philosophy and Other Essays*. New York: Monthly Review Press.

American Heritage Dictonary (Second College Edition). 1985. New York: Houghton Mifflin.

Apple, Michael. 1982. *Power and Ideology.* London: Routledge and Kegan Paul.

Bowles, Samuel, and Herbert Gintis. 1975. *Schooling in Capitalist America.* New York: Basic Books.

———. *Capitalism and Democracy.* 1986. New York: Basic Books.

Carnoy, Martin. 1984. *The State and Political Theory.* Princeton: Princeton University Press.

Carnoy, Martin, and Henry M. Levin. 1985. *Schooling and Work in the Democratic State.* Stanford: Stanford University Press.

Carnoy, Martin, and Joel Samoff. Forthcoming. *Education and Social Transformation in the Third World.*

Carnoy, Martin, Derek Shearer, and Russell Rumberger. 1983. *A New Social Contract.* New York: Harper and Row.

DeGrasse, Robert. 1983. *Military Expansion, Economic Decline.* New York: Council on Economic Priorities.

Durkheim, Emile. 1949. *The Division of Labor in Society.* Glencoe, Ill.: The Free Press.

Giroux, Henry A. 1981. *Ideology, Culture, and the Process of Schooling.* Philadelphia: Temple University Press.

Gramsci, Antonio. 1971. *Selections from Prison Notebooks.* New York: International Press.

Katz, Michael. 1970. *The Irony of Early School Reform.* Boston: Beacon Press.

Our Children at Risk. 1985. Cambridge, Mass.: National Coalition of Advocates for Students.

Poulantzas, Nicos. 1975. *Classes in Contemporary Capitalism.* London: New Left Books.

———. *State, Power, Socialism.* 1978. London: New Left Books.

Przeworski, Adam, and Michael Wallerstein. 1982. "The Structure of Class Conflict in Democratic Capitalist Societies," *American Political Science Review* 76 (2): 215–238.

Sennett, Richard, and Jonathan Cobb. 1972. *The Hidden Injuries of Class.* New York: Random House.

Skocpol, Theda. 1981. "Political Response to Capitalist Crisis: Neo-Marxist Theories of the State and the Case of the New Deal," *Politics and Society* 10 (2): 155–201.

Tyack, David. 1982. *Managers of Virtue: Public School Leadership in America, 1820–1980.* New York: Basic Books.

Willis, Paul. 1977. *Learning to Labor.* Lexington, Mass.: Heath.

Chapter 2.

1. We have developed this reasoning in some detail in our *Democracy and Capitalism: Property, Community, and the Contradictions of Modern Social Thought* (New York: Basic Books, 1986).

2. In Marshall Cohen (ed.), *The Philosophy of John Stuart Mill* (New York: Modern Library, 1961):197–198.

3. The reader may be surprised that we limit our critique of the liberal model of individual action to this one point. We are of course aware that the major criticisms leveled against the liberal model of the individual lie elsewhere — in its purported attribution of such traits as rationality, egotism, hedonism, subjectivism, instrumentalism, and atomism to the individual actor. We contend, however, that such critiques are either invalid, or can be more pointedly argued in terms of the liberal presumption of the givenness of wants. For an insightful exploration of the liberal model of choice complementary to that presented below, see Jan Elster, *Ulysses and the Sirens* (Cambridge: Cambridge University Press, 1979), and *Sour Grapes* (Cambridge: Cambridge University Press, 1983).

4. The logic of Mill's argument in no way depends upon the particular examples he has chosen — children and barbarians — and is scarcely discredited by what we might now consider a racist choice of terminology in apparently referring to non-European societies.

5. Marx, *Capital*, Vol. 1 (New York: Vintage, 1977):283.

6. Albert Hirschman, *Exit, Voice, and Loyalty* (Cambridge, MA: Harvard University Press, 1970). Liberal theory typically does not even address the remaining term of Hirschman's trilogy: loyalty.

7. Though quite foreign to the structure of liberal theory per se, this commonsense idea is hardly novel. It has been taken in interesting directions by Brian Fay, "How People Change Themselves: The Relationship Between Critical Theory and Its Audience," in T. Hall (ed.), *Political Theory and Praxis* (Minneapolis: University of Minnesota Press, 1977), among others.

8. Denis Patrick Obrien, *The Classical Economists* (Oxford: Oxford University Press, 1975):272.

9. Otto Gierke, *Political Theories of the Middle Ages* (F. W. Maitland, trans., (Cambridge: Cambridge University Press) 1958):87.

10. Samuel Bowles and Herbert Gintis, *Schooling in Capitalist America: Educational Reform and the Contradictions of Economic Life* (New York: Basic Books, 1976).

Chapter 3.

I would like to thank the Friday Seminar at the University of Wisconsin, Madison, for their comments on the various drafts of this chapter.

1. Stuart Hall, "The Toad in the Garden: Thatcherism Among the Theorists," in Cary Nelson and Lawrence Grossberg, eds., *Marxism and the Interpretation of Culture* (Urbana: University of Illinois Press, 1988), p. 42.

2. Ibid.

3. Michael W. Apple, *Teachers and Texts: A Political Economy of Class and Gender Relations in Education* (New York: Routledge and Kegan Paul, 1986).

4. Hall, "The Toad in the Garden," p. 35.

5. Ibid., p. 36.

6. See Apple, *Teachers and Texts*, and Henry Giroux, "Public Philosophy and the Crisis in Education," *Harvard Educational Review* 54 (May 1984), pp. 186–194.

7. Michael W. Apple, *Education and Power* (Boston: Routledge and Kegan Paul, 1982), and Apple, *Teachers and Texts*.

8. Herbert Gintis, "Communication and Politics," *Socialist Review* 10 (March–June 1980), p. 193.

9. Ibid., p. 194. See also Samuel Bowles and Herbert Gintis, *Democracy and Capitalism* (New York: Basic Books, 1986).

10. Apple, *Teachers and Texts*.

11. Mary Anderson, "Teachers Unions and Industrial Politics," doctoral thesis, School of Behavioral Sciences, Macquarie University, Sydney, 1985, pp. 6–8.

12. Ann Bastian, Norm Fruchter, Marilyn Gittell, Colin Greer, and Kenneth Haskins, *Choosing Equality: The Case for Democratic Schooling* (Philadelphia: Temple University Press, 1986), p. 14.

13. I wish to thank my colleague Walter Secada for his comments on this point.

14. Michael W. Apple, "National Reports on the Construction of Inequality," *British Journal of Sociology of Education* 7(no. 2, 1986), pp. 171–190.

15. Michael W. Apple, *Ideology and Curriculum* (Boston: Routledge and Kegan Paul, 1979); and Jorge Larrain, *Marxism and Ideology* (Atlantic Highlands, N.J.: Humanities Press, 1983).

16. Stuart Hall, "Authoritarian Populism: A Reply," *New Left Review* 151 (May–June 1985), p. 122.

17. See David Clark and Terry Astuto, "The Significance and Permanence of Changes in Federal Education Policy," *Educational Researcher* 15 (October 1986), pp. 4–13; Frances Piven and Richard Cloward, *The New Class War* (New York: Pantheon Books, 1982); and Marcus Raskin, *The Common Good* (New York: Routledge and Kegan Paul, 1986). Clark and Astuto point out that during the current Reagan term, the following initiatives have characterized its educational policies: reducing the federal role in education, stimulating competition among schools with the aim of "breaking the monopoly of the public school," fostering individual competition so that "excellence" is gained, increasing the reliance on performance standards for students and teachers, an emphasis on the "basics" in content, increasing parental choice "over what, where, and how their children learn," strengthening the teaching of "traditional values" in schools, and expanding the policy of transferring educational authority to the state and local levels (p. 8).

18. Stuart Hall and Martin Jacques, "Introduction," in Stuart Hall and Martin Jacques, eds., *The Politics of Thatcherism* (London: Lawrence and Wishart, 1983), p. 13.

19. Stuart Hall, "Popular Democratic vs. Authoritarian Populism: Two Ways of Taking Democracy Seriously," in Alan Hunt, ed., *Marxism and Democracy* (London: Lawrence and Wishart, 1980), pp. 160–161.

20. Ibid., p. 161.

21. I realize that there is a debate about the adequacy of this term. See Hall, "Authoritarian Populism," and B. Jessop, K. Bonnett, S. Bromley, and T. Ling, "Authoritarian Populism, Two Nations, and Thatcherism," *New Left Review* 147 (1984), pp. 33–60.

22. Michael Omi and Howard Winant, *Racial Formation in the United States* (New York: Routledge and Kegan Paul, 1986), p. 214.

23. Walter Dean Burnham, "Post-Conservative America," *Socialist Review* 13 (November–December 1983), p. 125.

24. Hall, "Authoritarian Populism," p. 117.

25. Ibid., p. 119.

26. Hall, "Popular Democratic vs. Authoritarian Populism," p. 166.

27. Hall, "The Toad in the Garden," p. 55.

28. Stuart Hall, "The Great Moving Right Show," in Stuart Hall and Martin Jacques, eds., *The Politics of Thatcherism*, pp. 19–39.

29. Apple, *Education and Power.*

30. Hall, "The Great Moving Right Show," pp. 29–30.

31. Ibid., pp. 36–37. For an illuminating picture of how these issues are manipulated by powerful groups, see Allen Hunter, "Virtue With a Vengeance: The Pro-Family Politics of the New Right," doctoral thesis, Department of Sociology, Brandeis University, Waltham, 1984.

32. Apple, *Teachers and Texts*.

33. Jessop, et al., "Authoritarian Populism, Two Nations, and Thatcherism," p. 49.

34. Hall, "The Great Moving Right Show," p. 21.

35. Allen Hunter, "The Politics of Resentment and the Construction of Middle America," unpublished paper, American Institutions Program, University of Wisconsin, Madison, 1987, pp. 1–3.

36. Ibid., p. 9.

37. Samuel Bowles, "The Post-Keynesian Capital-Labor Stalemate," *Socialist Review* 12 (September–October 1982), p. 51.

38. Hunter, "The Politics of Resentment and the Construction of Middle America," p. 12.

39. Omi and Winant, *Racial Formation in the United States*, pp. 214–215.

40. Raskin, *The Common Good*.

41. Omi and Winant, *Racial Formation in the United States*, pp. 215–216. See also Hunter, "Virtue With a Vengeance."

42. Omi and Winant, *Racial Formation in the United States*, p. 220. For a more complete discussion of how this has affected educational policy in particular, see Clark and Astuto, "The Significance and Permanence of Changes in Federal Education Policy," and Apple, *Teachers and Texts*.

43. Omi and Winant, *Racial Formation in the United States*, p. 221. I have elsewhere claimed, however, that some members of the new middle class—namely, efficiency experts, evaluators, testers, and many of those with technical and management expertise—will form part of the alliance with the New Right. This is simply because their own jobs and mobility depend on it. See Apple, *Teachers and Texts*.

44. Omi and Winant, *Racial Formation in the United States*, p. 227.

45. Ibid., p. 164.

46. Ibid. The discussion in Bowles and Gintis, *Democracy and Capitalism*, of the "transportability" of struggle over person rights from, say, politics to the economy is very useful here. I have extended and criticized some of their claims in Michael W. Apple, "Facing the Complexity of Power: For a Parallelist Position in

Critical Educational Studies," in Mike Cole, ed., *Rethinking Bowles and Gintis* (Philadelphia: Falmer Press, 1988).

47. See Apple, *Education and Power*, and Apple, *Teachers and Texts*.

48. Omi and Winant, *Racial Formation in the United States*, pp. 177–178.

49. Ibid.

50. Ibid., p. 180.

51. Ibid., p. 190.

52. Ibid.

53. Ibid.

54. Ibid., p. 252.

55. Ibid., p. 155.

56. Hunter, "The Politics of Resentment and the Construction of Middle America," p. 23.

57. Ibid., p. 30.

58. Ibid., p. 33.

59. Ibid., p. 34.

60. Ibid., p. 21.

61. Ibid., p. 37.

62. See Apple, "National Reports and the Construction of Inequality," and Apple, *Teachers and Texts*.

63. Stuart Hall, "Popular Culture and the State," in Tony Bennett, Colin Mercer, and Janet Woollacott, eds., *Popular Culture and Social Relations* (Milton Keynes: Open University Press, 1986), pp. 35–36.

64. Hall, "The Toad in the Garden," p. 40.

65. Ibid., p. 45.

66. Ibid.

67. Chantal Moffe, "Hegemony and New Political Subjects: Toward a New Concept of Democracy," in Nelson and Grossberg, eds., *Marxism and the Interpretation of Culture*, p. 96.

68. Ibid.

69. Omi and Winant, *Racial Formation in the United States*, p. 165.

70. Ibid., p. 166.

71. I say "new" here, but the continuity of, say, black struggles for freedom and equality also needs to be stressed. See the powerful treatment of the history of such struggles in Vincent Harding, *There is a River: The Black Struggle for Freedom in the United States* (New York: Vintage Books, 1981).

72. See David Hogan, "Education and Class Formation," in Michael W. Apple, ed., *Cultural and Economic Reproduction in Education* (Boston: Routledge and Kegan Paul, 1982), pp. 32–78, for a discussion of this in relationship to class dynamics.

73. Omi and Winant, *Racial Formation in the United States*, p. 166.

74. Apple, "National Reports and the Construction of Inequality."

75. Apple, *Teachers and Texts*, and Martin Carnoy, Derek Shearer, and Russell Rumberger, *A New Social Contract* (New York: Harper and Row, 1984).

76. Apple, "National Reports and the Construction of Inequality." For a comprehensive analysis of the logic of capitalism, one that compares it with other political and economic traditions, see Andrew Levine, *Arguing for Socialism* (Boston: Routledge and Kegan Paul, 1984).

77. Apple, *Education and Power,* and Apple, *Teachers and Texts*.

78. See Sara Freedman, Jane Jackson, and Katherine Boles, *The Effects of the Institutional Structure of Schools on Teachers* (Somerville, Mass.: Boston Women's Teachers' Group, 1982).

79. See Apple, *Teachers and Texts*; Bastian, et al., *Choosing Equality*; and David Livingstone, ed., *Critical Pedagogy and Cultural Power* (South Hadley, Mass.: Bergin and Garvey, 1987).

80. Hall, "The Great Moving Right Show," p. 120.

81. Apple, *Ideology and Curriculum*.

Chapter 4.

Best, Raphaela (1982). *We've All Got Scars Now*. Bloomington: Indiana University Press.

Bowles, Sam, and Gintis, Herb (1976). *Schooling in Capitalist America*. London: Routledge and Kegan Paul.

Coleman Report (1966). *On Equality of Educational Opportunity*. Washington, D.C.: U.S. Government Printing Office.

Coley, Sonia (1987). *Higher Education and Child Care.* Unpublished project in social sciences. London: South Bank Polytechnic.

David, Miriam (1980). *The State, The Family and Education.* London: Routledge and Kegan Paul.

———— (1984). Women, Family and Education. In S. Acker, J. Meganry, S. Nisbet, and E. Hoyle (eds.), *World Yearbook of Education 1984. Women and Education.* London: Kogan Page.

———— (1985). Motherhood and Social Policy–A Matter of Education? *Critical Social Policy* 12, pp. 28–44.

———— (1986a). Teaching Family Matters. *British Journal of the Sociology of Education* 7. (1), pp. 35–57.

———— (1986b). Morality and Maternity: Towards a Better Union than the Moral Right's Family Policy. *Critical Social Policy* 16, pp. 40–57.

———— (1987). The Dilemmas of Parent Education and Parental Skills for Sexual Equality. In S. Walker and L. Barton (eds.), *Changing Policies, Changing Teachers.* Milton Keynes: Open University Press.

Deem, Rosemary, ed. (1985). *Co-Education Reconsidered.* Milton Keynes: Open University Press.

Department of Education and Science (DES) (1986). *Health Education from 5 to 16.* Curriculum Matters 6. London: Her Majesty's Stationery Office.

Freedman, Sarah and Barton, L. (1987). Burntout or Beached: Weeding Women Out of Women's True Profession. In S. Walker (eds.), *Changing Policies, Changing Teachers.* Milton Keynes: Open University Press.

Griffith, Alison (1984). *Ideology, Education and Single Parent Families: The Normative Ordering of Families through Schooling.* Ph.D dissertation. University of Toronto.

Griffith, Alison, and Smith, Dorothy (1986). Constructing Cultural Knowledge: Mothering as Discourse. Paper presented at Women and Education conference. Faculty of Education, University of British Columbia, Vancouver, B.C., June 12.

Grubb, Norton, and Lazerson, Marvin (1983). *Broken Promises.* New York: Basic Books.

Hall, Stuart (1983). Education in Crisis. In A. M. Wolpe and J. Donald (eds.), *Is There Anyone Here From Education?* London: Pluto Press.

Hargreaves Report (1985). *Improving Secondary Schools.* London: ILEA.

Her Majesty's Inspectors (HMI) (1985). *The Effects of Local Authority Expenditure Policies on Education Provision in England.* London: DES.

Honeyford, Ray (1983). Multi-Ethnic Intolerance. *The Salisbury Review* 4, pp. 12–13.

Honeyford, Ray (1984). Education and Race: An Alternative View. *The Salisbury Review* 6, pp. 30–32.

Jencks, Christopher, et al. (1972). *Inequality: A Reassessment of Family and Schooling in America*. New York: Basic Books.

Knight, Christopher (1987). The Conservative Educationalists. Chapter of dissertation. London: South Bank Polytechnic.

Land, Hilary (1986). *Women Won't Benefit*. London: National Council for Civil Liberties.

New, Caroline, and David, Miriam 1985. *For the Children's Sake: Making Child Care More Than Women's Business*. Harmondsworth: Penguin.

Pollert, Anna (1983). *Girl's Lives, Factory Lives*. London: George Allen and Unwin.

Pugh, Gillian, and De'Ath, Erica (1984). *The Needs of Parents: Practice and Policy in Parent Education*. London: MacMillan.

Sharpe, Sue (1987). *Falling for Love: Teenage Mothers Talk*. London: Virgo Press.

Shaw, Jenny (1980). Education and the Individual: Schooling for Girls or Mixed Schooling–A Mixed Blessing. In R. Deem (ed.), *Schooling for Women's Work*. London: Routledge and Kegan Paul.

Smith, Dorothy (1984). *Women, Class and Family*. London: Socialist Register.

Spender, Dale (1980). *Man-Made Language*. London, Routledge and Kegan Paul.

Spender, Dale, and Sarah, Elizabeth, eds. (1980). *Learning to Lose: Sexism and Education*. London: the Woman's Press.

Swann Report (1985). *Education for All*. Cmnd 9453, London: HMSO.

Tyack, David, and Strober, Myra (1980). Why Do Men Manage and Women Teach? *Signs: Journal of Women and Culture*, 5, 3, pp. 494–504.

Wenman, Suzanne (1987). Personal communication. London: South Bank Polytechnic.

Women's National Commission (WNC) (1984). *The Other Half of Our Future*. London: Cabinet Office.

Zellman, Gail (1981). *A Title IX Perspective on the Schools' Response to Teenage Pregnancy and Parenthood*. Santa Monica, Calif.: Rand Corporation.

Chapter 5.

1. The National Commission on Excellence in Education, *A Nation at Risk*, Washington, D. C.: U. S. Government Printing Office, 1983.

2. It is instructive to remember that in the 1970s even President Nixon was advocating a national health insurance bill. A recent survey by Arthur D. Little Inc. of 125 experts in health care found a shared belief that the public would shortly abandon its goal of equal health care. As reported in the *Champaign-Urbana News Gazette*, Saturday, June 1, 1985.

3. The National Science Board/The National Science Foundation, *Today's Problems Tomorrow's Crises*, Washington, D. C.: National Science Board, 1982.

4. Twentieth Century Fund Task Force on Federal Elementary and Secondary Educational Policy, *Making the Grade*, New York: Twentieth Century Fund, 1983, p. 3.

5. National Commission, *A Nation at Risk*, p. 17.

6. For others who claim the same link, see, for example, those of the National Science Board and the Twentieth Century Fund, op. cit. Also see Business-Higher Education Forum, *America's Competitive Challenge: The Need for a National Response,* (Business Higher Education Forum: Washington, D.C., 1983. The last of these deals largely with postsecondary education.

7. These interviews took place in December, 1984.

8. This is a body appointed by the prime minister and has a somewhat analogous function to that of our National Commission on Excellence in Education.

9. High school education is not compulsory in Japan. However, Japanese schools actually graduate a significantly higher percentage of high-school-age students than do schools in the United States. Somewhere over 90 percent of high-school-age children attend school in Japan, and, of these, about 97 percent graduate. Hindenuri Fujita, "A Crisis of Legitimacy in Japanese Education: Meritocracy and Cohesiveness," paper presented at the annual meeting of the Comparative and International Education Society, March 22, 1984, at Houston, Texas.

10. Ibid., p. 14.

11. For a critical analysis of these schools and the role that they play in the Japanese economy, see Michio Morishima, *Why has Japan 'Succeeded'? Western Technology and the Japanese Ethos*, Cambridge, England: Cambridge University Press, 1984, pp. 184–193.

12. In Korea the penalty for tutoring is, for the child, expulsion from school: for the father, loss of any government job; and for the tutor, six months in jail.

13. Rokuro Hidaka, *The Price of Affluence: Dilemmas of Contemporary Japan,* Tokyo: Kodansha International, LTD., 1984, p. 107.

14. Twentieth Century Fund Task Force, *Making the Grade*, p. 6.

15. Paul E. Peterson, "Background Paper," in *Making the Grade*, p. 157.

16. Ibid., p. 158.

17. Ibid., p. 118.

18. Ibid., p. 157.

19. Twentieth Century Fund Task Force, *Making the Grade*, p. 6.

20. Ibid.

21. Henry M. Levin and Russell W. Rumberger, *The Educational Implications of High Technology*, Stanford: Institute of Research on Educational Finance and Governance, 1983.

22. See Twentieth Century Fund Task Force, *Making the Grade*, p. 11.

23. Mortimer J. Adler, *The Paideia Proposal: An Educational Manifesto*, New York: Macmillan, 1982.

24. Adler (ed.), *The Paideia Program: An Educational Syllabus*, New York: Macmillan, 1984.

25. Adler, *The Paideia Proposal*, pp. 23–24.

26. Ibid., pp. 16–17.

27. These include Ernest Boyer and Theodore Sizer.

28. In November 1983, I chaired a panel with Adler and a number of his critics for the annual meeting of the American Educational Studies Association. The substance of much of this criticism was that Adler's proposal did not take into account individual differences. His reponse, as I recall it, was essentially that he recognized that there were different limits to the speed and the amount that different children could learn. However, there are some essentially humanizing experiences, and to deny children the opportunity to participate in these is truly discriminatory.

29. For those who are concerned that Adler would neglect craft work, driver's education, and other such areas, they should be reassured that Adler's school will find a place for many of these areas, including automobile repair, driver's education, metalworking, sewing, cooking, and typing. See *The Paideia Proposal*, p. 33.

30. John I. Goodlad, *A Place Called School: Prospects for the Future*, New York, McGraw-Hill, 1984.

31. Theodore R. Sizer, *Horace's Compromise: The Dilemma of the American High School*, Boston: Houghton Mifflin, 1984.

32. Ernest L. Boyer, *High School: A Report on Secondary Education in America*, New York: Harper and Row, 1983.

33. Goodlad, *A Place Called School*, p. 140.

34. Boyer, *High School*, p. 5.

35. Sizer, *Horace's Compromise,* p. 6.

36. Goodlad, *A Place Called School*, pp. 146–147.

37. Ibid., p. 149.

38. Ibid., p. 160.

39. Ibid., p. 161.

40. Ibid., p. 150.

41. Ibid., p. 161.

42. I suspect that the practice of firing both nontenured and tenured teachers at the end of the year in order to meet budgetary constraints, together with a decline in purchasing power, has been one of the major reasons for the decline in the attractiveness of the teaching profession.

43. Sizer, *Horace's Compromise.*

Chapter 6.

Alexander, K. L., and Cook, M. A. (1982), Curricula and Coursework: A Surprise Ending to a Familiar Story, *American Sociological Review,* Vol. 47 (October), pp. 626–640.

Apple, M. W. (1982), *Education and Power,* Boston, Routledge and Kegan Paul.

Baudrillard, J. (1981), *For a Critique of the Political Economy of the Sign*, St. Louis, Mo., Telos Press.

Bernstein, B. (1987), Pedagogic Device, in *On Pedagogic Discourse.* Unpublished paper.

Bloom, A. (1987), *The Closing of the American Mind: How Higher Education Has Failed Democracy and Impoverished the Souls of Today's Students*, New York, Simon and Schuster.

Brown, R. (1973), *Knowledge, Education, and Cultural Change: Papers in the Sociology of Education*, published by British Sociological Association, Distributor, Harper and Row.

Callahan, R. E. (1962), *Education and the Cult of Efficiency*, Chicago, Chicago University Press.

Cheney, L. V. (1987), *American Memory: A Report on the Humanities in the Nation's Public Schools*, National Endowment in the Humanities.

Dreeben, R., and Barr, R. (1987), An Organizational Analysis of Curriculum and Instruction, in Hallinan, M.T., ed., *The Social Organization of Schools*, New York, Plenum Press.

Elias, N., Martins, H., and Whitley, R. (eds.) (1982), *Scientific Establishment and Hierarchies*, Holland, D. Reidel, Vol. 6.

Gamoran, A. (1987), The Stratification of High School Learning, *Sociology of Education*, Vol. 60, No. 3 (July), pp. 135–155.

Geertz, C. (1980), Blurred Genres: The Refiguration of Social Thought, *The American Scholar*, Spring, pp. 115–179.

Giroux, H. (1983), *Theory and Resistance in Education: A Pedagogy for the Opposition*, Massachusetts, Bergin and Garvey.

Goodson, I. (1987), *School Subjects and Curriculum Change: Studies in Curriculum History*, London, Falmer Press.

Gunn, G. (1987), *The Culture of Criticism and the Criticism of Culture*, New York, Oxford University Press.

Hallinan, M. T., ed., (1987), *The Social Organization of Schools: New Conceptualization of the Learning Process*, New York, Plenum Press.

Hirsch, E. D., Jr. (1987), *Cultural Literacy: What Every American Needs to Know*, Boston, Houghton Mifflin.

Horkheimer, M. (1972), *Critical Theory*, New York, Herder and Herder.

Horkheimer, M., and Adorno, T. W. (1972), *Dialectic of Enlightenment*, New York, Herder and Herder.

Knorr-Cetina, Karin, D., and Mulkay, M., eds. (1983), *Science Observed*, Beverly Hills, Calif., SAGE Publications Inc.

Latour, B. (1983), Give Me a Laboratory and I Will Raise the World, in Knorr-Cetina, Karin D., and Mulkay, M., eds., *Science Observed*, Beverly Hills, Calif., SAGE Publications Inc.

Lave, J. (1988), *Cognition in Practice: Mind, Mathematics, and Culture in Everyday Life*, New York, Cambridge University Press.

Lave, J., Murtaugh, M., and de la Rocha, O. (1984), The Dialectic of Arithmetic in Grocery Shopping, in Rogoff, B., and Lave, J., eds., *Everyday Cognition: Its Development in Social Context*, Cambridge, Mass., Harvard University Press.

Lesko, N. (1987), *Invisible Essentials*, in press, Falmer Press.

Luke, T. (1986), Televisual Democracy, *Telos*, Vol. 70 (Winter) pp. 59–79.

Lyotard, J. F. (1984), *The Post-Modern Condition: A Report on Knowledge*, Translated by Bennington, G., and Massumi, B., "Theory and History of Literature" Series, Vol. 10, Minneapolis, University of Minnesota Press.

Marcuse, H. (1968), The Affirmative Character of Culture, in *Negations*, Boston, Beacon Press.

Mendelsohn, E., Weingart, P., and Whitley, R., eds. (1977), *The Social Production of Scientific Knowledge*, Holland, D. Reidel.

Meyer, J. J. (1977), The Effects of Education as an Institution, *American Journal of Sociology*, Vol. 83, No. 1, pp. 55–77.

Meyerowitz, J. (1985), *No Sense of Place: The Impact of Electronic Media on Social Behavior*, New York, Oxford University Press.

Newman, C. (1985), *The Post-Modern Aura: The Act of Fiction in an Age of Inflation*, Evanston, Ill., Northwestern University Press.

Popkewitz, T. S., ed. (1987), *The Formation of the School Subjects: The Struggle for Creating an American Institution*, New York, Falmer Press.

Prigogine, I., and Stengers, I. (1984), *Order out of Chaos: Man's New Dialogue with Nature*, New York, Bantam.

Rip, A. (1982), 'The Development of Restrictedness in the Sciences', in Elias, N., Martins, H. and Whitley, R. (eds), *Scientific Establishment and Hierarchies,* Holland, D. Reidel, Vol. 6, pp. 219–238 (see reference on previous page)

Rorty, R. (1982) *Consequences of Pragmatism*, Sussex, England: Harvester Press.

Schubert, W. H. (1986), *Curriculum: Perspective, Paradigm, and Possibility*, New York, Macmillan.

Schwab, J. J. (1978), *Science, Curriculum, and Liberal Education: Selected Essays*, Chicago, University of Chicago Press.

Shulman, L. S. (1986), Those Who Understand: Knowledge Growth in Teaching, *Educational Researcher*, Vol. 15, No. 2 (February), pp. 4–14.

Sorensen, A. B., and Hallinan, M. T. (1977), A Reconceptualization of School Effects, *Sociology of Education*, Vol. 50 (October), pp. 273–289.

Trow, G. W. S. (1980), Reflections Within the Context of No-context, *The New Yorker*, Vol. 56 (Nov. 17), pp. 63–171.

Wexler, P. (1987), Case Studies in the Social Dynamics of School Disaffection, talk prepared for the American Education Research Association (AERA) annual meeting in April 1987, unpublished.

Whitson, J. A. (1987), The Politics of "Non-Political" Curriculum: Heteroglossia and the Discourse of "Choice" and "Effectiveness," paper presented at the annual meeting of the American Education Research Association (AERA), in Washington, D. C., April 1987.

Whitty, G. (1987), Curriculum Research and Curricular Politics, *British Journal of Sociology of Education*, Vol. 8, No. 2, pp. 109–117.

Willis, P. (1977), *Learning to Labour: How Working Class Kids Get Working Class Jobs*, Westmead, England, Saxon House.

Young, M. F. D. (1973), Curricula and the Social Organization of Knowledge, in R. Brown, *Knowledge, Education and Cultural Change*, 1973), published by British Sociological Association, Distributor, Harper and Row.

Chapter 7.

Notes

1. By "discourse" we refer to a regulated system of statements that establish differences between, let us say, teacher education and law and between different forms of teacher education theory such as the psychological and sociological. Discourse is not simply words but is embodied in the practices of institutions, patterns of behavior, and forms of pedagogy. By "dominant" discourse we wish to register the concept that the dominant "is the discourse whose presence is defined by *the social impossibility of its absence*" (Terdiman, 1985, p. 61, italics in original).

2. By "avant-garde" we wish to register the notion of opposition between the primacy of producers and the primacy of marketings in the economy of teacher production: a distinction between newcomers and those who dominate. The avant-garde is the voice of counterdominance in the field of teacher education. See Bourdieu (1986) for an elaboration of this in the field of art.

3. "Genre" refers to the normatively structured sets of formal, contextual, and thematic features or rules that are characteristic of ways of speaking in particular situations. As social practices, they produce what is taken to be "proper" meaning, appropriate speech and action, in particular settings. Rules in this sense are selection principles that govern the content and processes of social settings, the relations of power and solidarity between speakers, and the semantic medium. These Frow (1986, p. 68) refers to as field, tenor, and mode, respectively. Every text participates in one or several genres while not being irreducibly identified with any one. Thus, realist pedagogic discourse is fundamentally a set of principles for embedding and relating discourses, a "principle" of delocating an element of discourse from its substantive practice and relocating it according to the genre's own principle of selective reordering and focusing (Bernstein, 1986, p. 210). In this metonymic transformation of reordering, the original discourse becomes an "imaginary" subject, signifying something other than itself, and pedagogic discourse remains a recontextualiz-

ing principle, a genre. Speakers, writers, and readers enter discourse by way of the subject positions presupposed by these principles in the structure of the genre. But the kind and degree of the implicit presuppositions given by field and tenor are always connected to other discourses so that discourse can be described as "a play of voices" (Frow, 1986, p. 159).

4. We draw on Australian experience here.

5. What we mean by this is that the sign, in this case the truth of the *meaning of teaching* lying in teacher practice, is the story told about it by Olsen: that is, the truth of Olsen's propositions lies in his *narrative production about* practicality rather than in teacher work as a preexisting object. See Terdiman (1982).

6. The authors do not necessarily agree with the ideological accents of this metaphor.

7. To reiterate, the business-as-usual of conventional classrooms is part of the definition of the nascent state as it is being employed here. Avant-garde teacher educators, if they are to be successful agitators, require that their discourses of hope and transformation be returned in the practice of student-teachers.

8. The practicum in Australia is more often than not incorporated by schools so that what is done may or may not realize what curriculum studies and foundations courses intend. Avant-garde theory is particularly disadvantaged in such a setting because it is apprehended as impractical. Perhaps the key strategic issue for the avant-garde in teacher education is the forming of alliances with schools so that collaborative practicums can become the "normal" experience.

References

Alberoni, F. (1984). *Movement and Institution*. New York: Columbia University Press.

Apple, M. W. (1986a). National Reports and the construction of inequality. *British Journal of Sociology of Education*. 7: 2, 171–190.

————. (1986b). *Teachers and Texts*. New York: Routledge and Kegan Paul.

Aronowitz, S., Giroux, H. (1987). Ideologies about schooling: Rethinking the nature of educational reform. *Journal of Curriculum Theorizing*. 7: 1, 7–38.

Australian Government (1985). *Quality of Education in Australia* (P. H. Karmel, Chairman, 'QERC' Report). Canberra: Australian Government Publishing Service.

Belsey, C. (1980). *Critical Practice*. London: Methuen.

Bernstein, B. (1986). On pedagogic discourse. In J. Richardson (ed.), *Handbook of Theory and Research for the Sociology of Education*. New York: Greenwood, 205–240.

Bourdieu, P. (1986). The production of belief: Contribution to an economy of symbolic goods. In R. Collins, J. Curran, N. Garnham, P. Scannell, P. Schlesinger, C. Sparkes (eds.), *Media Culture & Society*. London: Sage. 131–163.

Clandinin, D. J. (1985). Personal practical knowledge: A study of teachers' classroom images. *Curriculum Inquiry*. 15: 4, 361–385.

Connell, I. (1983). "Progressive" pedagogy?. *Screen* 24:3, 50–54.

Connell, R. W. (1983). *Teachers' Work*. Sydney: Allen and Unwin.

Connell, R. W., Ashendon, D. J., Kessler, S., Dowsett, G. (1982). *Making the Difference*. Sydney: Allen and Unwin.

Donald, J. (1985). Beacons of the future: Schooling, subjection and subjectification. In V. Beechey, J. Donald (eds.), *Subjectivity and Social Relations*. Milton Keynes: Open University Press.

Dow, G., Clegg, S., Boreham, P. (1984). From the politics of production to the production of politics. *Thesis Eleven*. 9: 16–32.

Foucault, M. (1980). *Power/Knowledge: Selected Interviews and Other Writings, 1972–1977*, ed. Colin Gordon. New York: Pantheon.

Freedman, S., Jackson, J., Boles, K. (1983). Teaching: An imperilled profession. In L. Schulman and G. Sykes (eds.), *Handbook of Teaching and Policy*. New York: Longman.

Frow, J. (1986). *Marxism and Literary History*. London: Blackwells.

Giroux, H. A. (1985). Critical pedagogy, cultural politics and the discourse of experience. *Journal of Education*. 167: 2, 22–41.

––––––. (1986). Authority, intellectuals, and the politics of practical learning. *Teachers College Record*. 88: 1, 22–40.

––––––. (in press). Solidarity, struggle and the discourse of hope: Theory, practice and experience in radical education, Part II. *The Review of Education*.

––––––. (in press). Literacy and the pedagogy of political empowerment: Introduction to *Literacy: Reading the World and the Word*. Miami University, Ohio: Unpublished MS.

Giroux, H. A., McLaren, P. (1986). Teacher education and the politics of engagement: The case for democratic schooling. *Harvard Educational Review*. 56: 3, 213–238.

Hall, S. (1983). Encoding/decoding. In S. Hall, D. Hobson, A. Lowe, P. Willis (eds.), *Culture, Media, Language*. London: Hutchison, 128–138.

––––––. (1985). The rediscovery of "ideology": Return to the repressed in media studies. In V. Beechey, J. Donald (eds.), *Subjectivity and Social Relations*. Milton Keynes: Open University Press. 23–55.

Henriques, J., Holloway, W., Urwin, C., Venn, C., Walkerdine, V. (1984). *Changing the Subject*. London: Methuen.

Huberman, M. (1985). What knowledge is worth most to teachers? A knowledge-use perspective. *Teaching and Teacher Education*. 1: 3, 251–262.

Jameson, F. (1985). Postmodernism and consumer society. In H. Foster (ed.), *Postmodern Culture*. London: Pluto, 111–125.

Kallos, D., Lundgren, U. (1979). The study of curriculum as a pedagogical problem. In *Curriculum As a Pedagogical Problem*. Stockholm: C. W. K. Gleerup, 14–33.

Laclau, E., Mouffe, C. (1985). *Hegemony and Socialist Strategy*. London: Verso.

Lampert, M. (1985). How do teachers manage to teach? Perspectives on problems in practice. *Harvard Educational Review*. 55: 2, 178–194.

Lasch, C. (1986). What's wrong with the Right. *Tikkun*. 1: 1, 23–29.

Lusted, D. (1986). Introduction—why pedagogy? *Screen*. 27: 5, 2–15.

McNeil, L. (1981). On the possibility of teachers as the source of an emancipatory pedagogy: A response to Henry Giroux. *Curriculum Inquiry*. 11: 3. 205–210.

Marginson, S. (1986). Free market education. *ATF Research Notes*. 18: 2–18.

Morley, D. (1980). *The Nationwide Audience: Structure and Decoding*. London: British Film Institute.

National Task Force on Educational Technology (1986). *Transforming American Education: Reducing the Risk to the Nation*. A report to the Secretary of Education, United States Department of Education.

Olsen, J. K. (1984). What makes teachers tick? In R. Halkes, J. K. Olsen (eds.), *Teacher Thinking: A New Perspective on Persisting Problems in Teacher Education*. Lisse: Swets and Zeitlinger, 35–42.

Panitch, L. (1977). The development of corporatism in liberal democracies. *Comparative Political Studies*. 10: 1, 61–90.

Pollard, A. (1980). Teacher interests and changing situations of survival threat in primary school classrooms. In P. Woods (ed.), *Teacher Strategies: Explorations in the Sociology of the School*. London: Croom Helm, 34–60.

Popkewitz, T., Pitman, A., Barry, A. (1986). Educational reform and its millenial quality. *Journal of Curriculum Studies*. 18: 3, 267–283.

Queensland Board of Teacher Education (1987). *Project 21: Teachers for the Twenty-first Century* (B. H. Watts, OBE, Chairman). Toowong, Brisbane.

Richards, C. (1986). Anti-racist initiatives. *Screen*. 27: 5, 74–79.

Sharp, R. (1982). Response to Wexler. *Interchange*. 13: 3, 68–75.

Smith, R. (1979). Myth and ritual in teacher education. In M. R. Pusey, R. E. Young (eds.), *Control and Knowledge*. Canberra: Australian National University Press, 97–123.

Smith, R., Sachs, J. (1988). "It really made me stop and think": Ethnography in teacher education. In J. Nias, S. Groundwater-Smith (eds.), *The Enquiring Teacher: Supporting and Sustaining Teacher Research*. Cambridge: Cambridge Institute of Education, pp. 71–84.

Task Force on Teaching as a Profession (1986). *A Nation Prepared: Teachers for the 21st Century*. New York: Carnegie Forum on Education and the Economy.

Terdiman, R. (1982). Deconstruction/mediation: A dialectical critique of Derrideanism. *Minnesota Review*. n.s. 19: 103–111.

———. (1985). *Discourse/Counter-Discourse: The Theory and Practice of Symbolic Resistance in Nineteenth-century France*. Ithaca, N.Y.: Cornell University Press.

Veenman, S. (1984). Perceived problems of beginning teachers. *Journal of Educational Research*. 54: 2, 143–178.

Volosinov, V. N. (1973). *Marxism and the Philosophy of Language*. New York: Seminar Press.

Westbury, I. (1983). How can curriculum guides guide teaching? *Journal of Curriculum Studies*. 15: 1, 5–16.

Wexler, P. (1985). Social change and the practice of social education. *Social Education*. May, 390–394.

———. (1986). Society and knowledge again. Speech to Sociology of Education Association. Monterey, California.

Whitty, G., Pollard, A., Barton, L. (1987). Ideology and control in teacher education: A review of recent experience in England. In T. Popkewitz (ed.), *Critical Studies in Teacher Education*. London: Falmer.

Williamson, J. (1985). Is there anyone here from a classroom? *Screen*. 26: 1, 90–95.

Wood, G. H. (1984). Schooling in a democracy: Transformation or reproduction? *Educational Theory*. 34: 3, 219–239.

Zeichner, K. M. (1983). Alternative paradigms of teacher education. *Journal of Teacher Education*. 34: 3, 3–9.

Zeichner, K. M., Liston, D. P. (1987). Teaching student teachers to reflect. *Harvard Educational Review*. 57: 1, 23–48.

Chapter 8.

1. Karl Marx, *A Contribution to the Critique of Political Economy*, ed. Maurice Dobbs (New York: International Publishers, 1964), p. 21.

2. The diverse positions that characterize these fields can be found in Hal Foster, ed., *The Anti-Aesthetic: Essays on Postmodern Culture* (Port Townsend, Wash.: Bay Press, 1983); John Fekete, ed., *The Structural Allegory: Reconstructive Encounters with the New French Thought* (Minneapolis: University of Minnesota Press, 1984); Jonathan Arac, ed., *Postmodernism and Politics* (Minneapolis: University of Minnesota Press, 1986); Julian Henriques et al., *Changing the Subject* (New York: Methuen Press, 1984); Fredric Jameson and contributors, *Formations of Pleasure* (London: Routledge and Kegan Paul, 1983); Cary Nelson, ed., *Theory in the Classroom* (Urbana: University of Illinois Press, 1986); Seyla Benhabib and Drucilla Cornell, eds., *Feminism as Critique* (Minneapolis: University of Minnesota Press, 1987); and Chris Weedon, *Feminist Practice and Poststructuralist Theory* (London: Basil Blackwell, 1987).

3. For a summative and critical analysis of this position, see Stanley Aronowitz and Henry A. Giroux, *Education Under Siege* (South Hadley, Mass.: Bergin and Garvey, 1985), especially chapter 6.

4. For a brilliant analysis of these concerns, see Richard Johnson, "What is Cultural Studies Anyway?" *Anglistica* 26: 1/2 (1983), pp. 1–75.

5. James Clifford and George E. Marcus, eds., *Writing Culture: The Poetics and Politics of Ethnography* (Berkeley: University of California Press, 1986); George Marcus and Michael Fischer, *Anthropology as Cultural Critique* (Chicago: University of Chicago Press, 1986); Stephen A. Tyler, *The Unspeakable: Discourse, Dialogue, and Rhetoric in the Postmodern World* (Madison: University of Wisconsin Press, 1987); James Clifford, *The Predicament of Culture* (Cambridge, Mass.: Harvard University Press, 1988).

6. For an overview of these two positions, see Stuart Hall, "Cultural Studies: Two Paradigms," in *Culture, Ideology and Social Process*, ed. Tony Bennett et al. (London: Batsford Academic, 1981); see also Henry A. Giroux, *Theory and Resistance in Education* (South Hadley, Mass.: Bergin and Garvey, 1983), especially pp. 119–167.

7. Stanley Aronowitz, *Crisis in Historical Materialism* (South Hadley, Mass.: Bergin and Garvey, 1981); Johnson, "What is Cultural Studies Anyway?"; Lawrence Grossberg and Stuart Hall, "On Postmodernism and Articulation," *Journal of Communication Inquiry* 10:2 (Summer, 1988), pp. 45–60.

8. Francis Mulhern, "Notes on Culture and Cultural Struggle," *Screen Education*, No. 34 (Spring, 1980), p. 33.

9. Some of the more well-known texts that emerged in the 1970s and early 1980s were M. F. D. Young, ed., *Knowledge and Control* (London: Collier-Macmillan, 1971); Basil Bernstein, *Class, Codes and Control*, Vol. 3 (London: Routledge and Kegan Paul, 1977); Sam Bowles and Herbert Gintis, *Schooling in Capitalist America* (New York: Basic Books, 1976); Michael Apple, *Ideology and Curriculum* (London: Routledge and Kegan Paul, 1977); and Henry A. Giroux, *Ideology, Culture, and the Process of Schooling* (Philadelphia: Temple University Press, 1981).

10. For an analysis of this position, see Giroux, *Ideology, Culture, and the Process of Schooling*.

11. The most celebrated example of this position can be found in Bowles and Gintis, *Schooling in Capitalist America*. The literature on schooling and the reproductive thesis is critically reviewed in Giroux, *Theory and Resistance in Education*.

12. For a recent analysis of this position, see Henry A. Giroux and David Purpel, eds., *The Hidden Curriculum and Moral Education* (Berkeley, Calif.: McCutchan, 1983). Also see Jeannie Oakes, *Keeping Track: How Schools Structure Inequality* (New Haven, Conn.: Yale University Press, 1985).

13. Michael Apple, *Education and Power* (London: Routledge and Kegan Paul, 1982).

14. The most influential book on this position has been Pierre Bourdieu and Jean Claude Passeron, *Reproduction in Education, Society, and Culture* (Beverly Hills, Calif.: Sage, 1977).

15. I develop these themes extensively in Henry A. Giroux, *Schooling and the Struggle for Public Life* (Minneapolis: University of Minnesota Press, 1988).

16. Philip Corrigan, "In/Forming Schooling," in David Livingstone and contributors, *Critical Pedagogy and Cultural Power* (South Hadley, Mass.: Bergin and Garvey, 1987), pp. 17–40.

17. Bruce Robbins, "The Politics of Theory," *Social Text* 6:3 (Winter, 1987/1988), p. 9.

18. Antonio Gramsci, *Selections from Prison Notebooks,* ed. Quinton Hoare and Geoffrey Smith (New York: International Publishers, 1971).

19. Nicos Poulantzas, *Classes in Contemporary Society* (London: New Left Books, 1975); Regis Debray, *Teachers, Writers, Celebrities: The Intellectuals of Modern France* (London: New Left Books, 1981); Alvin Gouldner, *The Future of Intellectuals and the Rise of the New Class* (New York: Seabury, 1979); George Konrad and Ivan Szelenyi, *The Intellectuals on the Road to Class Power* (Brighton, England: Harvester

Press, 1979); Rudolf Bahro, *The Alternative in Eastern Europe* (London: New Left Books, 1978); Russell Jacoby, *The Last Intellectuals: American Culture in the Age of Academe* (New York: Basic Books, 1987). For an excellent review of the work of these specific theorists, see Philip Schlesinger, "In Search of the Intellectuals: Some Comments on Recent Theory," in *Media, Culture, and Society*, ed. Richard Collins et al. (London: Sage, 1986), pp. 84–103.

20. This position is more fully elaborated in Giroux, *Schooling and the Struggle for Public Life*.

21. Cited in Colin Gordon, "Afterword," in Michel Foucault, *Power/Knowledge: Selected Interviews and Other Writings, 1972–1977*, ed. Colin Gordon (New York: Pantheon Press, 1980), p. 233.

22. John Dewey, *Democracy and Education* (New York: Macmillan, 1916); John Dewey, "Creative Democracy–The Task Before Us," reprinted in *Classic American Philosophers*, ed. Max Fisch (New York: Appleton-Century-Crofts, 1951); George S. Counts, *Dare the Schools Build a New Social Order* (New York: Day, 1932); see also Richard J. Bernstein, "Dewey, Democracy: The Task Ahead of Us," in *Post-Analytic Philosophy*, ed. John Rajchman and Cornell West (New York: Columbia University Press, 1985).

23. Benjamin Barber, *Strong Democracy: Participating Politics for a New Age* (Berkeley: University of California Press, 1984).

24. Sheldon Wolin, "Revolutionary Action Today," in Rajchman and West, *Post-Analytic Philosophy*, p. 256.

25. For an important discussion on these concepts, see Richard Lichtman, "Socialist Freedom," in *Socialist Perspectives*, ed. Phyllis and Julius Jacobson (New York: Kary-Cohl Publishing, 1983); for a more general theoretical discussion of these issues, see Landon E. Beyer and George Wood, "Critical Inquiry and Moral Action in Education," *Educational Theory* 36: 1 (Winter, 1986), pp. 1–14.

26. Doug White, "Education; Controlling the Participants," *Arena*, no. 72 (1985), p. 78.

27. Sharon Welch, *Communities of Resistance and Solidarity* (New York: Orbis Press, 1985), p. 31.

28. The concept of the engaged intellectual comes from Michael Walzer, *Interpretation and Social Criticism* (Cambridge, Mass.: Harvard University Press, 1987).

29. For a superb but politically skewed analysis of this issue, see Isaiah Berlin, "On the Pursuit of the Ideal," *The New York Review of Books*, 35:4 (March 17, 1988), pp. 11–18, 23.

30. Walzer, *Interpretation and Social Criticism*.

31. Jacoby, *The Last Intellectuals*.

32. Johnson, "What is Cultural Studies Anyway?", p. 11; this issue has been taken up extensively in a number of critical ethnographic studies: see Paul Willis, *Learning to Labor* (New York: Columbia University Press, 1981); Peter McLaren, *Life in Schools* (New York: Longman, 1989); and Henry A. Giroux, *Teachers as Intellectuals* (South Hadley, Mass.: Bergin and Garvey, 1988).

33. Teresa de Lauretis, *Technologies of Gender* (Bloomington: Indiana University Press, 1987), p. 18.

34. Ibid., p. 25.

35. Teresa de Lauretis, *Alice Doesn't* (Bloomington: Indiana University Press, 1985), p. 186.

36. V. N. Volosinov (M. Bakhtin), *Marxism and the Philosophy of Language* (New York: Seminar Press, 1973); Mikhail Bakhtin, *The Dialogic Imagination*, trans. Carl Emerson and Michael Holquist (Austin: University of Texas Press, 1981).

37. Linda Alcoff, "Cultural Feminism Versus Poststructuralism: The Identity Crisis in Feminist Theory," *Signs: Journal of Women in Culture and Society*, 13:3 (1988), p. 431.

38. Michel Foucault, *Language, Counter-Memory, Practice*, trans. Donald Bouchard (Ithaca, N. Y.: Cornell University Press, 1977), p. 22.

39. Chris Weedon, *Feminist Practice and Poststructuralist Theory*, p. 85.

40. Gary Peller, "Reason and the Mob: the Politics of Representation," *Tikkun* 2:3 (1987), p. 30.

41. These three forms of reading are developed in Robert Scholes, *Textual Power* (New Haven, Conn.: Yale University Press, 1985).

42. David Lusted, "Why Pedagogy," *Screen* 27:5 (September–October, 1986), p. 3.

43. Henry A. Giroux and Roger I. Simon, "Schooling, Popular Culture, and a Pedagogy of Possibility," *Journal of Education* (forthcoming).

44. Roger I. Simon, "Empowerment as a Pedagogy of Possibility," *Language Arts* 64:4 (April, 1987), pp. 37–38.

Chapter 9.

Notes

1. This research was made possible by a grant from the W. T. Grant Foundation, New York City, 1984 through 1985.

2. Personal communication with employee in the High Schools' Division, New York City Board of Education, in response to inquiry about why New York City does not maintain race/ethnicity sensitive statistics on dropping out and school achievement.

3. Columbus Avenue, on the upper West Side, has recently become a rapidly gentrified, elite neighborhood in Manhattan, displacing many low-income, particularly black and Hispanic, residents.

References

Advocates for Children (1985). *Report of the New York Hearings on the Crisis in Public Education*. New York.

Anyon, J. (1980). School curriculum: Political and economic structure and social change. *Social Practice*, Spring, 96–108.

————. (1983). Intersections of gender and class: Accomodation and resistance by working class and affluent females to contradictory sex role ideologies. In *Gender, Class and Education*. Edited by S. Walker and L. Barton. London: Falmer Press.

Apple, M. (1982). *Cultural and Economic Reproduction in Education*. Boston: Routledge and Kegan Paul.

Aronowitz, S., and Giroux, H. (1985). *Education Under Siege*. South Hadley, Mass.: Bergin and Garvey.

Aspira (1983). *Racial and Ethnic High School Dropout Rates in New York City: A Summary Report*. New York.

Bastian, A., Fruchter, N., Gittell, M., Greer, C., and Haskins, K. (1985). Choosing equality: The case for democratic schooling. *Social Policy*, Spring, 35–51.

Carnegie Forum of Education and the Economy (1986). *A Nation Prepared: Teachers for the 21st Century*. New York: Carnegie Foundation.

Carnoy, M., and Levin, H. (1985). *Schooling and Work in the Democratic State*. Stanford, Calif.: Stanford University Press.

Connell, R., Ashenden, D., Kessler, S., and Dowsett, G. (1982) *Making the Difference*. Sydney, Australia: George Allen and Unwin.

Cummins, J. (1986). Empowering minority students: A framework for intervention. *Harvard Education Review, 56*, 1, February.

Elliott, D., Voss, H., and Wendling, A. (1966). Capable dropouts and the social milieu of high school. *Journal of Educational Research, 60*, 180–186.

Felice, J. (1981). Black student dropout behaviors: Disengagement from school rejection and racial discrimination. *Journal of Negro Education, 50,* 415–424.

Fine, M. (1983). Perspectives on inequity: Voices from urban schools. In *Applied Social Psychology Annual IV.* Edited by L. Bickman. Beverly Hills, Calif.: Sage.

———. (1985). Dropping out of high school: An inside look. *Social Policy,* Fall, 43–50.

———. (1986). Why urban adolescents drop into and out of public high school. *Teachers College Record, 87,* 3, Spring.

Fine, M., and Rosenberg, P. (1983). Dropping out of high school: The ideology of school and work. *Journal of Education, 165,* 257–272.

Freire, P. (1985). *The Politics of Education.* South Hadley, Mass.: Bergin and Garvey.

Giroux, H. (1983). *Theory and Resistance in Education* (South Hadley, Mass.: Bergin and Garvey).

Giroux, H., and McLaren, P. (1986). Teacher education and the politics of engagement. *Harvard Educational Review, 56,* 3, August, 213–238.

Goodlad, J. (1984). *A Place called School: Prospects for the Future*: New York: McGraw Hill.

Gramsci, A. (1971). *Selections from Prison Notebooks.* New York: International.

Holmes Group (1986). *Tomorrow's Teachers.* East Lansing, Michigan. The Holmes Group.

Lightfoot, S. (1978). *Worlds Apart.* New York: Basic Books.

McNeil, L. (1981). Negotiating classroom knowledge: Beyond achievement and socialization. *Curriculum Studies, 13,* 313–328.

Militarism Resource Project (1985). *High School Military Recruiting: Recent Developments.* Philadelphia, Penn.

New York State Department of Education (1985). Memo from Dennis Hughes, State Administrator on High School Equivalency Programs. December 4, 1984. Albany, New York.

Ogbu, J. (1978). *Minority Education and Caste: The American System in Cross-Cultural Perspective.* New York: Academic Press.

Rich, A. (1979). *On Lies, Secrets and Silence.* New York: Norton Books.

Rosen, H. (1986). The importance of story. *Language Arts, 63,* 226–237.

Schor, I. (1980). *Critical Teaching and Everyday Life.* Boston: South End Press.

Sizer, T. (1985). *Horace's Compromise: The Dilemma of the American High School*. Boston: Houghton Mifflin.

Tobier, E. (1984). *The Changing Face of Poverty: Trends in New York City's Population in Poverty, 1960–1990*. New York: Community Service Society.

U. S. Commission on Civil Rights (1982). *Unemployment and Underemployment among Blacks, Hispanics and Women*. Washington, D. C.

U. S. Department of Labor (1983). *Time of Change: 1983 Handbook of Women Workers*. Washington, D. C.

Wexler, P. (1983). *Critical Social Psychology*. Boston: Routledge and Kegan Paul.

Young, A. (1983). Youth labor force marked turning point in 1982. U. S. Department of Labor, Bureau of Labor Statistics, Washington, D. C.

Zorn, J. (1982). Black English and the King decision. *College English, 44*, 3, March.

Chapter 10.

1. Good recent efforts at analyzing theories of ideology include S. Hanninen and L. Paldan (eds.), *Rethinking Ideology: A Marxist Debate* (New York: International General, 1983); and David McLellan, *Ideology* (Minneapolis: University of Minnesota Press, 1986).

2. See Michel Foucault, *Power/Knowledge: Selected Interviews and Other Writings, 1972–1977* C. Gordon (ed.) (New York: Pantheon Books, 1980). For a good commentary on Foucault's concept of ideology, see James Donald, "Beacons of the Future: Schooling, Subjection and Subjectification," in V. Beechey and J. Donald (eds.), *Subjectivity and Social Relations* (Milton Keynes: Open University Press, 1986). Foucault would consider the concept of ideology to be somewhat redundant, given that subjectification relies on mechanisms of power within institutions and apparatuses of knowledge and not on the manipulation of ideas and beliefs that constitute consciousness. See Donald, "Beacons of the Future," 217.

3. See Catherine Belsey, *Critical Practice* (London and New York: Methuen, 1980): 46. In Belsey's view, language must be recognized as a coding system that constitutes one of many ideological forms.

4. Stanley Aronowitz, "Theory and Socialist Strategy," *Social Text* (Winter 1986/87): 11. Foucault's position contravenes the positivistic approach, which maintains that truth can best be ascertained by bracketing subjective elements, including political and ethical dimensions, and by paying attention to empirical data alone.

5. Ibid., 12.

6. Ibid., 11–12.

7. Ibid.

8. Michel Foucault, *Power/Knowledge: Selected Interviews and Other Writings, 1972–1977*, C. Gordon (ed.) (New York: Pantheon Books, 1980): 84–85. Here is where Foucault's coupling of "discourse/practice" corrects, as Mark Poster claims, the Western Marxist tendency to separate material life from signification and consciousness, thereby bringing a new perspective to the debate between Hegelian Marxists such as Jameson and Lukas and structural Marxists such as Althusser. See Jon Klancher, "What Critical Intellectuals Do Now," *College English*, 69(2), 1987: 202–208. See also John Rajchman, "Ethics After Foucault," *Social Text*, 5(1/2), 1986: 165–183.

9. Barry Smart, *Foucault, Marxism and Critique* (London: Routledge and Kegan Paul, 1983): 80.

10. *Subjectivity*, as I am using the term, is best defined by Simon as follows:

Subjectivity includes both conceptually organized articulated knowledge and elements that move us without being consciously expressed. These elements include both pre-conscious taken-for-granted knowledge and the radical and sedimented needs and desires that are expressed in our demands on ourselves and others. As an active ongoing construction, subjectivity is always a material and discursive rendering of these forms of knowledge. Subjectivity is not viewed as unitary but is divided by both the repression of that which cannot and refuses to be expressed and the constant processes of reorganization that construct a fragmented, contradictory consciousness. In its manifestation in practice, subjectivity expresses a non-unitary social identity accomplished through the historically produced social forms through which people live. Hence subjectivity reflects both objective conditions and a socially constructed representation of everyday life.

Roger I. Simon, "Work Experience," in David Livingstone (ed.), *Critical Pedagogy and Cultural Power* (South Hadley, MA: Bergin and Garvey, 1986): 157.

11. Philip Wexler, "Structure, Text, and Subject: A Critical Sociology of School Knowledge," in Michael Apple (ed.), *Cultural and Economic Reproduction in Education: Essays on Class, Ideology and the State* (London: Routledge and Kegan Paul, 1982): 285.

12. As early as the sixth century, metaphysical realism was predetermined as the only possible philosophical stance. Since that time, a number of thinkers have challenged the dominant assumption that knowledge must in some fundamental way reflect reality. Within this line of reasoning, orthodox explanations of ideology can be interrogated to reveal the archaeological stratifications, "breakdowns," or constraints from which they are constructed. In light of the poststructuralist advances in this area, the persistently empirical stance of orthodox Marxists, which submits to theory virtually on the basis of specifiable and verifiable epistemological criteria, is rendered eminently problematic: that is, their pursuit of objec-

tivity tends to separate knowledge from subjectivity, object from subject, and fact from value.

13. Working within a logic of identity (in the tradition of transcendental philosophy from Descartes through Kant to Husserl), classical Marxists manage to theoretically sidestep criticisms directed at this tradition by thinkers such as Derrida, Adorno, Kristeva, and others. In fact, the "classical realist" stance was successfully challenged decades ago by Wittgenstein.

14. Ernesto Laclau, "The Impossibility of Society," *Canadian Journal of Political and Social Theory*, 7(1/2), 1983: 22. See also Ernesto Laclau and Chantal Mouffe, *Hegemony and Socialist Strategy* (London: Verso Press, 1985).

15. Laclau, "Impossibility," pp. 21–22.

16. Ibid., 21.

17. Ibid., 22.

18. Ibid., 23.

19. Aronowitz, "Theory and Socialist Strategy," 11. See also Norman Geras's recent criticism of Laclau and Mouffe's work in "Post-Marxism?" *New Left Review*, *163*, May/June, 1987: 40–82.

20. Gayatri Spivak, *In Other Worlds: Essays in Cultural Politics* (New York: Methuen, 1987): 78.

21. Stanley Aronowitz, "Relativity of Theory," *The Village Voice*, December 27, 1983: 60.

22. Ibid.

23. Stanley Aronowitz, "Science and Ideology," *Current Perspectives in Social Theory*, *1*, 1980: 75–101.

24. Ibid.

25. Ibid.

26. Ibid.

27. Veronica Beechey and James Donald, "Introduction," in V. Beechey and J. Donald (eds.), *Subjectivity and Social Relations* (Milton Keynes: Open University Press, 1985): xvi.

28. Aronowitz, "Science and Ideology," 100.

29. Terry Eagleton, "Marxism, Structuralism, and Post-Structuralism," *Diacritics*, Winter, 1985: 10–11.

30. Aronowitz, "Theory and Socialist Strategy," 7.

31. Rejecting traditional Marxism's view of ideology as a form of false con-

sciousness, Fredric Jameson subscribes to a view of ideology as a *strategy of containment*, or a way of achieving a unitary positioning of the subject by closing reality to the truth of history and by repressing the contradictions generated by both history and necessity. In so doing, Jameson rejects Althusser's attack on the semi-autonomy of various levels of the social structure (via expressive causality and homology) on the grounds that one cannot discuss differences without recognizing a prior unity. See F. Jameson, *The Political Unconscious: Narrative as a Socially Symbolic Act* (Ithaca, NY: Cornell University Press, 1981).

32. Paul Hirst, "Ideology, Culture and Personality," *Canadian Journal of Political and Social Theory,* 7(1/2), 1983: 129.

33. Wayne Hudson, "Ernst Bloch: 'Ideology' and Postmodern Philosophy," *Canadian Journal of Political and Social Theory,* 7(1/2), 1983: 133.

34. Ibid., 133–134.

35. Ibid., 134.

36. Ibid.

37. Aronowitz, "Theory and Socialist Strategy," 9.

38. See Stuart Hall, "The Problem of Ideology–Marxism Without Guarantees," in B. Matthews (ed.), *Marx: A Hundred Years On* (Atlantic Highlands, NJ: Humanities Press, 1983): 82–83.

39. See the debate on this issue between Henry A. Giroux and Daniel P. Liston. See Liston, "Marxism and Schooling: A Failed or Limited Tradition?" *Educational Theory,* 35(3), 1985, pp. 307–12 and Giroux's trenchant response, "Toward a Critical Theory of Education: Beyond a Marxism with Guarantees," *Educational Theory,* 35(3), 1985: 313–319.

40. Michael Dale, "Stalking a Conceptual Chameleon: Ideology in Marxist Studies of Education," *Educational Theory,* 36(3), 1986: 257.

41. The classical orthodox position on ideology is also reflected in the writings of educational theorists Daniel Liston and Madan Sarup. See Daniel P. Liston, "Have We Explained the Relationship Between Curriculum and Capitalism? An Analysis of the Selective Tradition," *Educational Theory,* 34(3), 1984, and his "On Facts and Values: An Analysis of Radical Curriculum Studies," *Educational Theory,* 36(2), 1986: 137–152. Also see Madan Sarup, *Marxism and Education* (London: Routledge and Kegan Paul, 1978).

42. Henry A. Giroux, *Theory and Resistance in Education: A Pedagogy for the Opposition* (South Hadley, MA: Bergin and Garvey, 1983): 145. See also Giroux and Aronowitz's discussion of ideology in Stanley Aronowitz and Henry Giroux, *Education Under Siege* (South Hadley, MA: Bergin and Garvey, 1985).

43. Giroux, *Theory and Resistance*, 145.

44. Douglas Kellner, "Ideology, Marxism, and Advanced Capitalism," *Socialist Review*, 8(6), 1978: 38.

45. Gibson Winter, *Liberating Creation: Foundations of Religious Social Ethics* (New York: Crossroad, 1981): 97.

46. James Donald and Stuart Hall, "Introduction," in J. Donald and S. Hall (eds.), *Politics and Ideology* (Milton Keynes, England, and Philadelphia, PA: Open University Press, 1986): ix–x.

47. Ibid.

48. Ibid.

49. John. B. Thompson, "Language and Ideology: A Framework for Analysis," *The Sociological Review*, 35(3), August, 1987: 517–536.

50. Giroux, *Theory and Resistance*, 145.

51. Ibid., 143.

52. Ibid.

53. Ibid.

54. Ibid., 144.

55. Ibid., 146.

56. Ibid., 156.

57. Ibid.

58. For a similar position, see Judith Newton and Deborah Rosenfelt, "Toward a Materialist-Feminist Criticism," in J. Newton and D. Rosenfelt (eds.), *Feminist Criticism and Social Change* (New York: Methuen, 1985): xv–xxxi.

59. Stanley Aronowitz, *The Crisis in Historical Materialism* (South Hadley, MA: Bergin and Garvey, 1981).

60. Dean MacCannell, *The Tourist: A New Theory of the Leisure Class* (New York: Schocken, 1976).

61. Ibid.

62. See David Buckingham, "Against Demystification: A Reponse to 'Teaching the Media,'" *Screen*, 27(5), 1986: 80–95.

63. Peter McLaren, *Schooling as a Ritual Performance: Towards a Political Economy of Educational Symbols and Gestures* (London and New York: Routledge and Kegan Paul, 1986): 34–48.

64. Dean MacCannell, "Deconstructing Ritual," James A. Becker Alumni Lecture, Cornell University, Ithaca, New York, October 23, 1981.

65. Ibid.

66. Ibid.

67. Ibid.

68. John W. Dixon, "The Physiology of Faith," *Anglican Theological Review*, 48(4), 1976: 407–431.

69. Evan M. Zuesse, "Meditation on Ritual," *Journal of the American Academy of Religion*, 43(3), 1975: 517–530.

70. McLaren, *Schooling as a Ritual Performance*, 214–229.

71. Robert B. Everhart, *Reading, Writing, and Resistance: Adolescence and Labor in a Junior High School* (New York: Routledge and Kegan Paul, 1983). See also Robert B. Everhart, "Understanding Student Disruption and Classroom Control," *Harvard Educational Review*, 57(1), 1987: 77–83.

72. Everhart, *Reading, Writing, and Resistance.*

73. Ibid.

74. Lauren B. Resnick, "The 1987 Presidential Address: Learning In School and Out," *Educational Researcher*, 16(9), December, 1987: 13–20.

75. David Michael Levin, "Moral Education: The Body's Felt Sense of Value," *Teachers College Record*, 84(2), 1982: 287.

76. R.W. Connell, *Gender and Power: Society, the Person, and Sexual Politics* (Stanford, CA: Stanford University Press), 87.

77. Dixon, "The Physiology of Faith," 407–431.

78. Bryan Turner, *The Body and Society: Explorations in Social Theory* (Oxford: Basil Blackwell, 1984): 233.

79. Ibid.

80. Paul Smith, *Discerning the Subject* (Minneapolis: University of Minnesota Press, 1988): 107.

81. Ibid.

82. Ibid.

83. Rosalind O'Hanlon, "Recovering the Subject: Subaltern Studies and Histories of Resistance in Colonial South Asia," *Modern Asian Studies*, 22(1): 1988: 222–223.

84. Ibid., 223.

85. Ibid.

86. Ibid. This point is one which critics of resistance theory often fail to understand. Such a failure renders many of their insights on the subject trivial and quite silly. For a particularly good example of such a cripplingly narrow and nondialectical understanding of resistance, see Peter Gronn's "On the Side of the Angels," *Curriculum Inquiry 18*(3) 1988:355–367. For a further critique of Gronn's simplistic position, see my rejoinder, "No Light, But Rather Darkness Visible: Language and the Politics of Criticism," in the same issue.

87. Richard Harvey Brown, *Society as Text: Essays on Rhetoric, Reason, and Reality* (Chicago: University of Chicago Press, 1987): 187.

88. Terry Eagleton, *Walter Benjamin: Or Towards a Revolutionary Criticism* (London: Verso Editions and NLB, 1981): 160

89. Brown, *Society as Text*, 190.

90. Ibid., 191.

91. Lawrence Grossberg, "Teaching the Popular," in C. Nelson (ed.), *Theory in the Classroom* (Urbana: University of Illinois Press, 1986): 42.

92. Lawrence Grossberg, "The In-difference of Television," *Screen, 28*(2), Spring, 1987: 41.

93. Teresa de Lauretis, *Technologies of Gender* (Bloomington and Indianapolis: Indiana University Press, 1987): 3.

94. Benjamin Barber, *Strong Democracy: Participating Politics for a New Age Theology of Liberation* (Berkeley: University of California Press, 1984).

95. Henry A. Giroux, "Solidarity, Struggle, and the Public Sphere: Beyond the Politics of Anti-Utopianism in Radical Education, Part 1," *The Review of Education, 12*(3), 1986: 167.

96. Giroux, *Theory and Resistance.*

97. Ibid., 9.

98. Patrick H. Hutton, "Foucault, Freud, and the Technologies of the Self," in L. H. Martin, H. Gutman, P. H. Hutton (eds.), *Technologies of the Self* (Amherst: University of Massachusetts Press, 1988): 121–144.

Chapter 11.

Agee, H., and Galda, L. (eds.) 1983. Response to literature: Empirical and theoretical studies. *Journal of Research and Development in Education, 16(3)*, 1–75.

Allen, M. P. (1949). *Battle Lanterns*. Longmans Green and Co.

Anyon, J. M. (1979). Ideology and United States history textbooks. *Harvard Educational Review, 49*, 361–386.

———. (1981). Social class and school knowledge. *Curriculum Inquiry, 11*, 3–42.

Apple, M. W. (1982). *Education and Power*. Boston: Routledge and Kegan Paul.

———. (1986). *Teachers and Texts: A Political Economy of Class and Gender Relations in Education*. London: Routledge and Kegan Paul.

Apple, M. W. (1979). *Ideology and curriculum*. Boston: Routledge and Kegan Paul.

Aronowitz, S., and Giroux, H. (1987). Ideologies about schooling: Rethinking the nature of educational reform. *Journal of Curriculum Theorizing, 7(1)*, 7–38.

Avi (1984). *The Fighting Ground*. New York: Lippincott.

Beyer, L. (1983). Aesthetic curriculum and cultural reproduction. In *Ideology and Practice in Schooling*, ed. M. Apple and L. Weis. Philadelphia: Temple University Press.

Bourdieu, P. (1971). The thinkable and the unthinkable. *Times Literary Supplement*, October 15, 1255–1256.

Campbell, P. B., and Wirtenberg, J. (1980). How books influence children: What research shows. *Interracial Books for Children Bulletin, 11(6)*, 3–6.

Caudill, R. (1949). *Tree of Freedom*. New York: Viking.

Christian-Smith, L. (1984). Becoming a woman through romance: Adolescent novels and the ideology of femininity. Doctoral dissertation: University of Wisconsin, Madison.

Collier, J. L., and Collier, C. (1974). *My Brother Sam is Dead*. New York: Scholastic Books.

Cooke, A. (1973) *Alistair Cooke's America*. New York: Alfred A. Knopf.

Council on Interracial Books for Children (1977). *Stereotypes, distortions and omissions in U. S. history textbooks*. New York: Racism and Sexism Resource Center for Educators.

Crownfield, G. (1930). *Freedom's Daughter*. New York: E. P. Dutton.

Dixon, Bob. (1977a). *Catching Them Young: Sex, Race, and Class in Children's Fiction*. London: Pluto Press.

———. (1977b). *Catching Them Young: Political Ideas in Children's Fiction*. London: Pluto Press.

Eagleton, T. (1976). *Marxism and Literary Criticism*. Berkeley: University of California Press.

Edwards, S. (1972). *When the World's on Fire*. New York: Coward, McCann and Geoghegan.

Everhart, R. (1983). *Reading, Writing and Resistance: Adolescence and Labor in a Junior High School*. Boston: Routledge and Kegan Paul.

Finlayson, A. (1971). *Redcoat in Boston*. New York: Frederick Warne and Co.

Fitzgerald, F. (1979). *America Revised: History Schoolbooks in the Twentieth Century*. Boston: Little Brown.

Forbes, E. (1943). *Johnny Tremain*. New York: Dell.

Fritz, J. (1967). *Early Thunder*. New York: Coward, McCann and Geoghegan.

Giroux, H. (1983). *Theory and Resistance in Education: A Pedagogy for the Opposition*. South Hadley, MA: Bergin and Garvey Publishers.

Gitlin, T. (1979). Prime time ideology: The hegemonic process in television entertainment. *Social Problems, 26*, 251–266.

Harris, V. (1986). The Brownies' book: Challenge to the selective tradition in children's literature. Doctoral dissertation: University of Georgia.

Hawthorne, H. (1937). *Rising Thunder*. Longmans, Green and Co.

Kammen, M. (1978). *A Season of Youth: The American Revolution and the Historical Imagination*. New York: Alfred A. Knopf.

Kelly, R. G. (1970). Mother was a lady: Strategy and order in selected American children's periodicals, 1865–1890. Doctoral dissertation: University of Iowa.

———. (1974). Literature and the historian. *American Quarterly, 26*, 141–159.

———. (1984). Literary and cultural values in the evaluation of books for children. *The Advocate, 4(2)*, 84–100.

Klein, G. (1985). *Reading into Racism: Bias in Children's Literature and Learning Materials*. London: Routledge and Kegan Paul.

Morgan, E. S. (1976). Slavery and freedom: The American paradox. In *Conflict and Consensus in Early American History*, ed. A. Davis and H. Woodman. Lexington, MA: D. C. Heath.

O'Dell, F. A. (1978). *Socialization through Children's Literature in the Soviet Example*. New York: Cambridge University Press.

Rosenblatt, L. M. (1978). *The Reader, the Text, the Poem: The Transactional Theory of the Literary Work*. Carbondale, IL: Southern Illinois University Press.

Sebestyen, O. (1979). *Words by Heart*. New York: Bantam.

Sharp, R., and Green, A. (1975). *Education and Social Control: A Study in Progressive Primary Education*. London: Routledge and Kegan Paul.

Sims, R. (1980). *Words by Heart*: A black perspective. *Interracial Books for Children Bulletin, 11(7)*, 12–15, 17.

———. (1982). *Shadow and Substance: Afro-American Experience in Contemporary Children's Books*. Urbana, IL: NCTE.

———. (1984). A question of perspective. *The Advocate, 3(3)*, 145–156.

Snow, R. (1976). *Freelon Starbird*. Boston: Houghton Mifflin.

Taxel, J. (1981). The outsiders of the American revolution: The selective tradition in children's fiction. *Interchange, 12*, 206–228.

———. (1984). The American revolution in children's fiction: An analysis of historical meaning and narrative structure. *Curriculum Inquiry, 14*, 7–55.

———. (1986). The black experience in children's fiction: Controversies surrounding award winning books. *Curriculum Inquiry, 16(3)*, 245–281.

———. (1987). Teaching children's literature. *Teaching Education, 1(1)*, 12–15.

Taylor, M. (1976). *Roll of Thunder, Hear My Cry*. New York: Avon Press.

Wald, A. (1981). Hegemony and literary tradition in America. *Humanities in Society, 4(4)*, 419–429.

Wexler, P. (1982). Structure, text, and subject: A critical sociology of school knowledge. In *Cultural and Economic Reproduction in Education: Essays on Class, Ideology and the State*, ed. M. Apple. London: Routledge and Kegan Paul.

Williams, R. 1977. *Marxism and Literature*. London: Oxford University Press.

Willis, P. (1977). *Learning to Labor: How Working Class Kids Get Working Class Jobs*. Lexington: D. C. Heath.

Wright, W. (1975). *Sixguns and Society: A Structural Study of the Western*. Berkeley: University of California Press.

Zimet, S. G. (1976). *Print and Prejudice*. London: Hodder and Stoughton.

Zipes, J. (1983). *Fairy Tales and the Art of Subversion: The Classical Genre for Children and the Process of Civilization*. New York: Wildman Press.

Chapter 12.

Notes

1. Although some critics (e.g., Marsh, 1979) use the terms *rock* and *rock'n'roll* to refer to different genres or periods of popular music, I observe no such distinction in this essay.

2. Rock critics, not surprisingly, have usually dismissed Adorno's critique. For a more sympathetic reading, see Gendron (1986).

3. For a critique of Bloom from the perspective of rock'n'roll and youth culture, see Greider (1987).

4. Frith (1981) provides a good overview of the various elements of this system of production and consumption.

References

Adorno, Theodor W. (1941), On Popular Music, *Studies in Philosophy and Social Sciences*, 9, pp. 17–48.

———. (1967), *Prisms*, trans. Samuel and Shierry Weber, Cambridge, Mass.: MIT Press.

———. (1975), The Culture Industry Reconsidered, *New German Critique*, 6, pp. 12–19.

Adorno, Theodor W., and Horkheimer, M. (1972), *Dialectic of Enlightenment*, trans. John Cumming, New York: Seabury.

Barol, Bill, et al. (1985), He's On Fire, *Newsweek*, August 5, pp. 48–54.

Belz, Carl (1972), *The Story of Rock*, 2nd ed., New York: Harper.

Benjamin, Walter (1969), The Work of Art in the Age of Mechanical Reproduction, in H. Arendt (ed.), *Illuminations*, New York: Schocken.

Bloom, Allan (1987), *The Closing of the American Mind: How Higher Education Has Failed Democracy and Impoverished the Souls of Today's Students*, New York: Simon and Schuster.

Durant, Alan (1984), *Conditions of Music*, Albany: SUNY Press.

Felman, Shoshana (1982), Psychoanalysis and Education: Teaching Terminable and Interminable, *Yale French Studies*, 63, pp. 21–44.

Foucault, Michel (1977), *Discipline and Punish*, trans. Alan Sheridan, New York: Random House.

Frith, Simon (1981), *Sound Effects: Youth, Leisure, and the Politics of Rock'n'Roll*, New York: Random House.

Gendron, Bernard (1986), Theodor Adorno Meets the Cadillacs, in T. Modleski (ed.), *Studies in Entertainment: Critical Approaches to Mass Culture*, Bloomington: Indiana University Press.

Giroux, Henry A. (1983), *Theory and Resistance in Education: A Pedagogy for the Opposition*, South Hadley, Mass.: Bergin and Garvey.

Greider, William (1987), Bloom and Doom, *Rolling Stone*, October 8, pp. 39–40.

Grossberg, Lawrence (1984), "I'd Rather Feel Bad Than Not Feel Anything at All": Rock and Roll, Pleasure and Power, *Enclitic*, 8, pp. 94–111.

———. (1986), Teaching the Popular, in C. Nelson (ed.), *Theory in the Classroom*, Urbana: University of Illinois Press.

Hebdige, Dick (1979), *Subculture: The Meaning of Style*, London: Methuen.

Horkheimer, Max (1972), *Critical Theory*, New York: Seabury Press.

MacCannell, Dean, and MacCannell, Juliet Flower (1982), *The Time of the Sign*, Bloomington: Indiana University Press.

Marsh, Dave (1979), *Born to Run: The Bruce Springsteen Story*, Garden City, N. Y.: Doubleday.

Penley, Constance (1986), Feminism and Psychoanalysis, in C. Nelson (ed.), *Theory in the Classroom*, Urbana: University of Illinois Press.

Radway, Janice (1984), *Reading the Romance: Women, Patriarchy, and Popular Literature*, Chapel Hill: University of North Carolina Press.

Chapter 13.

Aronowitz, S., and Giroux, H.A. (1985). *Education Under Seige*. South Hadley, MA: Bergin and Garvey.

Bennett, T. (1986). Popular culture and the turn to Gramsci. In T. Bennett, C. Mercer, and J. Woolacott (eds.), *Popular Cultural and Social Relations*. London: Open University Press.

Bloom, A. (1987). *The Closing of the American Mind*. New York: Simon and Schuster.

Chambers, I. (1985). Popular culture, popular knowledge. *One Two Three Four: A Rock and Roll Quarterly*, pp. 1–8.

Clifford, J. (1981). On ethnographic surrealism. *Comparative Studies in Society and History*, No. 18, pp. 539–564.

Clifford, J., and Marcus, G.E. (eds.) (1986). *Writing Culture: The Poetics and Politics of Ethnography.* Berkeley: University of California Press.

Fitting, P. (1987). The decline of the feminist utopian novel. *Border/Lines*, No. 7/8, pp. 17–19.

Foucault, M. (1980a). *The History of Sexuality:* Volume 1, *An Introduction.* New York: Vintage Books.

———. (1980b). Two lectures. *Knowledge/Power* (Colin Gordon, trans.). New York: Pantheon Press.

Giroux, H.A. (1988). *Schooling and the Struggle for Public Life.* Minneapolis: University of Minnesota Press.

Grossberg, L. (1986). Teaching the popular. In C. Nelson (ed.), *Theory in the Classroom.* Urbana: University of Illinois Press.

Hall, S. (1981). Notes on deconstructing 'the popular.' In R. Samuel (ed.), *People's History and Socialist Theory* (pp. 227–240). London: Routledge and Kegan Paul.

Hebdige, R. (1979). *Subculture: The Meaning of Style.* New York: Methuen.

Lewis, M., and Simon, R. I. (1986). A discourse not intended for her: Learning and teaching within patriarchy. *Harvard Educational Review, 56*(4), pp. 457–472.

Lusted, D. (1986). Introduction: Why pedagogy? *Screen, 27*(5), pp. 2–14.

McLaren, P. (1986). *Schooling as a Ritual Performance: Toward a Political Economy of Educational Symbols and Gestures.* New York: Routledge and Kegan Paul.

———. (1989). *Life in Schools.* New York: Longman.

Mills, A., and Rice, P. (1982). Quizzing the popular. *Screen Education*, No. 41, pp. 15–25.

Morgan, R. (1987). English studies as cultural production in Ontario, 1860–1920. Doctoral dissertation, Ontario Institute for Studies in Education, Toronto.

Radway, J. (1984). *Reading the Romance: Women, Patriarchy, and Popular Literature.* Chapel Hill: University of North Carolina Press.

Rockhill, K. (1987, February). Literacy as threat/desire: Longing to be somebody. Unpublished paper, Ontario Institute for Studies in Education.

Rowe, E. (1987, January). Desire and popular culture: The ego ideal and its influence in the production of subjectivity. Unpublished paper, Ontario Institute for Studies in Education.

Ryerson, E. (1968). Summary of a speech at the Ontario Literary Society. *Journal of Education* (Ontario), *21*, p. 72.

————. (1870). The general absence of good breeding. *The Hamilton Spectator, 29,* p. 53.

Simon, R.I. (1984). Signposts for a critical pedagogy: A review of Henry A. Giroux's *Theory and Resistance in Education. Educational Theory, 34*(4), pp. 379–388.

————. (1987). Empowerment as a pedagogy of possibility. *Language Arts, 64*(4), pp. 370–382.

Williamson, J. (1981–1982). How does girl number 20 understand ideology? *Screen Education*, No. 40, pp. 80–87.

CONTRIBUTORS

MICHAEL W. APPLE is a Professor of Curriculum and Instruction and Educational Policy Studies at the University of Wisconsin-Madison. He has written extensively in the area of curriculum studies and social thought and is the author of numerous publications which include *Ideology and Curriculum, Education and Power,* and *Teachers and Texts.* Professor Apple also edits the book series "Critical Social Thought" for Routledge (New York).

SAMUEL BOWLES is Professor of Economics in the Department of Economics at the University of Massachusetts at Amherst, Massachusetts. He is the author of numerous publications including *Democracy and Capitalism: Property, Community, and the Contradictions of Modern Social Thought* (with Herbert Gintis) and *Beyond the Wasteland: A Democratic Alternative to Economic Decline* (with David Gordon and Thomas Weisskopf).

MARTIN CARNOY is Professor of Education at the School of Education at Stanford University in Stanford, California. He publishes widely in the United States and Latin America and is the author of *The State and Political Theory* and *Schooling and Work in the Democratic State* (with Henry M. Levin). He is also co-author with Joel Samoff of *Education and Social Transformation in the Third World* (forthcoming).

MIRIAM DAVID is currently Head of the Social Sciences Department at the Polytechnic of the South Bank of London. She has done research on educational policy and the family in both Britain and the USA. Her current interests are in comparative social policy, gender and social policy and questions of educational management, particularly the role of women as academic leaders in higher education. Her publications include *The State, The Family and Education, School Rule in the USA,* and, with Caroline New, *For the Children's Sake: Making Child Care More Than Women's Business.*

WALTER FEINBERG is a Professor in the Bureau of Educational Research and the Department of Educational Policy Studies at the University of Illinois. He is President-elect of the Philosophy of Education Society for 1987–88. His latest books are *School and Society* (with Jonas Soltis) and *Understanding Education*.

MICHELLE FINE is a social psychologist interested in the ways in which race, class, and gender operate inside high schools, and inside the relationship of schools to community, facilitating and obstructing educational justice for adolescents. Her work has focussed on high school dropouts, race and sex segregation in public schools, and the construction of "community" within and beyond public schools. Active in both educational advocacy and courtroom testimony on school discrimination, she is the author of numerous publications which include *Disabled Women: Psychology From the Margins* (with A. Asch) and is editor of *School Dropouts: Patterns and Policies*.

HERBERT GINTIS is Professor of Economics in the Department of Economics at the University of Massachusetts at Amherst, Massachusetts. He is the author of numerous publications including *Schooling in Capitalist America: Educational Reform and the Contradictions of Economic Life* and *Democracy and Capitalism: Property, Community, and the Contradictions of Modern Social Thought* (both with Samuel Bowles).

HENRY GIROUX is Professor of Education in the Department of Educational Leadership at Miami University [Ohio]. He is also Director for the Center for Education and Cultural Studies and the Distinguished Scholar-in-Residence, extensively in the fields of cultural studies, critical pedagogy, curriculum theory, and the sociology of education. His many award-winning books include *Theory and Resistance in Education: A Pedagogy for the Opposition, Ideology, Culture, and the Process of Schooling, Education Under Siege* (with Stanley Aronowitz) and *Cultura, Sociedad y Escuela* (with Peter McLaren). Professor Giroux is co-editor with Paulo Freire of the book series "Critical Studies in Education," Bergin and Garvey Publishers, Inc. His most recent works include *Teachers as Intellectuals* and *Schooling and the Struggle for Public Life: Critical Pedagogy in the Modern Age*.

PETER MCLAREN is Associate Professor of Education in the Department of Educational Leadership at Miami University [Ohio]. He is also Associate Director of the Center for Education and Cultural Studies. Professor McLaren is the author of *Cries From the Corridor: The New Suburban Ghettos, Schooling as a Ritual Performance: Towards a Political Economy of Educational Symbols and Gestures*, and *Life in Schools: An Introduction to Critical Pedagogy in the Social Foundations of Education*. He is also co-author with Henry A.

Giroux of the forthcoming *Cultura, Sociedad y Escuela* and co-editor with Peter Leonard of *Paulo Freire: A Critical Encounter* (forthcoming). He is presently working on two new books, *Beyond Silence and Chaos: A Pedagogy of Hope and Transformation* and *Decentering Culture: Modern Theories of Power and Subjectivity.*.

ROGER SIMON is Associate Professor in the Department of Curriculum, Ontario Institute for Studies in Education, Toronto. His major professional interests lie in critical pedagogy and cultural studies. He is co-editor (with Henry Giroux) of *Popular Culture and Critical Pedagogy* (forthcoming).

DAVID R. SHUMWAY is Assistant Professor of English in the English Department of Carnegie Mellon University in Pittsburgh. He is also a member of the literary and cultural theory faculty. He is the author of numerous publications and the forthcoming book, *Michel Foucault* (in press).

RICHARD SMITH is chair of the Department of Social and Cultural Studies, School of Education, James Cook University of North Queensland. His major intellectual interests lie in the sociology of culture with particular emphases in Policy Studies, Teacher Education and Cultural Studies. His current projects include a long-term empirical and analysis of the "dominant ideology thesis;" the use made by young people of information technology and an analysis of possibilities for transformative pedagogies in schools.

JOEL TAXEL is an Associate Professor in the Department of Language Education at the University of Georgia. His published works have appeared in journals such as *Interchange, Curriculum Inquiry,* and *Research in the Teaching of English.* He has recently completed a study of Walt Disney's transformation of classic fairy tales and is editor of *The New Advocate,* a journal dealing with issues related to the writing, publication, and teaching of children's literature.

PHILIP WEXLER is Associate Professor of Education and Sociology and the Associate Dean of the Graduate School of Education and Human Development at the University of Rochester in Rochester, New York. He is the author of *The Sociology of Education: Beyond Equality, Critical Social Psychology,* and *The Social Analysis of Education: After the New Sociology* and is currently working on a new book, *Becoming Somebody: Studies in High School,* a social analysis of the symbolic economy of identity production.

ANNA ZANTIOTIS graduated with a B.A. (Humanities) from Griffith University, Brisbane, Australia in 1978. She completed a Diploma in Education at the University of Queensland before teaching English as a second language to migrants in 1983. In 1984 she taught English and Social Sciences at a rural high school before joing the staff at Inala High, classified as a "disadvantaged school." Her major interests have been the development of curricula and pedagogies to create with students and student-teachers "really useful knowledge" in Social Science, English and Film and TV studies. Her current concern is to expand the counter-dominant practice of working in the "gap": identifying and exploiting potentially transformative breaks in the seemingly rigid government educational policy and practice.

INDEX

Ideology (*cont.*)
superstructure model, 184–86;
characteristics of, 13; and culture,
10–20; definition, 11; operation
of, 32; and ritual, 190–91; shift of,
72

Laclau, Ernesto: on ideology, 179–81
Language: construction, 133; of stu-
dent experience, 150
Lauretis, Teresa de: pedagogy of and
pedagogy for difference, 142–43
Liberal education, 71
Liberalism, 24–25; types of action ac-
cessible to, 26
Literature, children's: and the black
issue, 210–11; of the American
Revolution, 208–14; selective tradi-
tion in, 207–8, 220–21

Mass culture: and rock'n'roll, 222–25
McLaren, Peter, 174–202
Mill, John Stuart: and liberalism, 26
Mulhern, Francis: cultural politics,
127

Naming, 157; consequences of not,
159–60
Nascent state, 118; achievement of,
119
New Right: aims of, 37; and education, 38; resurgence, 39–41

Orthodox Marxist: base-superstructure
model, 184–86; on ideology, 177–
81; ideology and science, 183

Paideia Proposal, 74, 83–84
Popular culture, 237–38; and class-

Popular culture (*cont.*)
room pedagogy, 238; definition,
244; and education, 241–42; and
pedagogy, 248–49; practices of,
245–46; and social difference, 247
Postmodernism, 97–99

Radical pedagogy: emergence, 128;
failures of, 130–32; form of cultural politics, 144; and school
knowledge, 129; search for, 141,
and student experience, 148–49
Reailty effect, 112
Resistance, 99; and hegemony, 197;
and ritual knowledge, 193, student, 194–95
Ritual: and ideology, 190–91; and
knowledge, 192–93
Rock'n'roll: and mass culture, 222–
25; and sexual politics, 234; and
schooling, 226–27, 229–30

School: and culture, 4; definition,
143; and education, 107; and family, 52; goals of, 70–71; as sites of
struggle, 237; and state, 4 6–10
Schooling: as a form of cultural politics, 141–42; and education, 5
Scientism, 95–96; pathways to, 102–3
Selective tradition, 206; about the
black experience, 220; in children's
literature, 207–8, 220–21
Shumway, David, 222–35
Silencing, 152; characterization of, 154;
practices in public schools, 153;
school-imposed, 168–69; student, 165
Simon, Roger: and Henry Giroux,
236–52
Sizer, Theodore, 84–85, 89
Smith, Dorothy, 54, 56
Smith, Richard: and Anna Zantiotis,
105–22

Printed in the United States
66154LVS00003B/178-195